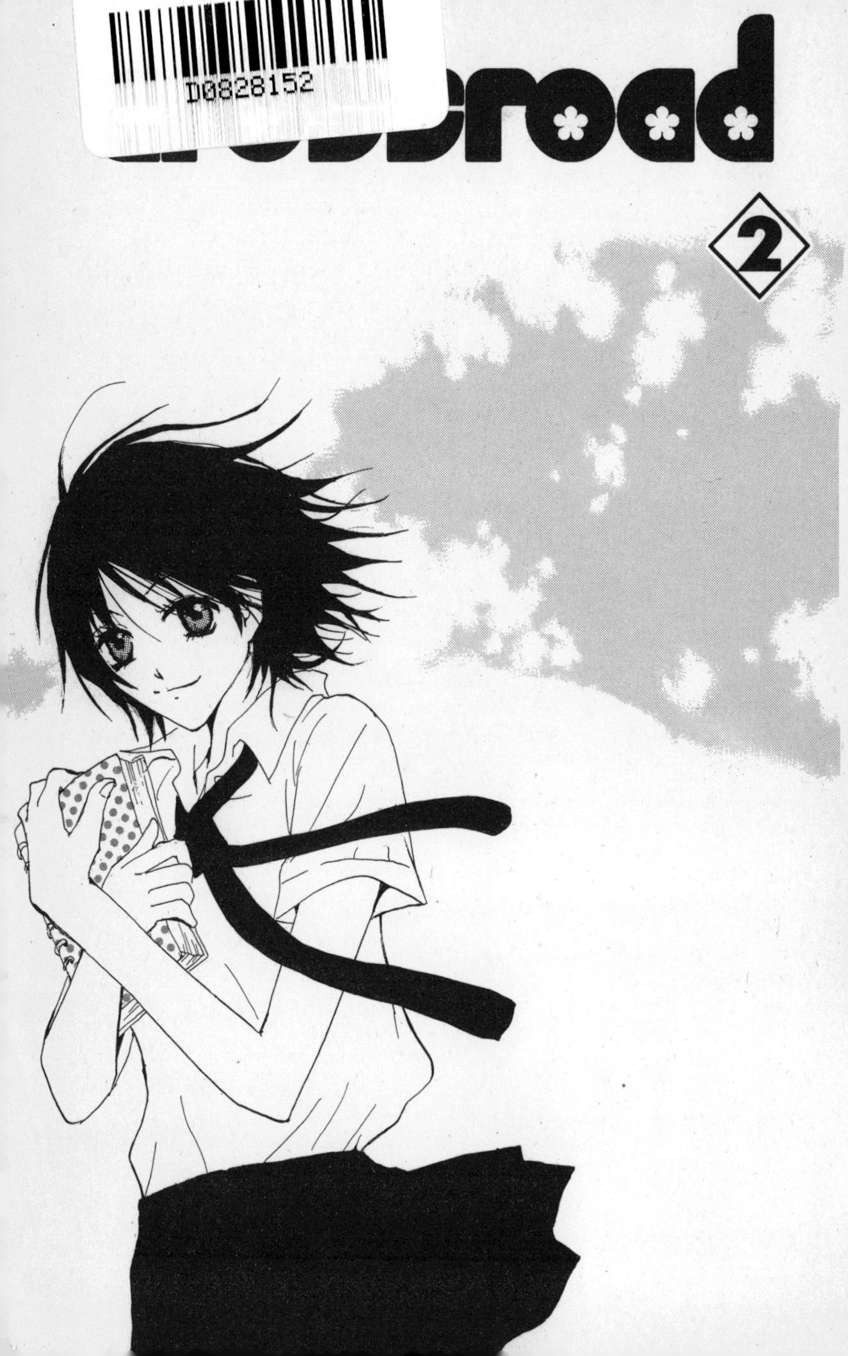
2

Translation – Kathy Schilling
Adaptation – Audry Taylor
Lettering & Design – Jake Forbes & Fawn Lau
Production Assistant – Mallory Reaves
Editor – Jake Forbes

A Go! Comi manga

Published by Go! Media Entertainment, LLC

Crossroad Volume 2
© SHIOKO MIZUKI 2004
Originally published in Japan in 2004 by Akita Publishing Co., Ltd., Tokyo.
English translation rights arranged with Akita Publishing Co., Ltd.
through TOHAN CORPORATION, Tokyo.

Visit us online at www.gocomi.com
e-mail: info@gocomi.com

ISBN 0-9768957-6-5

First printed in January 2006

1   2   3   4   5   6   7   8   9

Manufactured in the United States of America

crossroad

story and art by
SHIOKO MIZUKI

VOLUME 2

go!comi

Concerning Honorifics

At Go! Comi, we do our best to ensure that our translations read seamlessly in English while respecting the original Japanese language and culture. To this end, the original honorifics (the suffixes found at the end of characters' names) remain intact. In Japan, where politeness and formality are more integrated into every aspect of the language, honorifics give a better understanding of character relationships. They can be used to indicate both respect and affection. Whether a person addresses someone by first name or last name also indicates how close their relationship is.

Here are some of the honorifics you might encounter in reading this book:

-san: This is the most common and neutral of honorifics. The polite way to address someone you're not on close terms with is to use "-san." It's kind of like Mr. or Ms., except you can use "-san" with first or last names as easily as family names.

-chan: Used for friendly familiarity, mostly applied towards young girls. "-chan" also carries a connotation of cuteness with it, so it is frequently used with nicknames towards both boys and girls (such as "Na-chan" for "Natsu").

-kun: Like "-chan," it's an informal suffix for friends and classmates, only "-kun" is usually associated with boys. It can also be used in a professional environment by someone addressing a subordinate.

-sama: Indicates a great deal of respect or admiration.

Sempai: In school, "sempai" is used to refer to an upperclassman or club leader. It can also be used in the workplace by a new employee to address a mentor or staff member with seniority.

Sensei: Teachers, doctors, writers or any master of a trade are referred to as "sensei." When addressing a manga creator, the polite thing to do is attach "-sensei" to the manga-ka's name (as in Mizuki-sensei).

Onii: This is the more casual term for an older brother. Usually you'll see it with an honorific attached, such as "onii-chan."

Onee: The casual term for older sister, it's used like "onii" with honorifics.

[blank]: Not using an honorific when addressing someone indicates that the speaker has permission to speak intimately with the other person. This relationship is usually reserved for close friends and family.

crossroad

— Table of Contents —

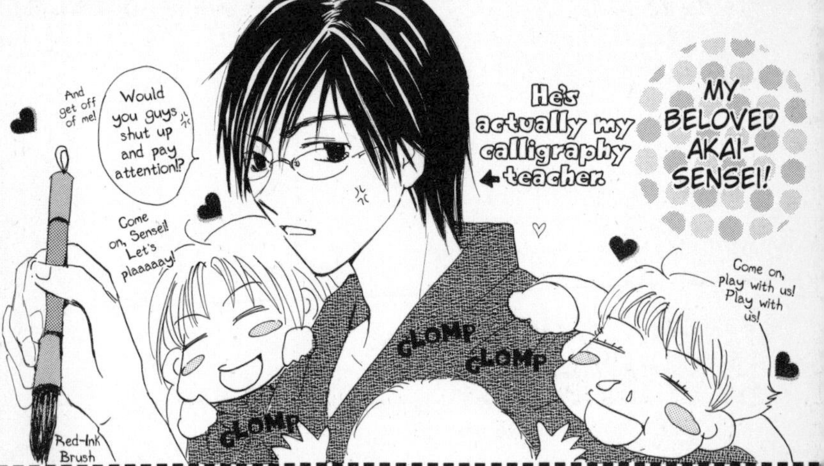
MY BELOVED AKAI-SENSEI!
He's actually my calligraphy teacher.
Come on, Play with us! Play with us!
GLOMP
GLOMP
Would you guys shut up and pay attention!?
And get off of me!
Come on, Sensei! Let's plaaaaay!
GLOMP
Red-Ink Brush

crossroad

Cast of Characters

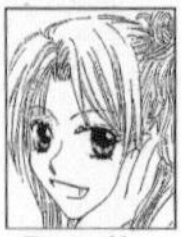
Rumiko Toda

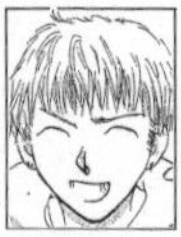
Taro Toda

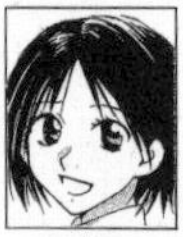
Kajitsu Toda

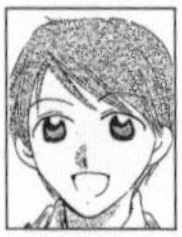
Tokihito Imanakajima

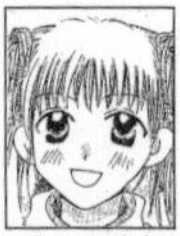
Satsuki Toda

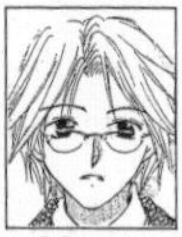
Natsu Toda

The Story So Far...

With the death of her kindly grandmother, 15-year-old Kajitsu Toda finds herself sharing her home with a little sister she's never met before and two step-brothers she hasn't seen since childhood. All four of them have been abandoned by their legal mother, Rumiko ("Run-Run"), who has run-run off with another in a series of deadbeat dads. Older brother Taro takes charge and immediately implements strict rules that no one upholds, while Kajitsu's younger brother Natsu enrolls in the same high school as her, to her deep embarrassment: back when they were kids, Kajitsu had a major crush on Natsu, but eventually sent him a nasty letter that ended their friendship. Forced now to live with each other, the two find that they no longer bear the grudges they used to – but that doesn't mean things won't heat up between them in an entirely different way...

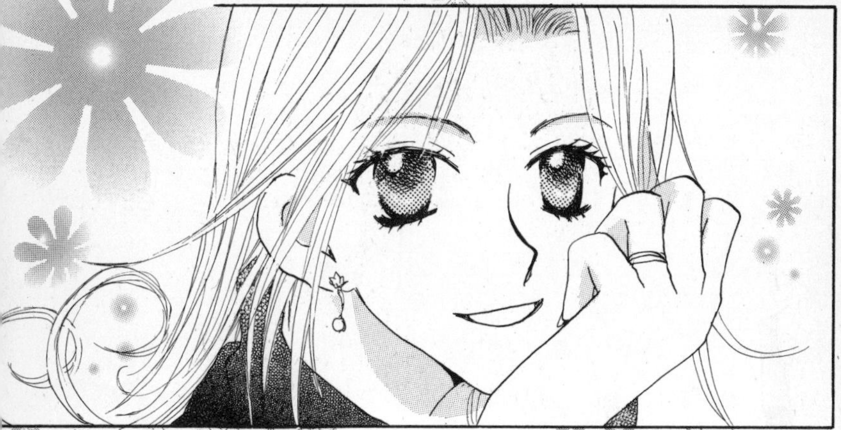

#6

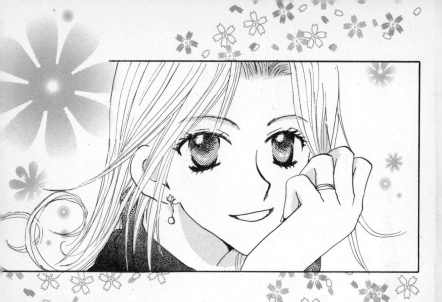

Mother

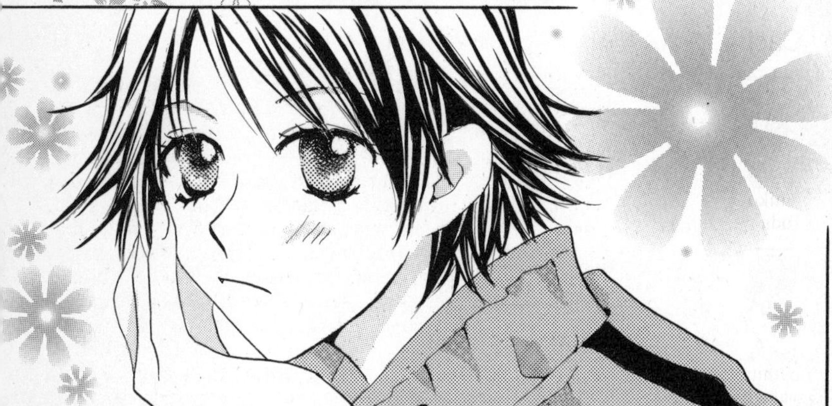

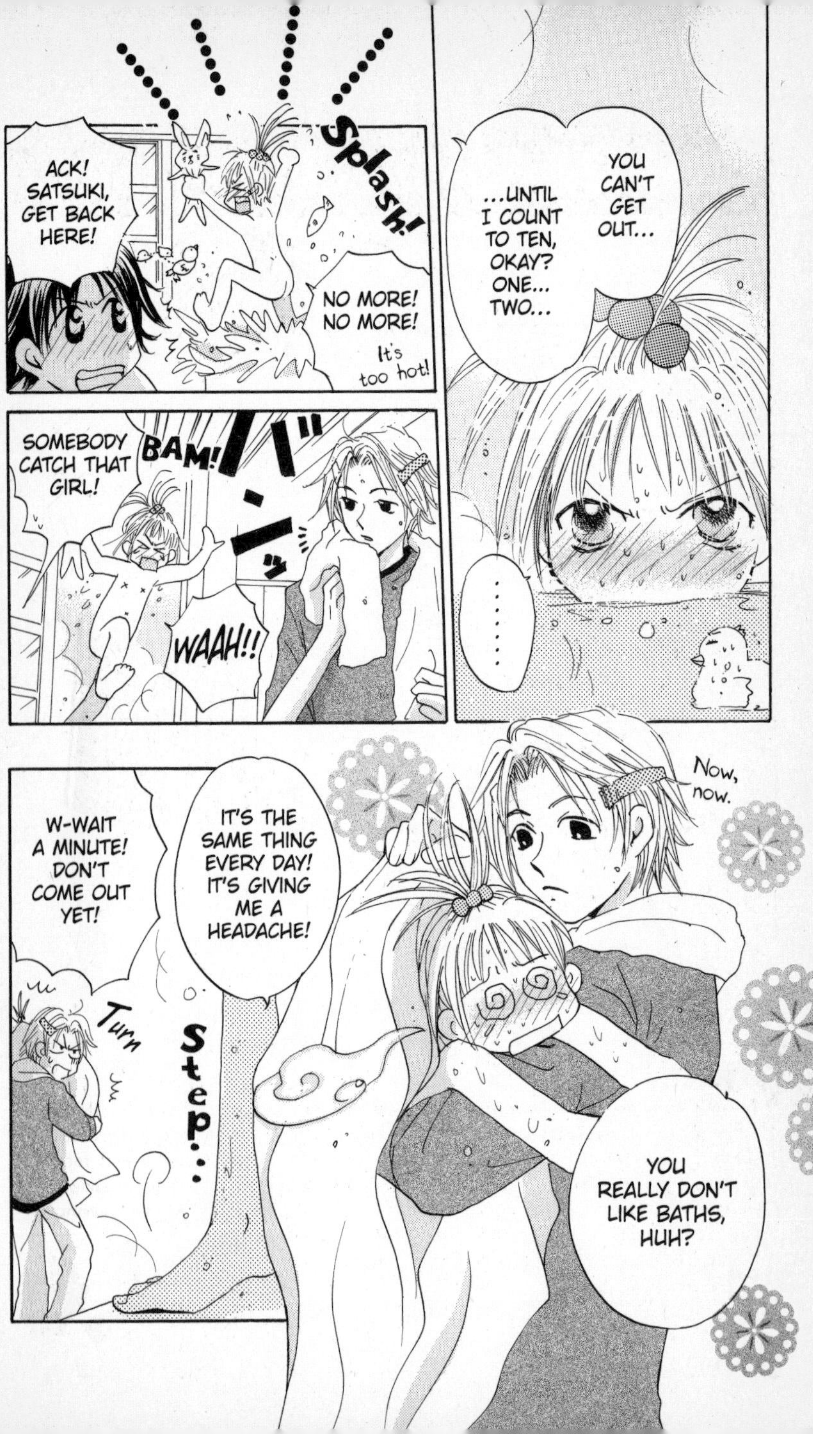
YOU CAN'T GET OUT...
...UNTIL I COUNT TO TEN, OKAY? ONE... TWO...
......
Splash!
NO MORE! NO MORE!
It's too hot!
ACK! SATSUKI, GET BACK HERE!
BAM!
WAAH!!
SOMEBODY CATCH THAT GIRL!
Now, now.
IT'S THE SAME THING EVERY DAY! IT'S GIVING ME A HEADACHE!
W-WAIT A MINUTE! DON'T COME OUT YET!
Turn
Step..
YOU REALLY DON'T LIKE BATHS, HUH?

crossroad Chapter 6: Mother

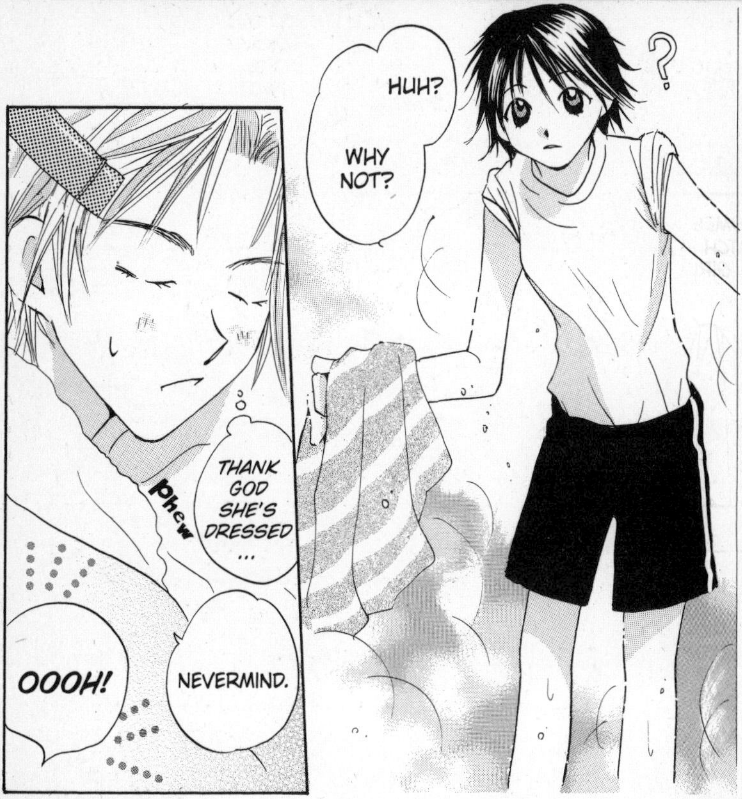
HUH?
WHY NOT?
THANK GOD SHE'S DRESSED...
Phew
NEVERMIND.
OOOH!

The Feudal Lord and I

1

Now I'm going to tell a little story about when I was a shrine maiden at a Shinto shrine. One day, my intstructor told me, "The feudal lord is coming today!!" "F-fuedal lord!?" I was so excited, I ran right out of the shrine to look, but found myself face to face with a regular-looking, nice old man. It turned out this man was a descendent of the feudal lord which had built this temple way back in the day. I remember running out all excited thinking it was a genuine "feudal lord" but it was really just a "futile lord." And that was my first experience with a so-called "real" feudal lord.

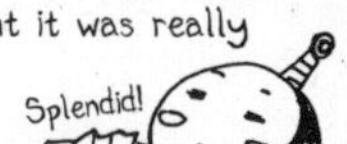
Splendid!

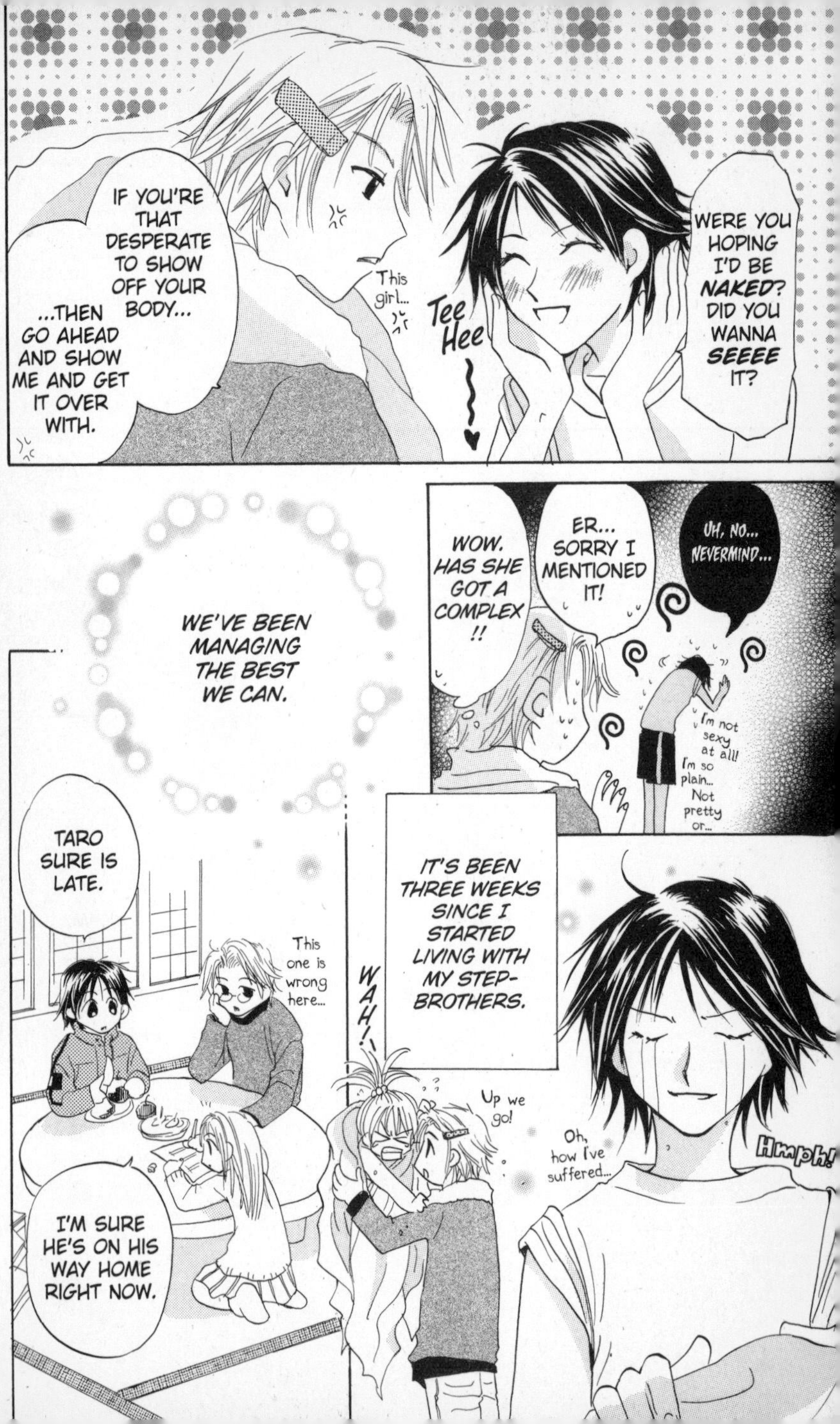
WERE YOU HOPING I'D BE *NAKED*? DID YOU WANNA *SEEEE* IT?
Tee Hee ~~~♥
This girl...
IF YOU'RE THAT DESPERATE TO SHOW OFF YOUR BODY...
...THEN GO AHEAD AND SHOW ME AND GET IT OVER WITH.
UH, NO... NEVERMIND...
ER... SORRY I MENTIONED IT!
WOW. HAS SHE GOT A COMPLEX !!
I'm not sexy at all! I'm so plain... Not pretty or...
WE'VE BEEN MANAGING THE BEST WE CAN.
Hmph!
IT'S BEEN THREE WEEKS SINCE I STARTED LIVING WITH MY STEP-BROTHERS.
Oh, how I've suffered...
Up we go!
WAH!!
TARO SURE IS LATE.
This one is wrong here...
I'M SURE HE'S ON HIS WAY HOME RIGHT NOW.

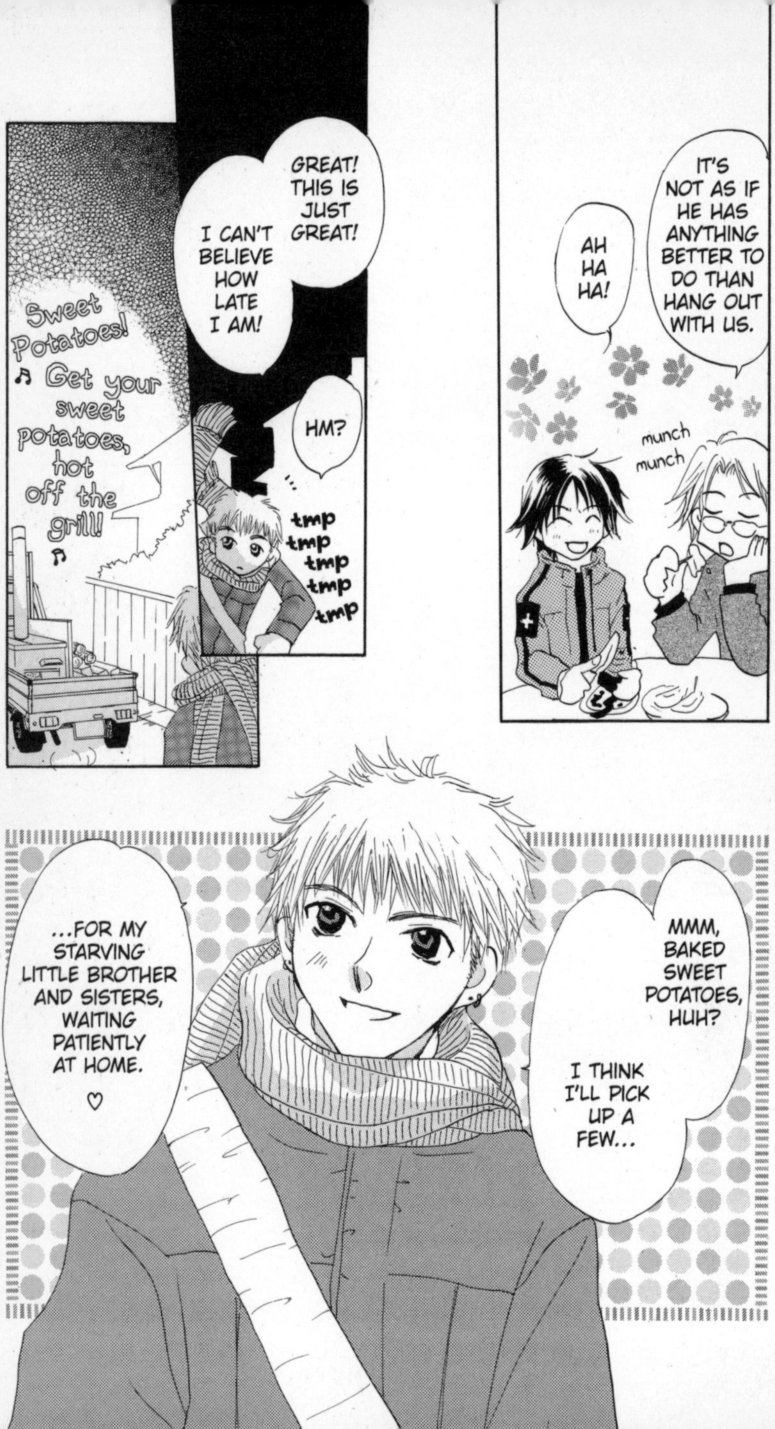
IT'S NOT AS IF HE HAS ANYTHING BETTER TO DO THAN HANG OUT WITH US.
AH HA HA!
munch munch
GREAT! THIS IS JUST GREAT!
I CAN'T BELIEVE HOW LATE I AM!
Sweet Potatoes! ♫ Get your sweet potatoes, hot off the grill! ♫
HM?
tmp tmp tmp tmp tmp
MMM, BAKED SWEET POTATOES, HUH?
I THINK I'LL PICK UP A FEW...
...FOR MY STARVING LITTLE BROTHER AND SISTERS, WAITING PATIENTLY AT HOME. ♡

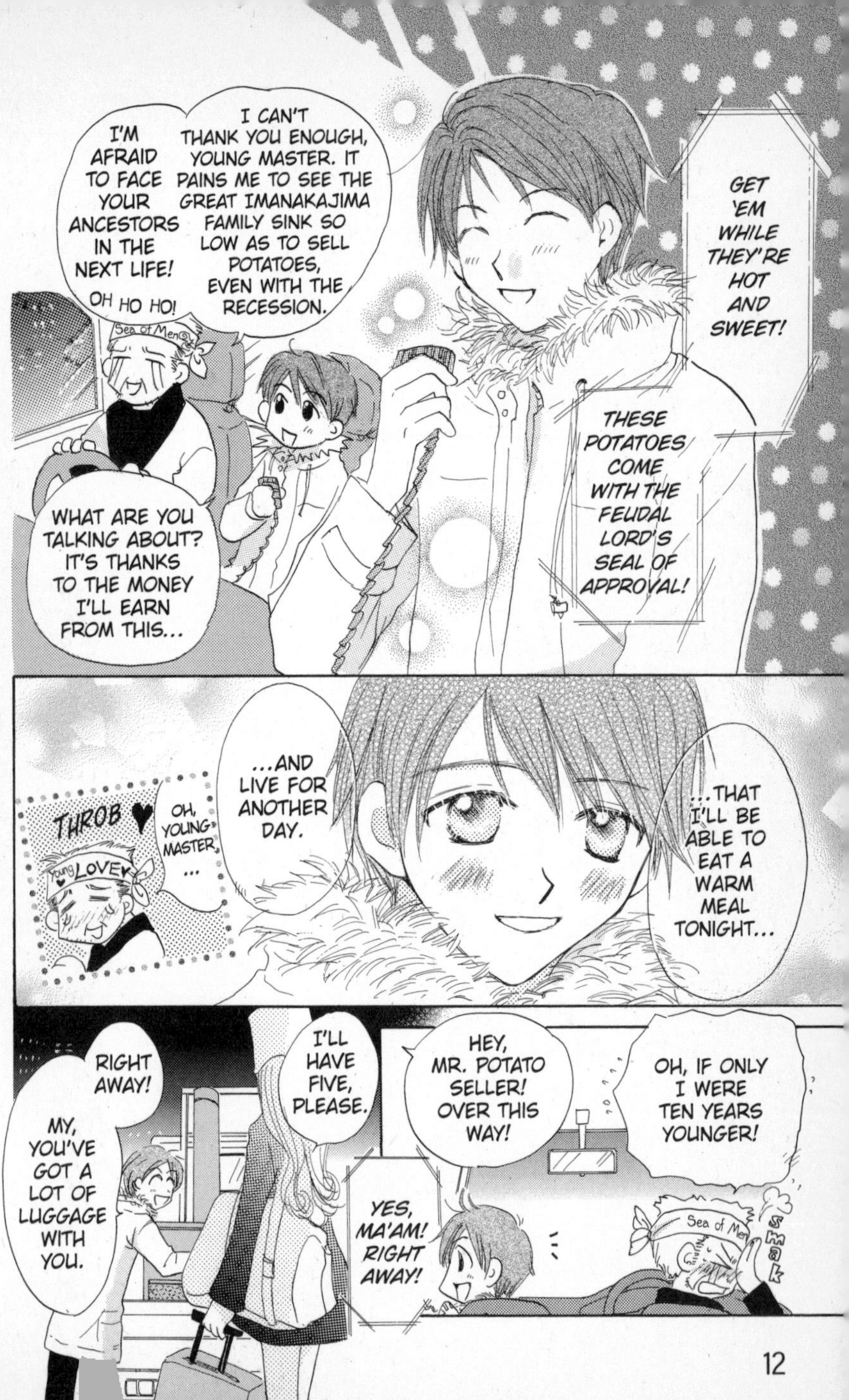
GET 'EM WHILE THEY'RE HOT AND SWEET!
THESE POTATOES COME WITH THE FEUDAL LORD'S SEAL OF APPROVAL!
I CAN'T THANK YOU ENOUGH, YOUNG MASTER. IT PAINS ME TO SEE THE GREAT IMANAKAJIMA FAMILY SINK SO LOW AS TO SELL POTATOES, EVEN WITH THE RECESSION.
I'M AFRAID TO FACE YOUR ANCESTORS IN THE NEXT LIFE!
OH HO HO!
Sea of Men
WHAT ARE YOU TALKING ABOUT? IT'S THANKS TO THE MONEY I'LL EARN FROM THIS...
...THAT I'LL BE ABLE TO EAT A WARM MEAL TONIGHT...
...AND LIVE FOR ANOTHER DAY.
OH, YOUNG MASTER, ...
THROB
Young LOVE
OH, IF ONLY I WERE TEN YEARS YOUNGER!
HEY, MR. POTATO SELLER! OVER THIS WAY!
Sea of Men
Smak
YES, MA'AM! RIGHT AWAY!
I'LL HAVE FIVE, PLEASE.
RIGHT AWAY!
MY, YOU'VE GOT A LOT OF LUGGAGE WITH YOU.

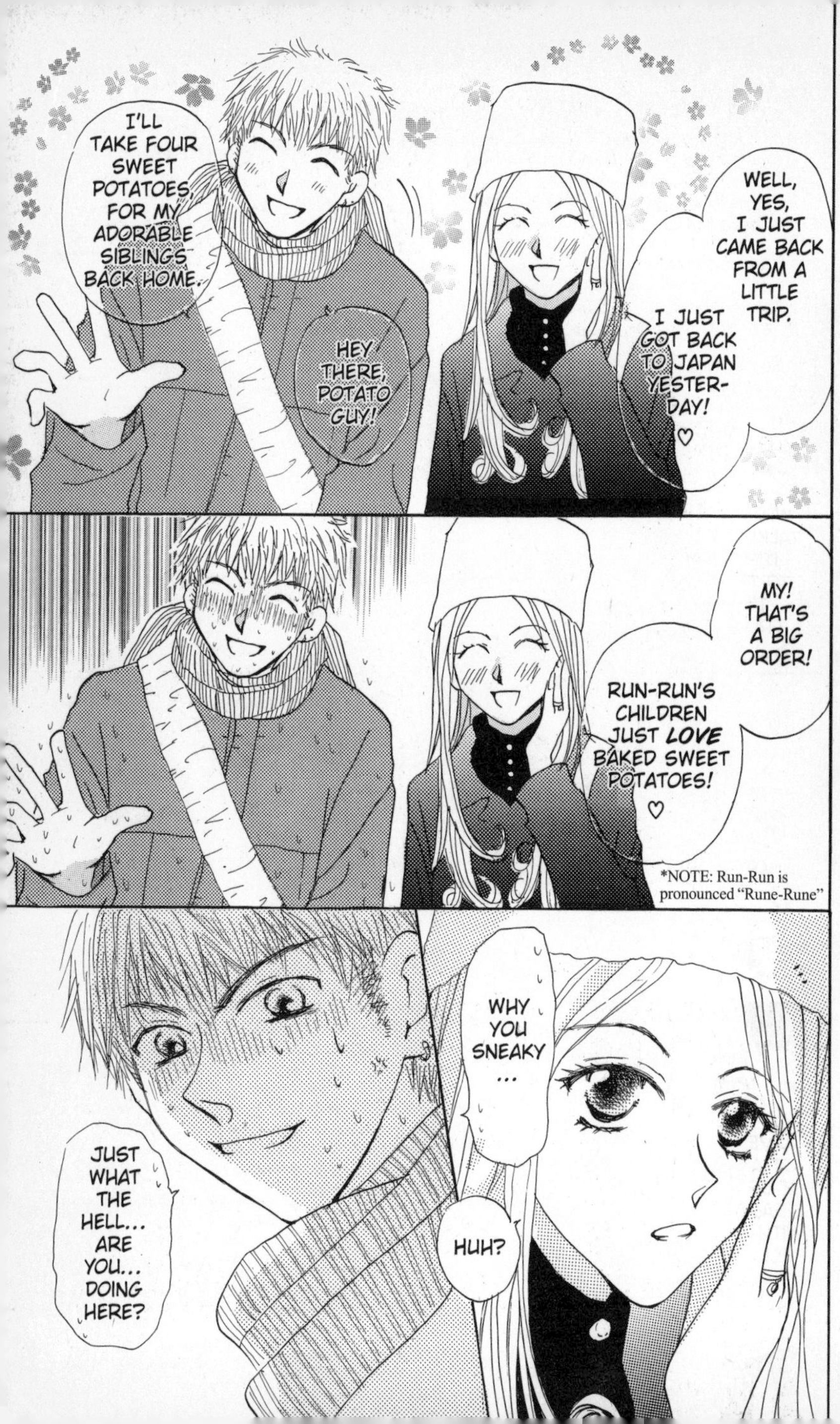
WELL, YES, I JUST CAME BACK FROM A LITTLE TRIP.
I JUST GOT BACK TO JAPAN YESTER-DAY! ♡
HEY THERE, POTATO GUY!
I'LL TAKE FOUR SWEET POTATOES, FOR MY ADORABLE SIBLINGS BACK HOME.
MY! THAT'S A BIG ORDER!
RUN-RUN'S CHILDREN JUST *LOVE* BAKED SWEET POTATOES! ♡
*NOTE: Run-Run is pronounced "Rune-Rune"
WHY YOU SNEAKY...
HUH?
JUST WHAT THE HELL... ARE YOU... DOING HERE?

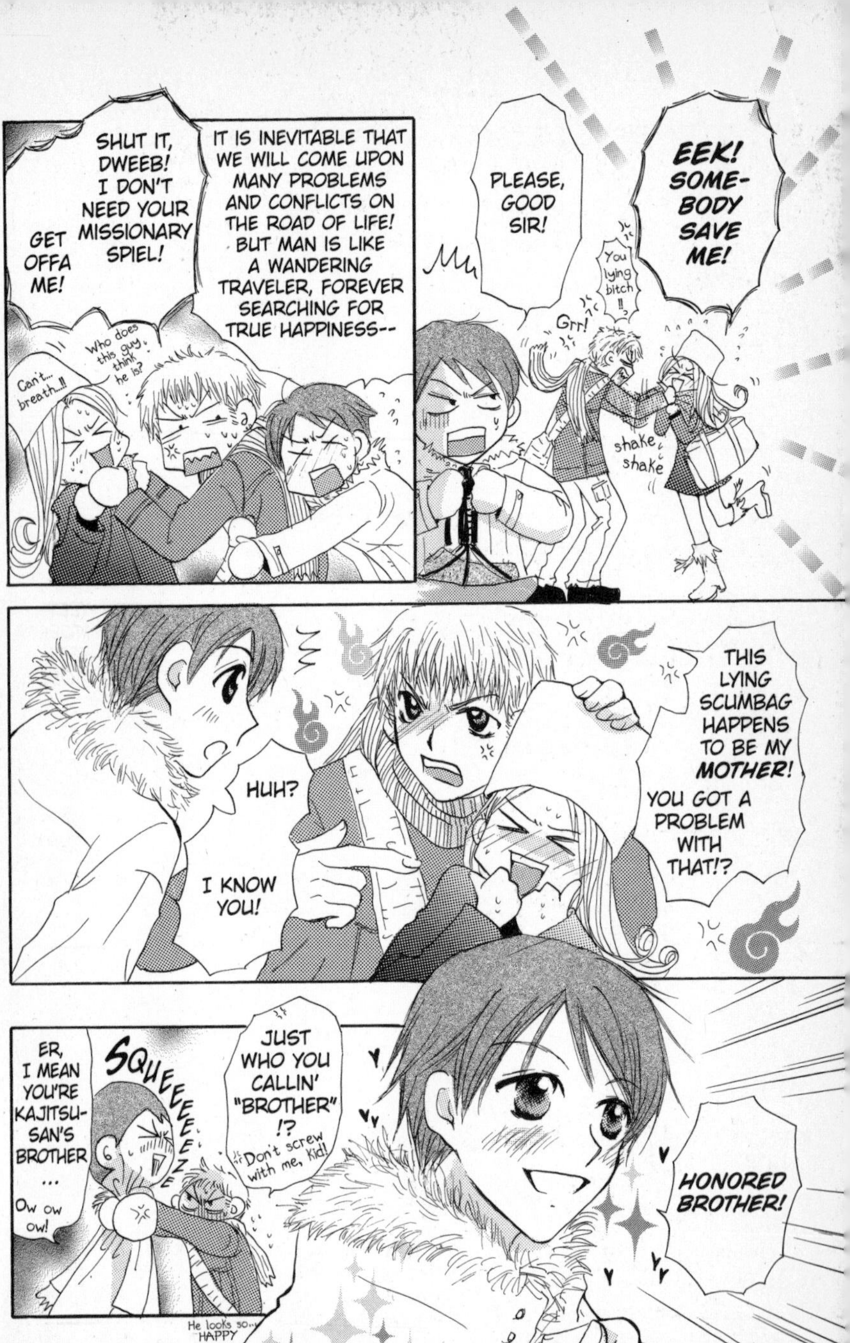
EEK! SOMEBODY SAVE ME!
You lying bitch!!
PLEASE, GOOD SIR!
Grr!
shake shake
IT IS INEVITABLE THAT WE WILL COME UPON MANY PROBLEMS AND CONFLICTS ON THE ROAD OF LIFE! BUT MAN IS LIKE A WANDERING TRAVELER, FOREVER SEARCHING FOR TRUE HAPPINESS--
SHUT IT, DWEEB! I DON'T NEED YOUR MISSIONARY SPIEL!
GET OFFA ME!
Who does this guy think he is?
Can't... breath...!!
THIS LYING SCUMBAG HAPPENS TO BE MY MOTHER!
YOU GOT A PROBLEM WITH THAT!?
HUH?
I KNOW YOU!
HONORED BROTHER!
JUST WHO YOU CALLIN' "BROTHER" !?
Don't screw with me, Kid!
SQUEEEEEEEZE
ER, I MEAN YOU'RE KAJITSU-SAN'S BROTHER ...
Ow ow ow!
He looks so... HAPPY

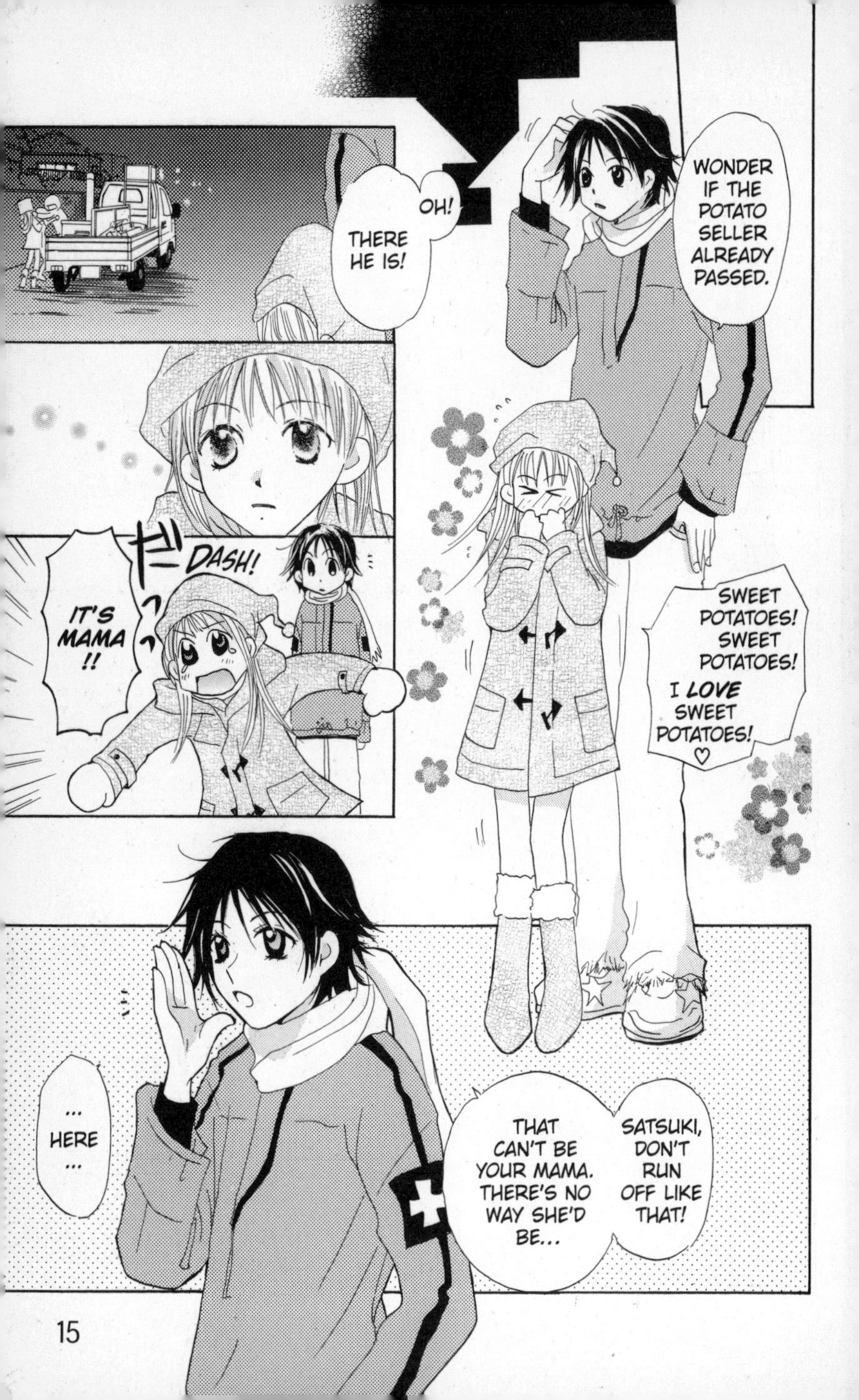

WONDER IF THE POTATO SELLER ALREADY PASSED.
OH!
THERE HE IS!
SWEET POTATOES! SWEET POTATOES! I *LOVE* SWEET POTATOES! ♡
DASH!
IT'S MAMA !!
SATSUKI, DON'T RUN OFF LIKE THAT!
THAT CAN'T BE YOUR MAMA. THERE'S NO WAY SHE'D BE...
... HERE ...

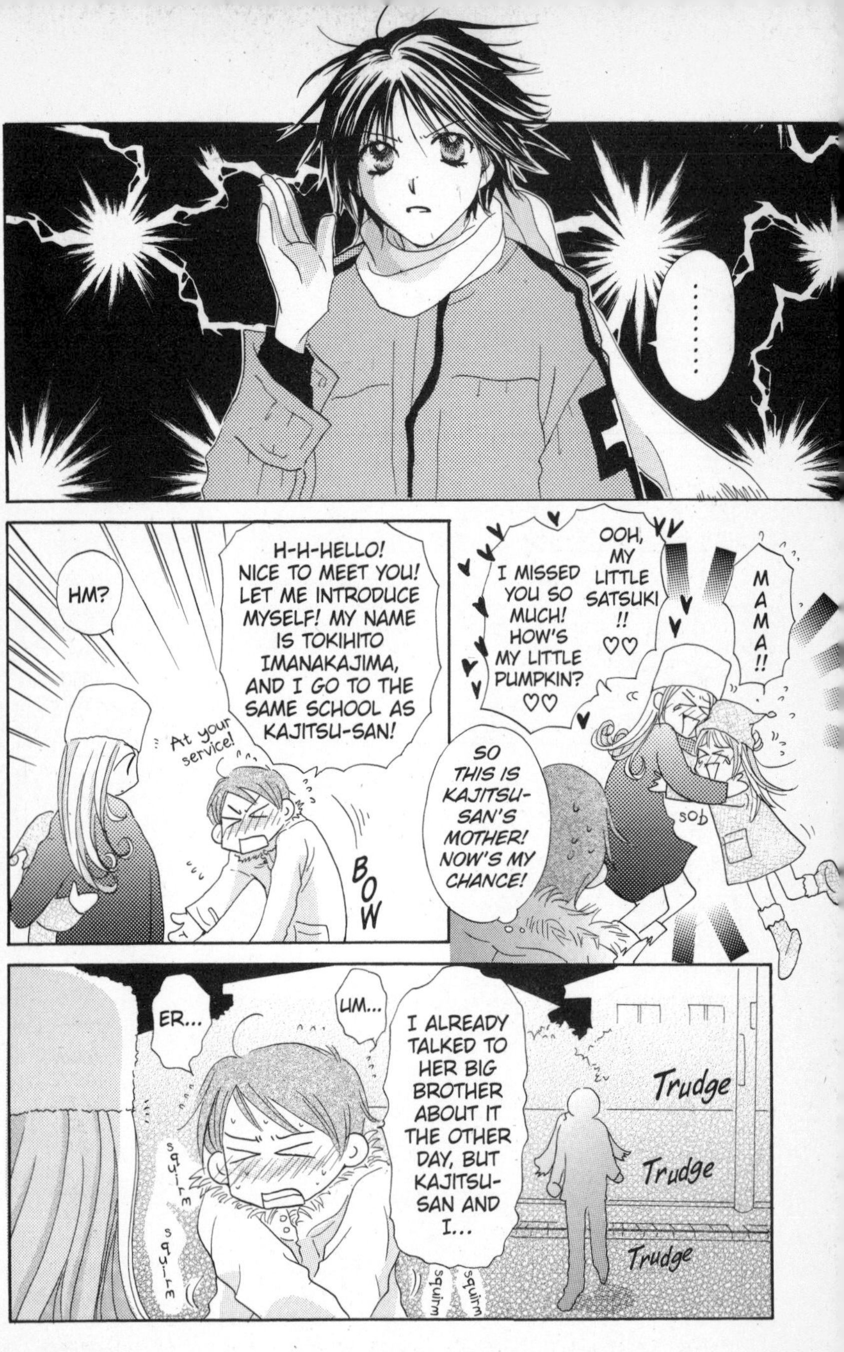
......
MAMA!!
OOH, MY LITTLE SATSUKI!! ♡♡
I MISSED YOU SO MUCH! HOW'S MY LITTLE PUMPKIN? ♡♡
sob
SO THIS IS KAJITSU-SAN'S MOTHER! NOW'S MY CHANCE!
H-H-HELLO! NICE TO MEET YOU! LET ME INTRODUCE MYSELF! MY NAME IS TOKIHITO IMANAKAJIMA, AND I GO TO THE SAME SCHOOL AS KAJITSU-SAN!
HM?
At your service!
BOW
Trudge
Trudge
Trudge
I ALREADY TALKED TO HER BIG BROTHER ABOUT IT THE OTHER DAY, BUT KAJITSU-SAN AND I...
squirm
squirm
UM...
ER...
squirm
squirm

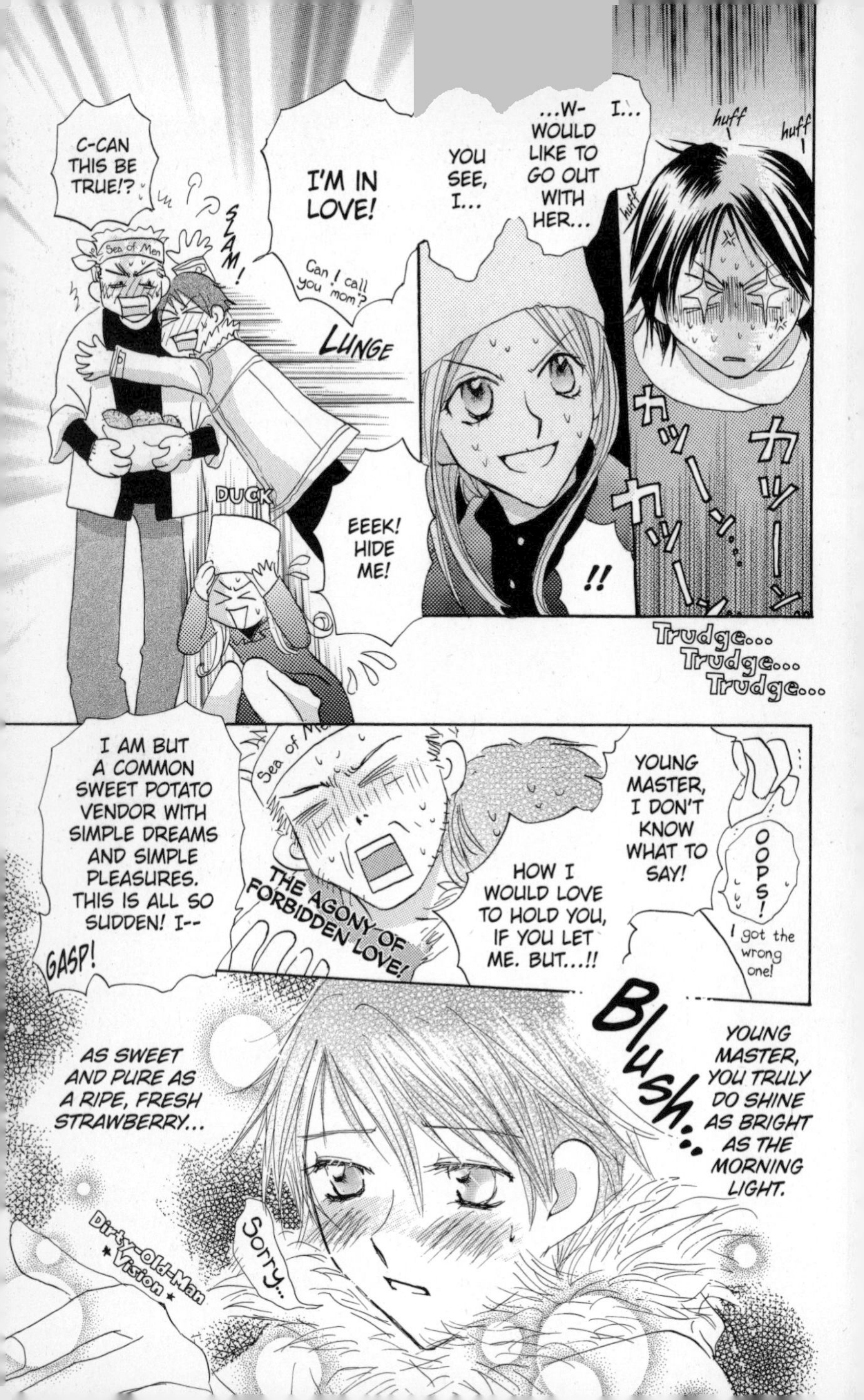
huff
huff
huff
!!
I...
...W- WOULD LIKE TO GO OUT WITH HER...
YOU SEE, I...
I'M IN LOVE!
Trudge... Trudge... Trudge...
C-CAN THIS BE TRUE!?
SLAM!
Can I call you mom?
LUNGE
DUCK
EEEK! HIDE ME!
OOPS!
I got the wrong one!
YOUNG MASTER, I DON'T KNOW WHAT TO SAY!
HOW I WOULD LOVE TO HOLD YOU, IF YOU LET ME. BUT...!!
THE AGONY OF FORBIDDEN LOVE!
Sea of Men
I AM BUT A COMMON SWEET POTATO VENDOR WITH SIMPLE DREAMS AND SIMPLE PLEASURES. THIS IS ALL SO SUDDEN! I--
GASP!
Blush...
YOUNG MASTER, YOU TRULY DO SHINE AS BRIGHT AS THE MORNING LIGHT.
AS SWEET AND PURE AS A RIPE, FRESH STRAWBERRY...
Sorry...
Dirty-Old-Man ★ Vision ★

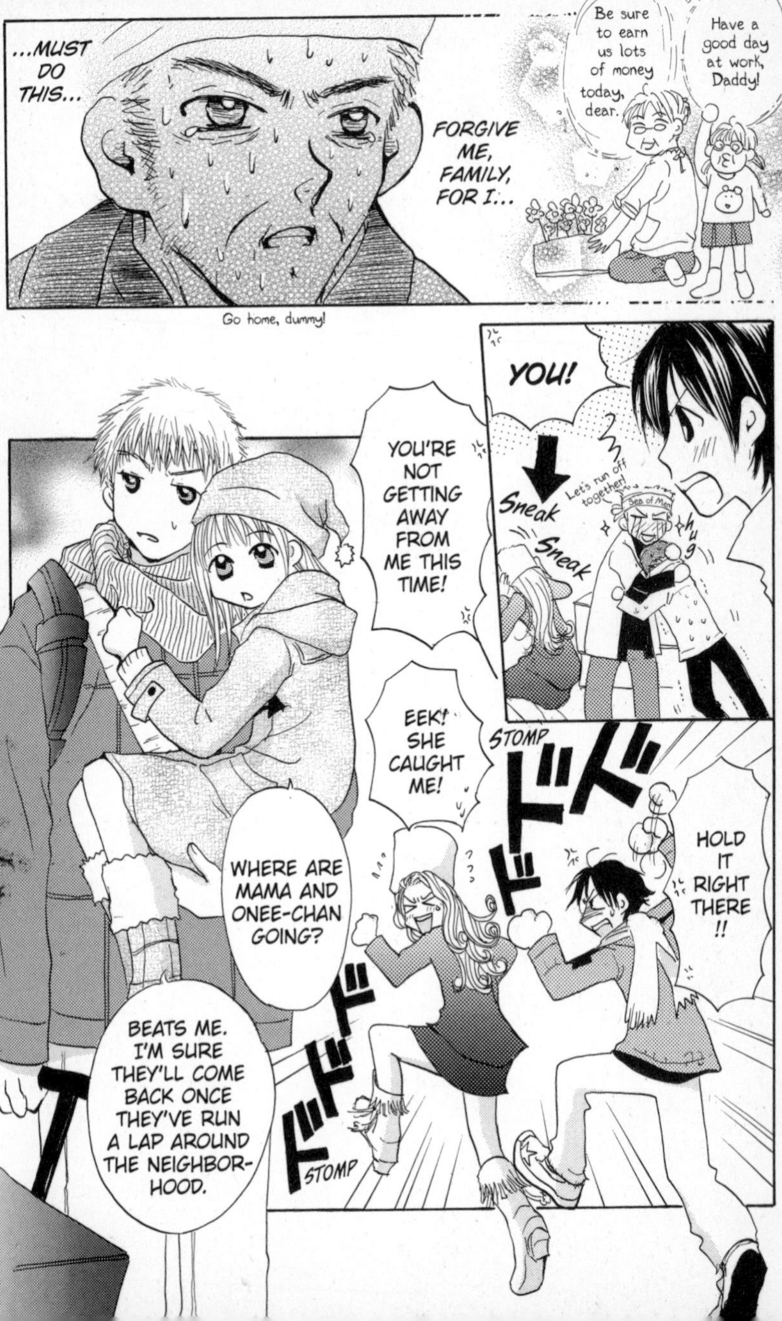
Have a good day at work, Daddy!
Be sure to earn us lots of money today, dear.
FORGIVE ME, FAMILY, FOR I...
...MUST DO THIS...
Go home, dummy!
YOU!
Let's run off together!
Sea of Men
hug
Sneak
Sneak
YOU'RE NOT GETTING AWAY FROM ME THIS TIME!
HOLD IT RIGHT THERE!!
STOMP
ドドド
EEK! SHE CAUGHT ME!
ドドド
STOMP
WHERE ARE MAMA AND ONEE-CHAN GOING?
BEATS ME. I'M SURE THEY'LL COME BACK ONCE THEY'VE RUN A LAP AROUND THE NEIGHBOR-HOOD.

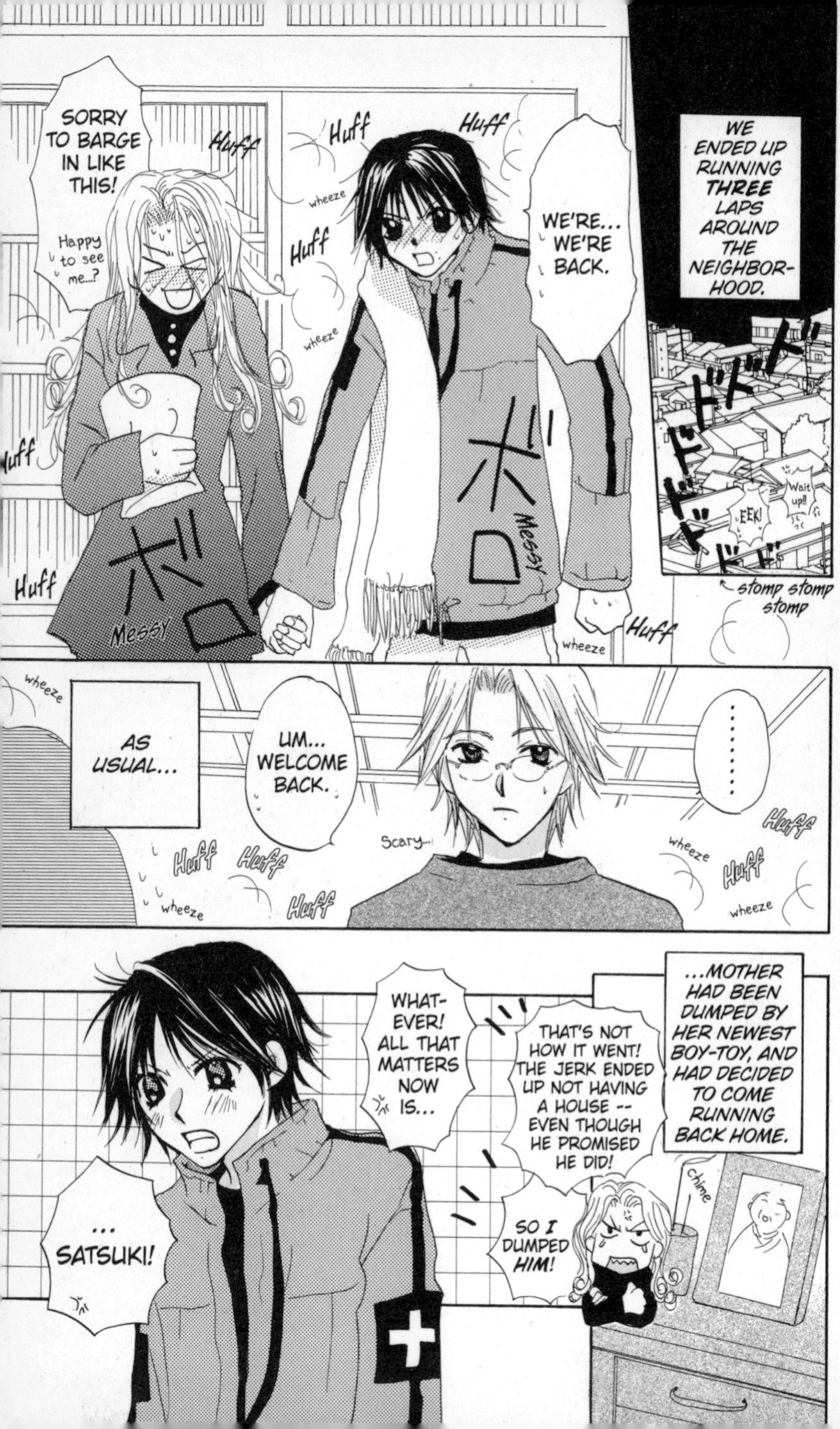
WE ENDED UP RUNNING THREE LAPS AROUND THE NEIGHBOR-HOOD.
EEK!
Wait up!!
stomp stomp stomp
WE'RE... WE'RE BACK.
Huff
wheeze
SORRY TO BARGE IN LIKE THIS!
Happy to see me...?
Messy
Messy
......
UM... WELCOME BACK.
Scary...
AS USUAL...
Huff
wheeze
...MOTHER HAD BEEN DUMPED BY HER NEWEST BOY-TOY, AND HAD DECIDED TO COME RUNNING BACK HOME.
THAT'S NOT HOW IT WENT! THE JERK ENDED UP NOT HAVING A HOUSE -- EVEN THOUGH HE PROMISED HE DID!
SO I DUMPED HIM!
chime
WHAT-EVER! ALL THAT MATTERS NOW IS...
...SATSUKI!

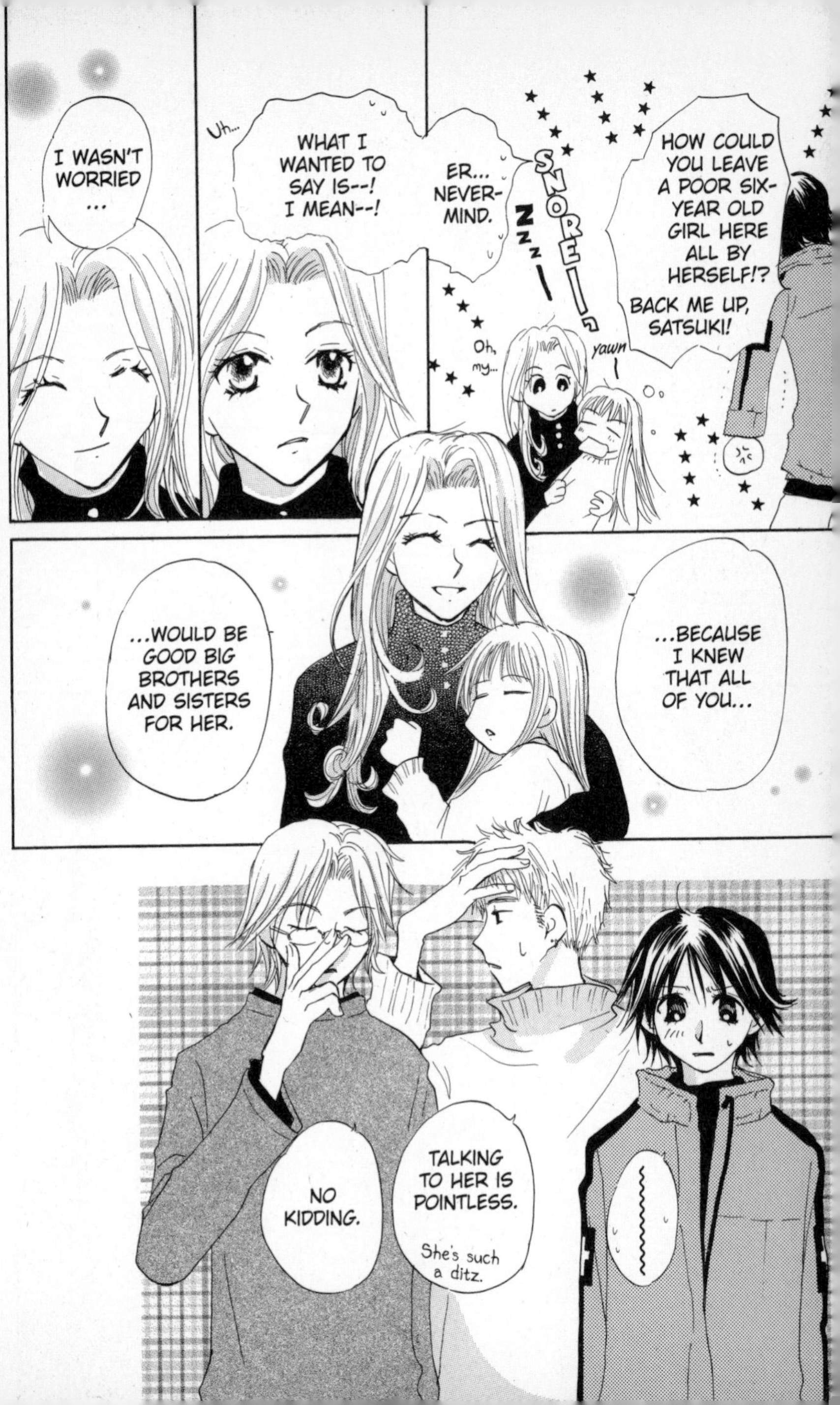
HOW COULD YOU LEAVE A POOR SIX-YEAR OLD GIRL HERE ALL BY HERSELF!?
BACK ME UP, SATSUKI!
SNORE
ZZZ
yawn
Oh, my...
ER... NEVER-MIND.
Uh...
WHAT I WANTED TO SAY IS--! I MEAN--!
I WASN'T WORRIED ...
...BECAUSE I KNEW THAT ALL OF YOU...
...WOULD BE GOOD BIG BROTHERS AND SISTERS FOR HER.
TALKING TO HER IS POINTLESS.
She's such a ditz.
NO KIDDING.

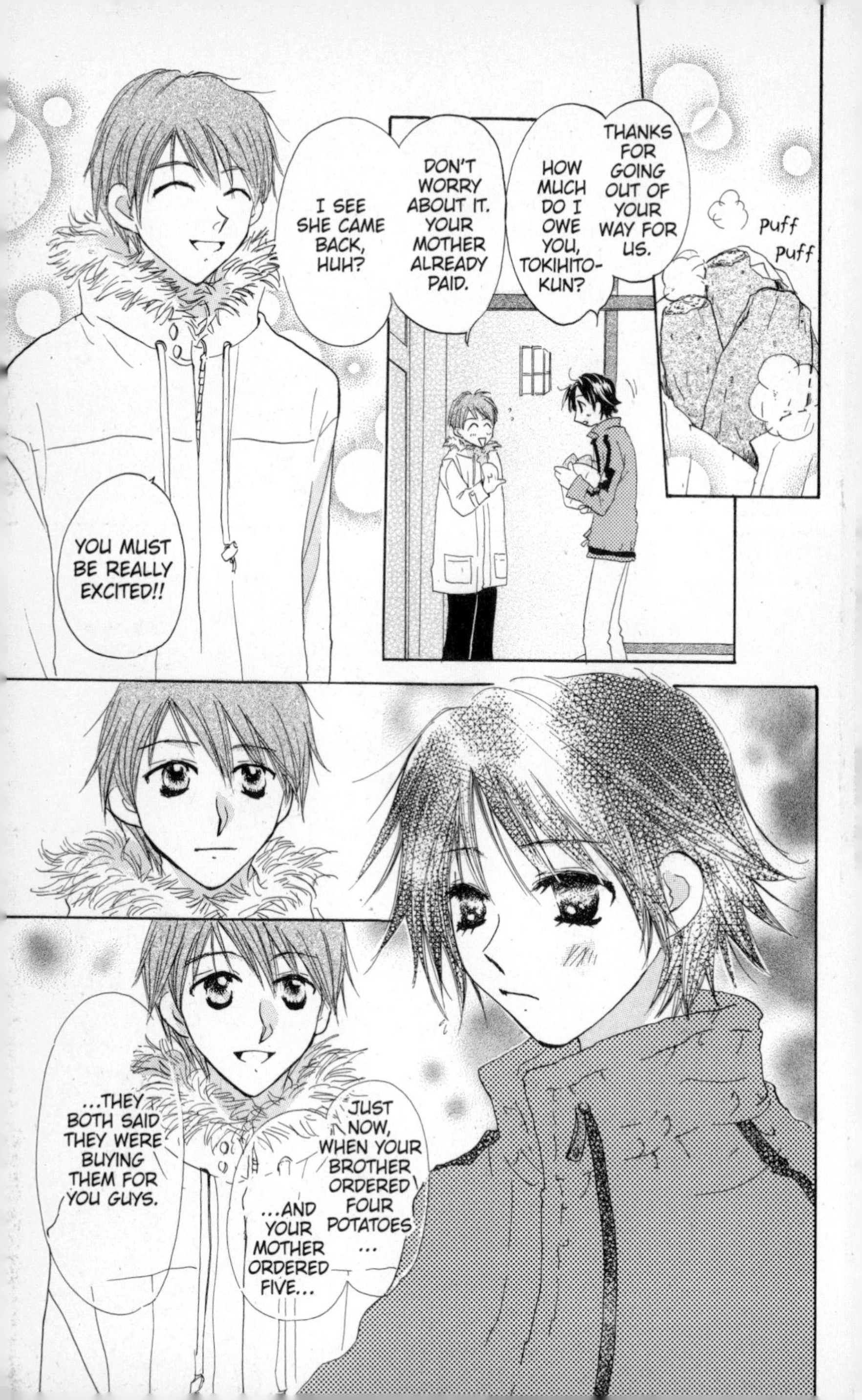
puff
puff
THANKS FOR GOING OUT OF YOUR WAY FOR US.
HOW MUCH DO I OWE YOU, TOKIHITO-KUN?
DON'T WORRY ABOUT IT. YOUR MOTHER ALREADY PAID.
I SEE SHE CAME BACK, HUH?
YOU MUST BE REALLY EXCITED!!
JUST NOW, WHEN YOUR BROTHER ORDERED FOUR POTATOES...
...AND YOUR MOTHER ORDERED FIVE...
...THEY BOTH SAID THEY WERE BUYING THEM FOR YOU GUYS.

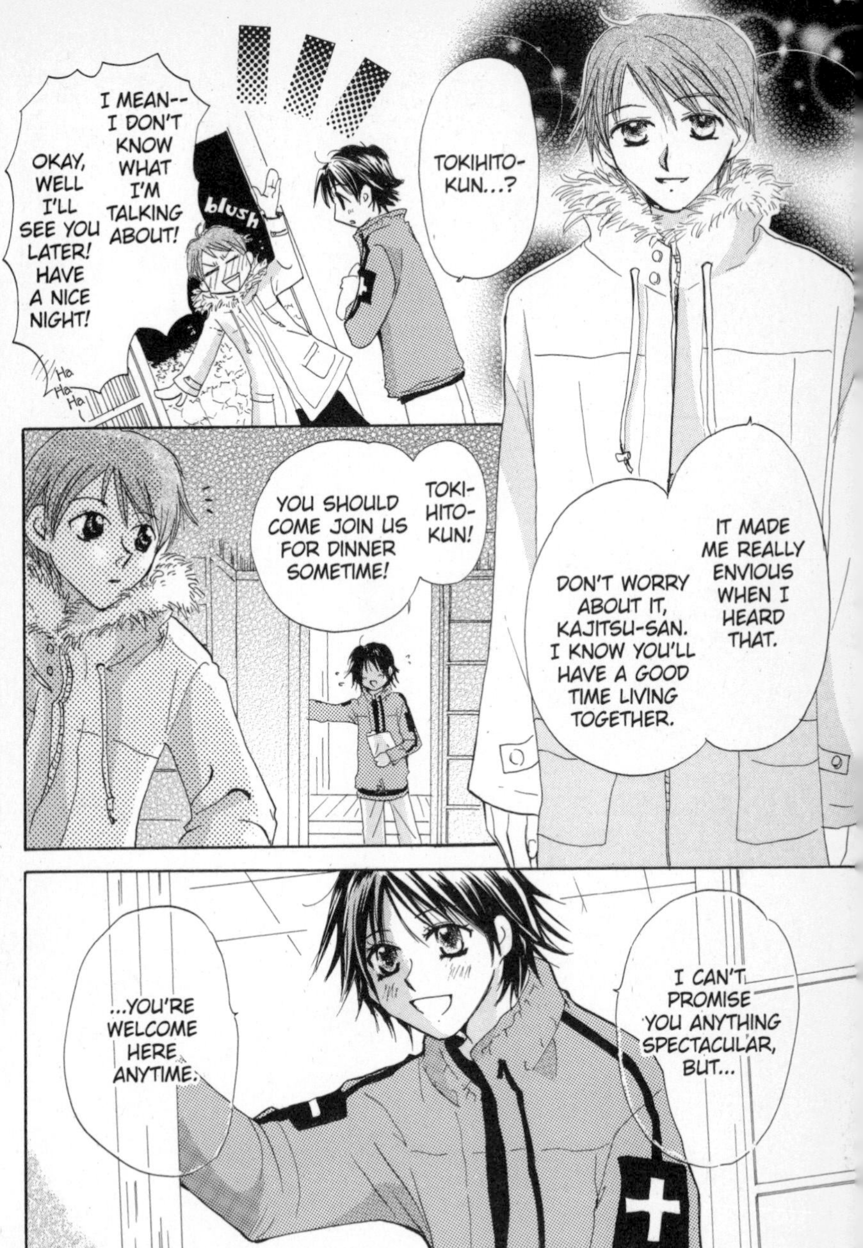
IT MADE ME REALLY ENVIOUS WHEN I HEARD THAT.
DON'T WORRY ABOUT IT, KAJITSU-SAN. I KNOW YOU'LL HAVE A GOOD TIME LIVING TOGETHER.
TOKIHITO-KUN...?
blush
I MEAN-- I DON'T KNOW WHAT I'M TALKING ABOUT!
OKAY, WELL I'LL SEE YOU LATER! HAVE A NICE NIGHT!
Ha Ha Ha
TOKI-HITO-KUN!
YOU SHOULD COME JOIN US FOR DINNER SOMETIME!
I CAN'T PROMISE YOU ANYTHING SPECTACULAR, BUT...
...YOU'RE WELCOME HERE ANYTIME.

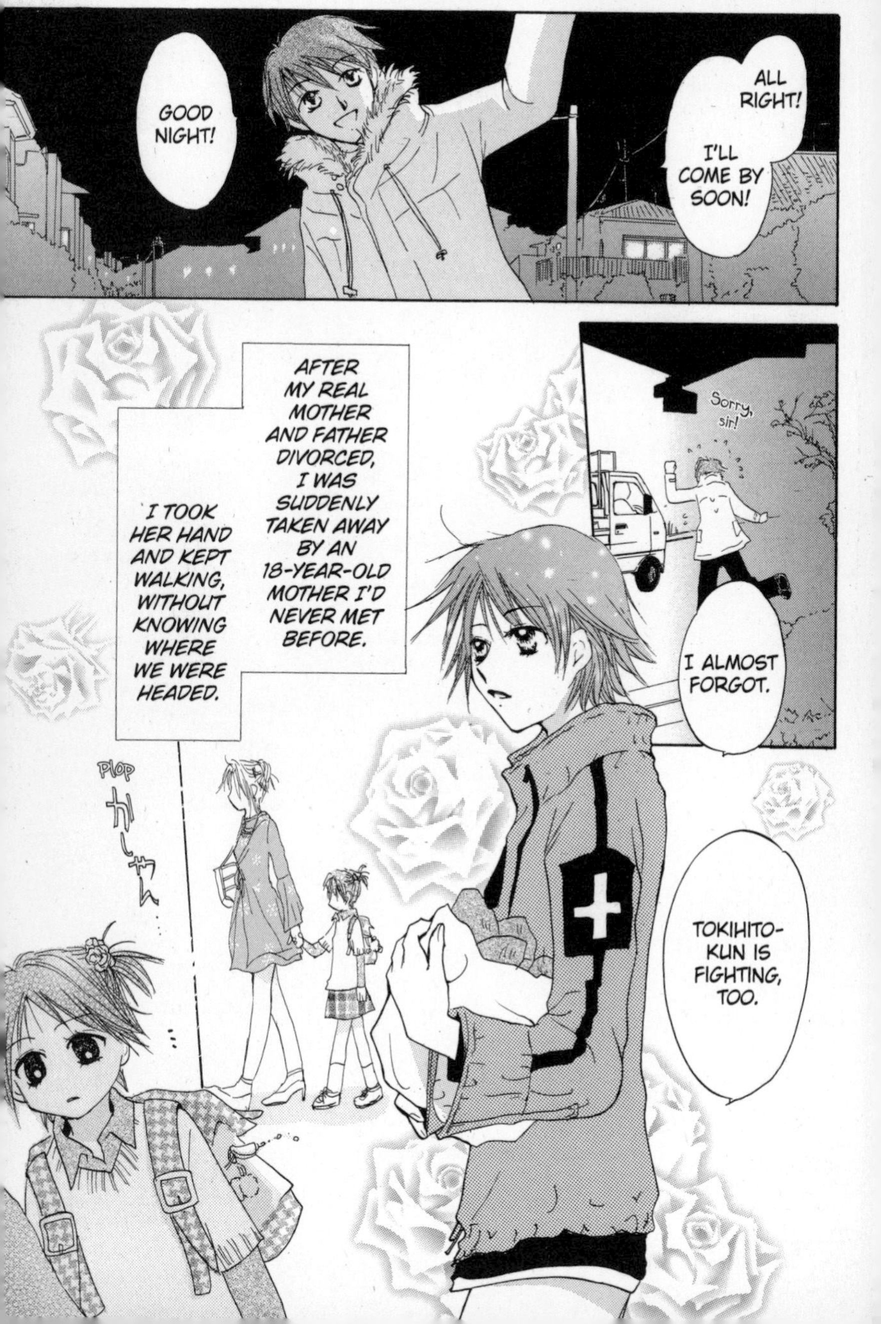
ALL RIGHT!
I'LL COME BY SOON!
GOOD NIGHT!
Sorry, sir!
I ALMOST FORGOT.
TOKIHITO-KUN IS FIGHTING, TOO.
AFTER MY REAL MOTHER AND FATHER DIVORCED, I WAS SUDDENLY TAKEN AWAY BY AN 18-YEAR-OLD MOTHER I'D NEVER MET BEFORE.
I TOOK HER HAND AND KEPT WALKING, WITHOUT KNOWING WHERE WE WERE HEADED.
PLOP
かしゃん
...

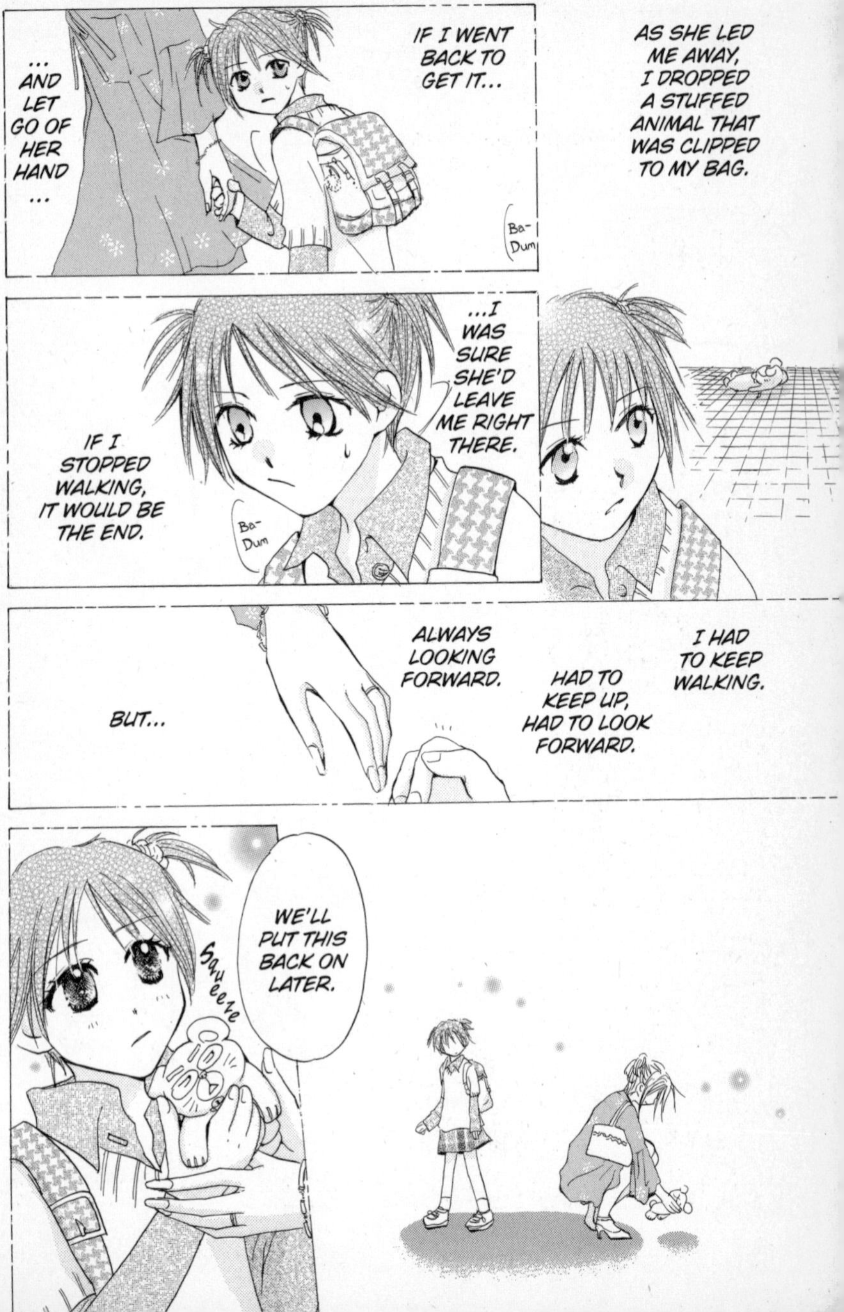
AS SHE LED ME AWAY, I DROPPED A STUFFED ANIMAL THAT WAS CLIPPED TO MY BAG.
IF I WENT BACK TO GET IT...
Ba-Dum
...AND LET GO OF HER HAND...
...I WAS SURE SHE'D LEAVE ME RIGHT THERE.
Ba-Dum
IF I STOPPED WALKING, IT WOULD BE THE END.
I HAD TO KEEP WALKING.
HAD TO KEEP UP, HAD TO LOOK FORWARD.
ALWAYS LOOKING FORWARD.
BUT...
WE'LL PUT THIS BACK ON LATER.
Squeeze

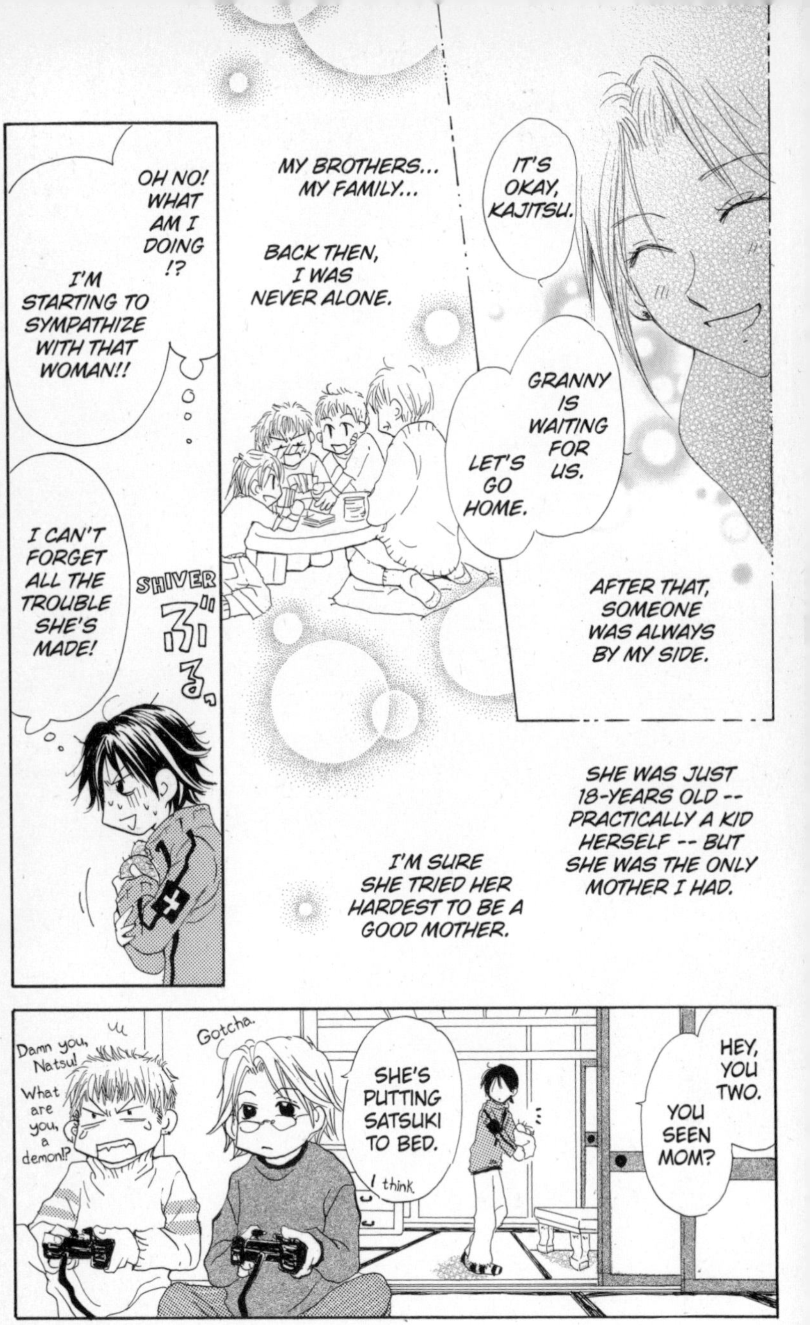
IT'S OKAY, KAJITSU.
GRANNY IS WAITING FOR US.
LET'S GO HOME.
AFTER THAT, SOMEONE WAS ALWAYS BY MY SIDE.
MY BROTHERS... MY FAMILY...
BACK THEN, I WAS NEVER ALONE.
SHE WAS JUST 18-YEARS OLD -- PRACTICALLY A KID HERSELF -- BUT SHE WAS THE ONLY MOTHER I HAD.
I'M SURE SHE TRIED HER HARDEST TO BE A GOOD MOTHER.
OH NO! WHAT AM I DOING !?
I'M STARTING TO SYMPATHIZE WITH THAT WOMAN!!
I CAN'T FORGET ALL THE TROUBLE SHE'S MADE!
SHIVER
HEY, YOU TWO.
YOU SEEN MOM?
SHE'S PUTTING SATSUKI TO BED.
I think.
Gotcha.
Damn you, Natsu!
What are you, a demon!?

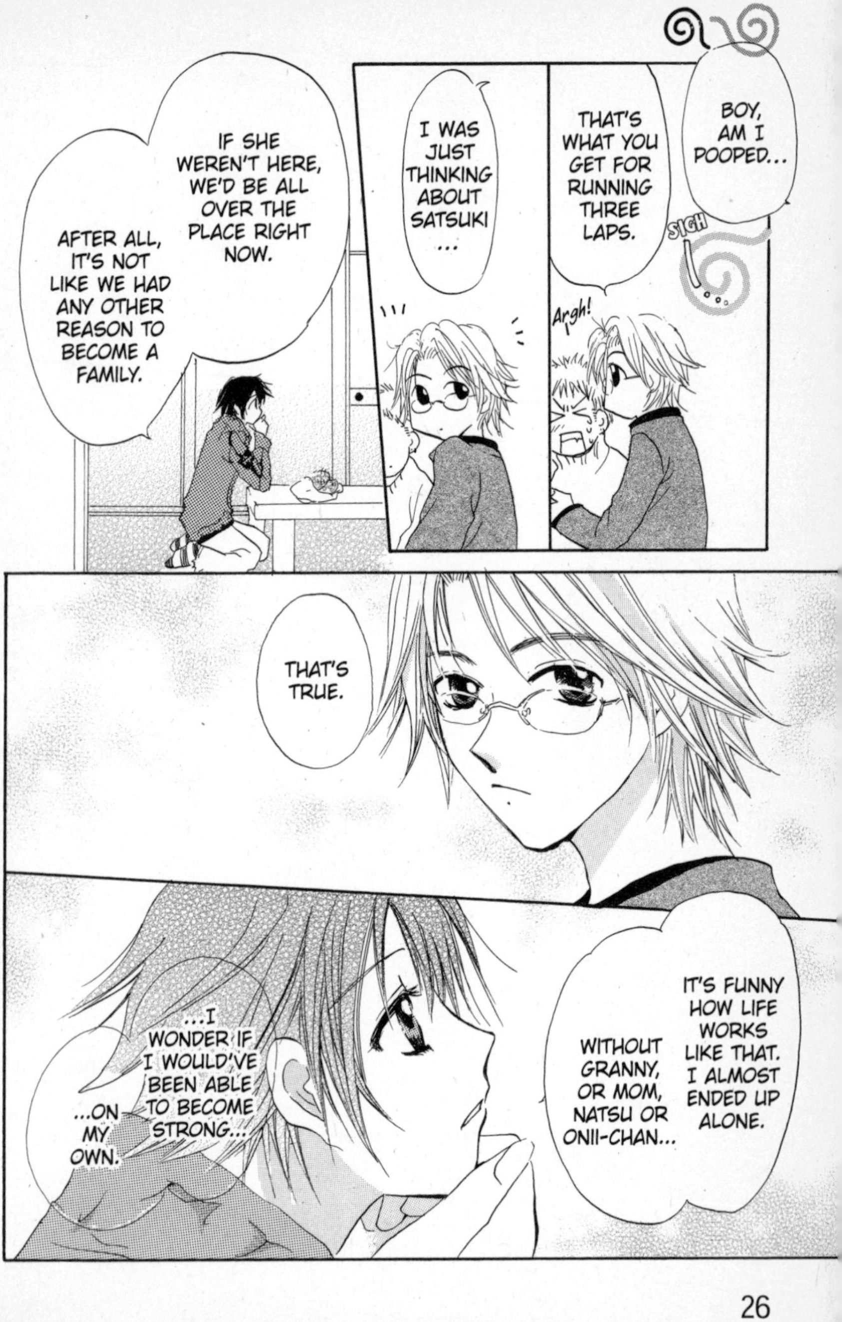
BOY, AM I POOPED...
SIGH
THAT'S WHAT YOU GET FOR RUNNING THREE LAPS.
Argh!
I WAS JUST THINKING ABOUT SATSUKI ...
IF SHE WEREN'T HERE, WE'D BE ALL OVER THE PLACE RIGHT NOW.
AFTER ALL, IT'S NOT LIKE WE HAD ANY OTHER REASON TO BECOME A FAMILY.
THAT'S TRUE.
IT'S FUNNY HOW LIFE WORKS LIKE THAT. I ALMOST ENDED UP ALONE.
WITHOUT GRANNY, OR MOM, NATSU OR ONII-CHAN...
...I WONDER IF I WOULD'VE BEEN ABLE TO BECOME STRONG...
...ON MY OWN.

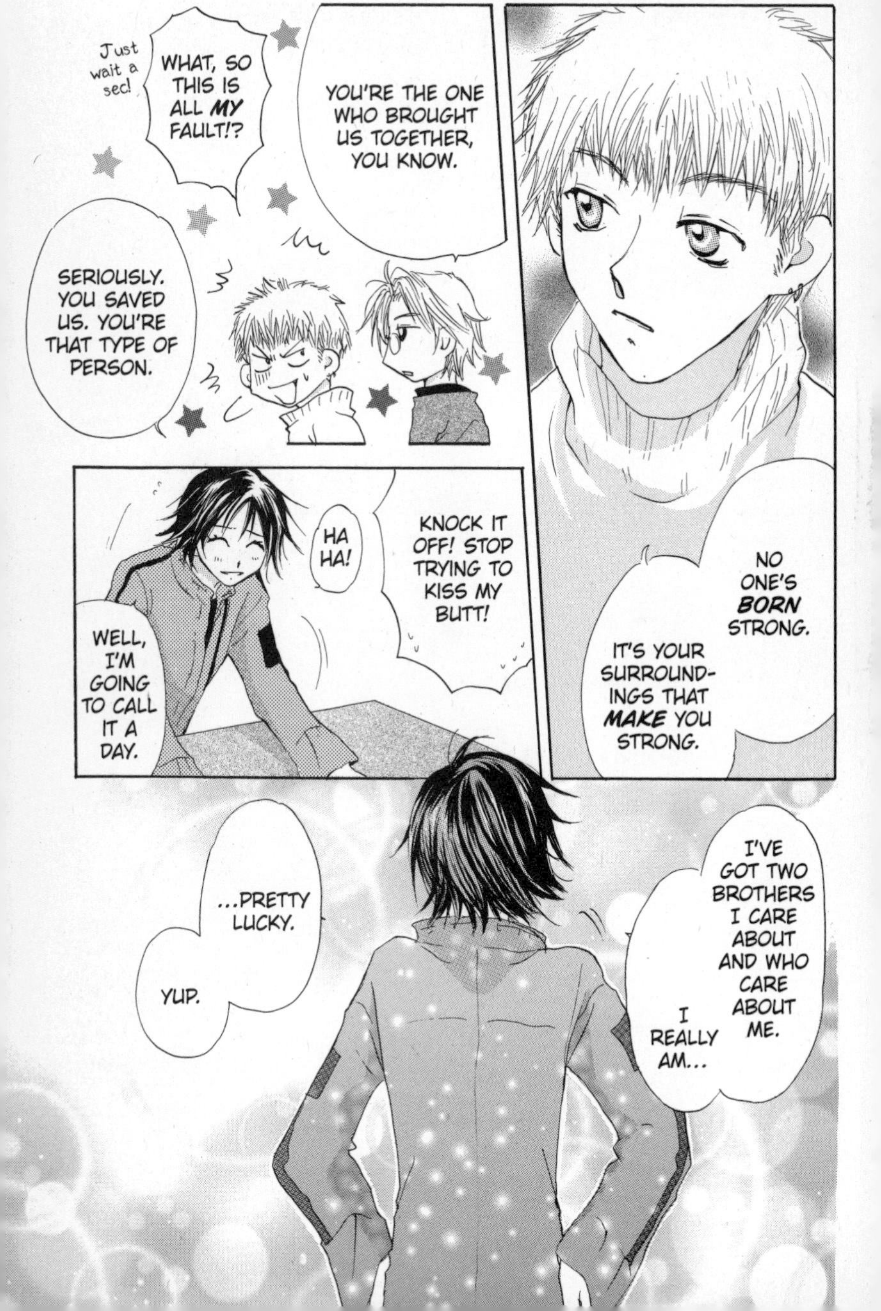
NO ONE'S **BORN** STRONG.
IT'S YOUR SURROUNDINGS THAT **MAKE** YOU STRONG.
YOU'RE THE ONE WHO BROUGHT US TOGETHER, YOU KNOW.
WHAT, SO THIS IS ALL **MY** FAULT!?
Just wait a sec!
SERIOUSLY. YOU SAVED US. YOU'RE THAT TYPE OF PERSON.
KNOCK IT OFF! STOP TRYING TO KISS MY BUTT!
HA HA!
WELL, I'M GOING TO CALL IT A DAY.
I'VE GOT TWO BROTHERS I CARE ABOUT AND WHO CARE ABOUT ME.
I REALLY AM...
...PRETTY LUCKY.
YUP.

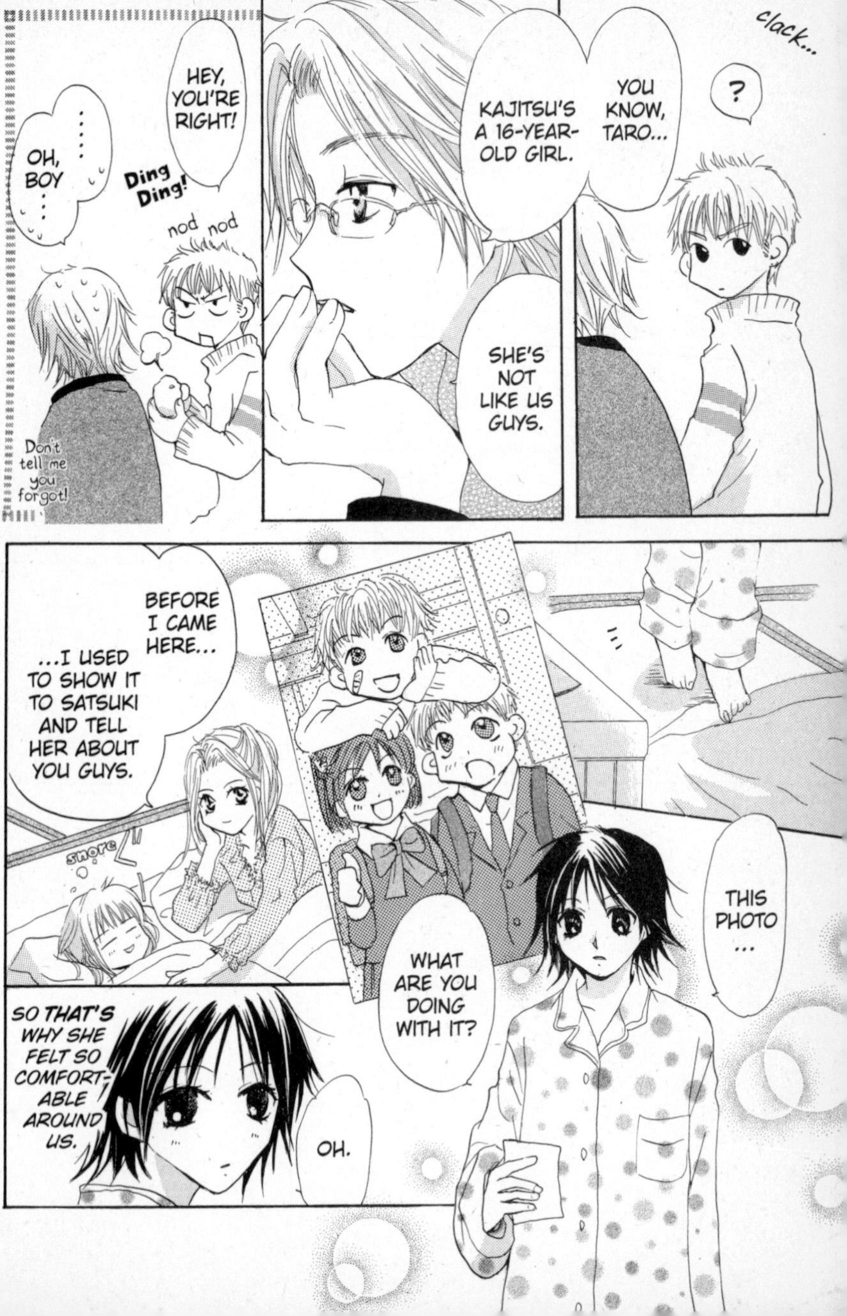
clack...
?
YOU KNOW, TARO...
KAJITSU'S A 16-YEAR-OLD GIRL.
SHE'S NOT LIKE US GUYS.
HEY, YOU'RE RIGHT!
Ding Ding!
nod nod
OH, BOY ......
Don't tell me you forgot!
THIS PHOTO ...
WHAT ARE YOU DOING WITH IT?
BEFORE I CAME HERE...
...I USED TO SHOW IT TO SATSUKI AND TELL HER ABOUT YOU GUYS.
snore
OH.
SO THAT'S WHY SHE FELT SO COMFORT-ABLE AROUND US.

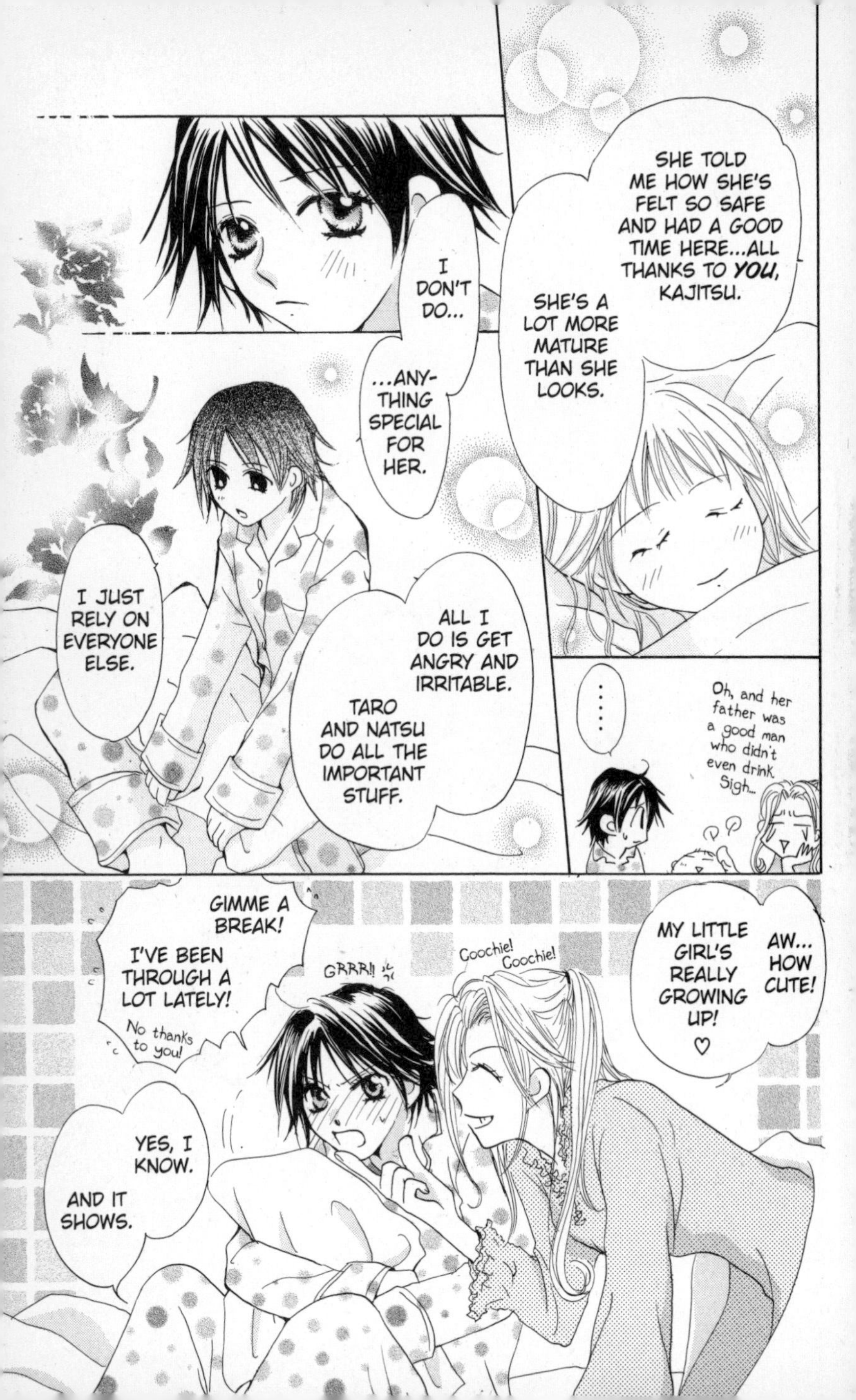
SHE TOLD ME HOW SHE'S FELT SO SAFE AND HAD A GOOD TIME HERE...ALL THANKS TO *YOU*, KAJITSU.
SHE'S A LOT MORE MATURE THAN SHE LOOKS.
I DON'T DO...
...ANY-THING SPECIAL FOR HER.
ALL I DO IS GET ANGRY AND IRRITABLE.
TARO AND NATSU DO ALL THE IMPORTANT STUFF.
I JUST RELY ON EVERYONE ELSE.
......
Oh, and her father was a good man who didn't even drink. Sigh...
AW... HOW CUTE!
MY LITTLE GIRL'S REALLY GROWING UP! ♡
Coochie! Coochie!
GRRR!!
GIMME A BREAK!
I'VE BEEN THROUGH A LOT LATELY!
No thanks to you!
YES, I KNOW.
AND IT SHOWS.

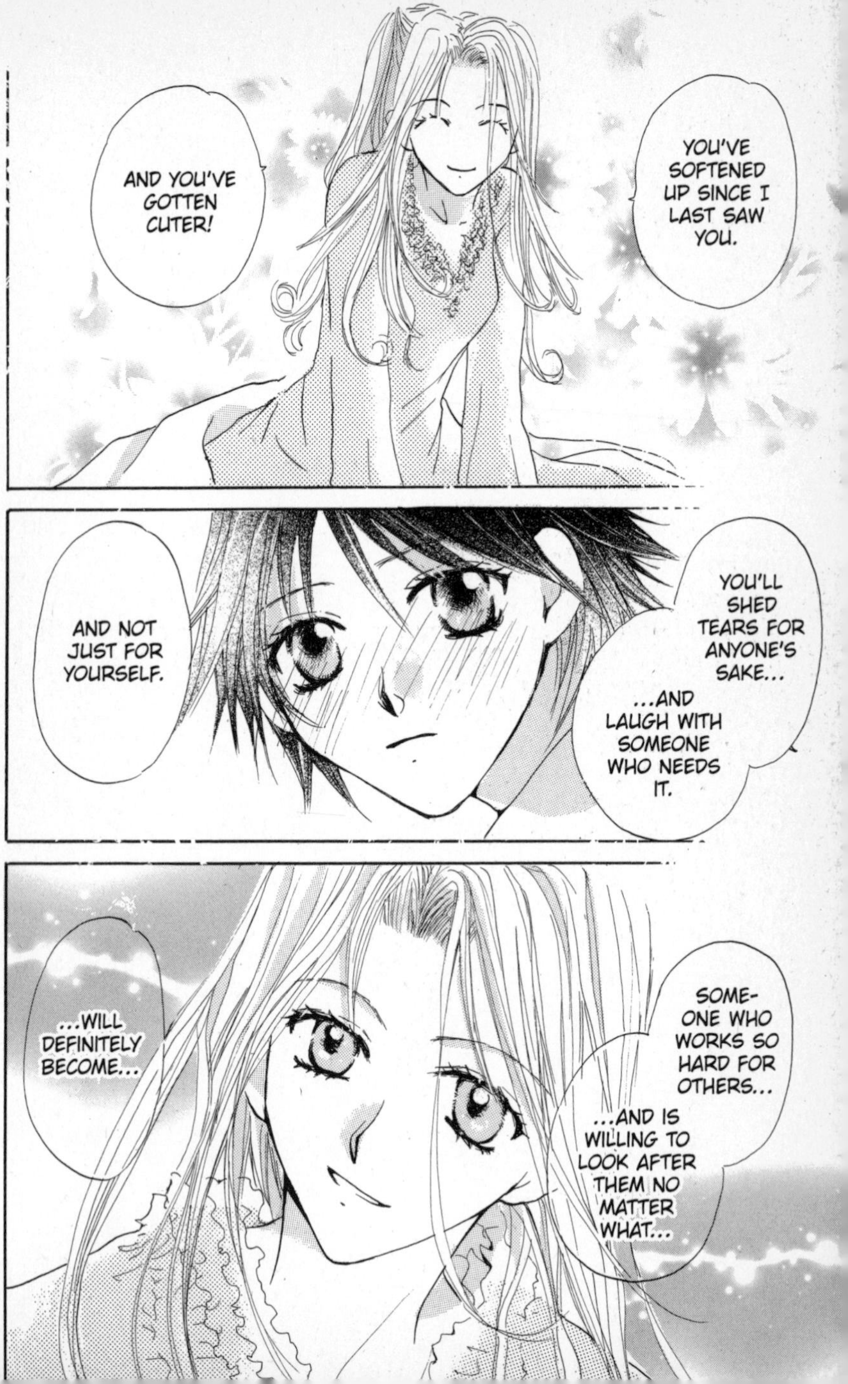
YOU'VE SOFTENED UP SINCE I LAST SAW YOU.
AND YOU'VE GOTTEN CUTER!
YOU'LL SHED TEARS FOR ANYONE'S SAKE...
...AND LAUGH WITH SOMEONE WHO NEEDS IT.
AND NOT JUST FOR YOURSELF.
SOME-ONE WHO WORKS SO HARD FOR OTHERS...
...AND IS WILLING TO LOOK AFTER THEM NO MATTER WHAT...
...WILL DEFINITELY BECOME...

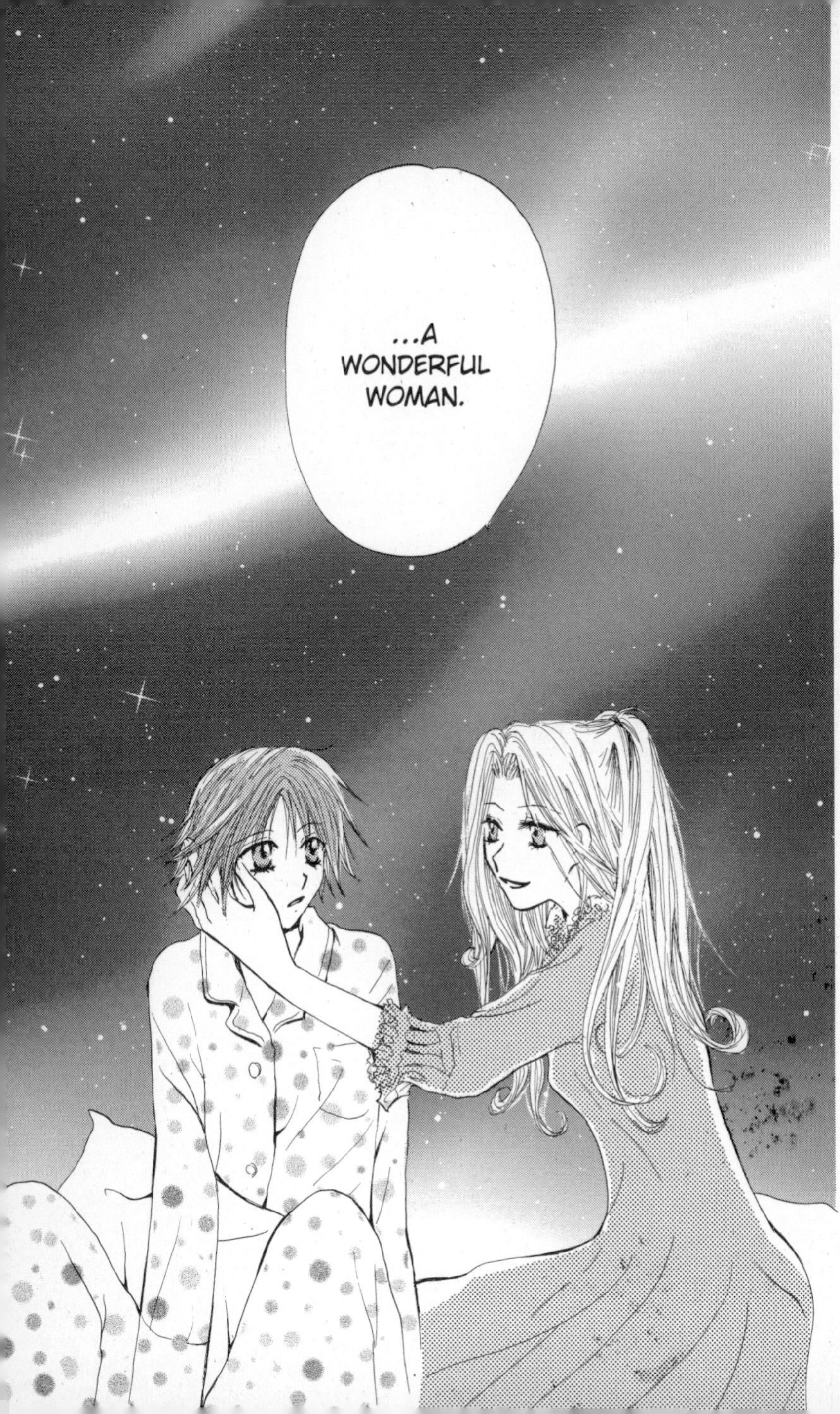
...A WONDERFUL WOMAN.

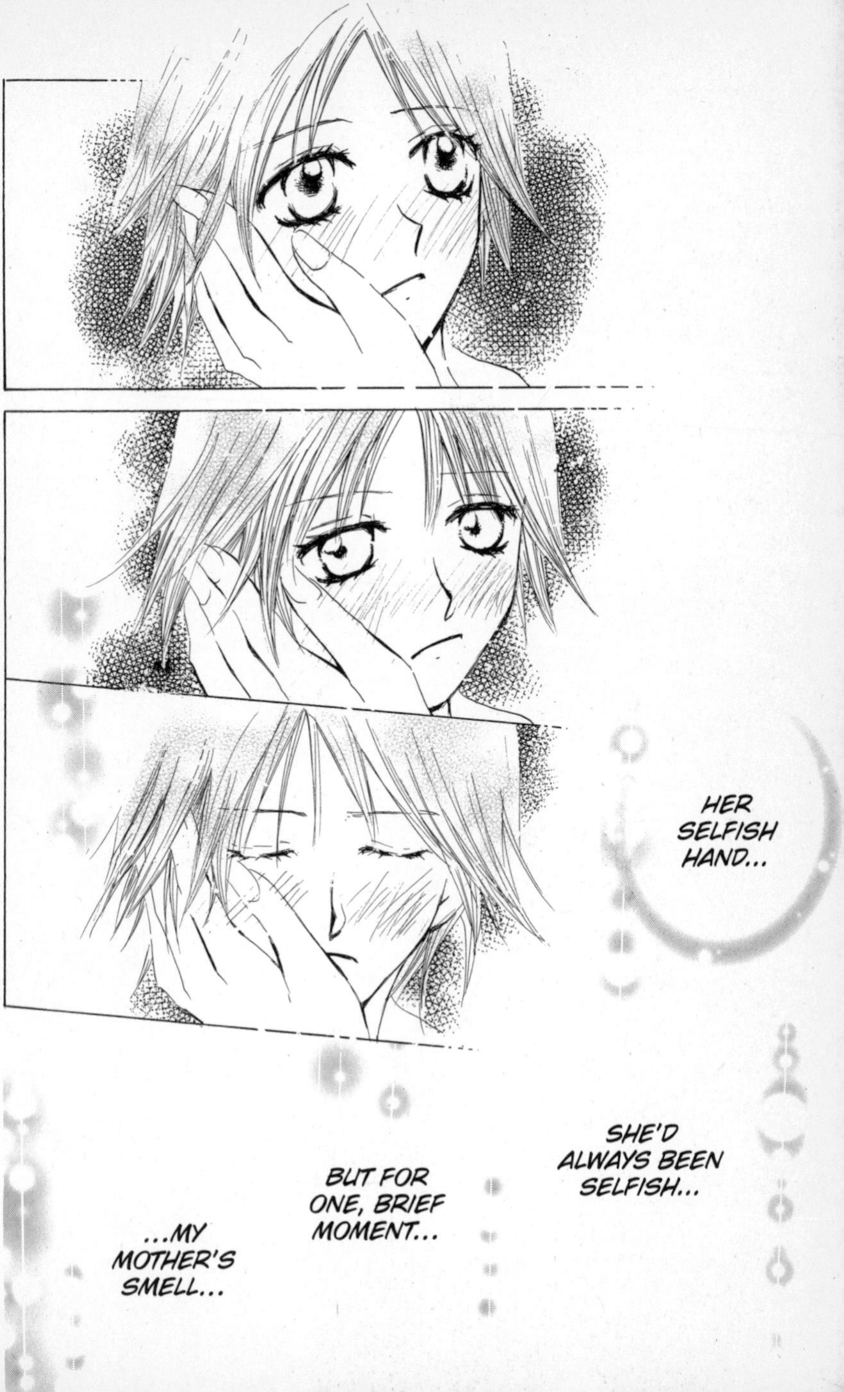
HER SELFISH HAND...
SHE'D ALWAYS BEEN SELFISH...
BUT FOR ONE, BRIEF MOMENT...
...MY MOTHER'S SMELL...

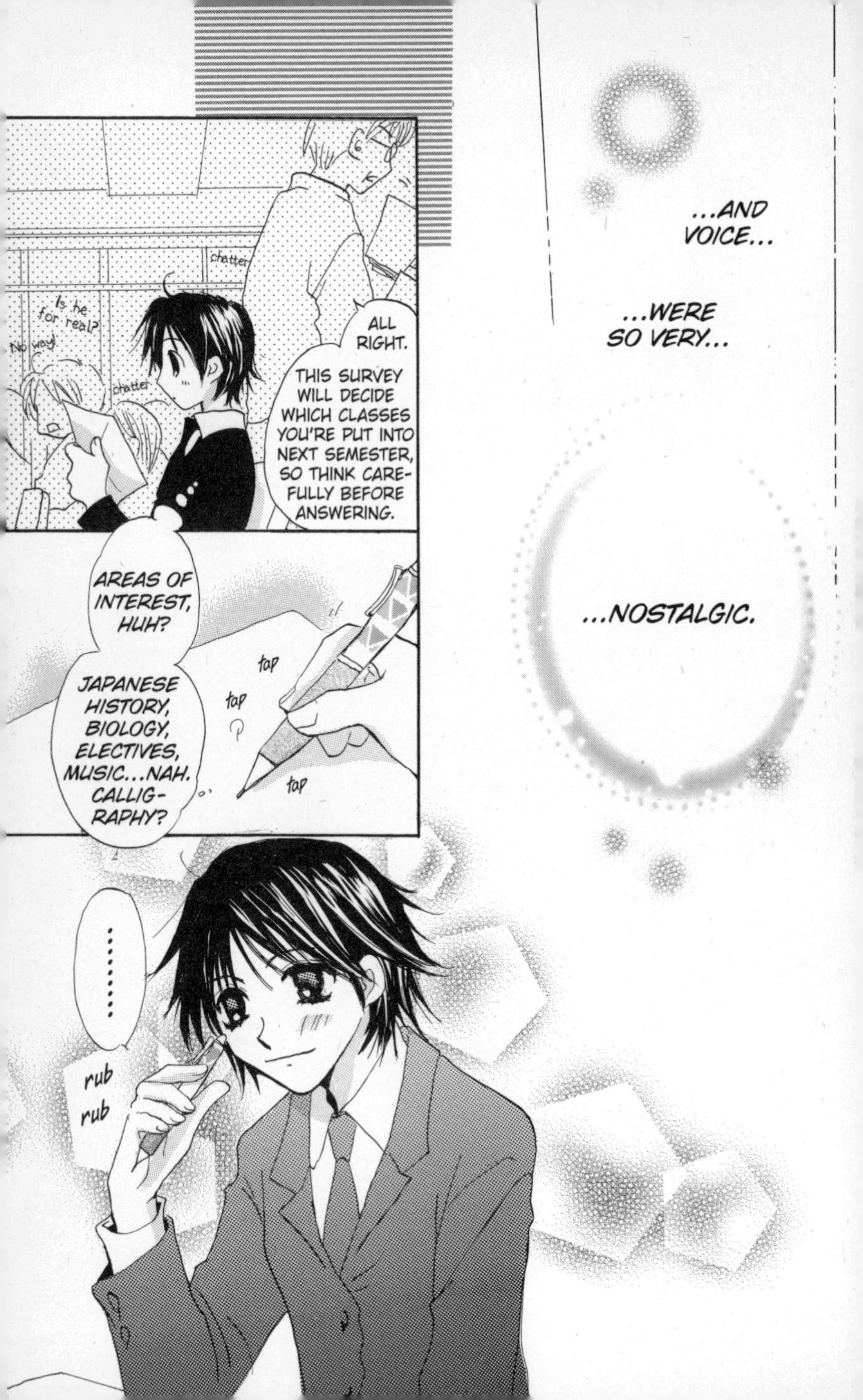
...AND VOICE...
...WERE SO VERY...
...NOSTALGIC.
chatter
ALL RIGHT. THIS SURVEY WILL DECIDE WHICH CLASSES YOU'RE PUT INTO NEXT SEMESTER, SO THINK CAREFULLY BEFORE ANSWERING.
Is he for real?
No way!
chatter
tap
tap
tap
AREAS OF INTEREST, HUH?
JAPANESE HISTORY, BIOLOGY, ELECTIVES, MUSIC...NAH. CALLIGRAPHY?
......
rub rub

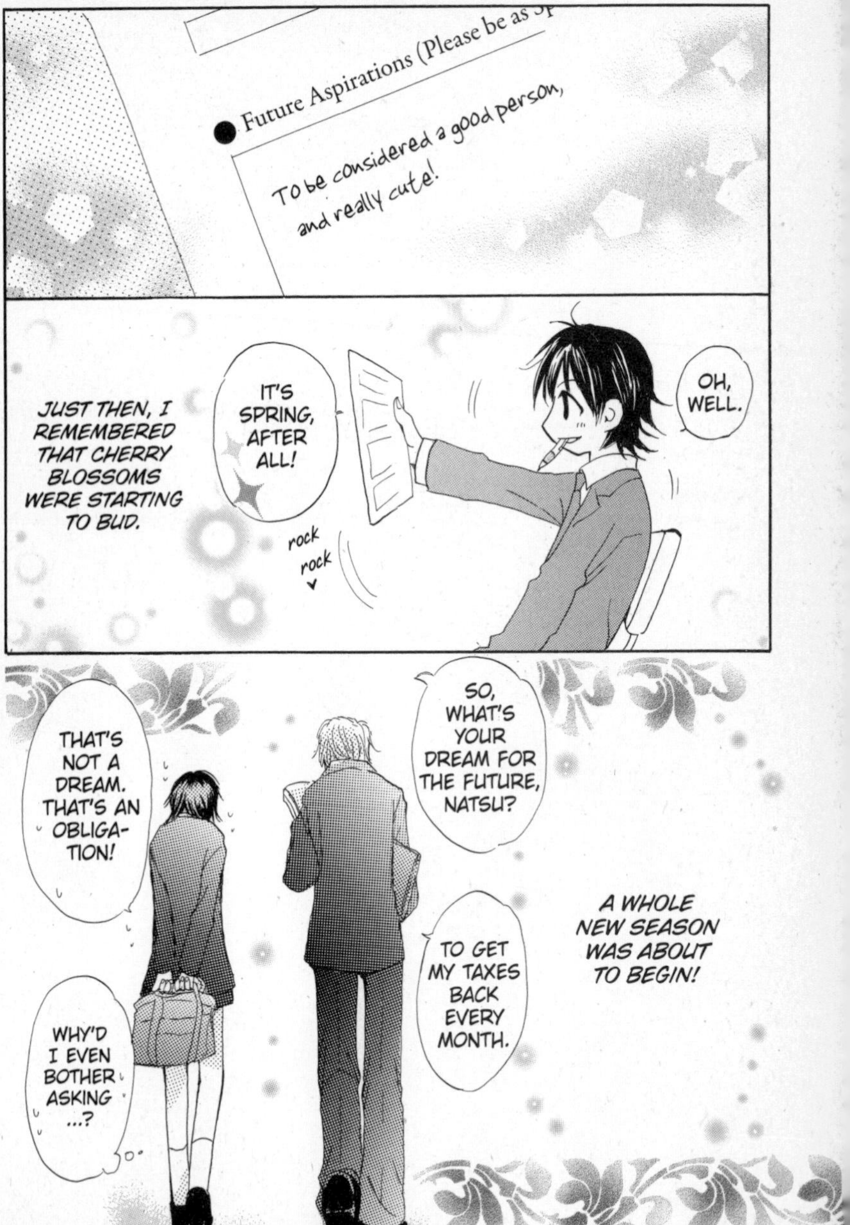
Future Aspirations (Please be as Sp
To be considered a good person, and really cute!
OH, WELL.
IT'S SPRING, AFTER ALL!
rock rock
JUST THEN, I REMEMBERED THAT CHERRY BLOSSOMS WERE STARTING TO BUD.
SO, WHAT'S YOUR DREAM FOR THE FUTURE, NATSU?
TO GET MY TAXES BACK EVERY MONTH.
THAT'S NOT A DREAM. THAT'S AN OBLIGATION!
WHY'D I EVEN BOTHER ASKING ...?
A WHOLE NEW SEASON WAS ABOUT TO BEGIN!

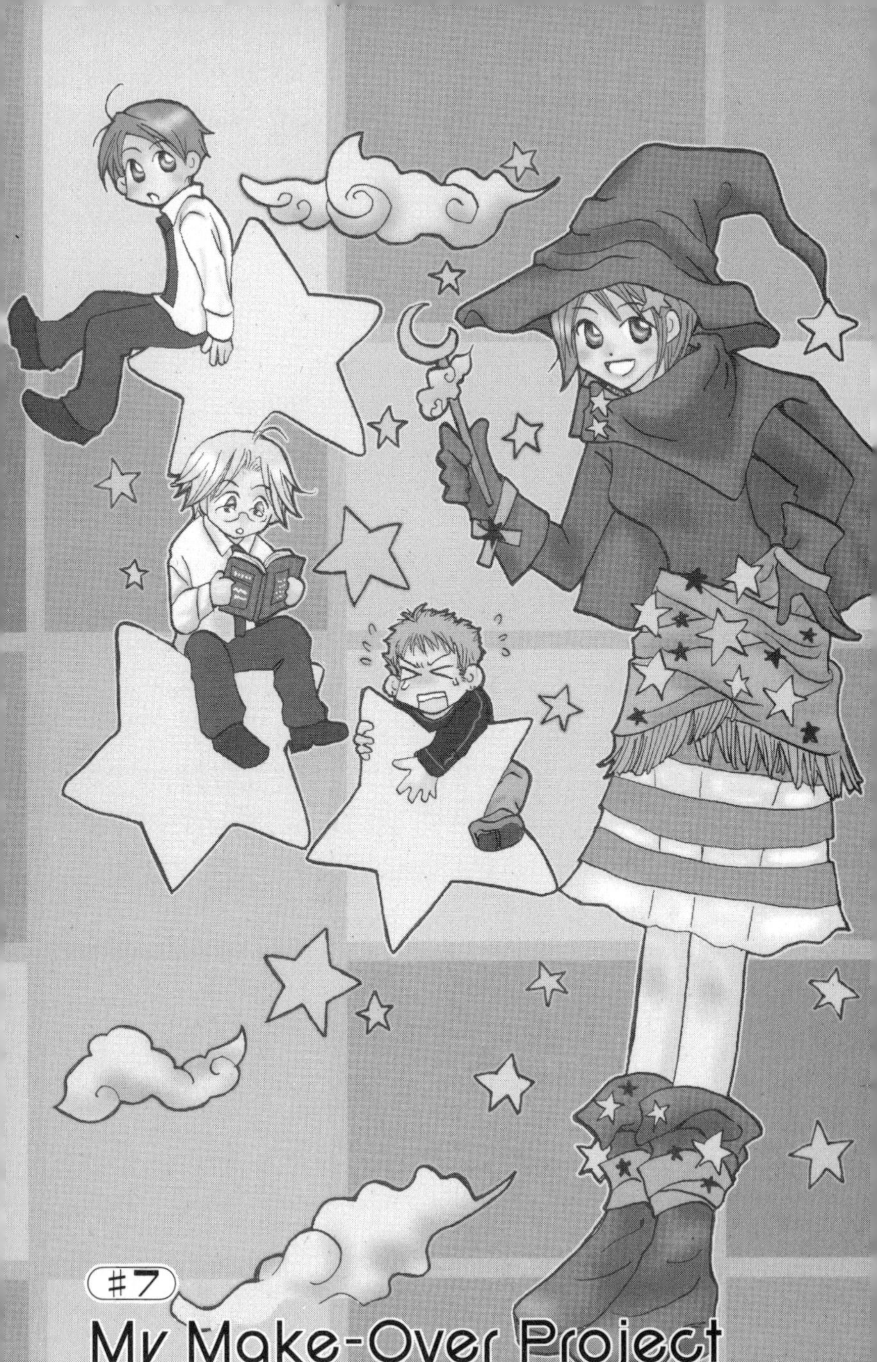

#7 My Make-Over Project

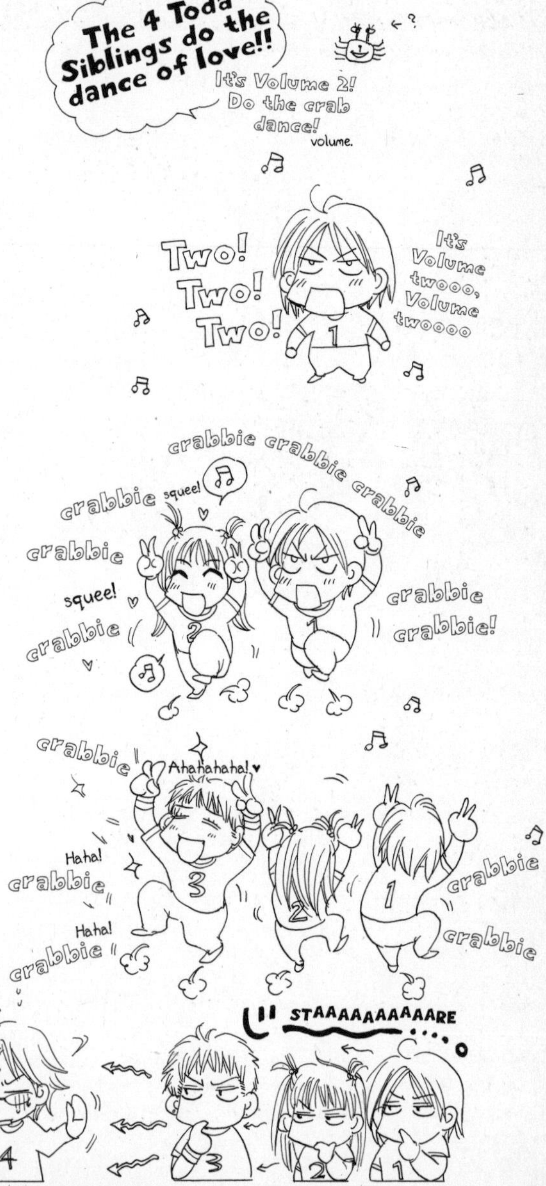

The 4 Toda Siblings do the dance of love!!
?
It's Volume 2! Do the crab dance!
volume.
It's Volume twooo, Volume twoooo
Two! Two! Two!
crabbie crabbie crabbie
crabbie
squee!
crabbie
squee!
crabbie
crabbie crabbie!
crabbie
Ahahahaha!♥
crabbie
crabbie
Haha!
crabbie
Haha!
crabbie
STAAAAAAAAAARE
Y-yes, I know what you want, but I'm not going to do it.
This is already embarrassing enough.
Geez, your stares are so heated...
THE END

crossroad Chapter 7: My Make-Over Project

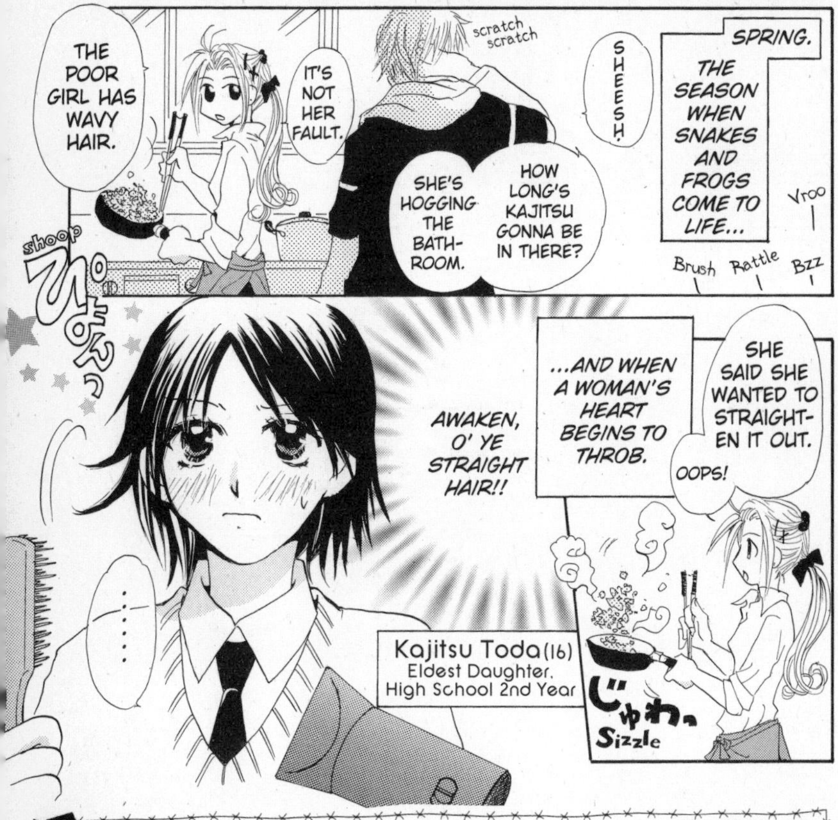
SPRING.
THE SEASON WHEN SNAKES AND FROGS COME TO LIFE...
Vroo
Brush
Rattle
Bzz
SHEESH.
scratch scratch
HOW LONG'S KAJITSU GONNA BE IN THERE?
SHE'S HOGGING THE BATH-ROOM.
IT'S NOT HER FAULT.
THE POOR GIRL HAS WAVY HAIR.
shoop
SHE SAID SHE WANTED TO STRAIGHT-EN IT OUT.
OOPS!
じゅわっ
Sizzle
...AND WHEN A WOMAN'S HEART BEGINS TO THROB.
AWAKEN, O' YE STRAIGHT HAIR!!
Kajitsu Toda(16)
Eldest Daughter, High School 2nd Year
......

Teachers ②

The model I used for Akai-Sensei was some random guy I saw on a trip to Beijing, China. He was letting a bunch of kids hitch a ride on the back of his truck as he puffed away on his cigarette, with his shirt halfway unbuttoned. Of course I thought he looked just AMAZING on the spot. As for Toma-Kun, he's based on a celebrity, but if I said that the only difference is his hair style, then I'm sure a lot of his fans would be angry at me, so I'm not going to say who it is... Whenever I think about what Toma-Kun would say, I always try to give him a "dirty old man" voice. I fear I might get carried away with it, so I'd better apologize while I still can. Just like a dirty old man would. Sorrrrrry~

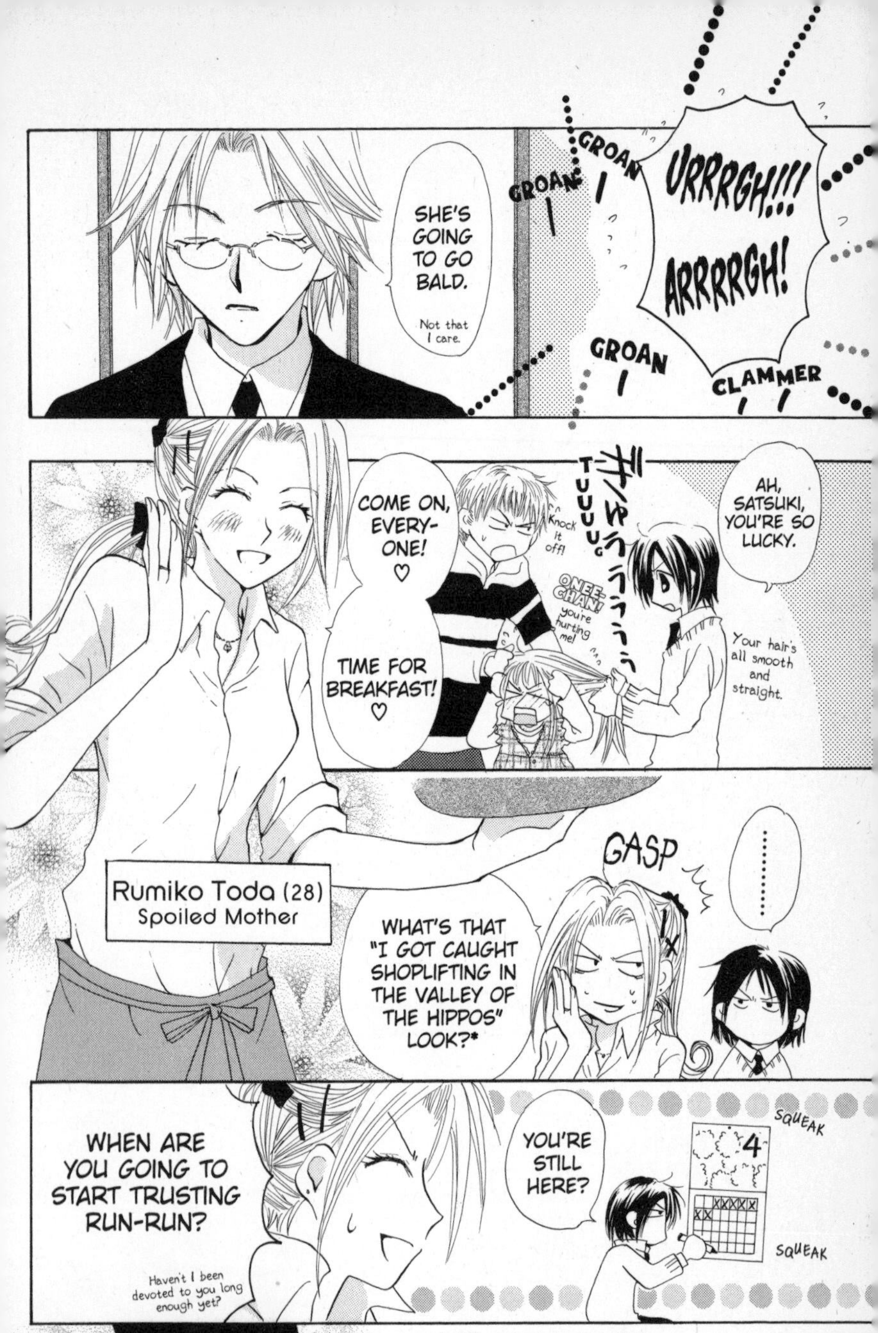
URRRGH!!! ARRRRGH!
GROAN
GROAN
GROAN
CLAMMER
SHE'S GOING TO GO BALD.
Not that I care.
AH, SATSUKI, YOU'RE SO LUCKY.
Your hair's all smooth and straight.
TUUUUG
ONEE-CHAN! you're hurting me!
Knock it off!
GASP
......
WHAT'S THAT "I GOT CAUGHT SHOPLIFTING IN THE VALLEY OF THE HIPPOS" LOOK?*
COME ON, EVERY-ONE! ♡
TIME FOR BREAKFAST! ♡
Rumiko Toda (28)
Spoiled Mother
SQUEAK
4
SQUEAK
YOU'RE STILL HERE?
WHEN ARE YOU GOING TO START TRUSTING RUN-RUN?
Haven't I been devoted to you long enough yet?

* SEE TRANSLATOR'S NOTE

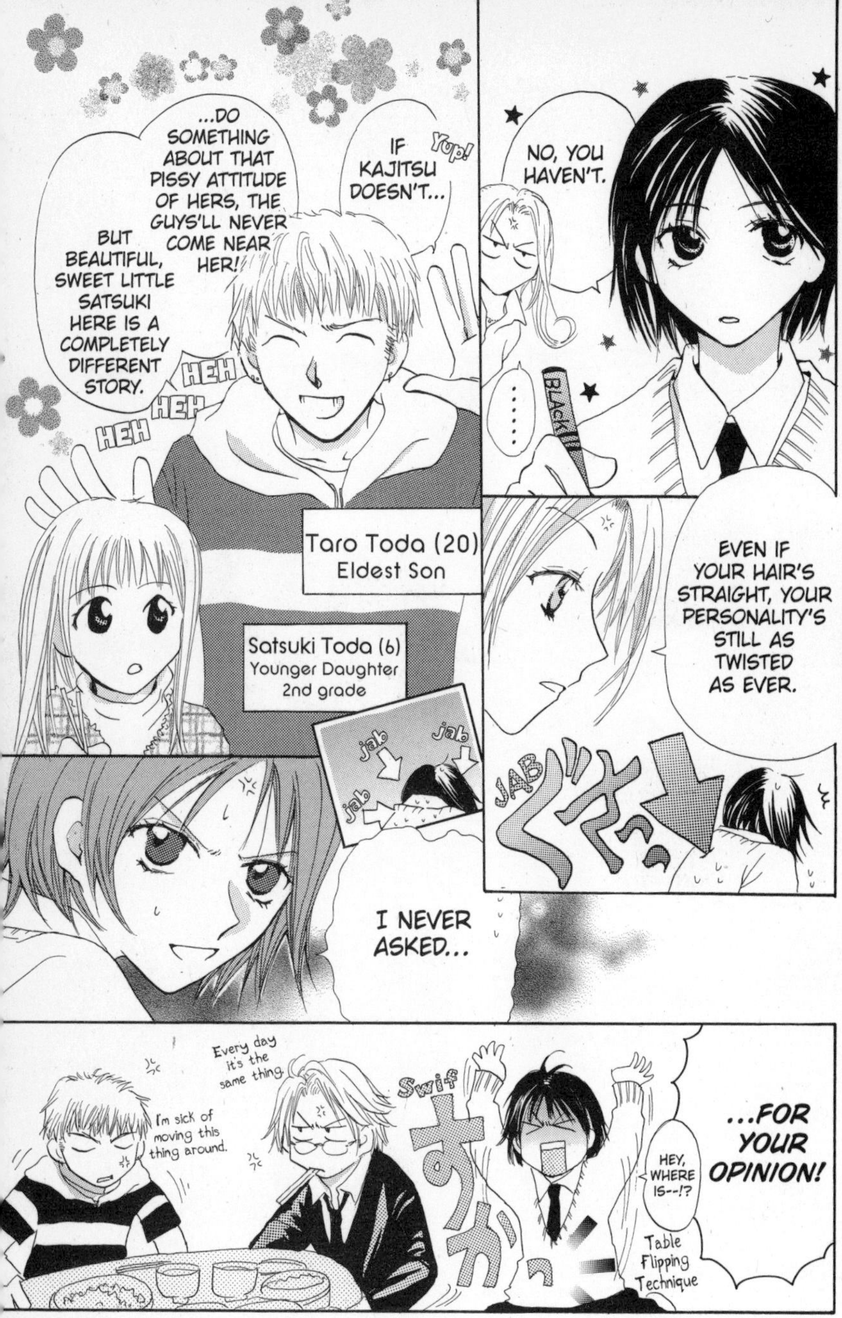
NO, YOU HAVEN'T.
......
BLACK
EVEN IF YOUR HAIR'S STRAIGHT, YOUR PERSONALITY'S STILL AS TWISTED AS EVER.
JAB
IF KAJITSU DOESN'T...
Yup!
...DO SOMETHING ABOUT THAT PISSY ATTITUDE OF HERS, THE GUYS'LL NEVER COME NEAR HER!
BUT BEAUTIFUL, SWEET LITTLE SATSUKI HERE IS A COMPLETELY DIFFERENT STORY.
HEH
HEH
HEH
Taro Toda (20)
Eldest Son
Satsuki Toda (6)
Younger Daughter
2nd grade
jab
jab
jab
I NEVER ASKED...
...FOR YOUR OPINION!
HEY, WHERE IS--!?
Table Flipping Technique
Swif
Every day it's the same thing.
I'm sick of moving this thing around.

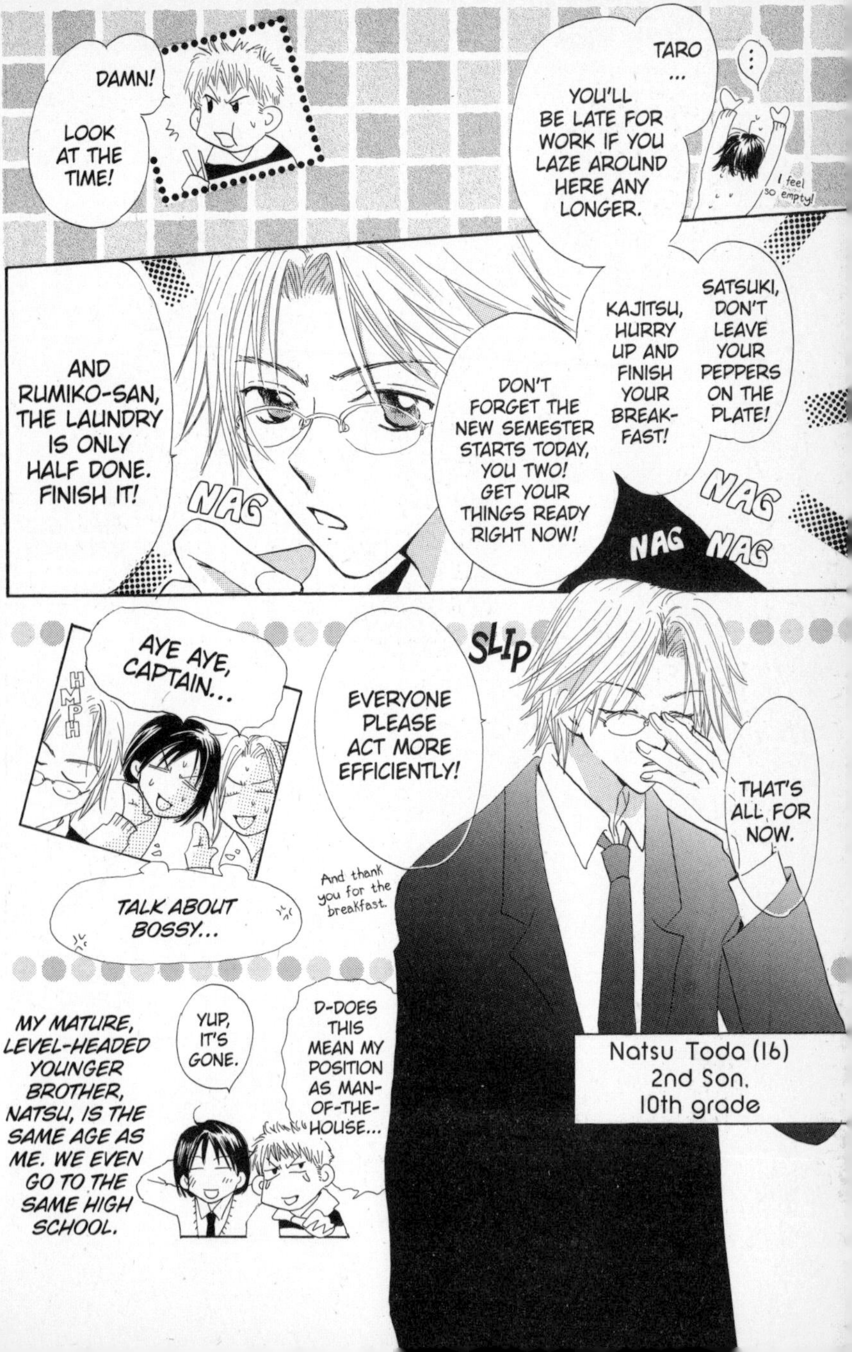
TARO ...
YOU'LL BE LATE FOR WORK IF YOU LAZE AROUND HERE ANY LONGER.
...
I feel so empty!
DAMN!
LOOK AT THE TIME!
SATSUKI, DON'T LEAVE YOUR PEPPERS ON THE PLATE!
KAJITSU, HURRY UP AND FINISH YOUR BREAK-FAST!
DON'T FORGET THE NEW SEMESTER STARTS TODAY, YOU TWO! GET YOUR THINGS READY RIGHT NOW!
NAG
NAG NAG
AND RUMIKO-SAN, THE LAUNDRY IS ONLY HALF DONE. FINISH IT!
NAG
SLIP
THAT'S ALL FOR NOW.
EVERYONE PLEASE ACT MORE EFFICIENTLY!
And thank you for the breakfast.
Natsu Toda (16)
2nd Son.
10th grade
AYE AYE, CAPTAIN...
HMPH
TALK ABOUT BOSSY...
D-DOES THIS MEAN MY POSITION AS MAN-OF-THE-HOUSE...
YUP, IT'S GONE.
MY MATURE, LEVEL-HEADED YOUNGER BROTHER, NATSU, IS THE SAME AGE AS ME. WE EVEN GO TO THE SAME HIGH SCHOOL.

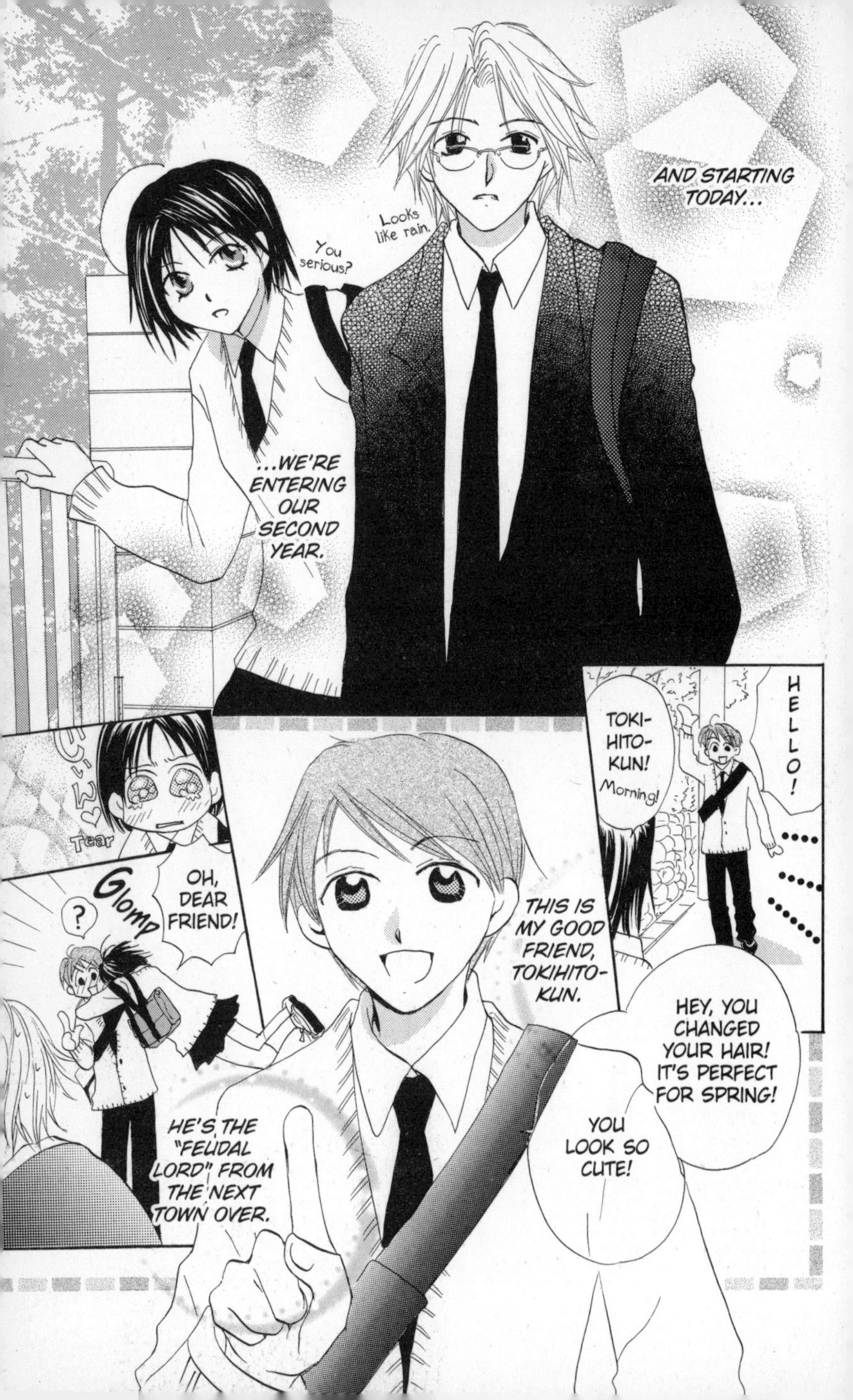
AND STARTING TODAY...
Looks like rain.
You serious?
...WE'RE ENTERING OUR SECOND YEAR.
HELLO!
TOKI-HITO-KUN!
Morning!
....
HEY, YOU CHANGED YOUR HAIR! IT'S PERFECT FOR SPRING!
YOU LOOK SO CUTE!
THIS IS MY GOOD FRIEND, TOKIHITO-KUN.
Tear
OH, DEAR FRIEND!
Glomp
?
HE'S THE "FEUDAL LORD" FROM THE NEXT TOWN OVER.

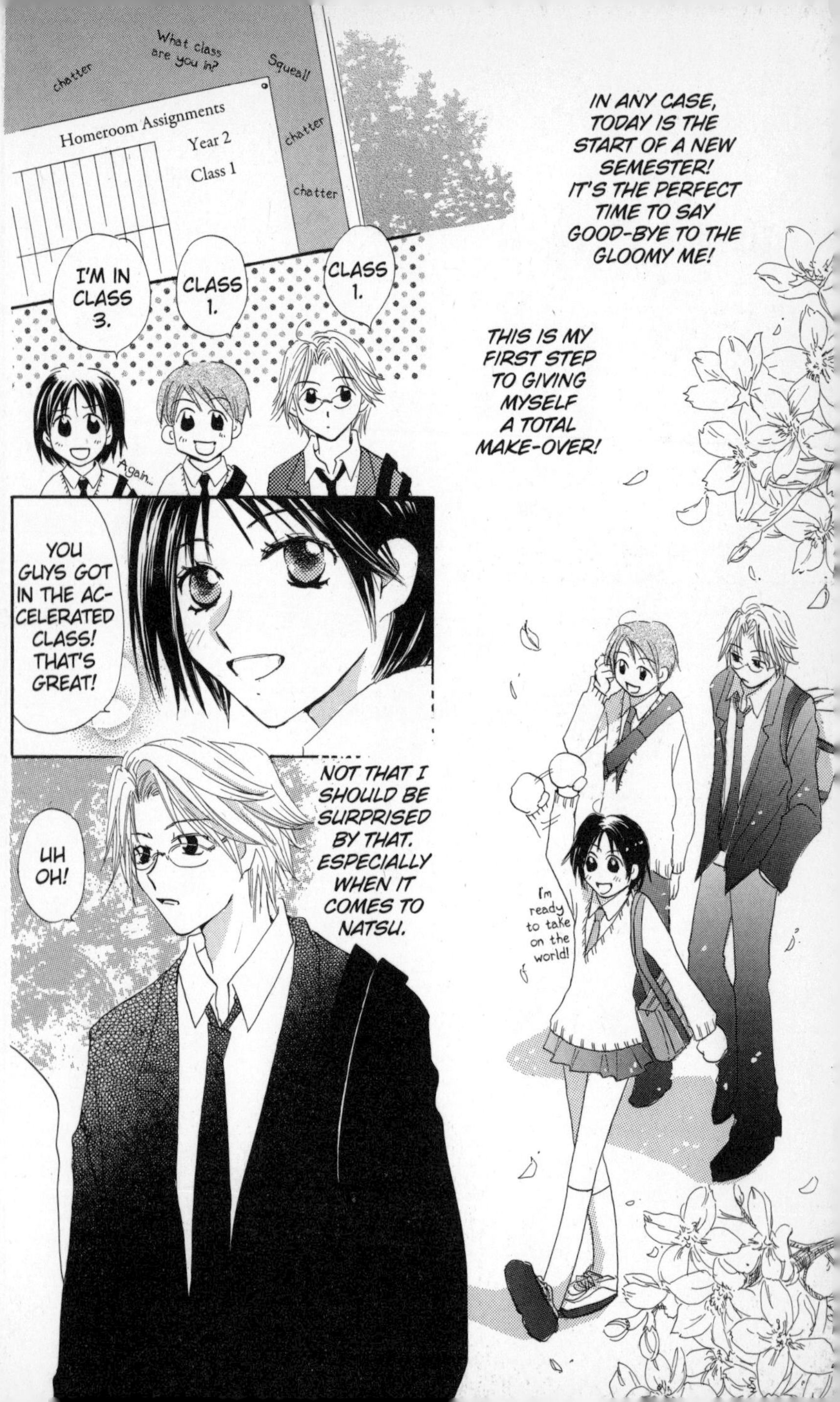
IN ANY CASE, TODAY IS THE START OF A NEW SEMESTER! IT'S THE PERFECT TIME TO SAY GOOD-BYE TO THE GLOOMY ME!
THIS IS MY FIRST STEP TO GIVING MYSELF A TOTAL MAKE-OVER!
I'm ready to take on the world!
Squeal!
What class are you in?
chatter
Homeroom Assignments
Year 2
Class 1
chatter
chatter
CLASS 1.
CLASS 1.
I'M IN CLASS 3.
Again...
YOU GUYS GOT IN THE ACCELERATED CLASS! THAT'S GREAT!
NOT THAT I SHOULD BE SURPRISED BY THAT. ESPECIALLY WHEN IT COMES TO NATSU.
UH OH!

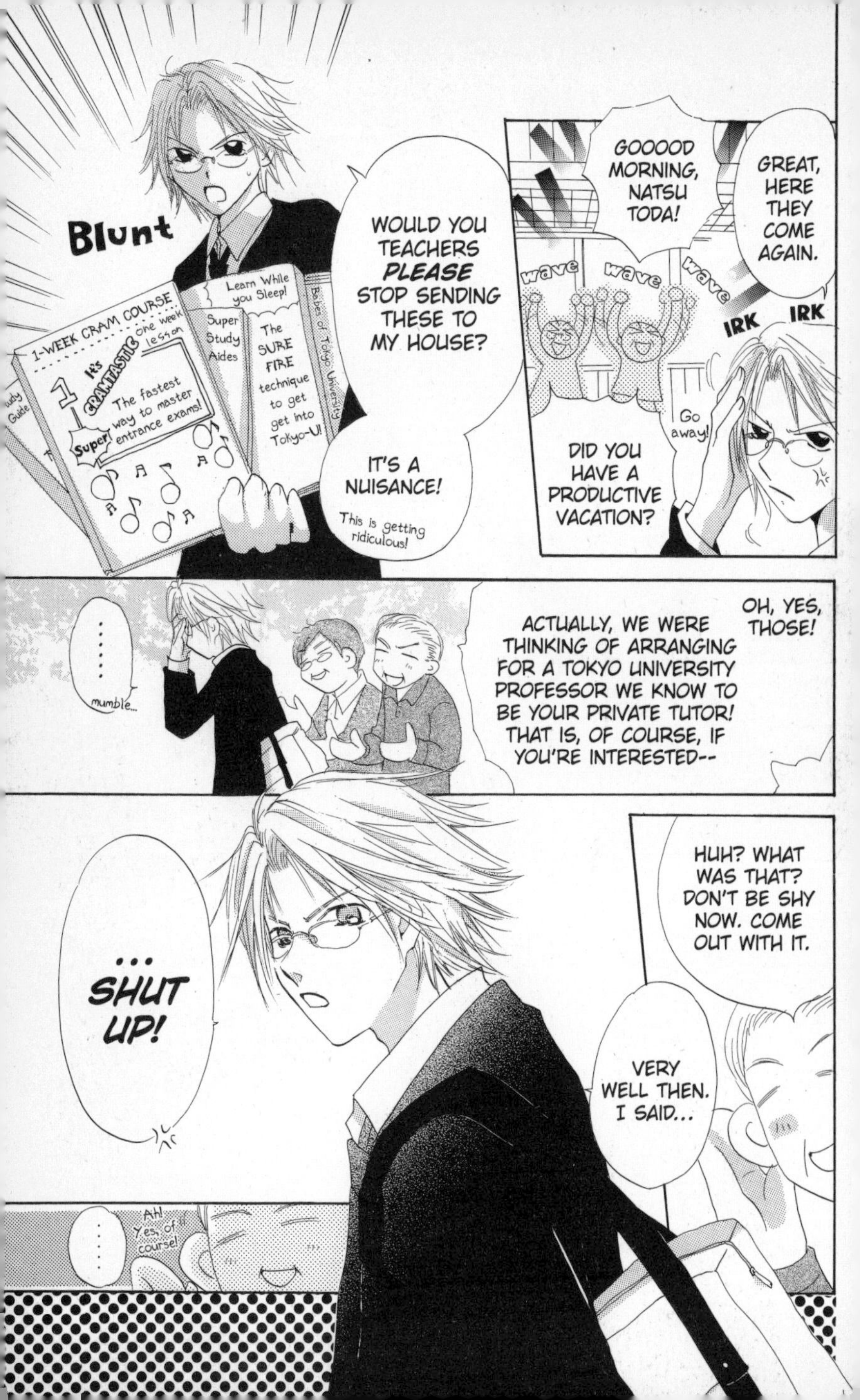
GREAT, HERE THEY COME AGAIN.
GOOOOD MORNING, NATSU TODA!
wave wave wave
IRK IRK
Go away!
DID YOU HAVE A PRODUCTIVE VACATION?
WOULD YOU TEACHERS *PLEASE* STOP SENDING THESE TO MY HOUSE?
IT'S A NUISANCE!
This is getting ridiculous!
Blunt
Babes of Tokyo University
Learn While you Sleep!
The SURE FIRE technique to get get into Tokyo-U!
Super Study Aides
1-WEEK CRAM COURSE
one week lesson
1 It's CRAMTASTIC
The fastest way to master entrance exams!
Super!
OH, YES, THOSE!
ACTUALLY, WE WERE THINKING OF ARRANGING FOR A TOKYO UNIVERSITY PROFESSOR WE KNOW TO BE YOUR PRIVATE TUTOR! THAT IS, OF COURSE, IF YOU'RE INTERESTED--
......
mumble...
HUH? WHAT WAS THAT? DON'T BE SHY NOW. COME OUT WITH IT.
VERY WELL THEN. I SAID...
... SHUT UP!
Ah! Yes, of course!
......

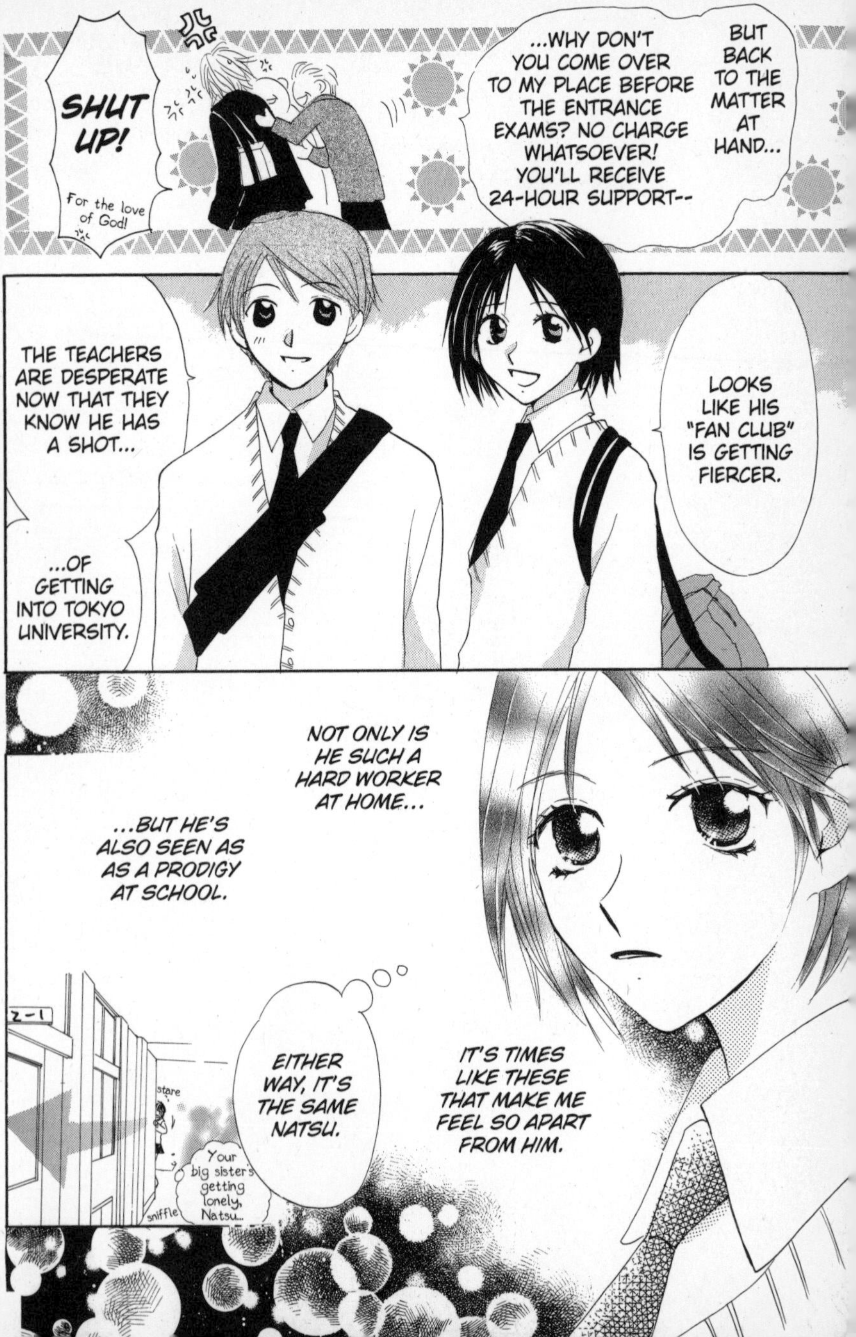
BUT BACK TO THE MATTER AT HAND...
...WHY DON'T YOU COME OVER TO MY PLACE BEFORE THE ENTRANCE EXAMS? NO CHARGE WHATSOEVER! YOU'LL RECEIVE 24-HOUR SUPPORT--
SHUT UP!
For the love of God!
LOOKS LIKE HIS "FAN CLUB" IS GETTING FIERCER.
THE TEACHERS ARE DESPERATE NOW THAT THEY KNOW HE HAS A SHOT...
...OF GETTING INTO TOKYO UNIVERSITY.
NOT ONLY IS HE SUCH A HARD WORKER AT HOME...
...BUT HE'S ALSO SEEN AS AS A PRODIGY AT SCHOOL.
IT'S TIMES LIKE THESE THAT MAKE ME FEEL SO APART FROM HIM.
EITHER WAY, IT'S THE SAME NATSU.
2-1
stare
Your big sister's getting lonely, Natsu...
sniffle

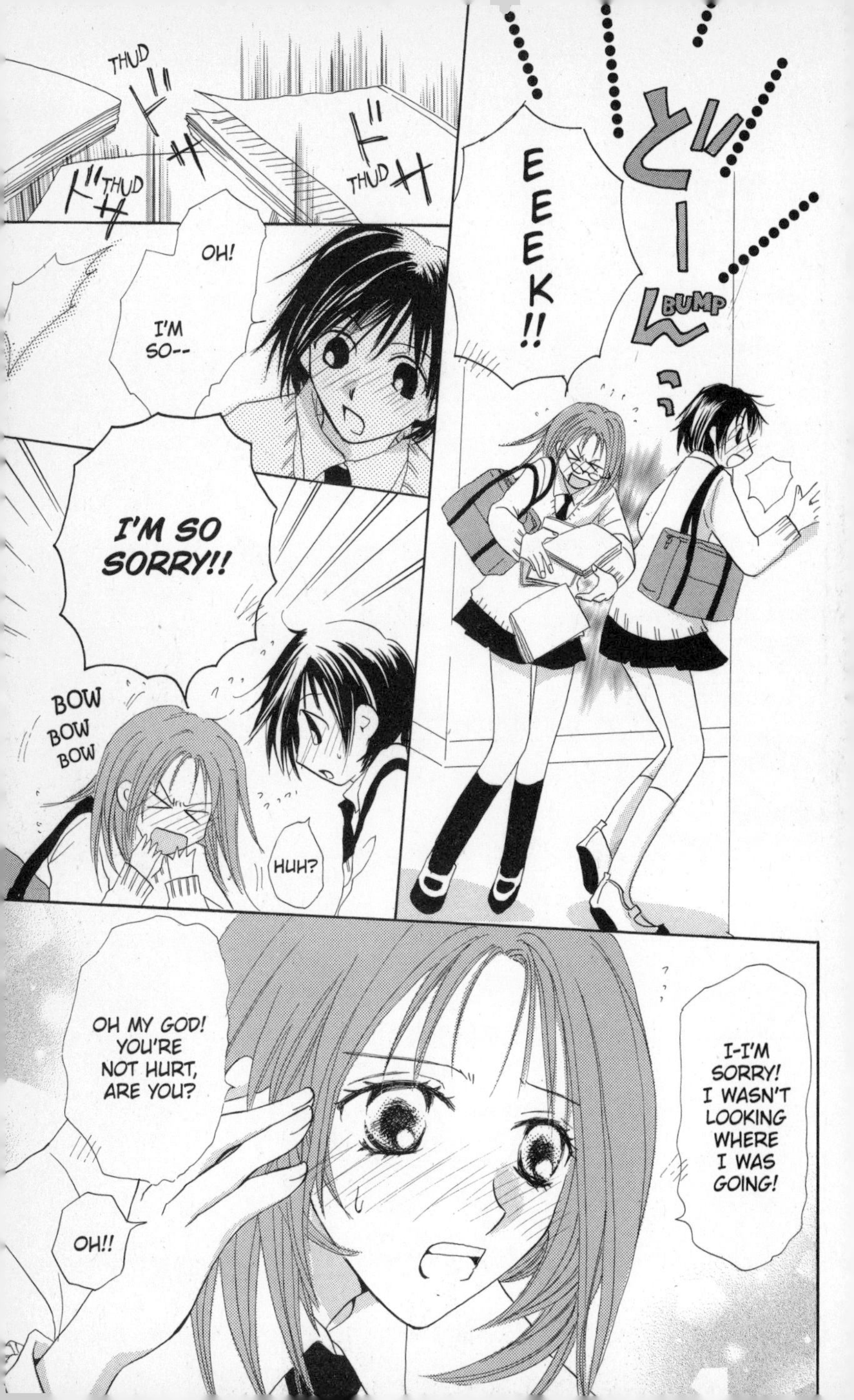

どーん
BUMP
EEEK!!
ドサ THUD
ドサ THUD
ドサ THUD
OH!
I'M SO--
I'M SO SORRY!!
BOW BOW BOW
HUH?
I-I'M SORRY! I WASN'T LOOKING WHERE I WAS GOING!
OH MY GOD! YOU'RE NOT HURT, ARE YOU?
OH!!

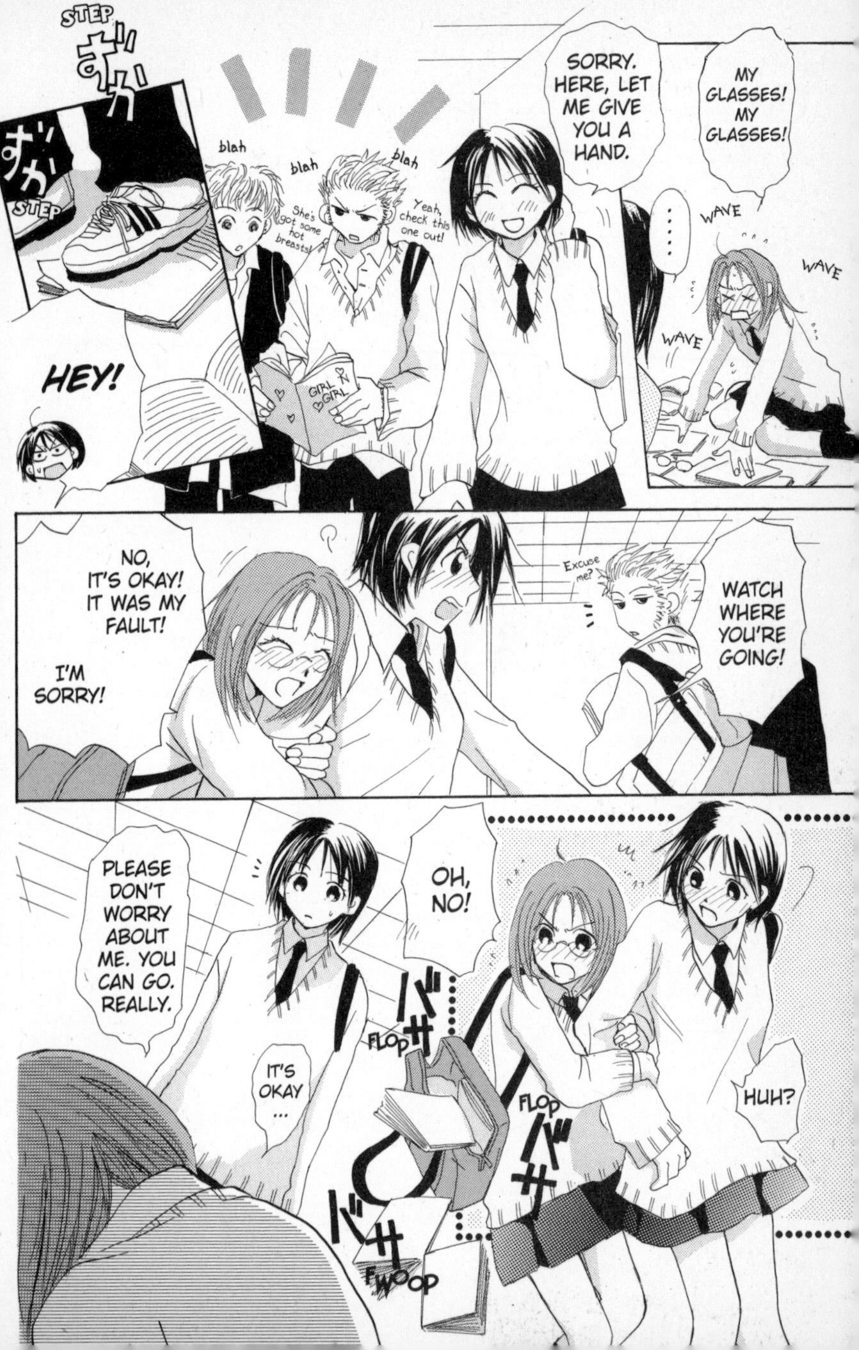

MY GLASSES! MY GLASSES!
......
WAVE
WAVE
WAVE
SORRY. HERE, LET ME GIVE YOU A HAND.
blah
Yeah, check this one out!
blah
She's got some hot breasts!
blah
GIRL N GIRL
STEP
STEP
HEY!
WATCH WHERE YOU'RE GOING!
Excuse me?
NO, IT'S OKAY! IT WAS MY FAULT!
I'M SORRY!
HUH?
OH, NO!
FLOP
FLOP
PLEASE DON'T WORRY ABOUT ME. YOU CAN GO. REALLY.
IT'S OKAY ...
FWOOP

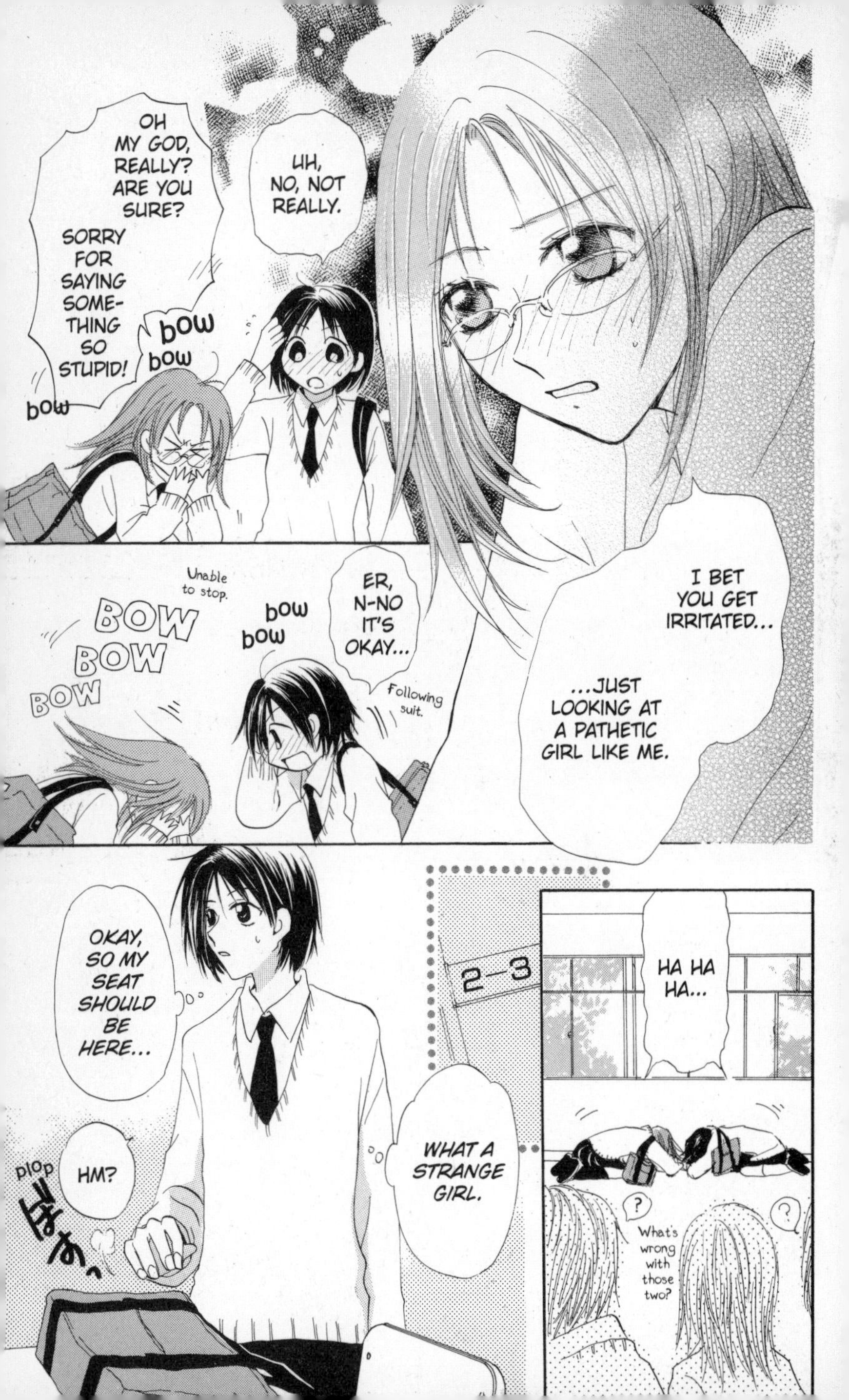

I BET YOU GET IRRITATED...
...JUST LOOKING AT A PATHETIC GIRL LIKE ME.
UH, NO, NOT REALLY.
OH MY GOD, REALLY? ARE YOU SURE?
SORRY FOR SAYING SOMETHING SO STUPID!
bow bow
bow
ER, N-NO IT'S OKAY...
Following suit.
bow bow
Unable to stop.
BOW BOW BOW
HA HA HA...
What's wrong with those two?
OKAY, SO MY SEAT SHOULD BE HERE...
WHAT A STRANGE GIRL.
HM?
plop

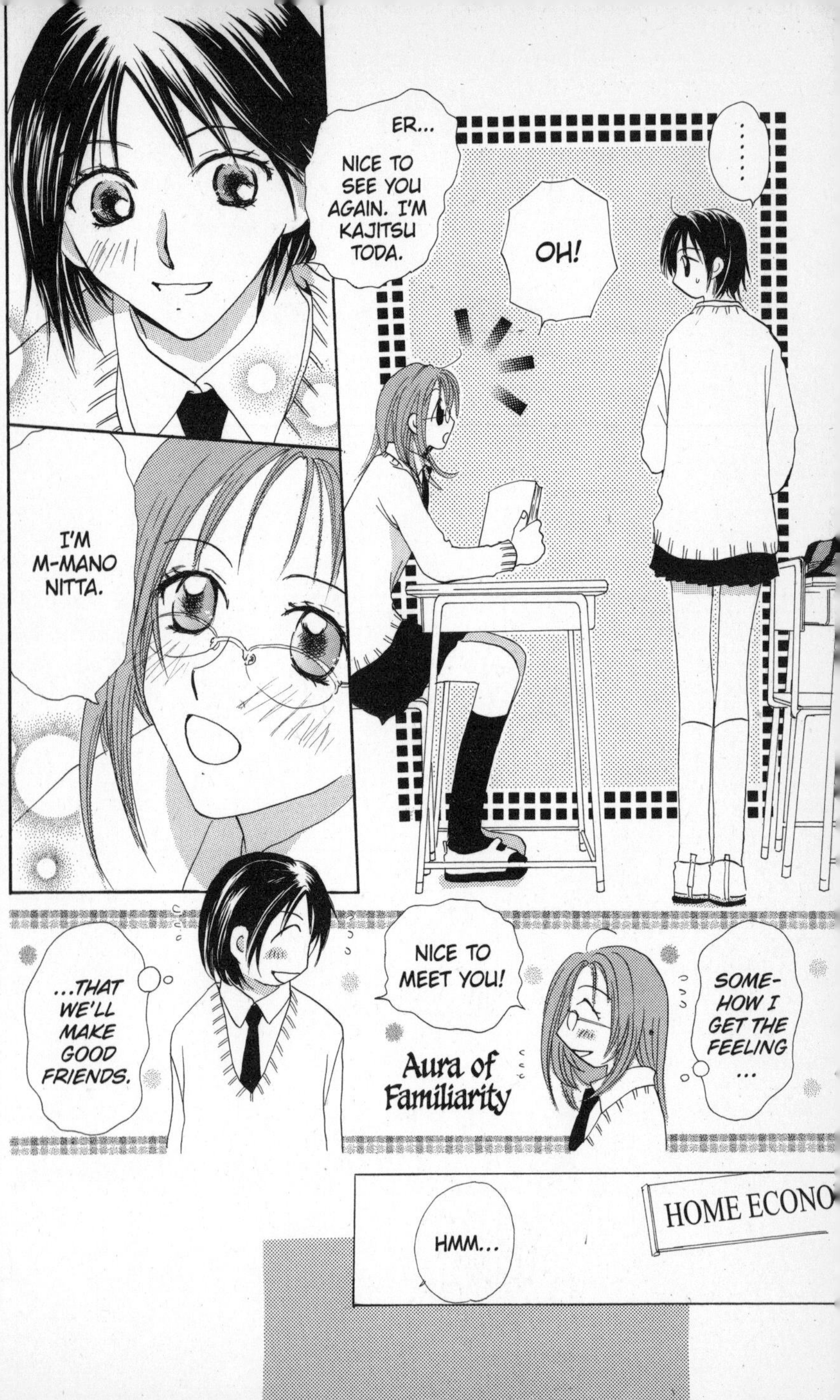
......
OH!
ER... NICE TO SEE YOU AGAIN. I'M KAJITSU TODA.
I'M M-MANO NITTA.
SOME-HOW I GET THE FEELING...
NICE TO MEET YOU!
Aura of Familiarity
...THAT WE'LL MAKE GOOD FRIENDS.
HOME ECONO
HMM...

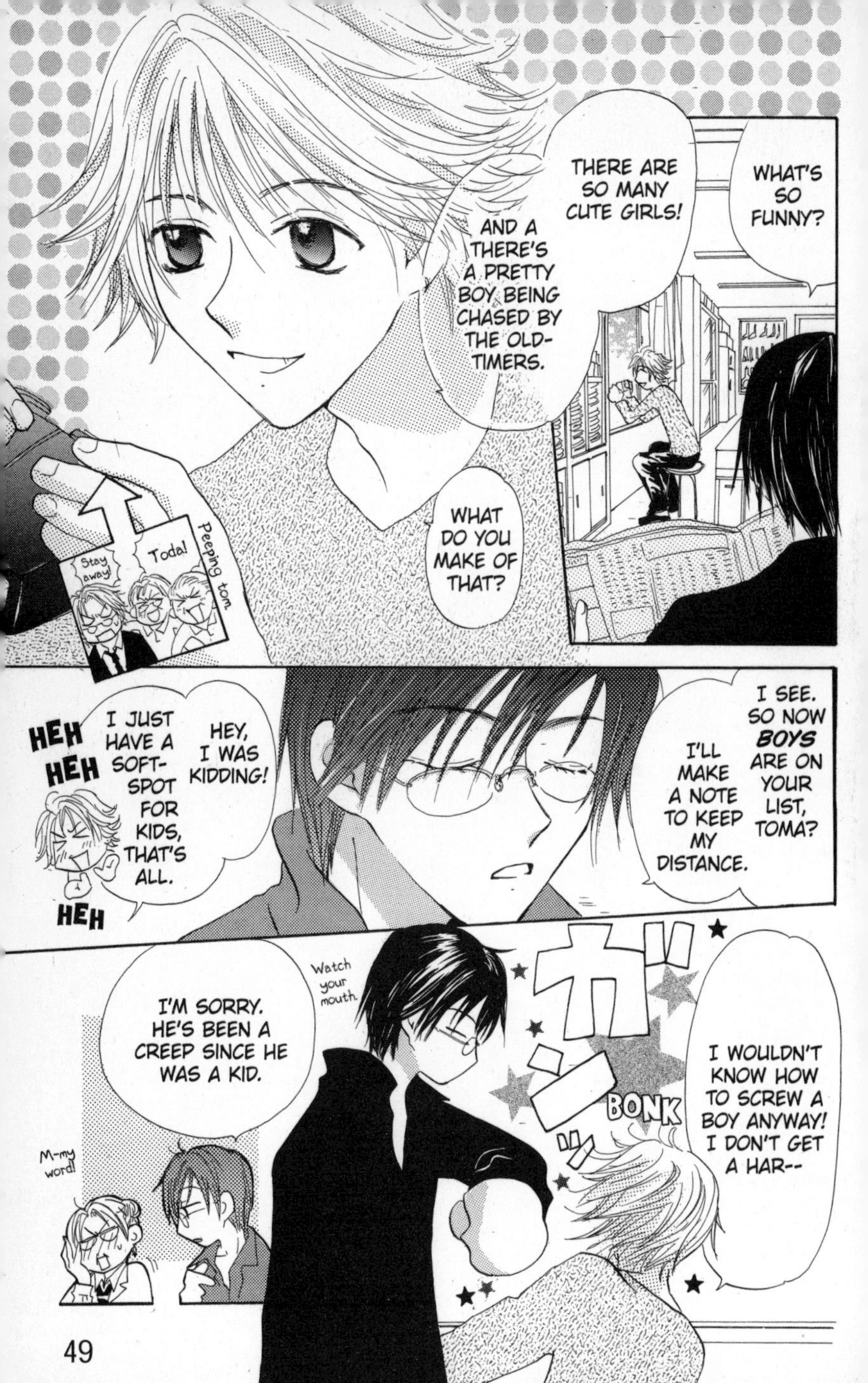
WHAT'S SO FUNNY?
THERE ARE SO MANY CUTE GIRLS!
AND A THERE'S A PRETTY BOY BEING CHASED BY THE OLD-TIMERS.
WHAT DO YOU MAKE OF THAT?
Peeping tom.
Toda!
Stay away!
I SEE. SO NOW *BOYS* ARE ON YOUR LIST, TOMA?
I'LL MAKE A NOTE TO KEEP MY DISTANCE.
HEY, I WAS KIDDING!
I JUST HAVE A SOFT-SPOT FOR KIDS, THAT'S ALL.
HEH HEH HEH
I WOULDN'T KNOW HOW TO SCREW A BOY ANYWAY! I DON'T GET A HAR--
BONK
Watch your mouth.
I'M SORRY. HE'S BEEN A CREEP SINCE HE WAS A KID.
M-my word!

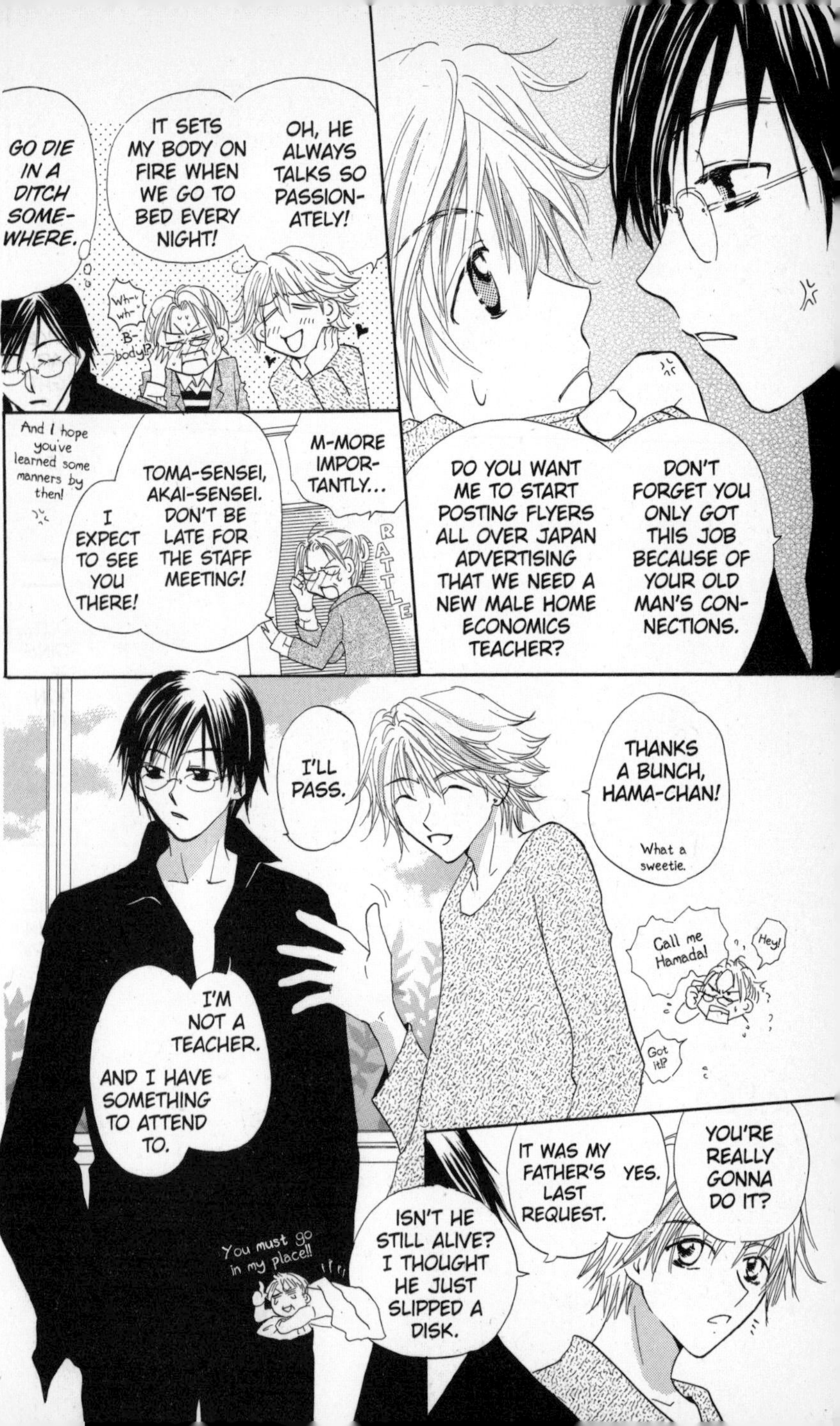
DON'T FORGET YOU ONLY GOT THIS JOB BECAUSE OF YOUR OLD MAN'S CONNECTIONS.
DO YOU WANT ME TO START POSTING FLYERS ALL OVER JAPAN ADVERTISING THAT WE NEED A NEW MALE HOME ECONOMICS TEACHER?
OH, HE ALWAYS TALKS SO PASSIONATELY!
IT SETS MY BODY ON FIRE WHEN WE GO TO BED EVERY NIGHT!
GO DIE IN A DITCH SOMEWHERE.
Wh- wh- B- body!?
M-MORE IMPORTANTLY...
RATTLE
TOMA-SENSEI, AKAI-SENSEI. DON'T BE LATE FOR THE STAFF MEETING!
I EXPECT TO SEE YOU THERE!
And I hope you've learned some manners by then!
THANKS A BUNCH, HAMA-CHAN!
What a sweetie.
Hey!
Call me Hamada!
Got it!?
I'LL PASS.
I'M NOT A TEACHER.
AND I HAVE SOMETHING TO ATTEND TO.
YOU'RE REALLY GONNA DO IT?
YES.
IT WAS MY FATHER'S LAST REQUEST.
ISN'T HE STILL ALIVE? I THOUGHT HE JUST SLIPPED A DISK.
You must go in my place!!

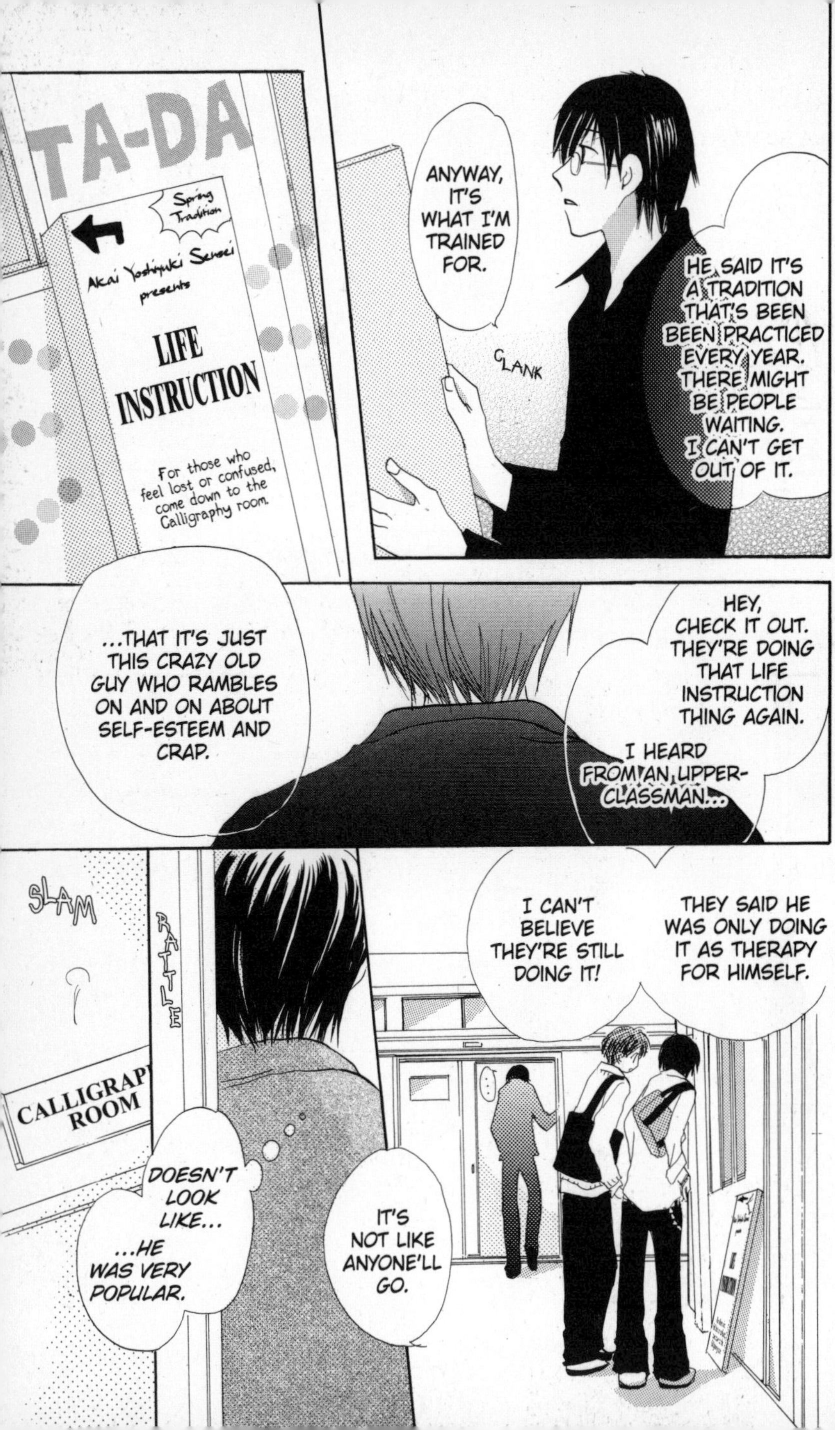
HE SAID IT'S A TRADITION THAT'S BEEN BEEN PRACTICED EVERY YEAR. THERE MIGHT BE PEOPLE WAITING. I CAN'T GET OUT OF IT.
ANYWAY, IT'S WHAT I'M TRAINED FOR.
CLANK
TA-DA
Spring Tradition
Akai Yoshiyuki Sensei presents
LIFE INSTRUCTION
For those who feel lost or confused, come down to the Calligraphy room.
HEY, CHECK IT OUT. THEY'RE DOING THAT LIFE INSTRUCTION THING AGAIN.
I HEARD FROM AN UPPER-CLASSMAN...
...THAT IT'S JUST THIS CRAZY OLD GUY WHO RAMBLES ON AND ON ABOUT SELF-ESTEEM AND CRAP.
THEY SAID HE WAS ONLY DOING IT AS THERAPY FOR HIMSELF.
I CAN'T BELIEVE THEY'RE STILL DOING IT!
...
RATTLE
SLAM
?
CALLIGRAP ROOM
IT'S NOT LIKE ANYONE'LL GO.
DOESN'T LOOK LIKE...
...HE WAS VERY POPULAR.

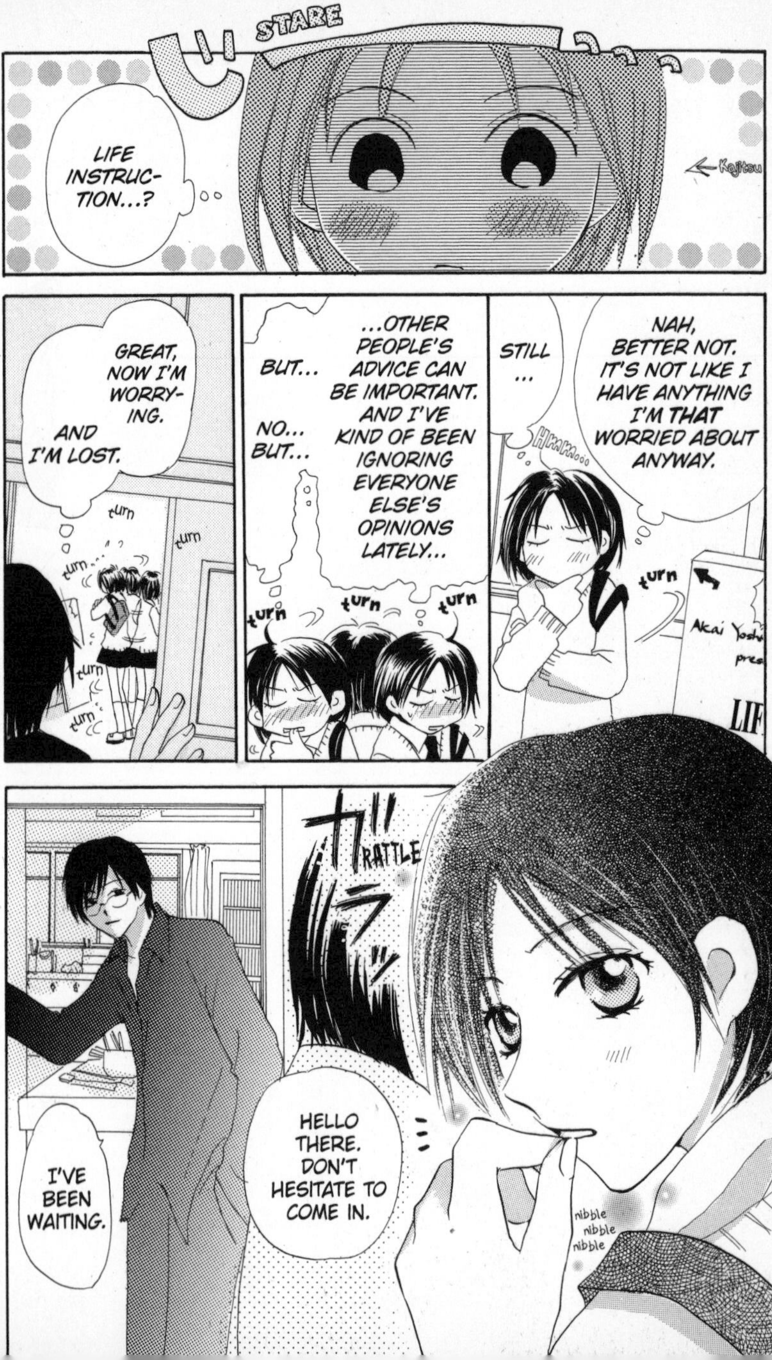
STARE
LIFE INSTRUCTION...?
Kajitsu
NAH, BETTER NOT. IT'S NOT LIKE I HAVE ANYTHING I'M THAT WORRIED ABOUT ANYWAY.
Hmm...
STILL ...
turn
BUT...
NO... BUT...
...OTHER PEOPLE'S ADVICE CAN BE IMPORTANT. AND I'VE KIND OF BEEN IGNORING EVERYONE ELSE'S OPINIONS LATELY...
turn turn turn
GREAT, NOW I'M WORRYING.
AND I'M LOST.
turn turn turn turn turn
RATTLE
nibble nibble nibble
HELLO THERE. DON'T HESITATE TO COME IN.
I'VE BEEN WAITING.

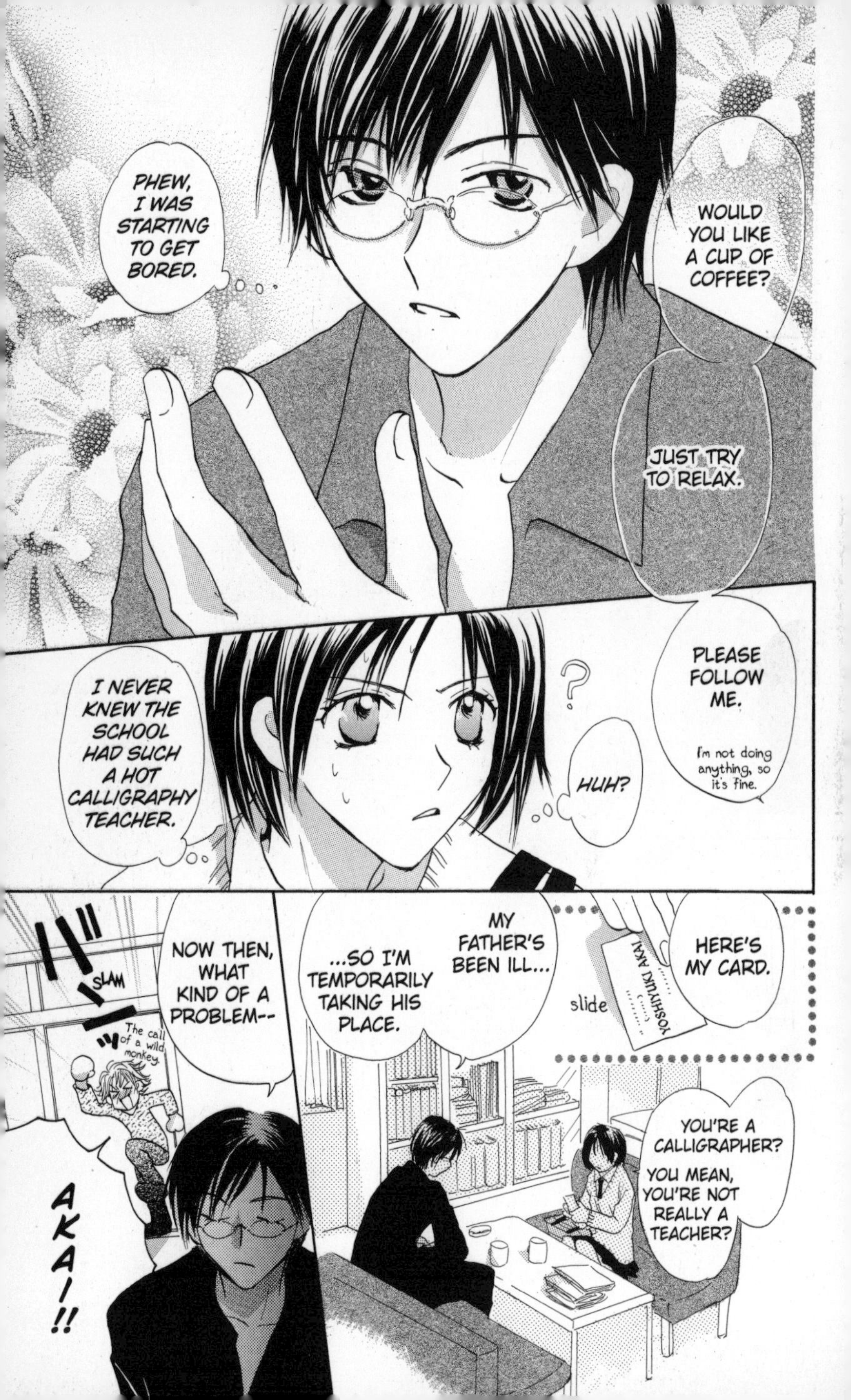
WOULD YOU LIKE A CUP OF COFFEE?
JUST TRY TO RELAX.
PHEW, I WAS STARTING TO GET BORED.
PLEASE FOLLOW ME.
I'm not doing anything, so it's fine.
?
HUH?
I NEVER KNEW THE SCHOOL HAD SUCH A HOT CALLIGRAPHY TEACHER.
HERE'S MY CARD.
YOSHIYUKI AKAI
slide
YOU'RE A CALLIGRAPHER? YOU MEAN, YOU'RE NOT REALLY A TEACHER?
MY FATHER'S BEEN ILL...
...SO I'M TEMPORARILY TAKING HIS PLACE.
NOW THEN, WHAT KIND OF A PROBLEM--
SLAM
The call of a wild monkey.
AKAI!!

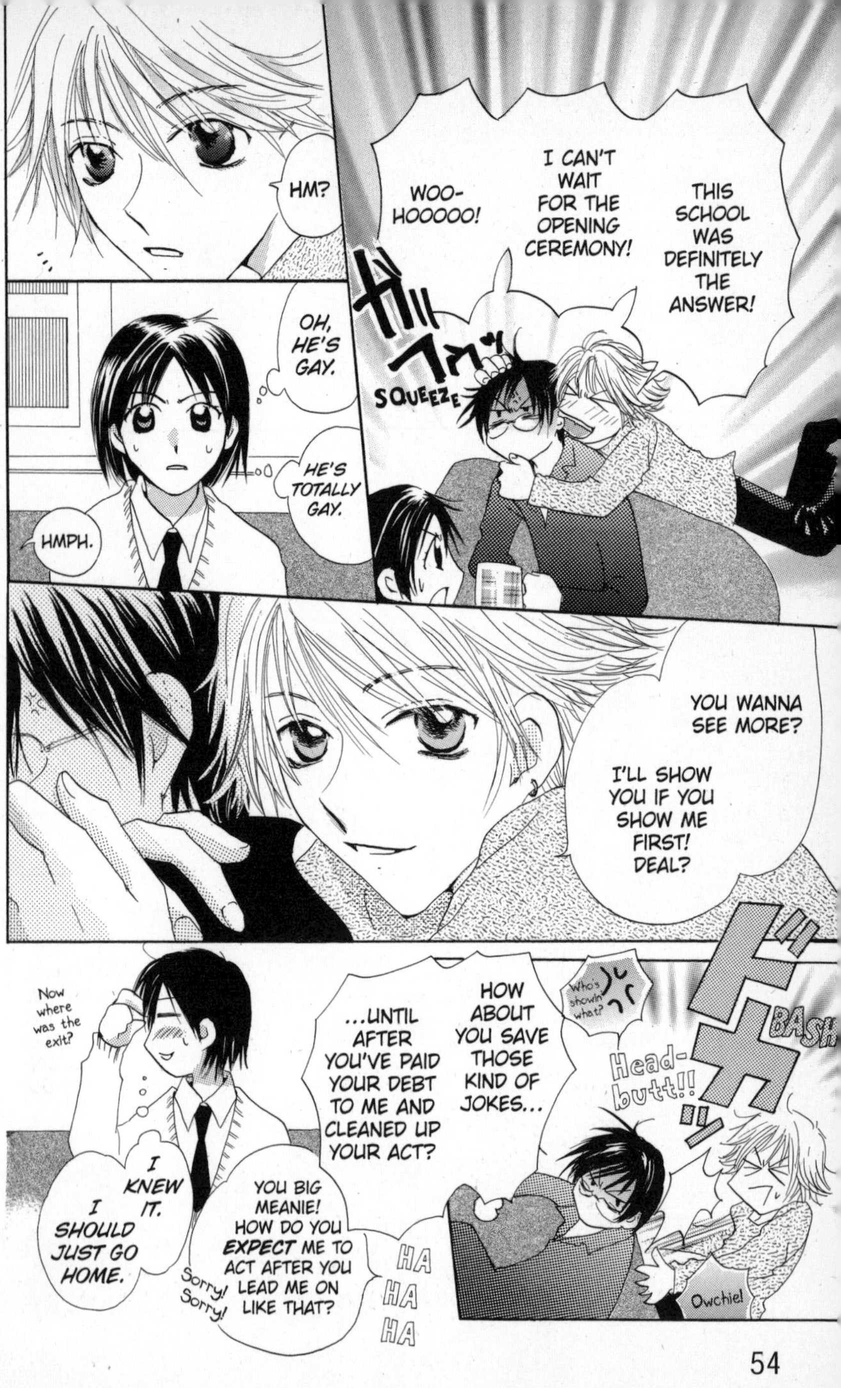
THIS SCHOOL WAS DEFINITELY THE ANSWER!
I CAN'T WAIT FOR THE OPENING CEREMONY!
WOO-HOOOOO!
SQUEEZE
HM?
OH, HE'S GAY.
HE'S TOTALLY GAY.
HMPH.
YOU WANNA SEE MORE?
I'LL SHOW YOU IF YOU SHOW ME FIRST! DEAL?
BASH
Head-butt!!
Who's shown what?
Owchie!
HOW ABOUT YOU SAVE THOSE KIND OF JOKES...
...UNTIL AFTER YOU'VE PAID YOUR DEBT TO ME AND CLEANED UP YOUR ACT?
YOU BIG MEANIE! HOW DO YOU *EXPECT* ME TO ACT AFTER YOU LEAD ME ON LIKE THAT?
Sorry! Sorry!
HA HA HA
I KNEW IT.
I SHOULD JUST GO HOME.
Now where was the exit?

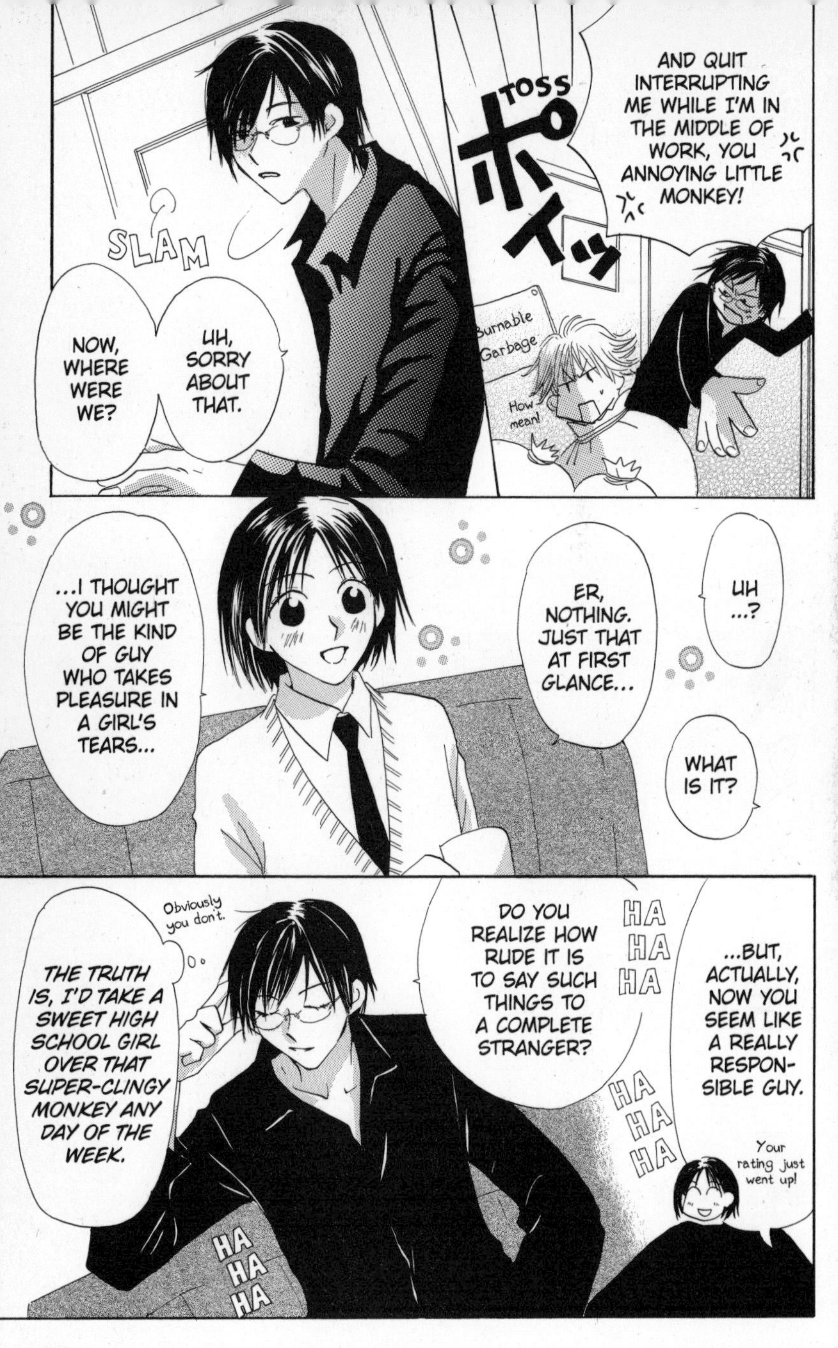
AND QUIT INTERRUPTING ME WHILE I'M IN THE MIDDLE OF WORK, YOU ANNOYING LITTLE MONKEY!
TOSS
Burnable Garbage
How mean!
SLAM
UH, SORRY ABOUT THAT.
NOW, WHERE WERE WE?
UH ...?
WHAT IS IT?
ER, NOTHING. JUST THAT AT FIRST GLANCE...
...I THOUGHT YOU MIGHT BE THE KIND OF GUY WHO TAKES PLEASURE IN A GIRL'S TEARS...
...BUT, ACTUALLY, NOW YOU SEEM LIKE A REALLY RESPON-SIBLE GUY.
Your rating just went up!
HA HA HA
HA HA HA
DO YOU REALIZE HOW RUDE IT IS TO SAY SUCH THINGS TO A COMPLETE STRANGER?
Obviously you don't.
THE TRUTH IS, I'D TAKE A SWEET HIGH SCHOOL GIRL OVER THAT SUPER-CLINGY MONKEY ANY DAY OF THE WEEK.
HA HA HA

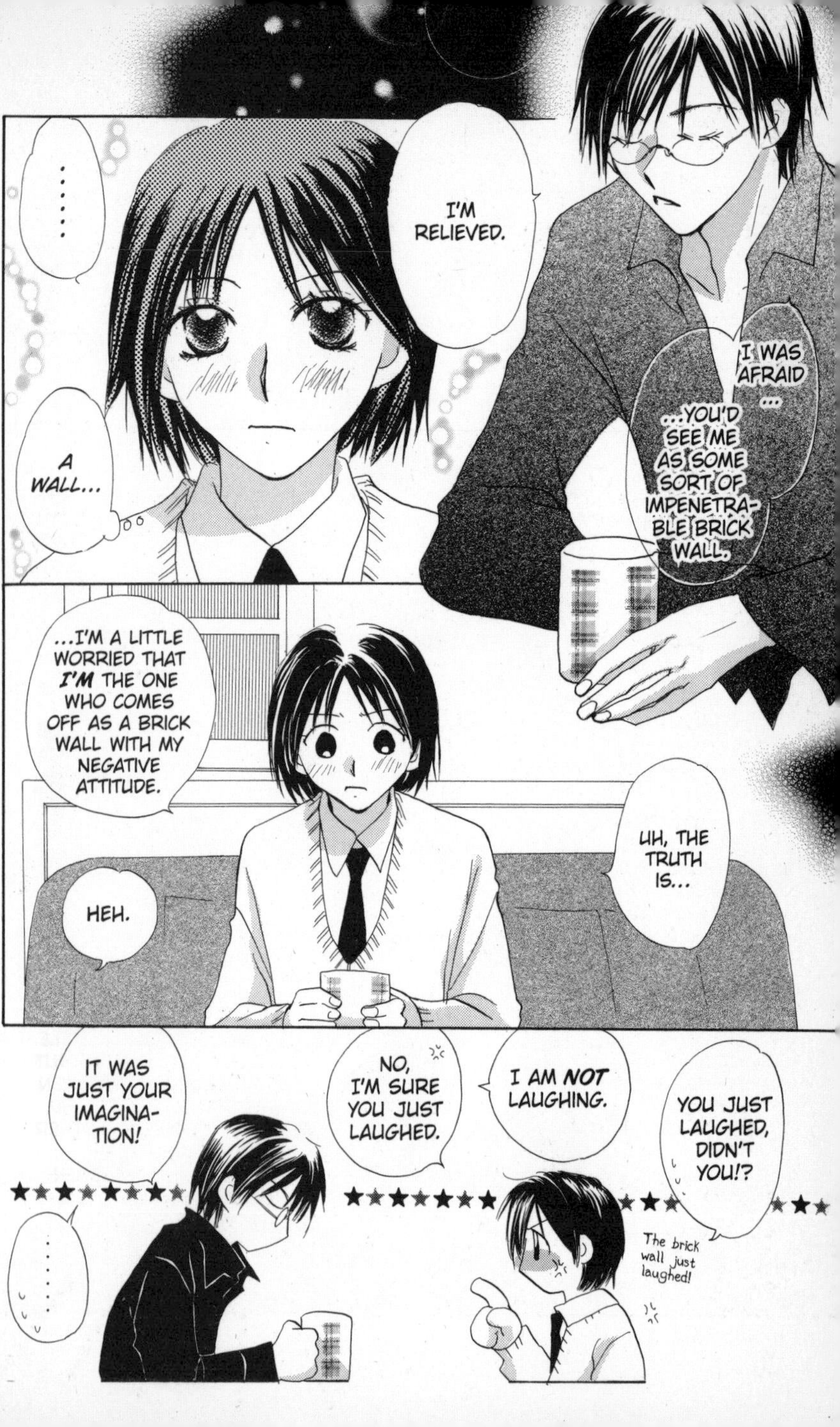
I'M RELIEVED.
I WAS AFRAID ...
...YOU'D SEE ME AS SOME SORT OF IMPENETRA-BLE BRICK WALL.
......
A WALL...
UH, THE TRUTH IS...
...I'M A LITTLE WORRIED THAT *I'M* THE ONE WHO COMES OFF AS A BRICK WALL WITH MY NEGATIVE ATTITUDE.
HEH.
YOU JUST LAUGHED, DIDN'T YOU!?
I AM **NOT** LAUGHING.
NO, I'M SURE YOU JUST LAUGHED.
IT WAS JUST YOUR IMAGINA-TION!
The brick wall just laughed!
......

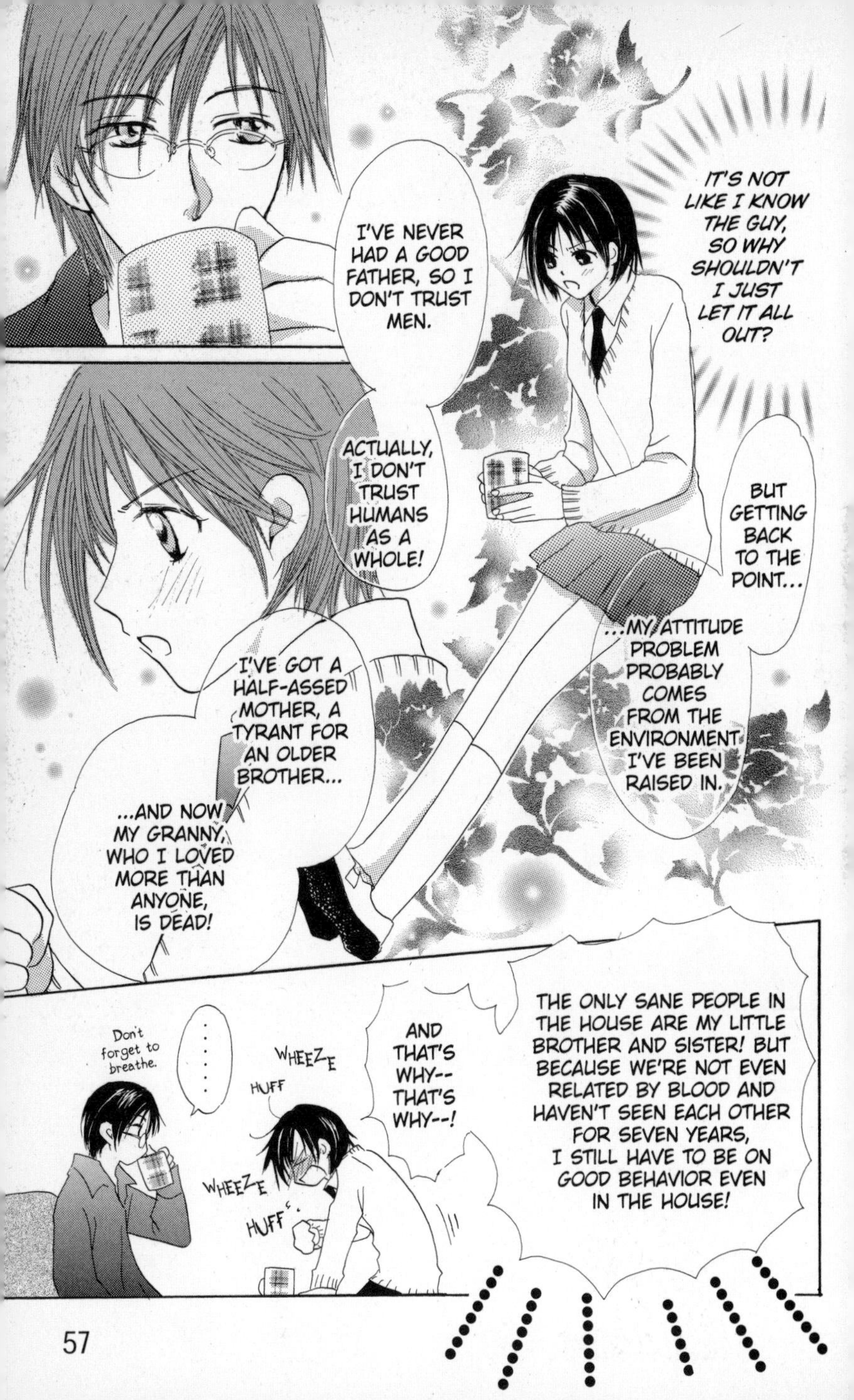

IT'S NOT LIKE I KNOW THE GUY, SO WHY SHOULDN'T I JUST LET IT ALL OUT?
I'VE NEVER HAD A GOOD FATHER, SO I DON'T TRUST MEN.
BUT GETTING BACK TO THE POINT...
...MY ATTITUDE PROBLEM PROBABLY COMES FROM THE ENVIRONMENT I'VE BEEN RAISED IN.
ACTUALLY, I DON'T TRUST HUMANS AS A WHOLE!
I'VE GOT A HALF-ASSED MOTHER, A TYRANT FOR AN OLDER BROTHER...
...AND NOW MY GRANNY, WHO I LOVED MORE THAN ANYONE, IS DEAD!
THE ONLY SANE PEOPLE IN THE HOUSE ARE MY LITTLE BROTHER AND SISTER! BUT BECAUSE WE'RE NOT EVEN RELATED BY BLOOD AND HAVEN'T SEEN EACH OTHER FOR SEVEN YEARS, I STILL HAVE TO BE ON GOOD BEHAVIOR EVEN IN THE HOUSE!
AND THAT'S WHY-- THAT'S WHY--!
WHEEZE
HUFF
WHEEZE
HUFF
......
Don't forget to breathe.

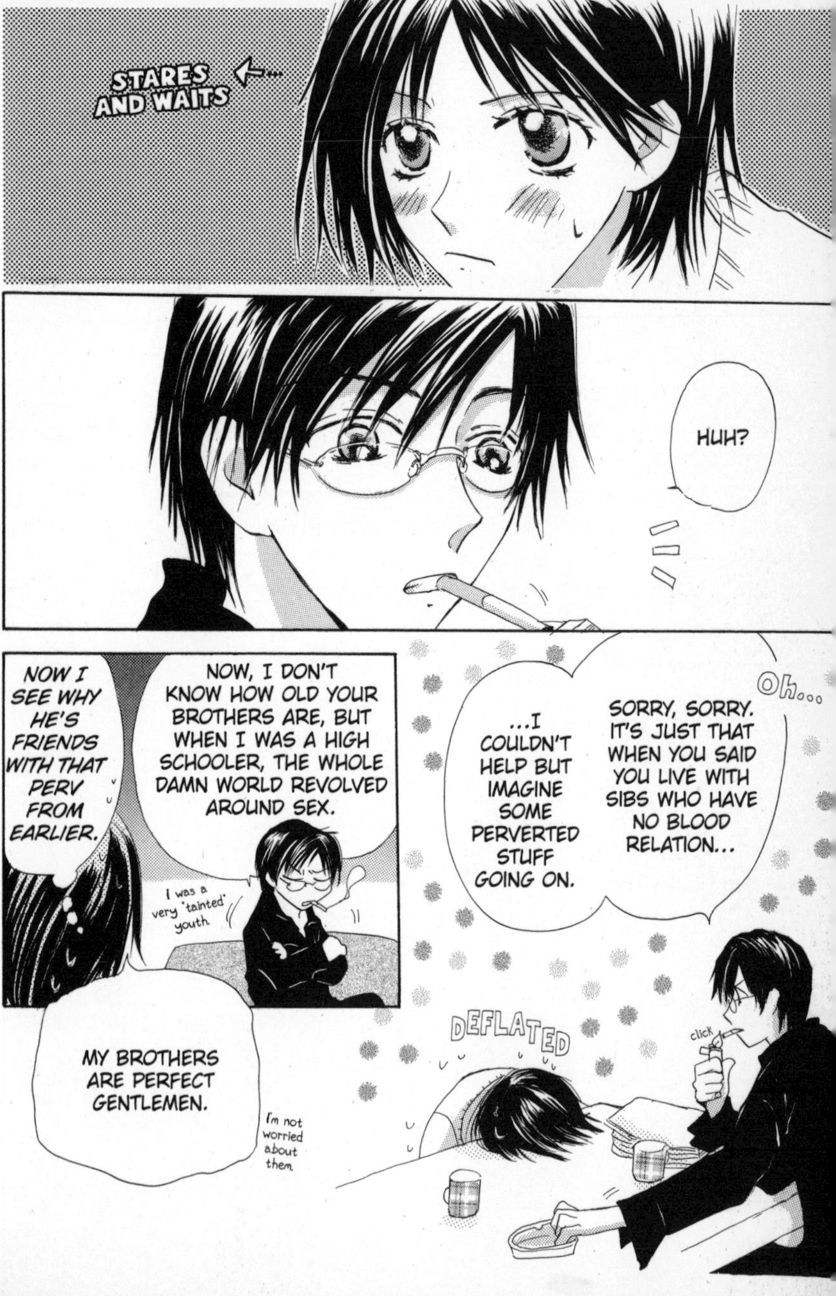

STARES AND WAITS
HUH?
Oh...
SORRY, SORRY. IT'S JUST THAT WHEN YOU SAID YOU LIVE WITH SIBS WHO HAVE NO BLOOD RELATION...
...I COULDN'T HELP BUT IMAGINE SOME PERVERTED STUFF GOING ON.
NOW, I DON'T KNOW HOW OLD YOUR BROTHERS ARE, BUT WHEN I WAS A HIGH SCHOOLER, THE WHOLE DAMN WORLD REVOLVED AROUND SEX.
NOW I SEE WHY HE'S FRIENDS WITH THAT PERV FROM EARLIER.
I was a very "tainted" youth.
MY BROTHERS ARE PERFECT GENTLEMEN.
I'm not worried about them.
DEFLATED
click

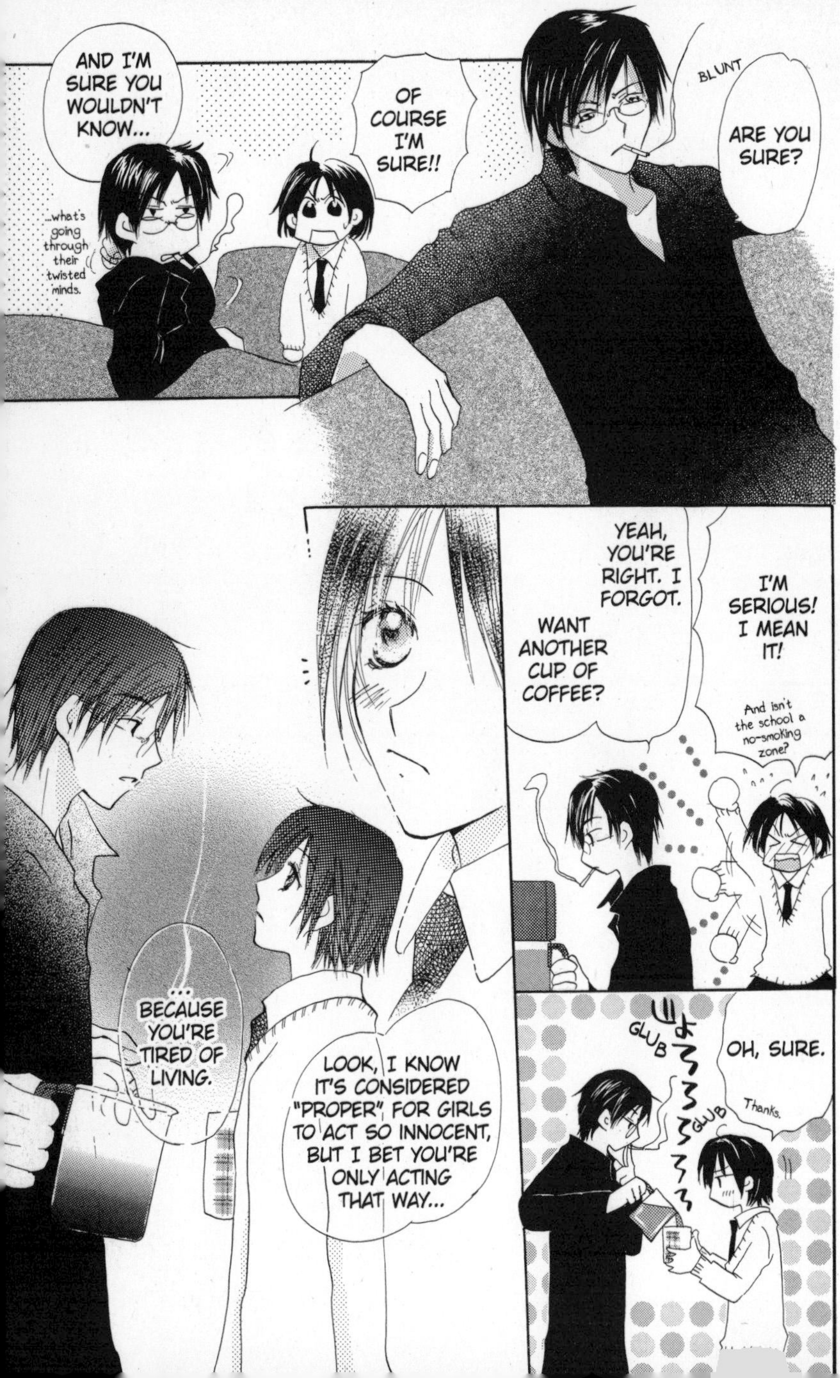
BLUNT
ARE YOU SURE?
OF COURSE I'M SURE!!
AND I'M SURE YOU WOULDN'T KNOW...
...what's going through their twisted minds.
I'M SERIOUS! I MEAN IT!
And isn't the school a no-smoking zone?
YEAH, YOU'RE RIGHT. I FORGOT.
WANT ANOTHER CUP OF COFFEE?
OH, SURE.
Thanks.
GLUB
GLUB
LOOK, I KNOW IT'S CONSIDERED "PROPER", FOR GIRLS TO ACT SO INNOCENT, BUT I BET YOU'RE ONLY ACTING THAT WAY...
...BECAUSE YOU'RE TIRED OF LIVING.

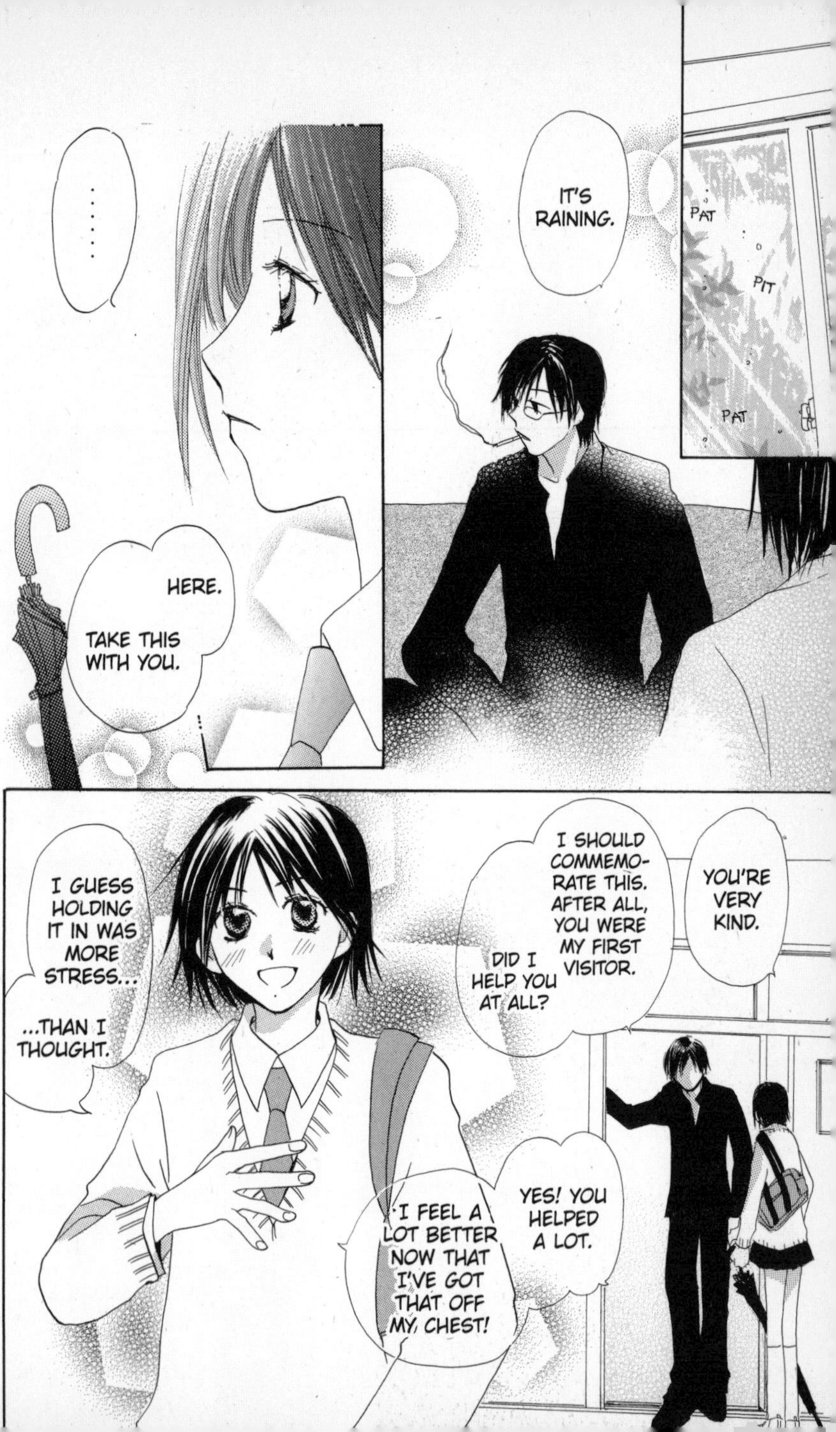
IT'S RAINING.
PAT
PIT
PAT
......
HERE.
TAKE THIS WITH YOU.
YOU'RE VERY KIND.
I SHOULD COMMEMORATE THIS. AFTER ALL, YOU WERE MY FIRST VISITOR.
DID I HELP YOU AT ALL?
YES! YOU HELPED A LOT.
I FEEL A LOT BETTER NOW THAT I'VE GOT THAT OFF MY CHEST!
I GUESS HOLDING IT IN WAS MORE STRESS...
...THAN I THOUGHT.

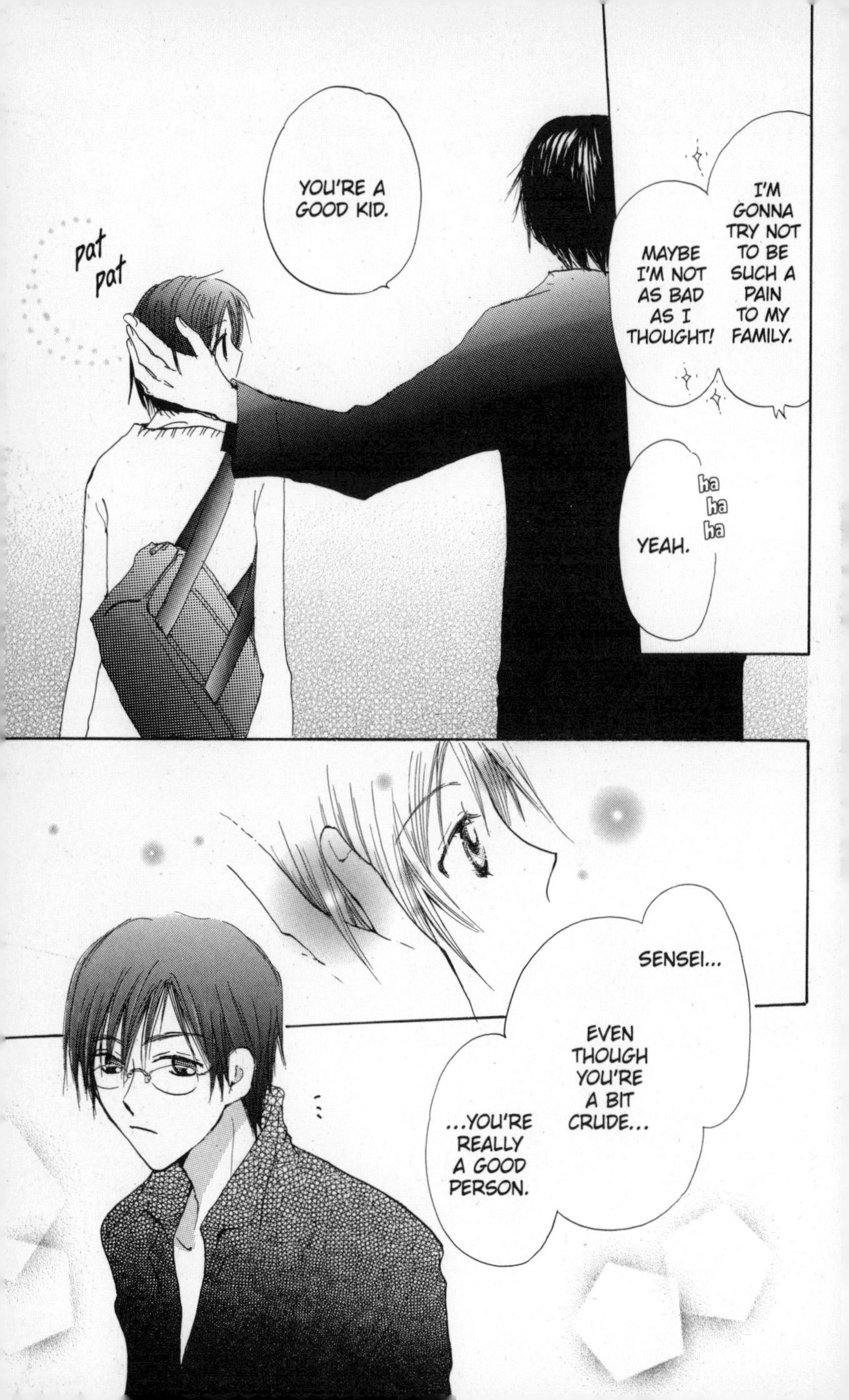
I'M GONNA TRY NOT TO BE SUCH A PAIN TO MY FAMILY.
MAYBE I'M NOT AS BAD AS I THOUGHT!
YEAH.
ha ha ha
YOU'RE A GOOD KID.
pat pat
SENSEI...
EVEN THOUGH YOU'RE A BIT CRUDE...
...YOU'RE REALLY A GOOD PERSON.

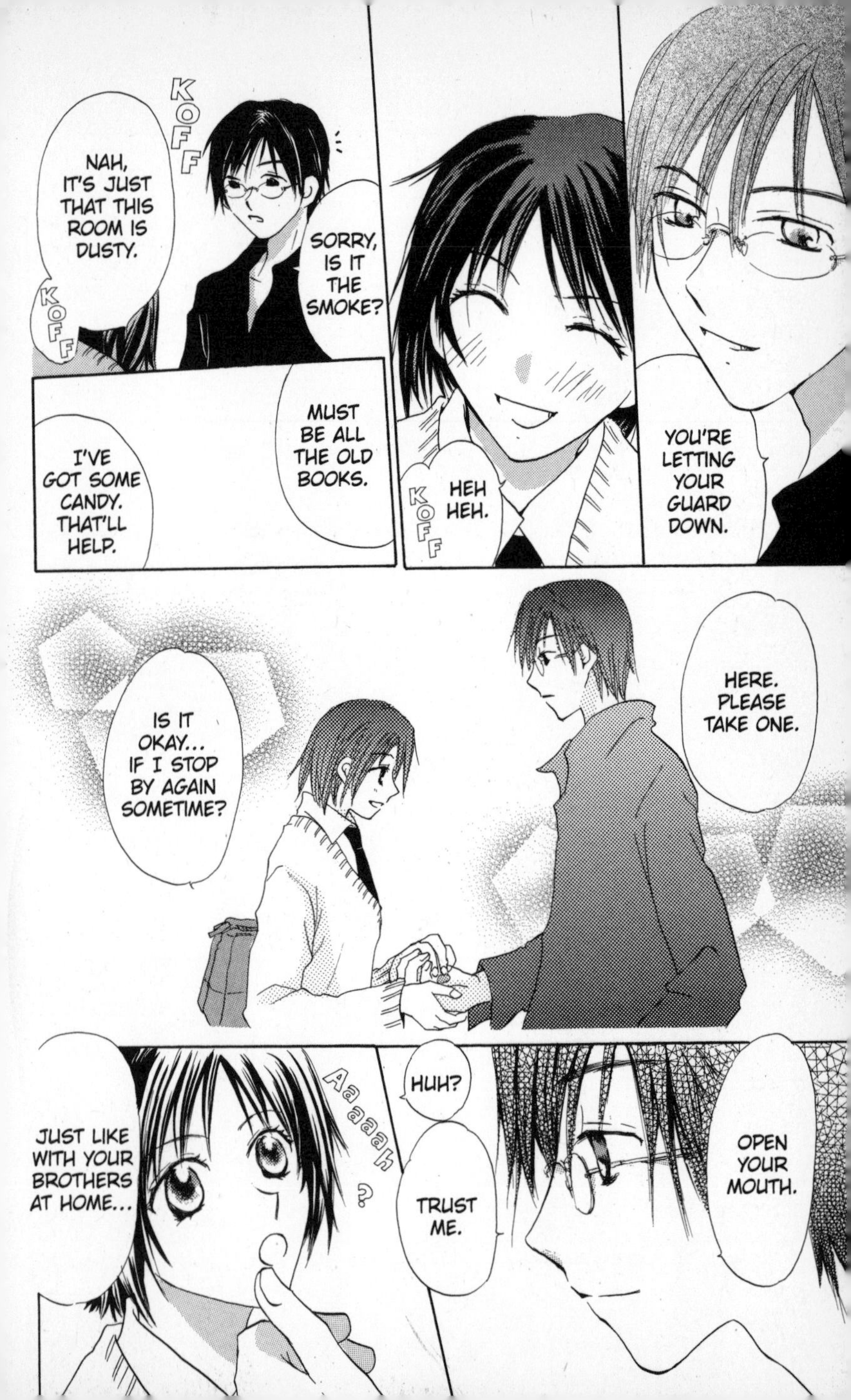
YOU'RE LETTING YOUR GUARD DOWN.
KOFF
HEH HEH.
SORRY, IS IT THE SMOKE?
KOFF
NAH, IT'S JUST THAT THIS ROOM IS DUSTY.
KOFF
MUST BE ALL THE OLD BOOKS.
I'VE GOT SOME CANDY. THAT'LL HELP.
HERE. PLEASE TAKE ONE.
IS IT OKAY... IF I STOP BY AGAIN SOMETIME?
OPEN YOUR MOUTH.
HUH?
TRUST ME.
Aaaaah?
JUST LIKE WITH YOUR BROTHERS AT HOME...

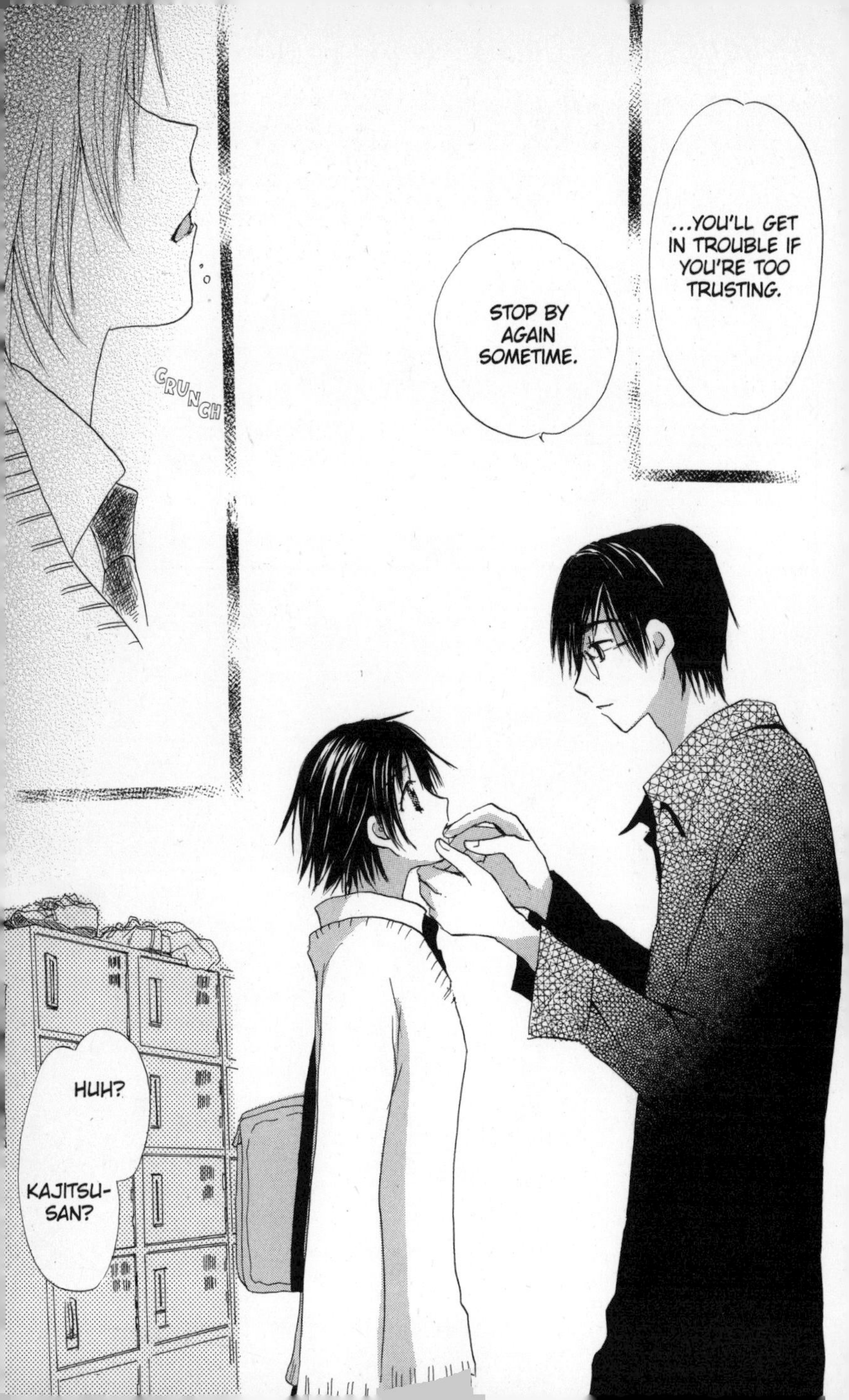
...YOU'LL GET IN TROUBLE IF YOU'RE TOO TRUSTING.
STOP BY AGAIN SOMETIME.
CRUNCH
HUH?
KAJITSU-SAN?

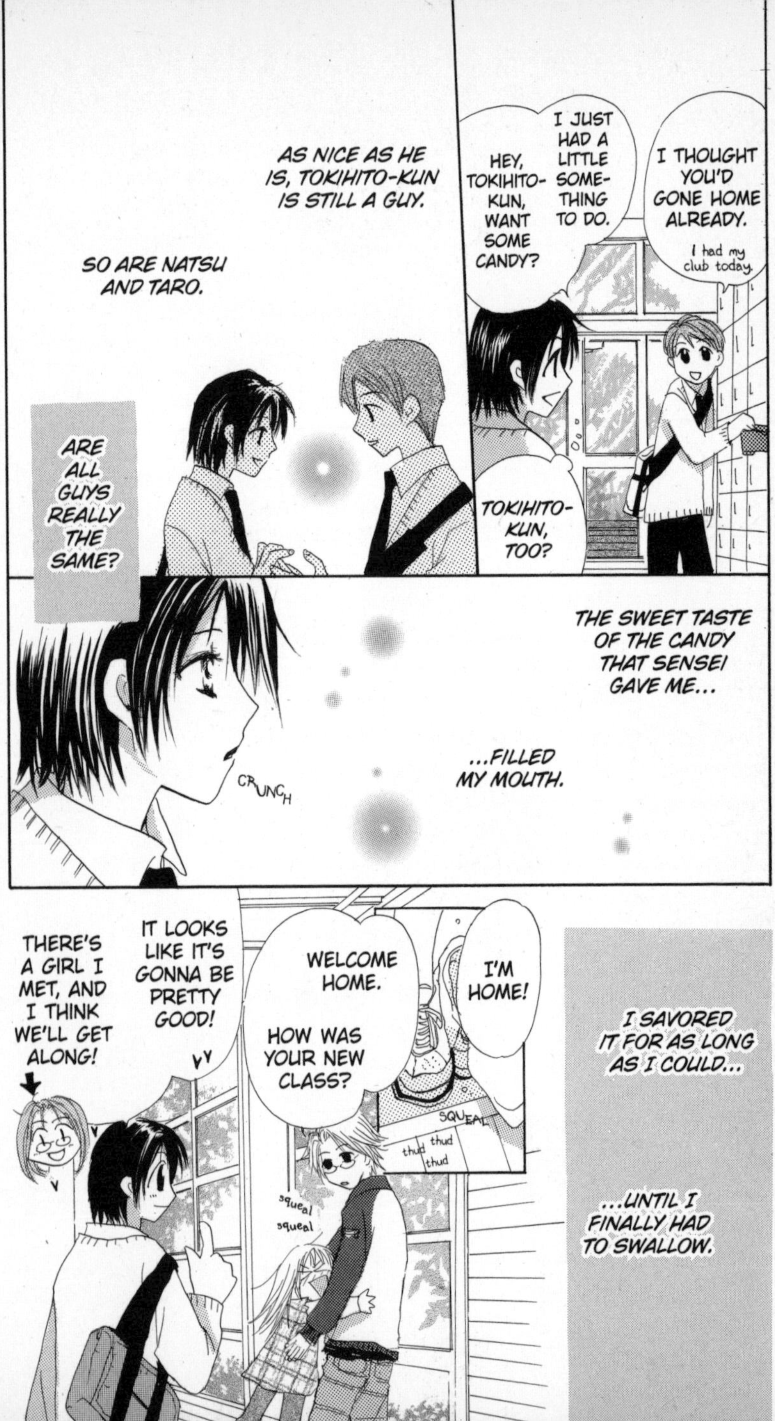
I THOUGHT YOU'D GONE HOME ALREADY.
I had my club today.
I JUST HAD A LITTLE SOMETHING TO DO.
HEY, TOKIHITO-KUN, WANT SOME CANDY?
TOKIHITO-KUN, TOO?
AS NICE AS HE IS, TOKIHITO-KUN IS STILL A GUY.
SO ARE NATSU AND TARO.
ARE ALL GUYS REALLY THE SAME?
THE SWEET TASTE OF THE CANDY THAT SENSEI GAVE ME...
...FILLED MY MOUTH.
CRUNCH
I SAVORED IT FOR AS LONG AS I COULD...
...UNTIL I FINALLY HAD TO SWALLOW.
I'M HOME!
SQUEAL
thud thud thud
WELCOME HOME.
HOW WAS YOUR NEW CLASS?
squeal squeal
IT LOOKS LIKE IT'S GONNA BE PRETTY GOOD!
THERE'S A GIRL I MET, AND I THINK WE'LL GET ALONG!

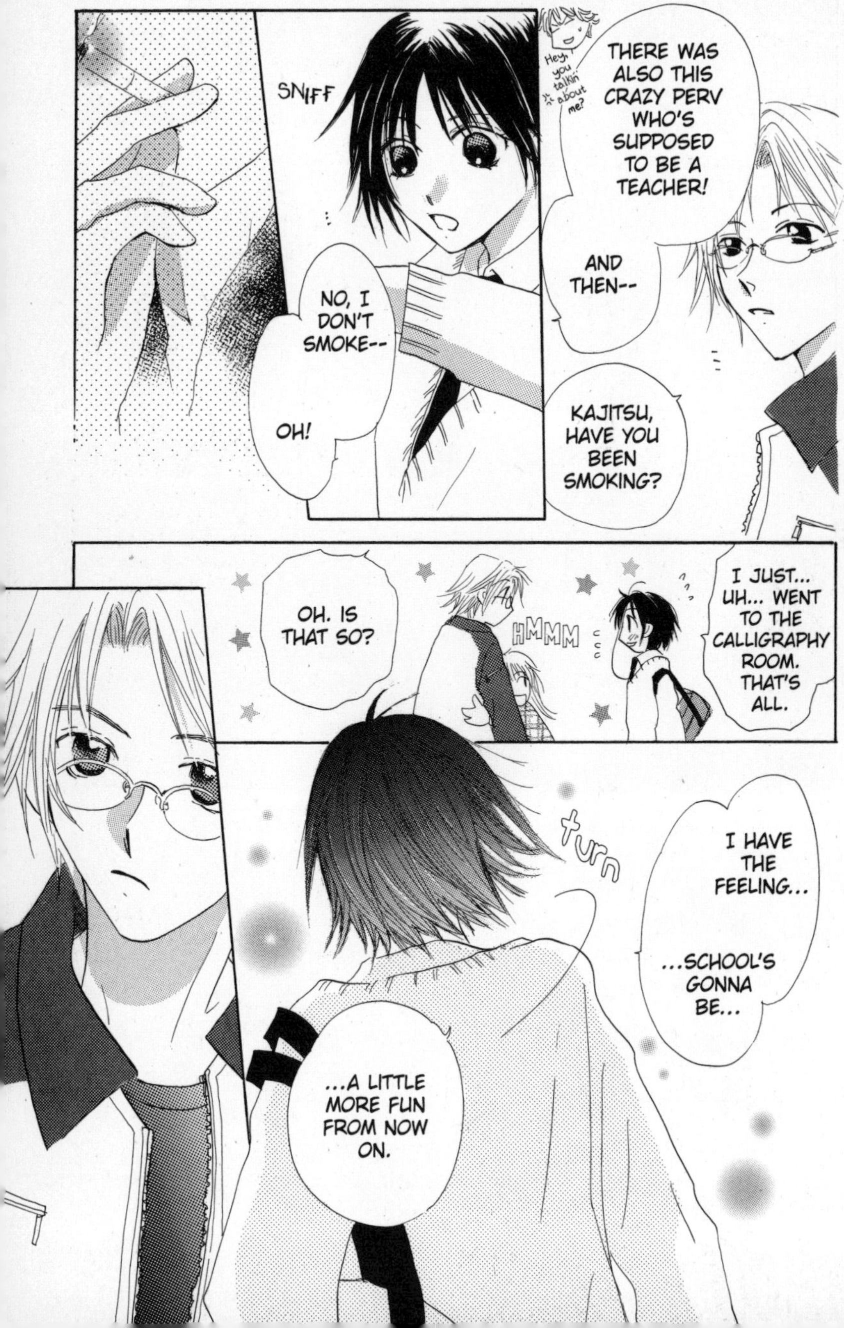
THERE WAS ALSO THIS CRAZY PERV WHO'S SUPPOSED TO BE A TEACHER!
Hey, you talkin' about me?
AND THEN--
KAJITSU, HAVE YOU BEEN SMOKING?
SNIFF
NO, I DON'T SMOKE--
OH!
I JUST... UH... WENT TO THE CALLIGRAPHY ROOM. THAT'S ALL.
HMMMM
OH. IS THAT SO?
turn
I HAVE THE FEELING...
...SCHOOL'S GONNA BE...
...A LITTLE MORE FUN FROM NOW ON.

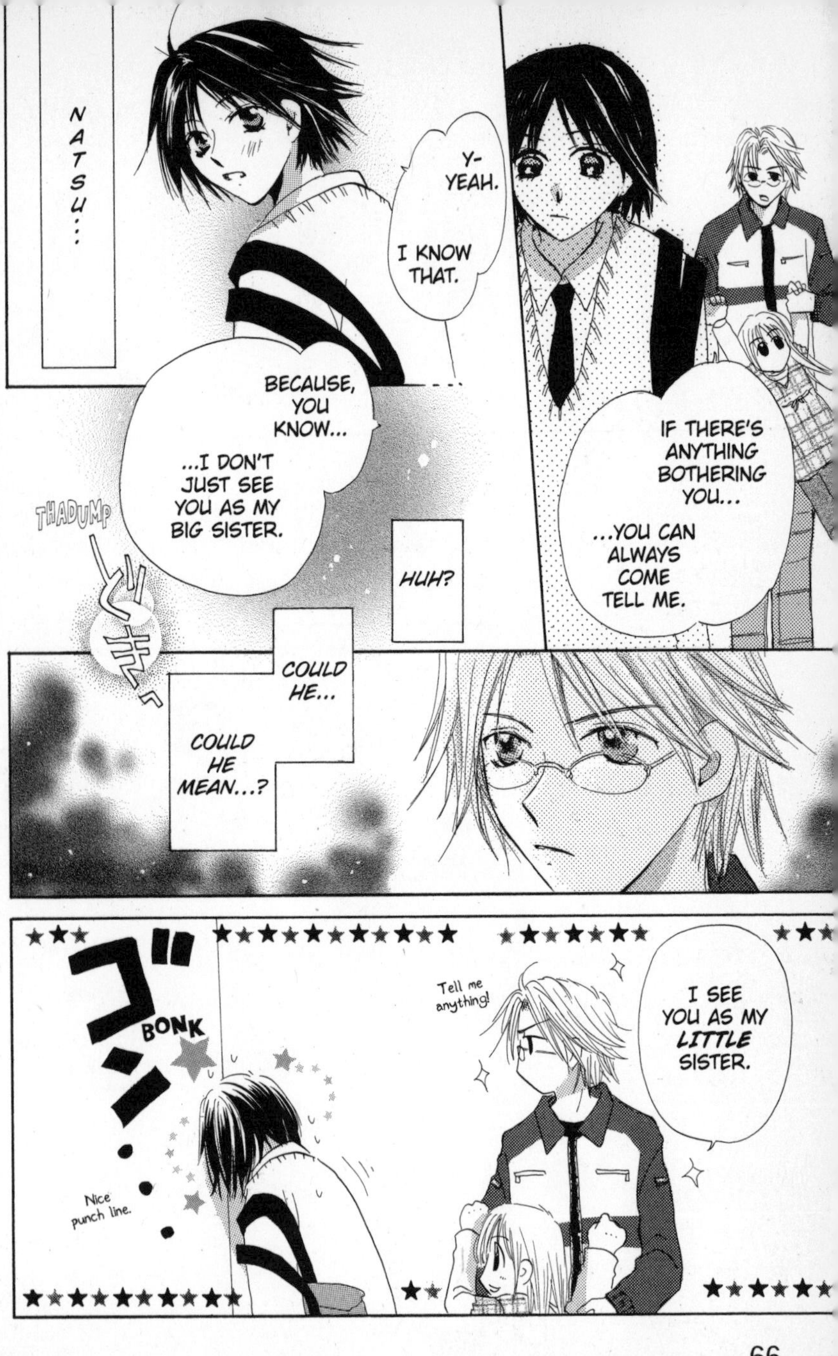
IF THERE'S ANYTHING BOTHERING YOU...
...YOU CAN ALWAYS COME TELL ME.
Y-YEAH.
I KNOW THAT.
NATSU...
BECAUSE, YOU KNOW...
...I DON'T JUST SEE YOU AS MY BIG SISTER.
HUH?
THADUMP
COULD HE...
COULD HE MEAN...?
I SEE YOU AS MY *LITTLE* SISTER.
Tell me anything!
BONK
Nice punch line.

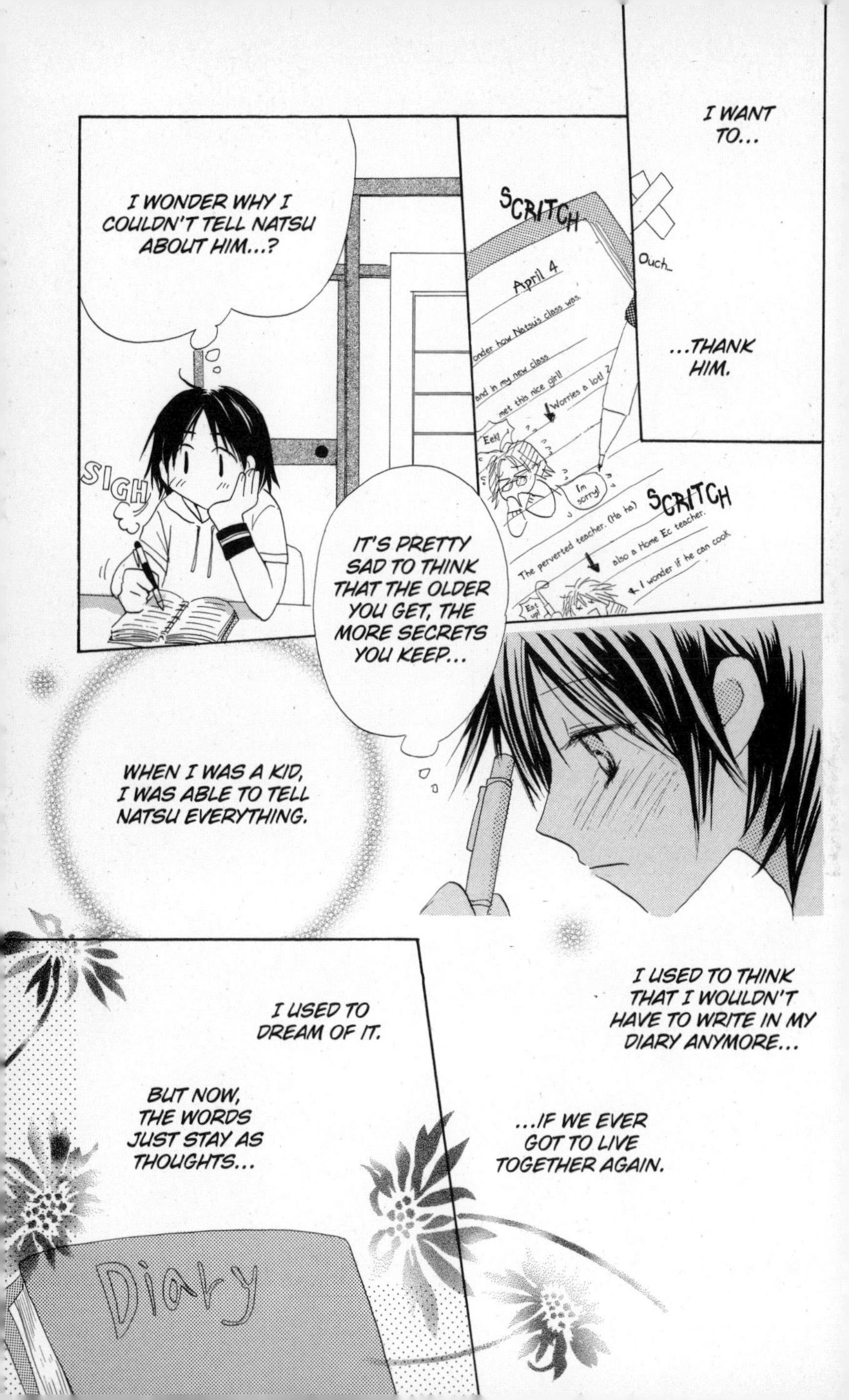
I WANT TO...
Ouch_
...THANK HIM.
SCRITCH
April 4
onder how Natsu's class was.
and in my new class
met this nice girl!
Worries a lot!
Eek!
I'm sorry!
SCRITCH
The perverted teacher. (Ha ha)
also a Home Ec teacher.
I wonder if he can cook.
Eat up!
I WONDER WHY I COULDN'T TELL NATSU ABOUT HIM...?
SIGH
IT'S PRETTY SAD TO THINK THAT THE OLDER YOU GET, THE MORE SECRETS YOU KEEP...
WHEN I WAS A KID, I WAS ABLE TO TELL NATSU EVERYTHING.
I USED TO THINK THAT I WOULDN'T HAVE TO WRITE IN MY DIARY ANYMORE...
...IF WE EVER GOT TO LIVE TOGETHER AGAIN.
I USED TO DREAM OF IT.
BUT NOW, THE WORDS JUST STAY AS THOUGHTS...
Diary

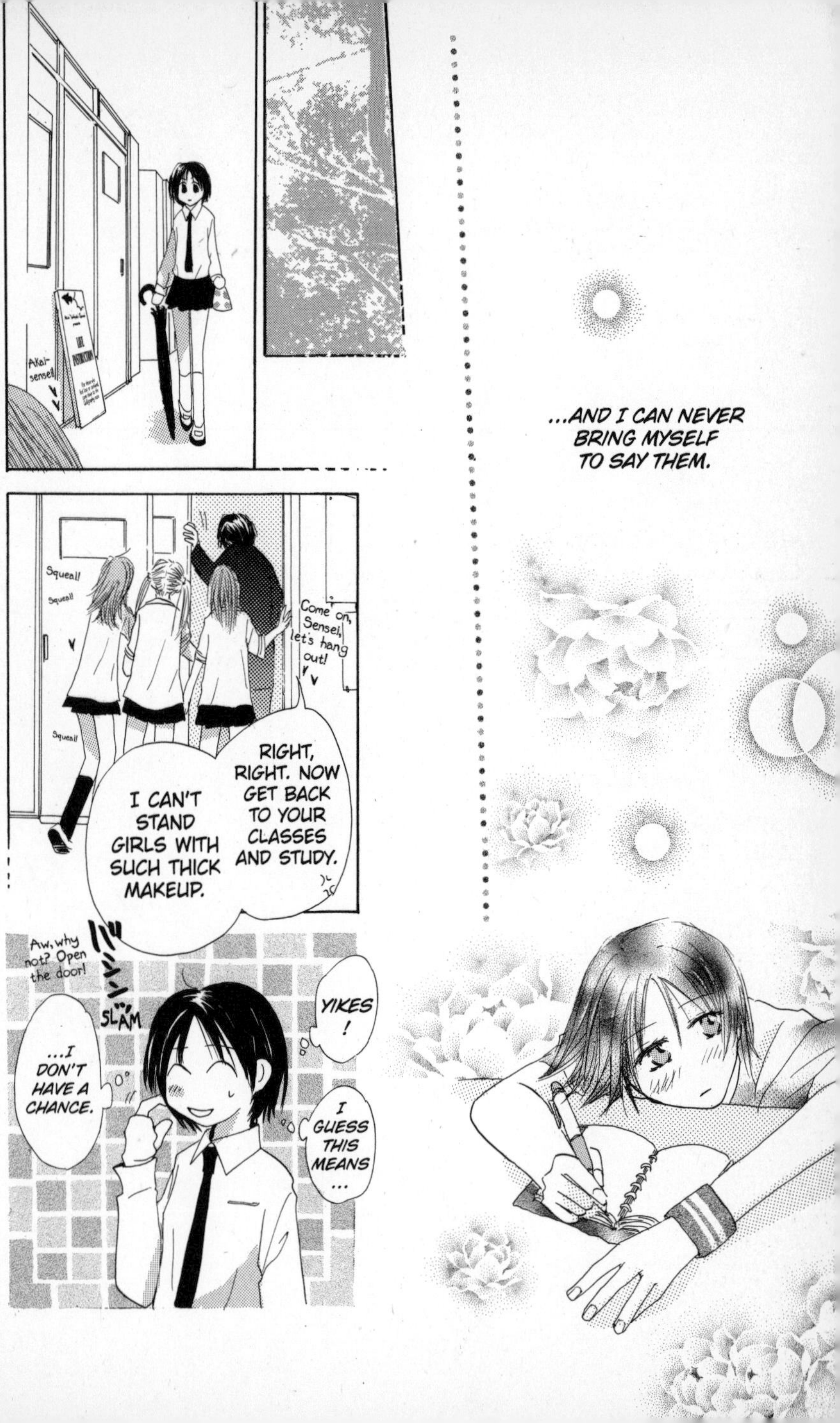
...AND I CAN NEVER BRING MYSELF TO SAY THEM.
Akai-sensei!
LIFE INSTRUCTION
Come on, Sensei, let's hang out!
RIGHT, RIGHT. NOW GET BACK TO YOUR CLASSES AND STUDY.
I CAN'T STAND GIRLS WITH SUCH THICK MAKEUP.
Squeal!
Squeal!
Squeal!
YIKES!
I GUESS THIS MEANS...
...I DON'T HAVE A CHANCE.
SLAM
Aw, why not? Open the door!

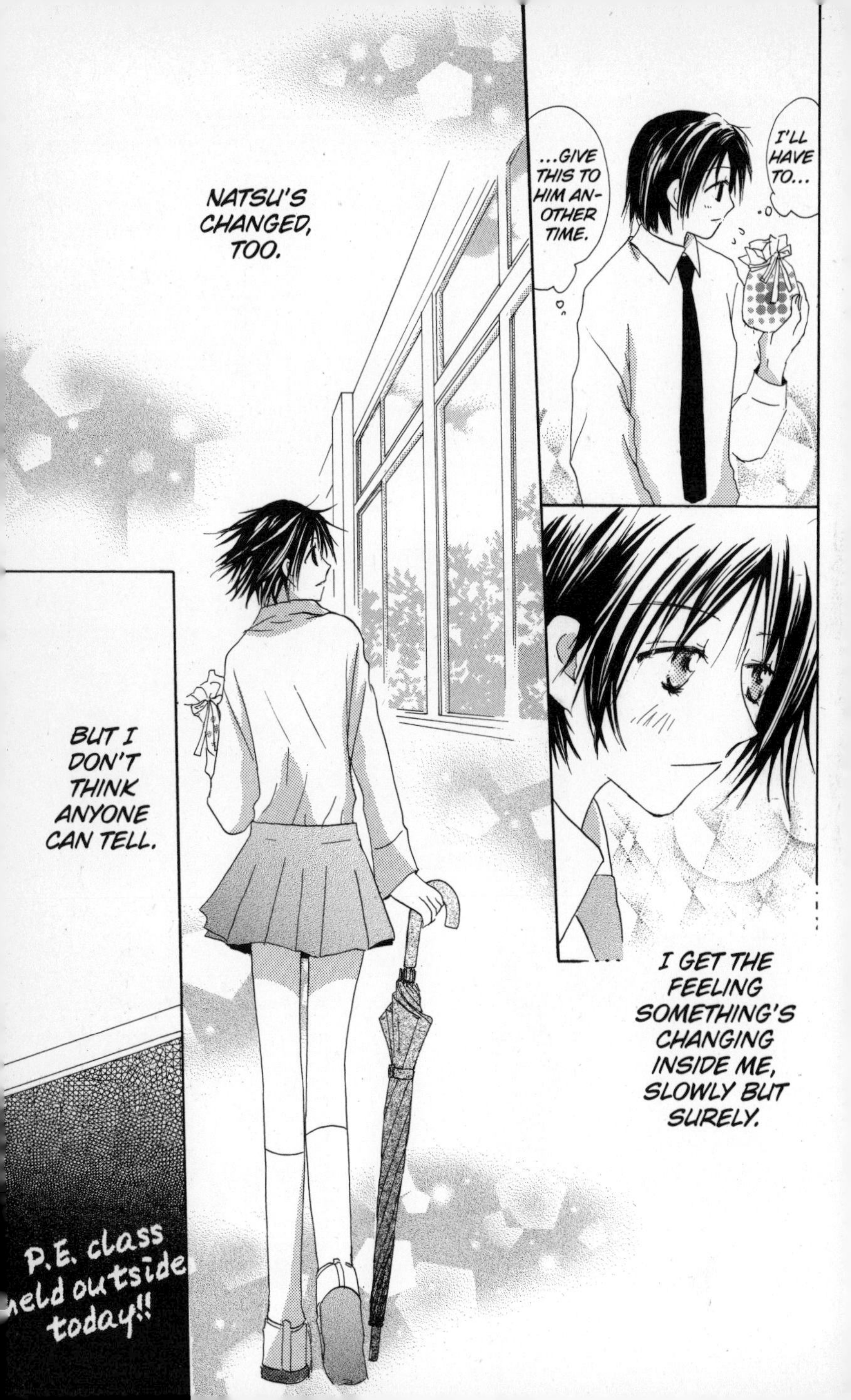
I'LL HAVE TO...
...GIVE THIS TO HIM ANOTHER TIME.
I GET THE FEELING SOMETHING'S CHANGING INSIDE ME, SLOWLY BUT SURELY.
NATSU'S CHANGED, TOO.
BUT I DON'T THINK ANYONE CAN TELL.
P.E. class held outside today!!

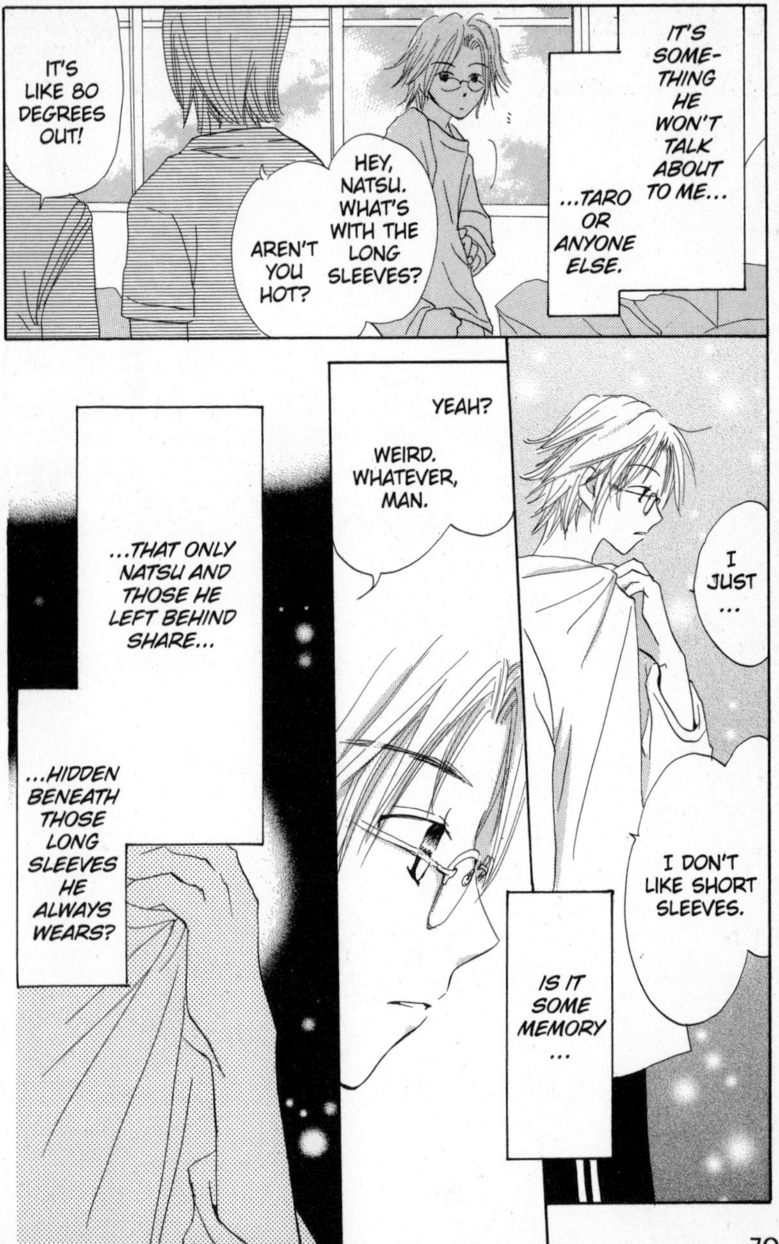
IT'S SOMETHING HE WON'T TALK ABOUT TO ME...
...TARO OR ANYONE ELSE.
HEY, NATSU. WHAT'S WITH THE LONG SLEEVES?
AREN'T YOU HOT?
IT'S LIKE 80 DEGREES OUT!
I JUST ...
I DON'T LIKE SHORT SLEEVES.
YEAH?
WEIRD. WHATEVER, MAN.
IS IT SOME MEMORY ...
...THAT ONLY NATSU AND THOSE HE LEFT BEHIND SHARE...
...HIDDEN BENEATH THOSE LONG SLEEVES HE ALWAYS WEARS?

Bonus Comic I: Don't Call me Mama!

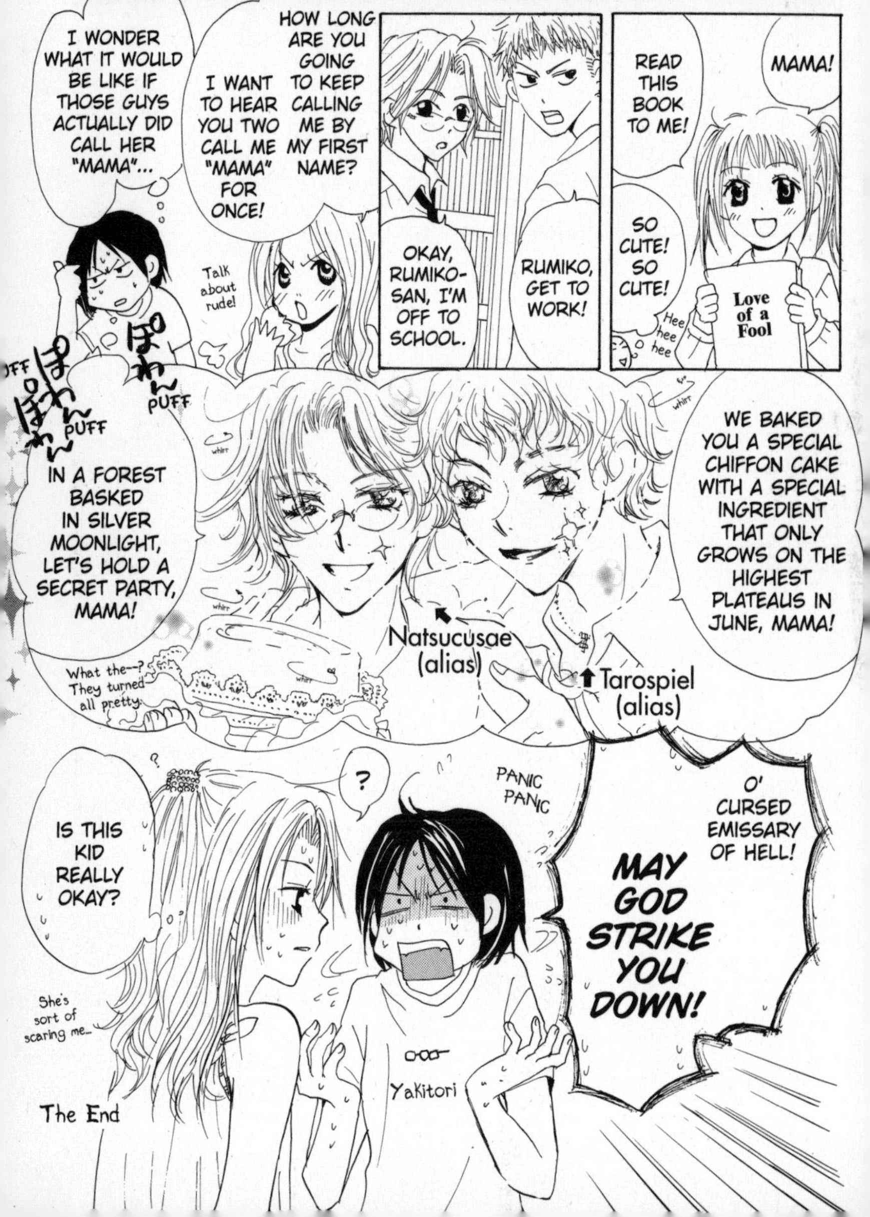

MAMA!
READ THIS BOOK TO ME!
SO CUTE! SO CUTE!
Hee hee hee
Love of a Fool
RUMIKO, GET TO WORK!
OKAY, RUMIKO-SAN, I'M OFF TO SCHOOL.
HOW LONG ARE YOU GOING TO KEEP CALLING ME BY MY FIRST NAME?
I WANT TO HEAR YOU TWO CALL ME "MAMA" FOR ONCE!
Talk about rude!
I WONDER WHAT IT WOULD BE LIKE IF THOSE GUYS ACTUALLY DID CALL HER "MAMA"...
ぽわん PUFF
ぽわん PUFF
ぽわん PUFF
WE BAKED YOU A SPECIAL CHIFFON CAKE WITH A SPECIAL INGREDIENT THAT ONLY GROWS ON THE HIGHEST PLATEAUS IN JUNE, MAMA!
whirr
Tarospiel (alias)
Natsucusae (alias)
IN A FOREST BASKED IN SILVER MOONLIGHT, LET'S HOLD A SECRET PARTY, MAMA!
whirr
What the--? They turned all pretty.
O' CURSED EMISSARY OF HELL!
MAY GOD STRIKE YOU DOWN!
PANIC PANIC
?
IS THIS KID REALLY OKAY?
She's sort of scaring me...
Yakitori
The End

Bonus Comic 2: Name Time!

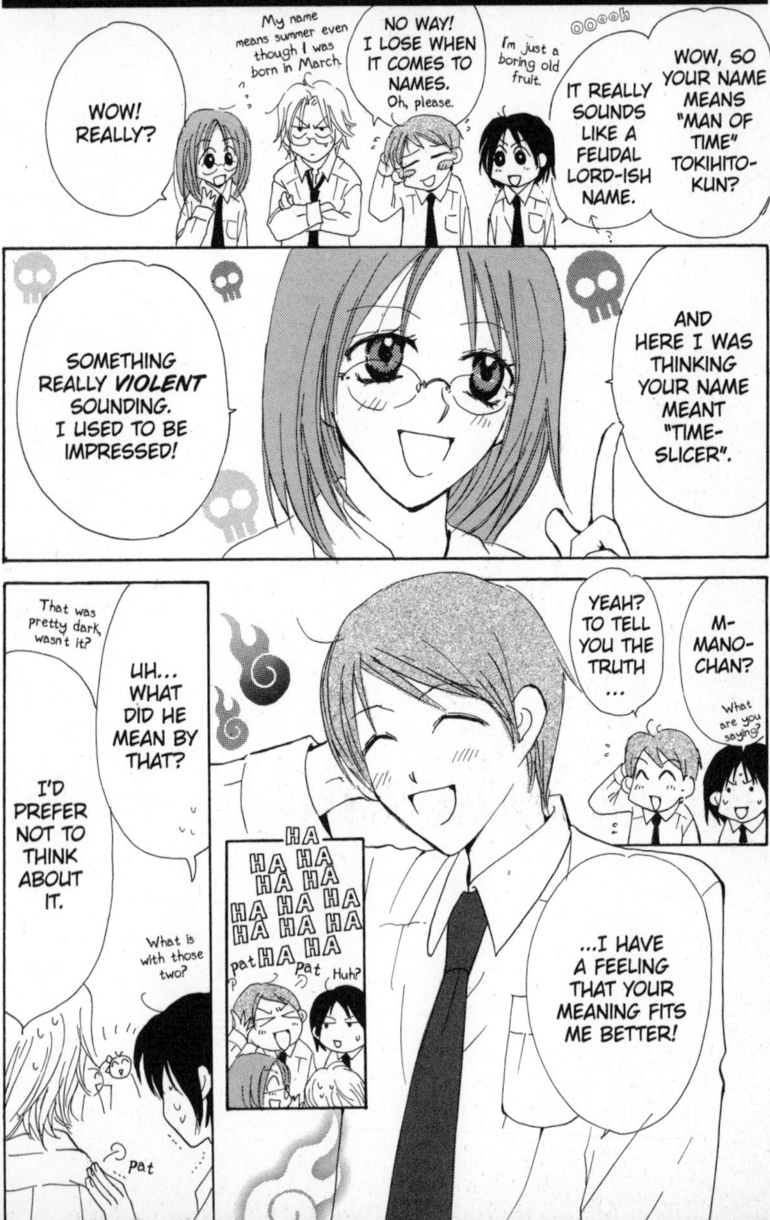
Oooh
WOW, SO YOUR NAME MEANS "MAN OF TIME" TOKIHITO-KUN?
IT REALLY SOUNDS LIKE A FEUDAL LORD-ISH NAME.
I'm just a boring old fruit.
NO WAY! I LOSE WHEN IT COMES TO NAMES.
Oh, please.
My name means summer even though I was born in March.
WOW! REALLY?
AND HERE I WAS THINKING YOUR NAME MEANT "TIME-SLICER".
SOMETHING REALLY VIOLENT SOUNDING. I USED TO BE IMPRESSED!
M-MANO-CHAN?
What are you saying?
YEAH? TO TELL YOU THE TRUTH ...
...I HAVE A FEELING THAT YOUR MEANING FITS ME BETTER!
HA HA HA HA HA HA HA HA HA HA HA HA HA HA
pat HA pat
Huh?
UH... WHAT DID HE MEAN BY THAT?
That was pretty dark, wasn't it?
I'D PREFER NOT TO THINK ABOUT IT.
What is with those two?
pat
The End

#8 Natsu's Memories (Part One)

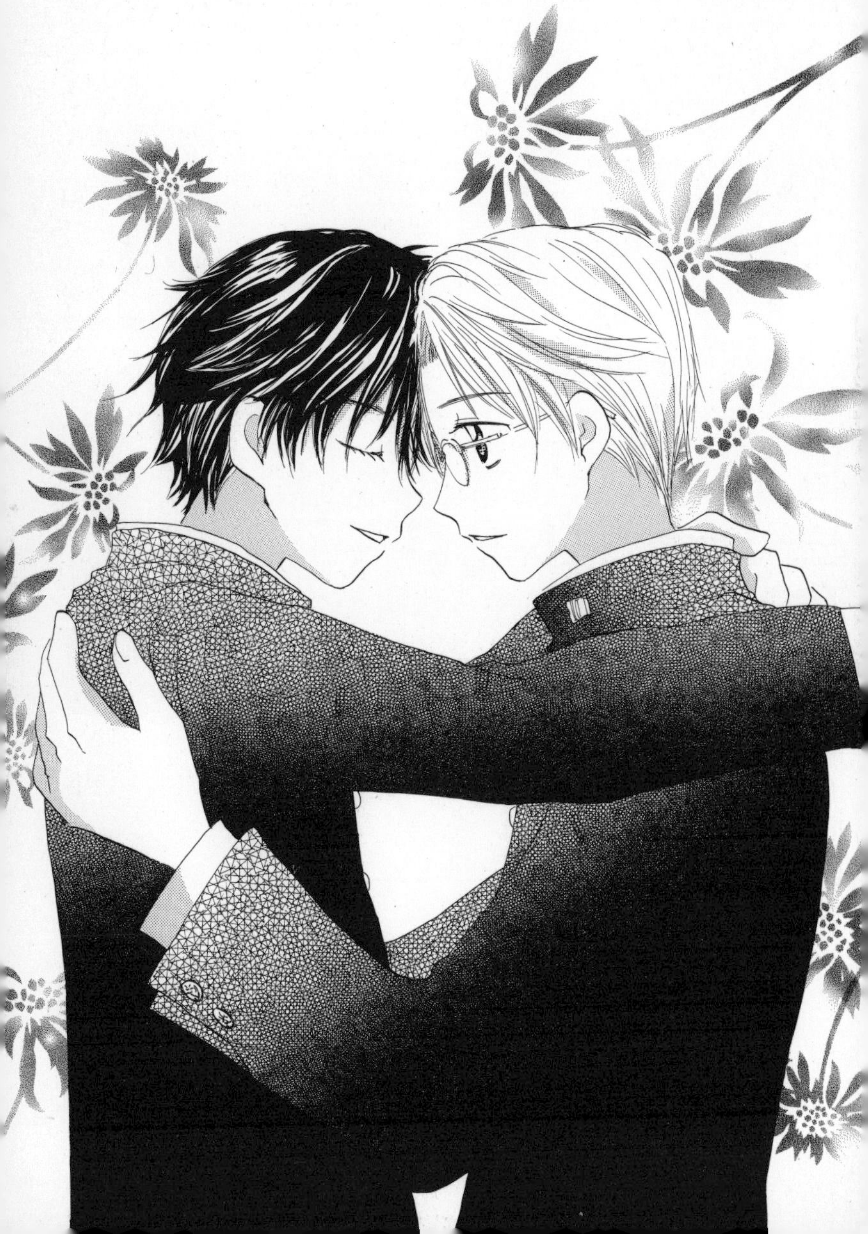

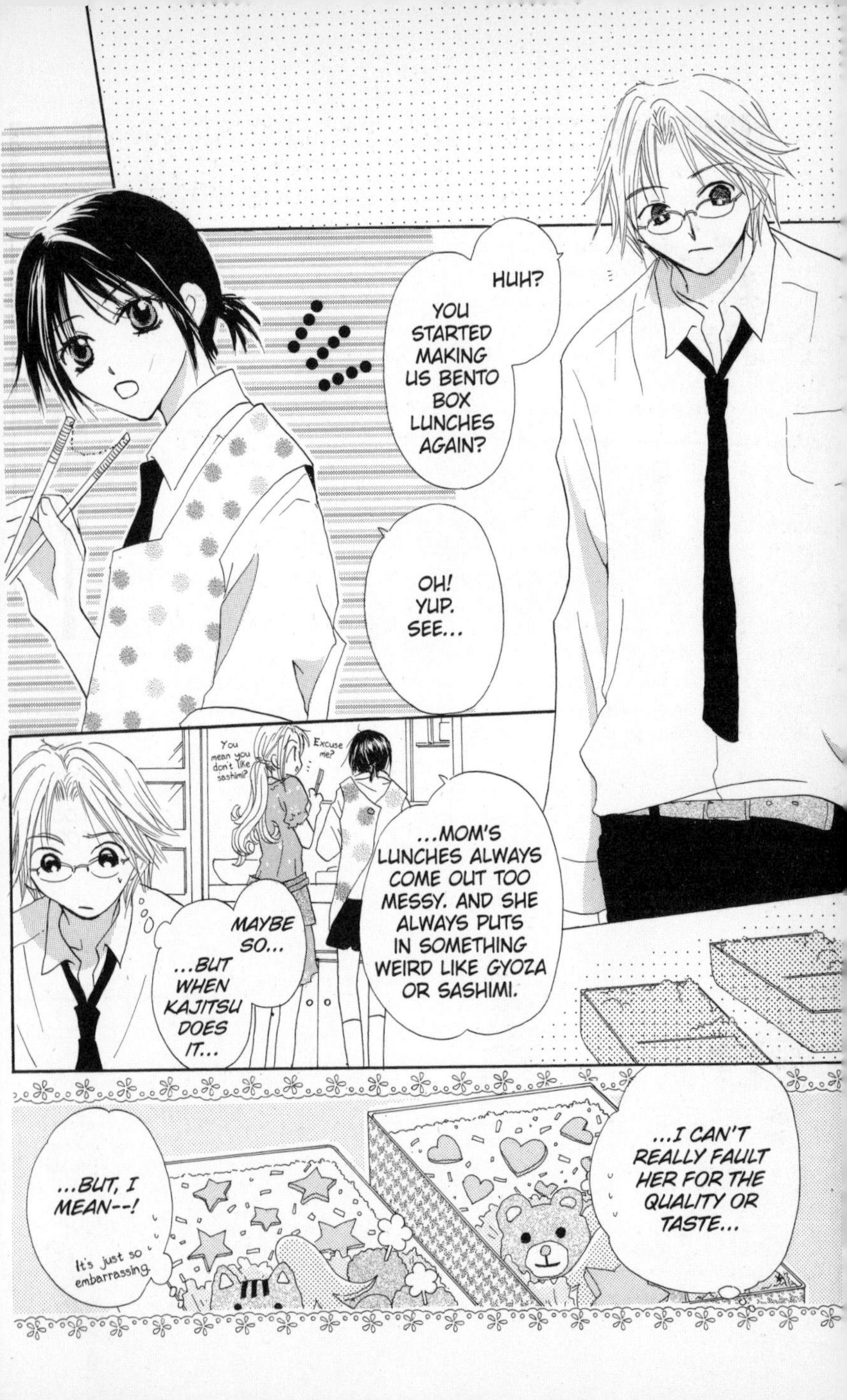
HUH?
YOU STARTED MAKING US BENTO BOX LUNCHES AGAIN?
OH! YUP. SEE...
...MOM'S LUNCHES ALWAYS COME OUT TOO MESSY. AND SHE ALWAYS PUTS IN SOMETHING WEIRD LIKE GYOZA OR SASHIMI.
Excuse me?
You mean you don't like sashimi?
MAYBE SO...
...BUT WHEN KAJITSU DOES IT...
...I CAN'T REALLY FAULT HER FOR THE QUALITY OR TASTE...
...BUT, I MEAN--!
It's just so embarrassing.

Crossroad Chapter 8: Natsu's Memories (Part I)

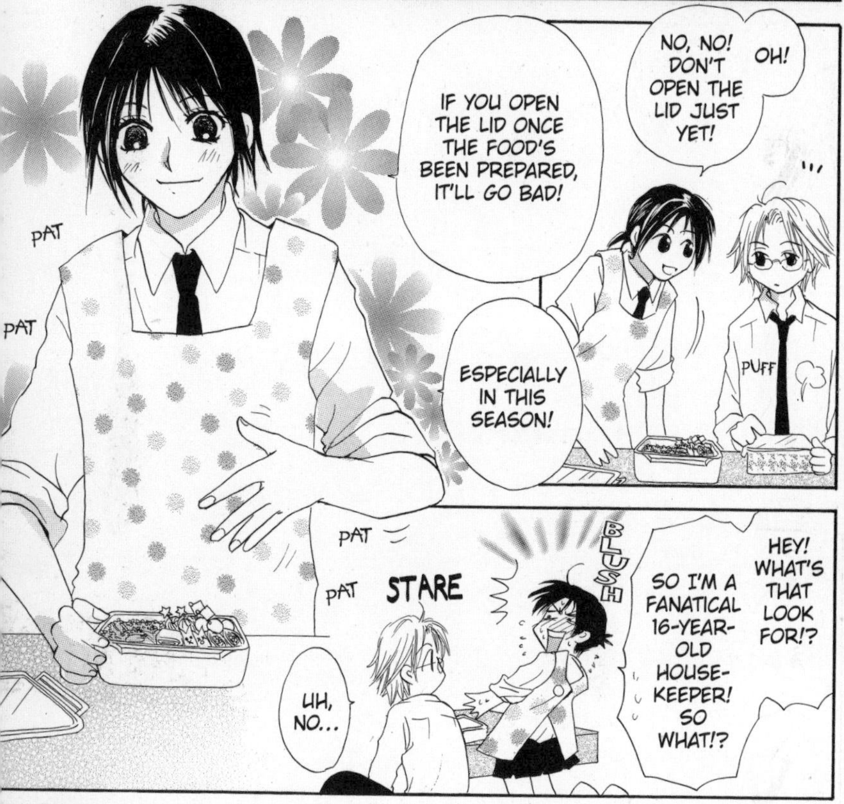
OH!
NO, NO! DON'T OPEN THE LID JUST YET!
...
IF YOU OPEN THE LID ONCE THE FOOD'S BEEN PREPARED, IT'LL GO BAD!
ESPECIALLY IN THIS SEASON!
PUFF
PAT
PAT
HEY! WHAT'S THAT LOOK FOR!?
SO I'M A FANATICAL 16-YEAR-OLD HOUSE-KEEPER! SO WHAT!?
BLUSH
STARE
PAT
PAT
UH, NO...

Scenery at a Crossroads 3

With there being a connection between "Natsu's Memories" and a railway crossing in this chapter, it made me wonder if in real life, there are such connections between railway crossings and the seasons of one's life. I was initially worried about doing this chapter because I didn't have any reference material for a railway crossing, so I had my assistant, Kise-san, take pictures of one that was near her house, and we both worked diligently to draw it. It was so grueling that my arm ended up in agony and Kise-san became exhausted, but we finished it in time. And then after we were done, totally out of the blue, my assistant was asked to draw a railway crossing for a completely unrelated project! Boy, was she surprised! But why in the same month? It must've been a sign from God! Not sure what it means, though. Just please keep sending us good messages, God!

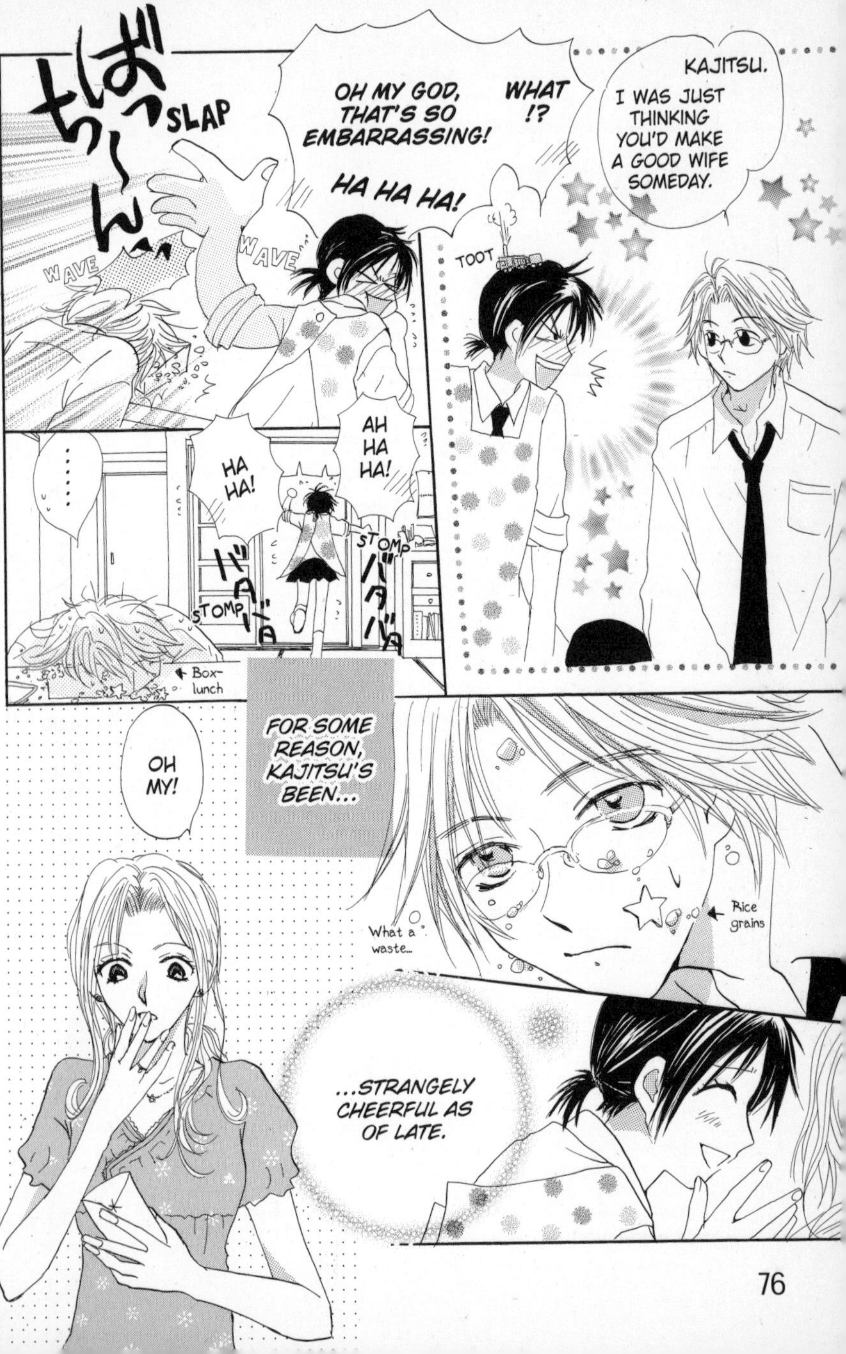
KAJITSU.
I WAS JUST THINKING YOU'D MAKE A GOOD WIFE SOMEDAY.
TOOT
WHAT!?
OH MY GOD, THAT'S SO EMBARRASSING!
HA HA HA!
ばっちぃ〜ん
SLAP
WAVE
WAVE
......
AH HA HA!
HA HA!
バタバタ
STOMP
STOMP
Box-lunch
FOR SOME REASON, KAJITSU'S BEEN...
Rice grains
What a waste...
...STRANGELY CHEERFUL AS OF LATE.
OH MY!

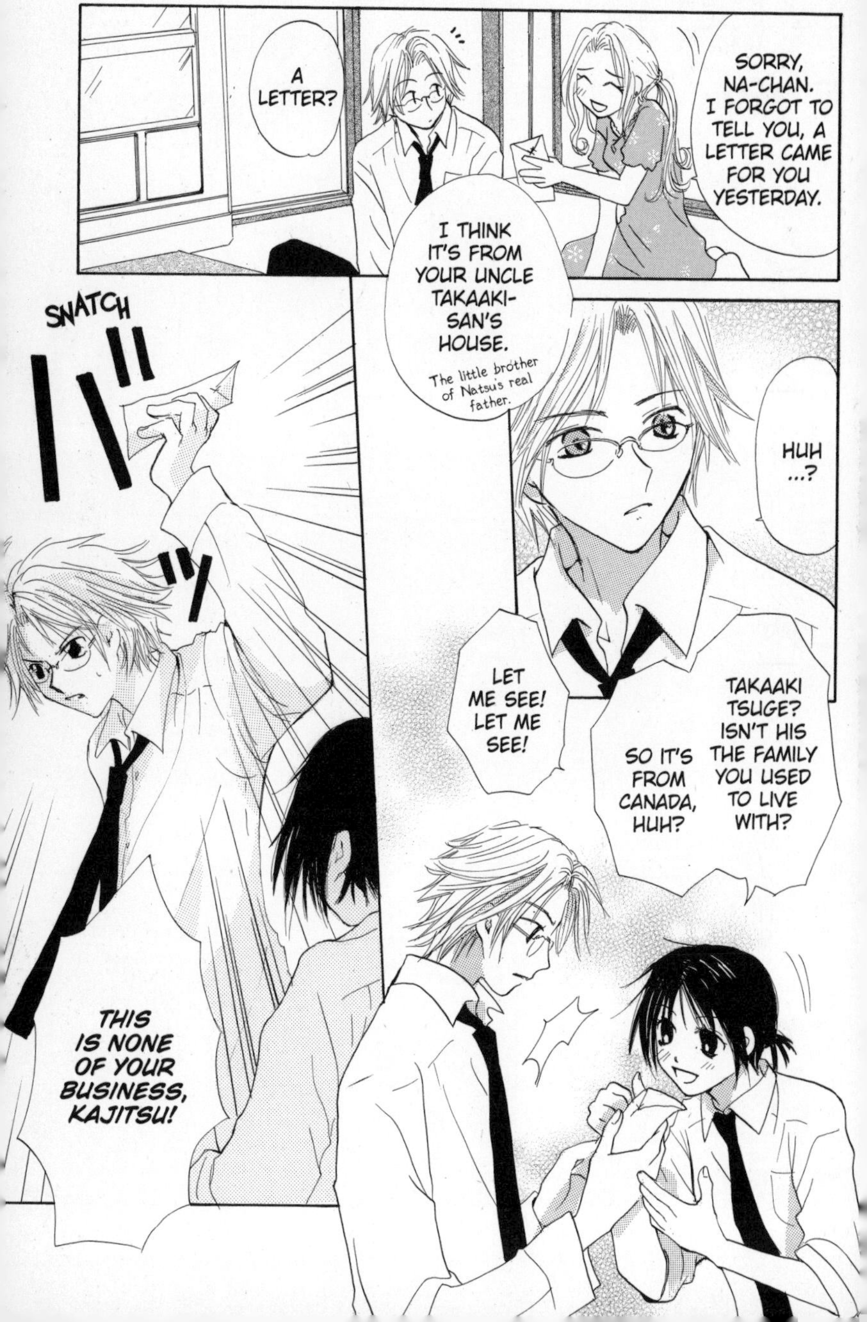
SORRY, NA-CHAN. I FORGOT TO TELL YOU, A LETTER CAME FOR YOU YESTERDAY.
A LETTER?
I THINK IT'S FROM YOUR UNCLE TAKAAKI-SAN'S HOUSE.
The little brother of Natsu's real father.
HUH ...?
TAKAAKI TSUGE? ISN'T HIS THE FAMILY YOU USED TO LIVE WITH?
SO IT'S FROM CANADA, HUH?
LET ME SEE! LET ME SEE!
SNATCH
THIS IS NONE OF YOUR BUSINESS, KAJITSU!

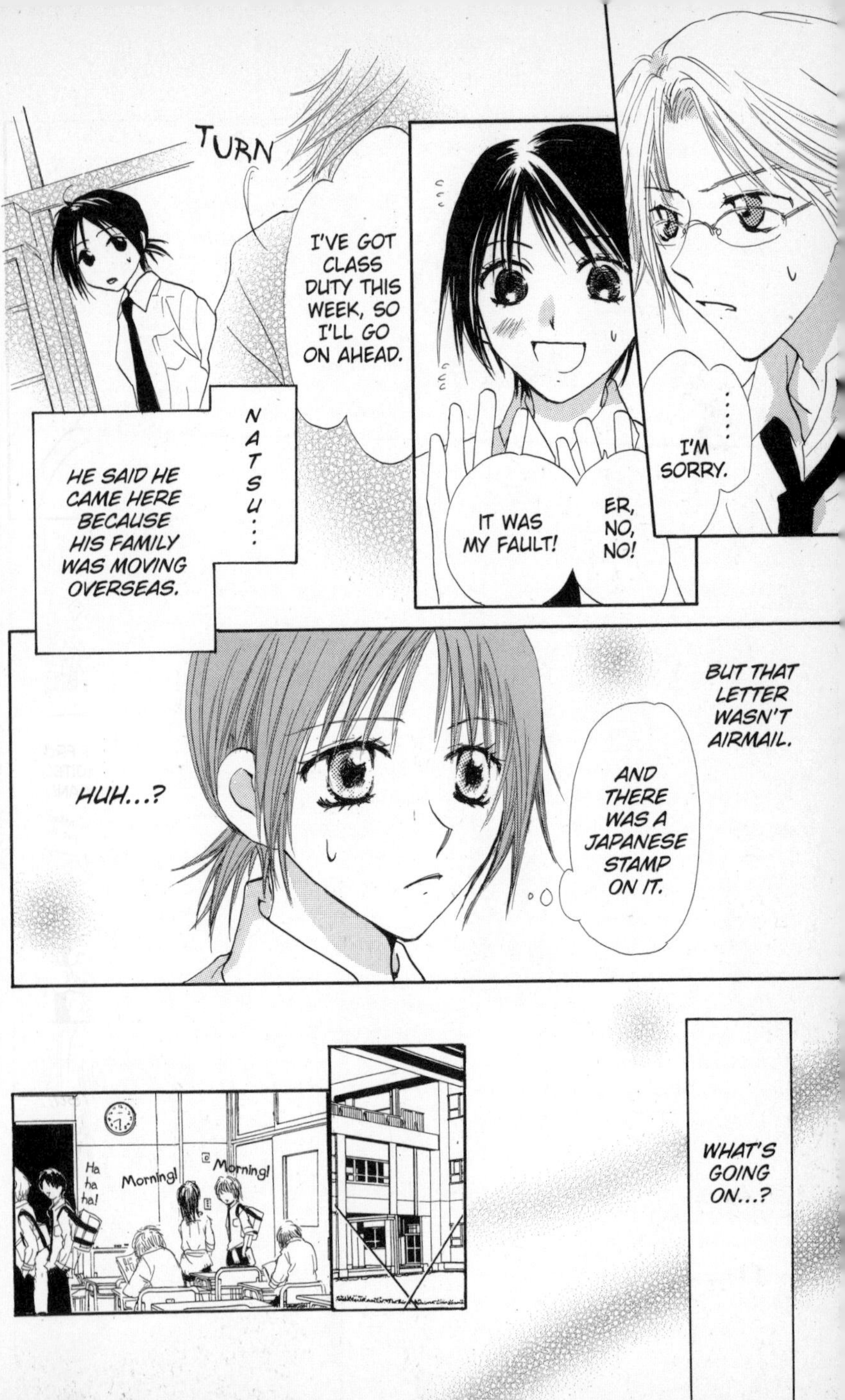
......
I'M SORRY.
ER, NO, NO!
IT WAS MY FAULT!
TURN
I'VE GOT CLASS DUTY THIS WEEK, SO I'LL GO ON AHEAD.
NATSU...
HE SAID HE CAME HERE BECAUSE HIS FAMILY WAS MOVING OVERSEAS.
BUT THAT LETTER WASN'T AIRMAIL.
AND THERE WAS A JAPANESE STAMP ON IT.
HUH...?
WHAT'S GOING ON...?
Morning!
Morning!
Ha ha ha!

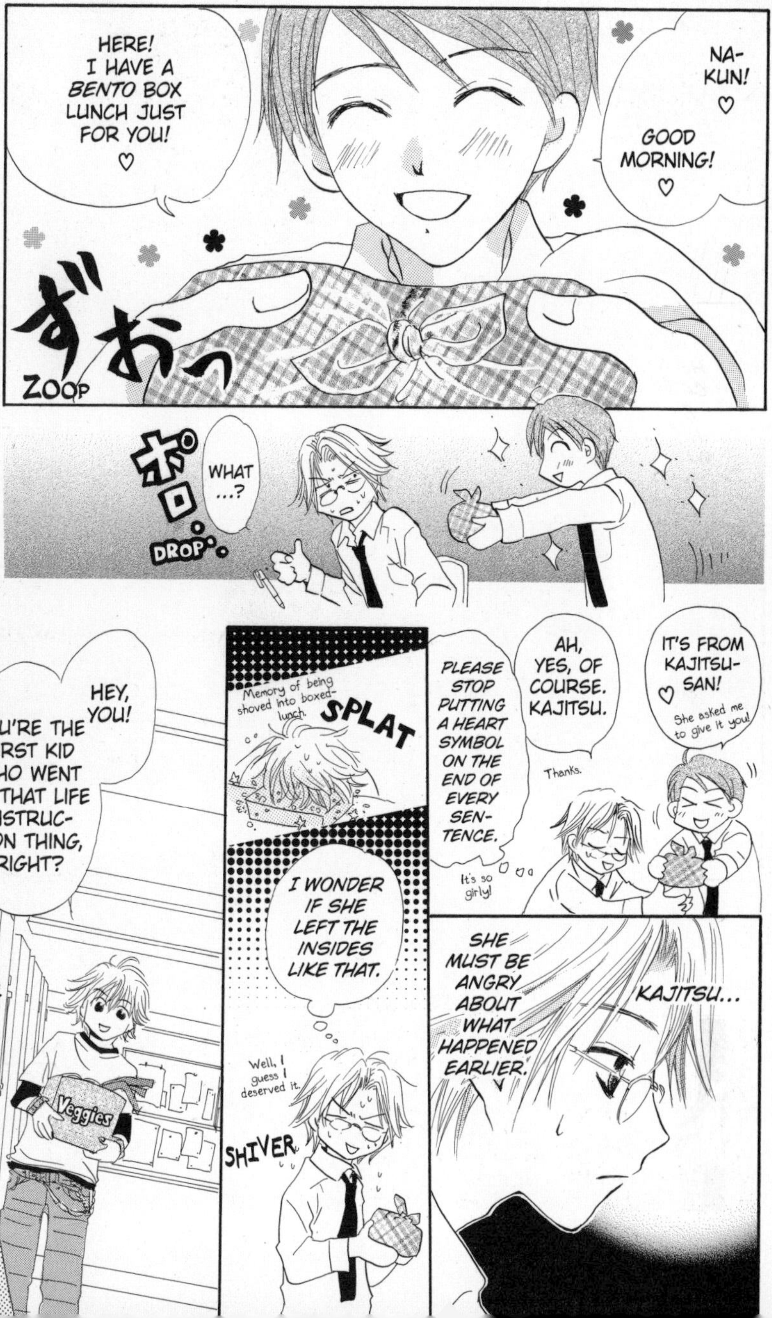
NA-KUN! ♡
GOOD MORNING! ♡
HERE! I HAVE A BENTO BOX LUNCH JUST FOR YOU! ♡
ずおっ
ZOOP
WHAT ...?
ポロ
DROP
IT'S FROM KAJITSU-SAN! ♡
She asked me to give it you!
AH, YES, OF COURSE. KAJITSU.
Thanks.
PLEASE STOP PUTTING A HEART SYMBOL ON THE END OF EVERY SENTENCE.
It's so girly!
KAJITSU...
SHE MUST BE ANGRY ABOUT WHAT HAPPENED EARLIER.
Memory of being shoved into boxed-lunch.
SPLAT
I WONDER IF SHE LEFT THE INSIDES LIKE THAT.
Well, I guess I deserved it.
SHIVER
HEY, YOU!
YOU'RE THE FIRST KID WHO WENT TO THAT LIFE INSTRUCTION THING, RIGHT?
Veggies

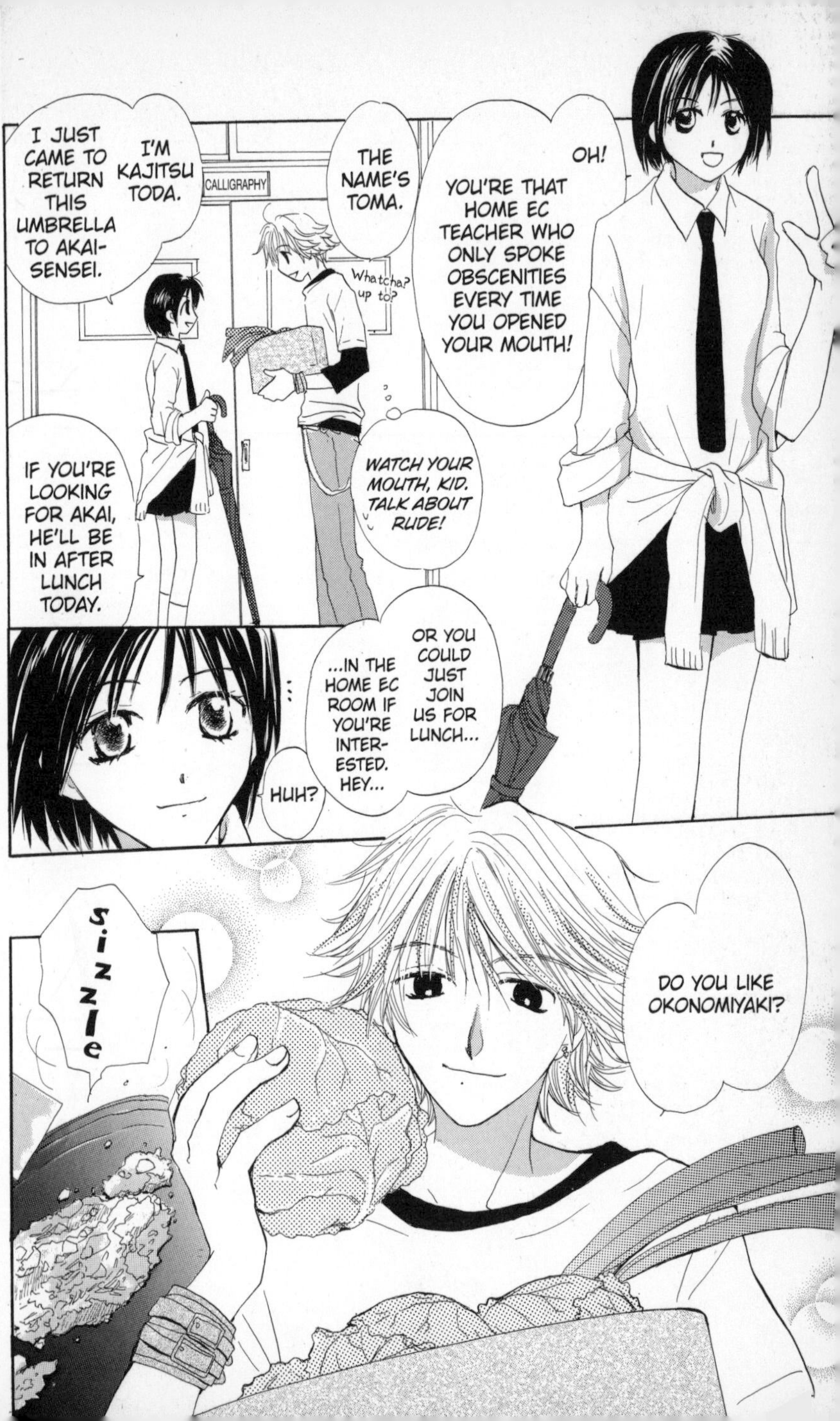
OH!
YOU'RE THAT HOME EC TEACHER WHO ONLY SPOKE OBSCENITIES EVERY TIME YOU OPENED YOUR MOUTH!
THE NAME'S TOMA.
Whatcha? up to?
I'M KAJITSU TODA.
I JUST CAME TO RETURN THIS UMBRELLA TO AKAI-SENSEI.
CALLIGRAPHY
WATCH YOUR MOUTH, KID. TALK ABOUT RUDE!
IF YOU'RE LOOKING FOR AKAI, HE'LL BE IN AFTER LUNCH TODAY.
OR YOU COULD JUST JOIN US FOR LUNCH...
...IN THE HOME EC ROOM IF YOU'RE INTER-ESTED. HEY...
HUH?
DO YOU LIKE OKONOMIYAKI?
sizzle

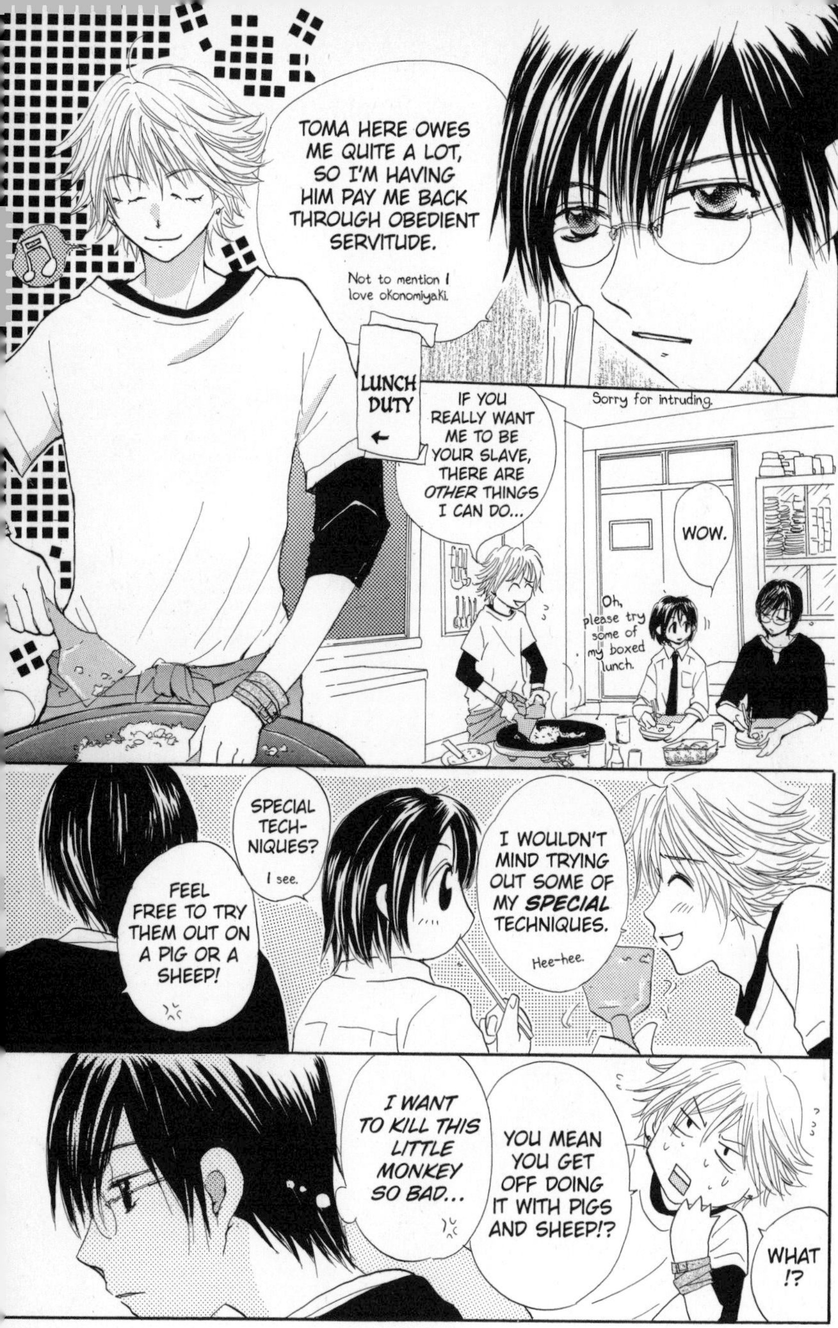
TOMA HERE OWES ME QUITE A LOT, SO I'M HAVING HIM PAY ME BACK THROUGH OBEDIENT SERVITUDE.
Not to mention I love oKonomiyaKi.
Sorry for intruding.
IF YOU REALLY WANT ME TO BE YOUR SLAVE, THERE ARE *OTHER* THINGS I CAN DO...
WOW.
Oh, please try some of my boxed lunch.
LUNCH DUTY ←
I WOULDN'T MIND TRYING OUT SOME OF MY ***SPECIAL*** TECHNIQUES.
Hee-hee.
SPECIAL TECH-NIQUES?
I see.
FEEL FREE TO TRY THEM OUT ON A PIG OR A SHEEP!
WHAT!?
YOU MEAN YOU GET OFF DOING IT WITH PIGS AND SHEEP!?
I WANT TO KILL THIS LITTLE MONKEY SO BAD...

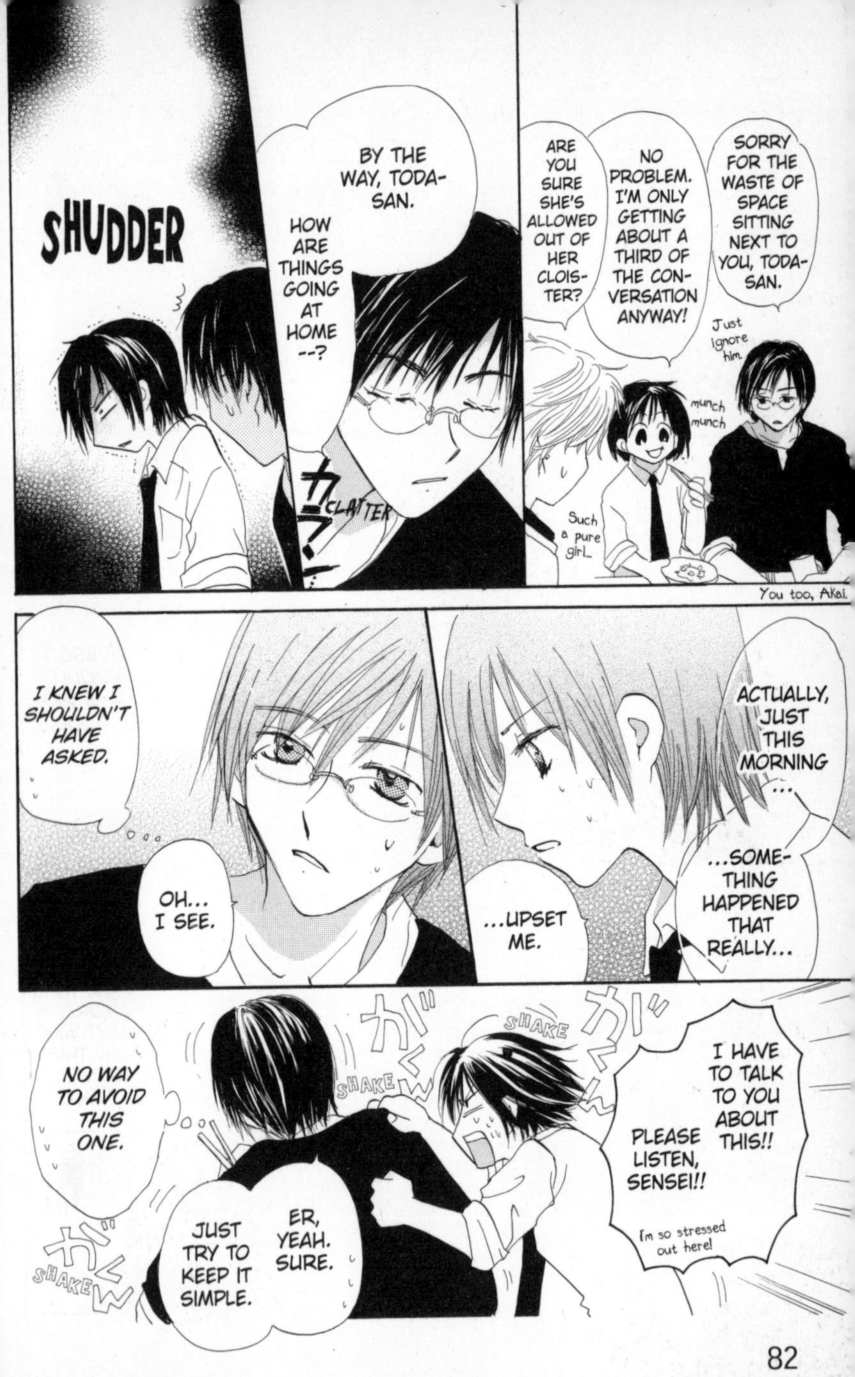
SORRY FOR THE WASTE OF SPACE SITTING NEXT TO YOU, TODA-SAN.
NO PROBLEM. I'M ONLY GETTING ABOUT A THIRD OF THE CONVERSATION ANYWAY!
ARE YOU SURE SHE'S ALLOWED OUT OF HER CLOISTER?
Just ignore him.
munch munch
Such a pure girl...
You too, Akai.
BY THE WAY, TODA-SAN.
HOW ARE THINGS GOING AT HOME --?
CLATTER
SHUDDER
ACTUALLY, JUST THIS MORNING...
...SOMETHING HAPPENED THAT REALLY...
...UPSET ME.
I KNEW I SHOULDN'T HAVE ASKED.
OH... I SEE.
I HAVE TO TALK TO YOU ABOUT THIS!!
PLEASE LISTEN, SENSEI!!
I'm so stressed out here!
SHAKE
SHAKE
ER, YEAH. SURE.
JUST TRY TO KEEP IT SIMPLE.
NO WAY TO AVOID THIS ONE.
SHAKE

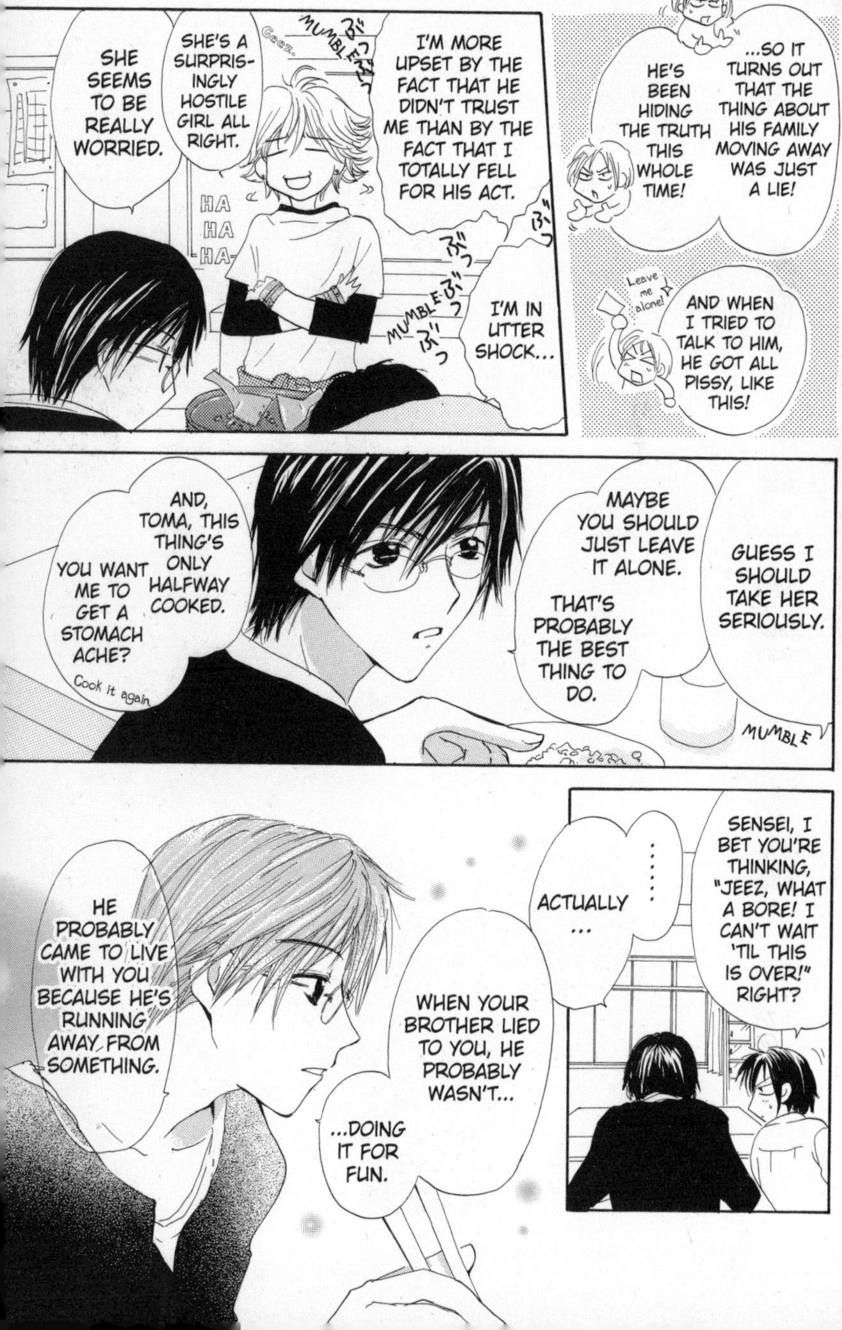
...SO IT TURNS OUT THAT THE THING ABOUT HIS FAMILY MOVING AWAY WAS JUST A LIE!
HE'S BEEN HIDING THE TRUTH THIS WHOLE TIME!
Leave me alone!
AND WHEN I TRIED TO TALK TO HIM, HE GOT ALL PISSY, LIKE THIS!
MUMBLE
I'M MORE UPSET BY THE FACT THAT HE DIDN'T TRUST ME THAN BY THE FACT THAT I TOTALLY FELL FOR HIS ACT.
MUMBLE
I'M IN UTTER SHOCK...
Geez.
SHE'S A SURPRISINGLY HOSTILE GIRL ALL RIGHT.
HA HA HA
SHE SEEMS TO BE REALLY WORRIED.
GUESS I SHOULD TAKE HER SERIOUSLY.
MUMBLE
MAYBE YOU SHOULD JUST LEAVE IT ALONE.
THAT'S PROBABLY THE BEST THING TO DO.
AND, TOMA, THIS THING'S ONLY HALFWAY COOKED.
YOU WANT ME TO GET A STOMACH ACHE?
Cook it again.
SENSEI, I BET YOU'RE THINKING, "JEEZ, WHAT A BORE! I CAN'T WAIT 'TIL THIS IS OVER!" RIGHT?
......
ACTUALLY...
WHEN YOUR BROTHER LIED TO YOU, HE PROBABLY WASN'T...
...DOING IT FOR FUN.
HE PROBABLY CAME TO LIVE WITH YOU BECAUSE HE'S RUNNING AWAY FROM SOMETHING.

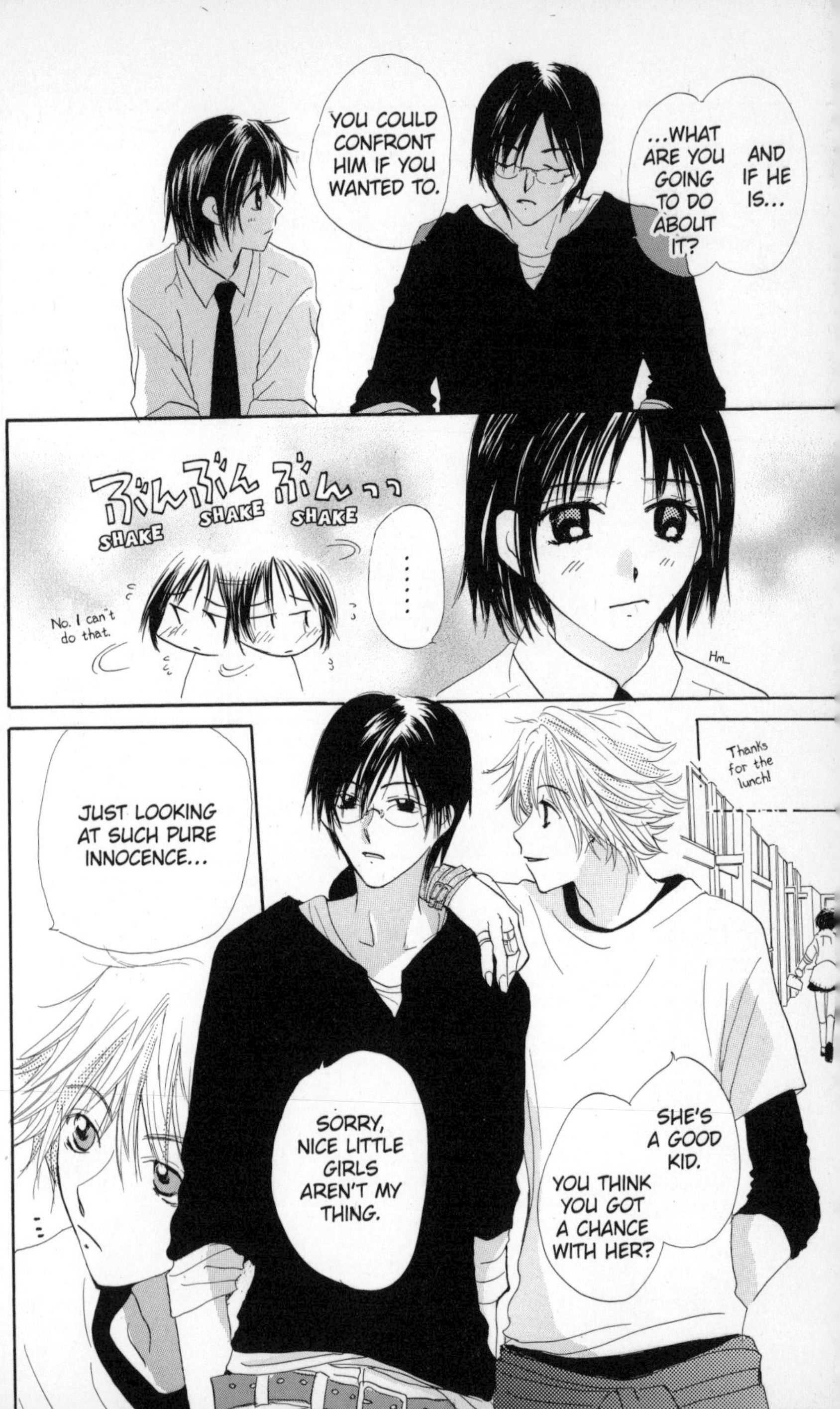
AND IF HE IS...
...WHAT ARE YOU GOING TO DO ABOUT IT?
YOU COULD CONFRONT HIM IF YOU WANTED TO.
Hm...
......
ぶんぶんぶんっっ
SHAKE SHAKE SHAKE
No. I can't do that.
Thanks for the lunch!
SHE'S A GOOD KID.
YOU THINK YOU GOT A CHANCE WITH HER?
SORRY, NICE LITTLE GIRLS AREN'T MY THING.
JUST LOOKING AT SUCH PURE INNOCENCE...
...

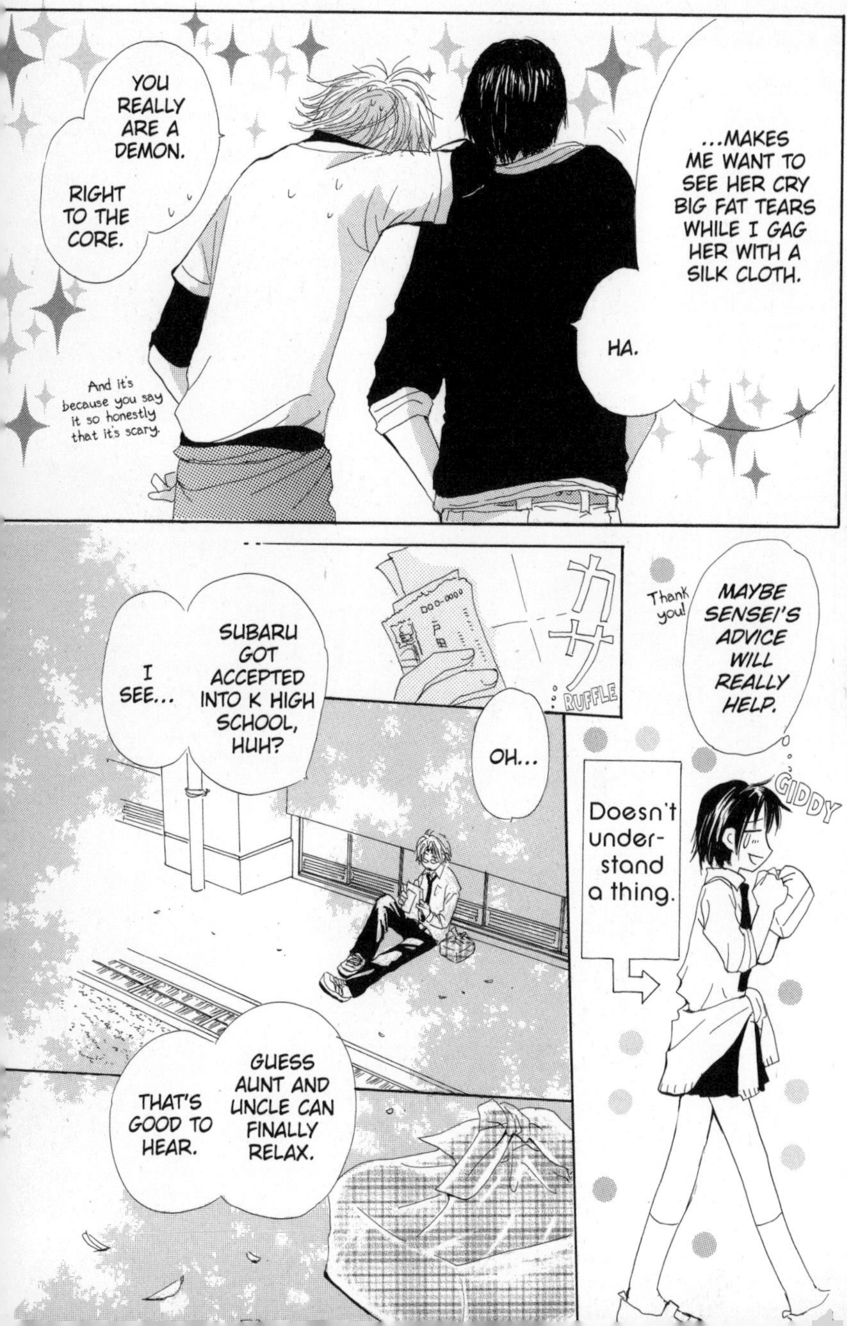
...MAKES ME WANT TO SEE HER CRY BIG FAT TEARS WHILE I GAG HER WITH A SILK CLOTH.
HA.
YOU REALLY ARE A DEMON.
RIGHT TO THE CORE.
And it's because you say it so honestly that it's scary.
MAYBE SENSEI'S ADVICE WILL REALLY HELP.
Thank you!
GIDDY
Doesn't under-stand a thing.
カサ
RUFFLE
OH...
I SEE... SUBARU GOT ACCEPTED INTO K HIGH SCHOOL, HUH?
GUESS AUNT AND UNCLE CAN FINALLY RELAX.
THAT'S GOOD TO HEAR.

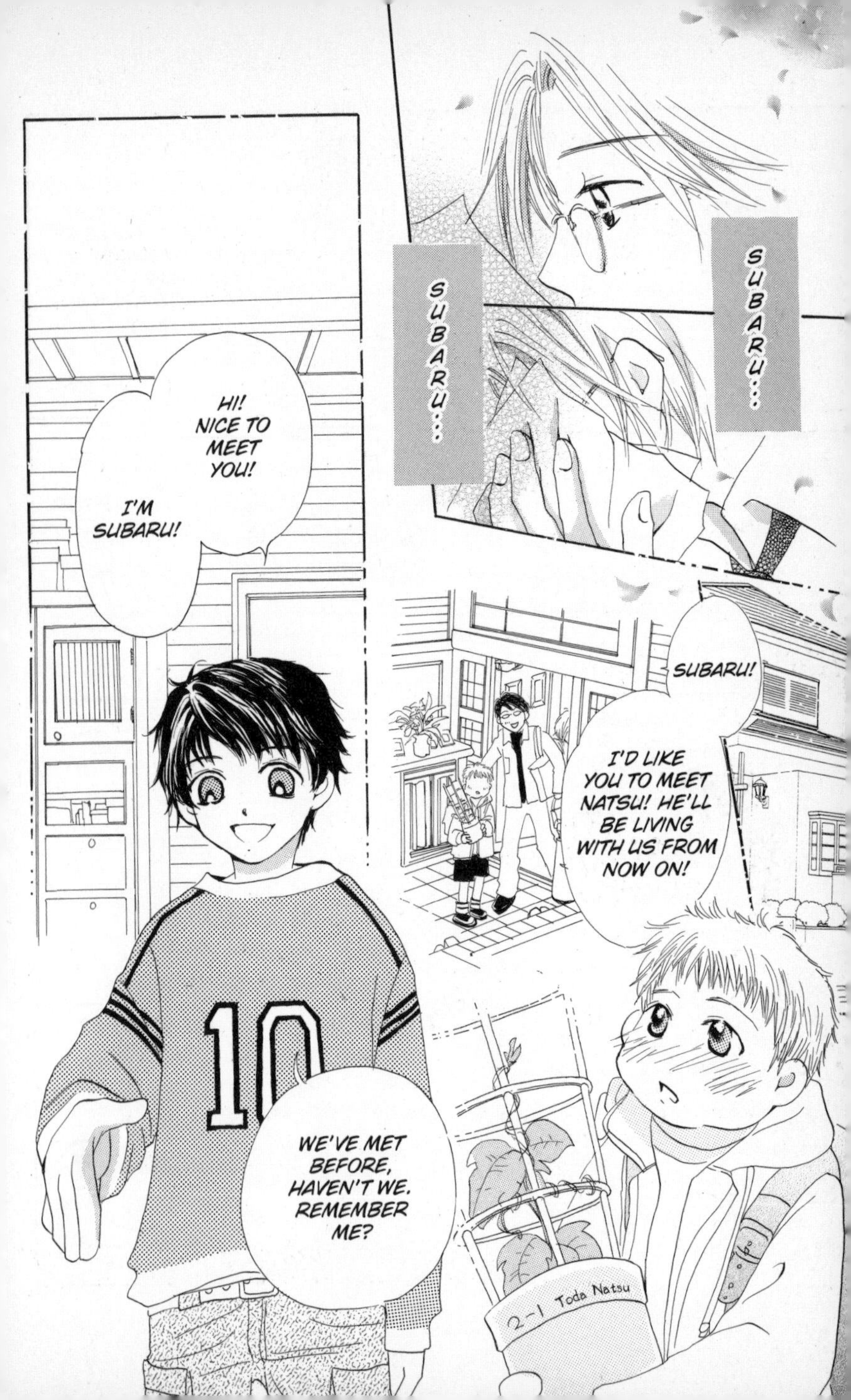
SUBARU...
SUBARU...
SUBARU!
I'D LIKE YOU TO MEET NATSU! HE'LL BE LIVING WITH US FROM NOW ON!
2-1 Toda Natsu
HI! NICE TO MEET YOU!
I'M SUBARU!
WE'VE MET BEFORE, HAVEN'T WE. REMEMBER ME?

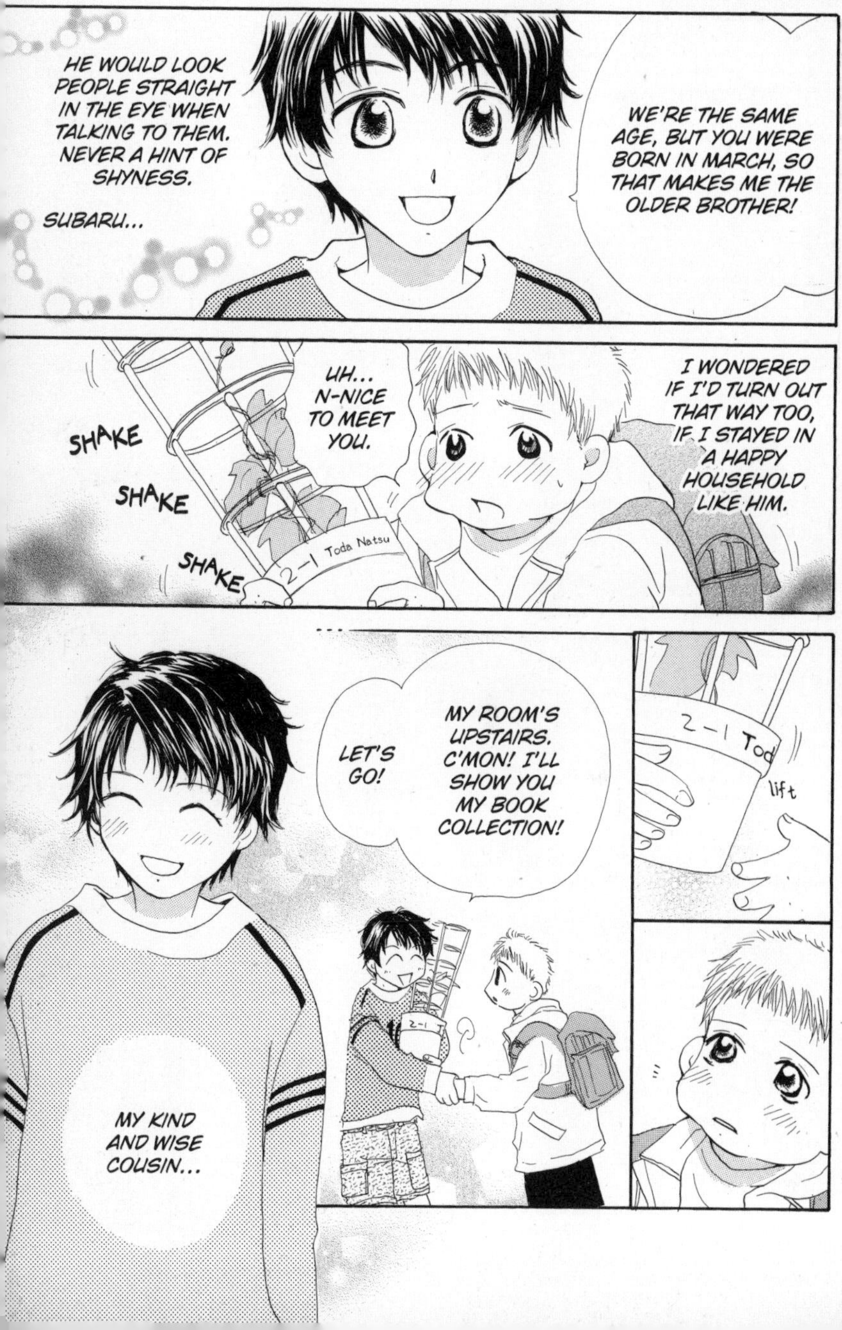
WE'RE THE SAME AGE, BUT YOU WERE BORN IN MARCH, SO THAT MAKES ME THE OLDER BROTHER!
HE WOULD LOOK PEOPLE STRAIGHT IN THE EYE WHEN TALKING TO THEM. NEVER A HINT OF SHYNESS.
SUBARU...
I WONDERED IF I'D TURN OUT THAT WAY TOO, IF I STAYED IN A HAPPY HOUSEHOLD LIKE HIM.
UH... N-NICE TO MEET YOU.
SHAKE
SHAKE
SHAKE
2-1 Toda Natsu
2-1 Tod
lift
MY ROOM'S UPSTAIRS. C'MON! I'LL SHOW YOU MY BOOK COLLECTION!
LET'S GO!
MY KIND AND WISE COUSIN...

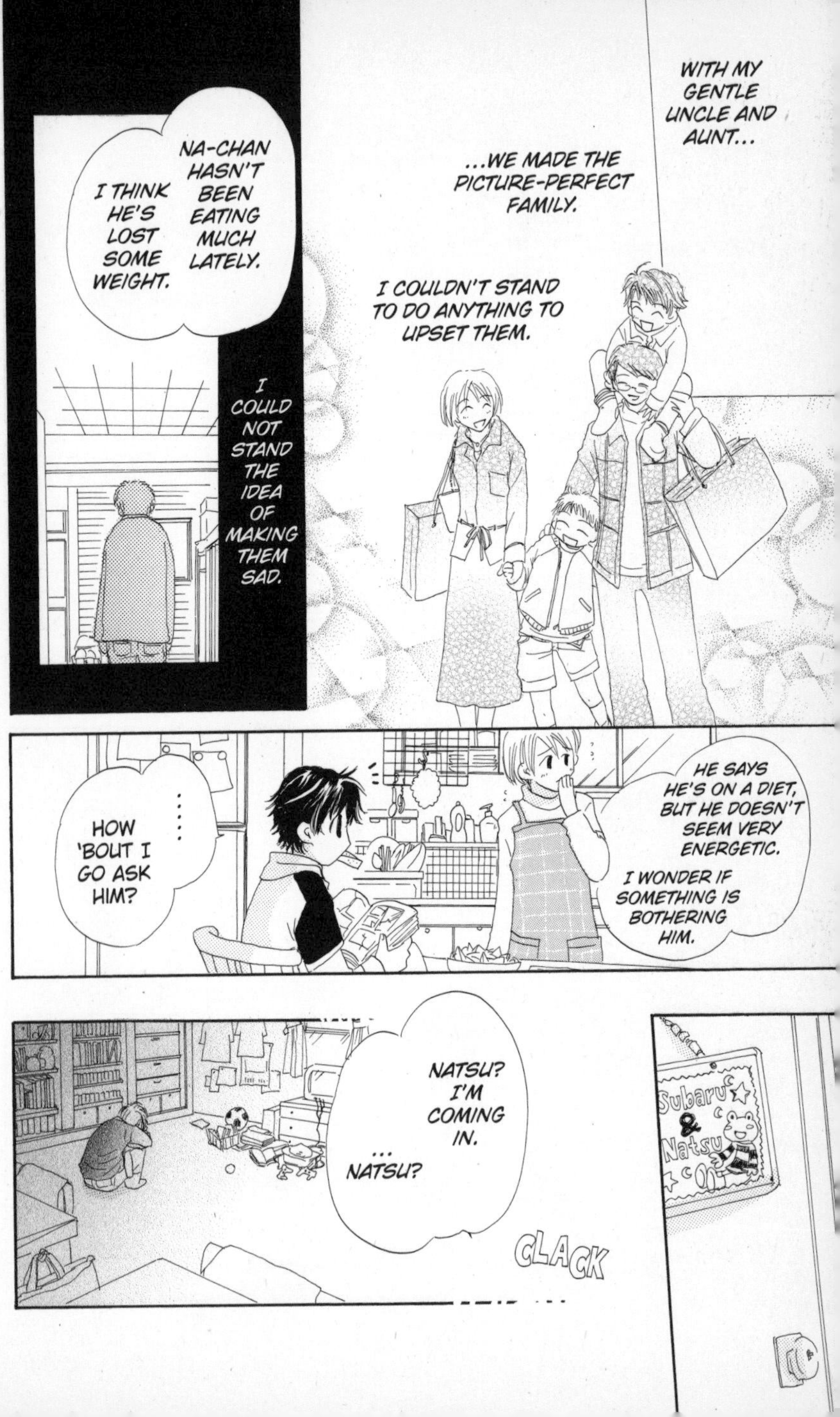
WITH MY GENTLE UNCLE AND AUNT...
...WE MADE THE PICTURE-PERFECT FAMILY.
I COULDN'T STAND TO DO ANYTHING TO UPSET THEM.
NA-CHAN HASN'T BEEN EATING MUCH LATELY. I THINK HE'S LOST SOME WEIGHT.
I COULD NOT STAND THE IDEA OF MAKING THEM SAD.
HE SAYS HE'S ON A DIET, BUT HE DOESN'T SEEM VERY ENERGETIC.
I WONDER IF SOMETHING IS BOTHERING HIM.
.....
HOW 'BOUT I GO ASK HIM?
Subaru & Natsu
NATSU? I'M COMING IN.
... NATSU?
CLACK

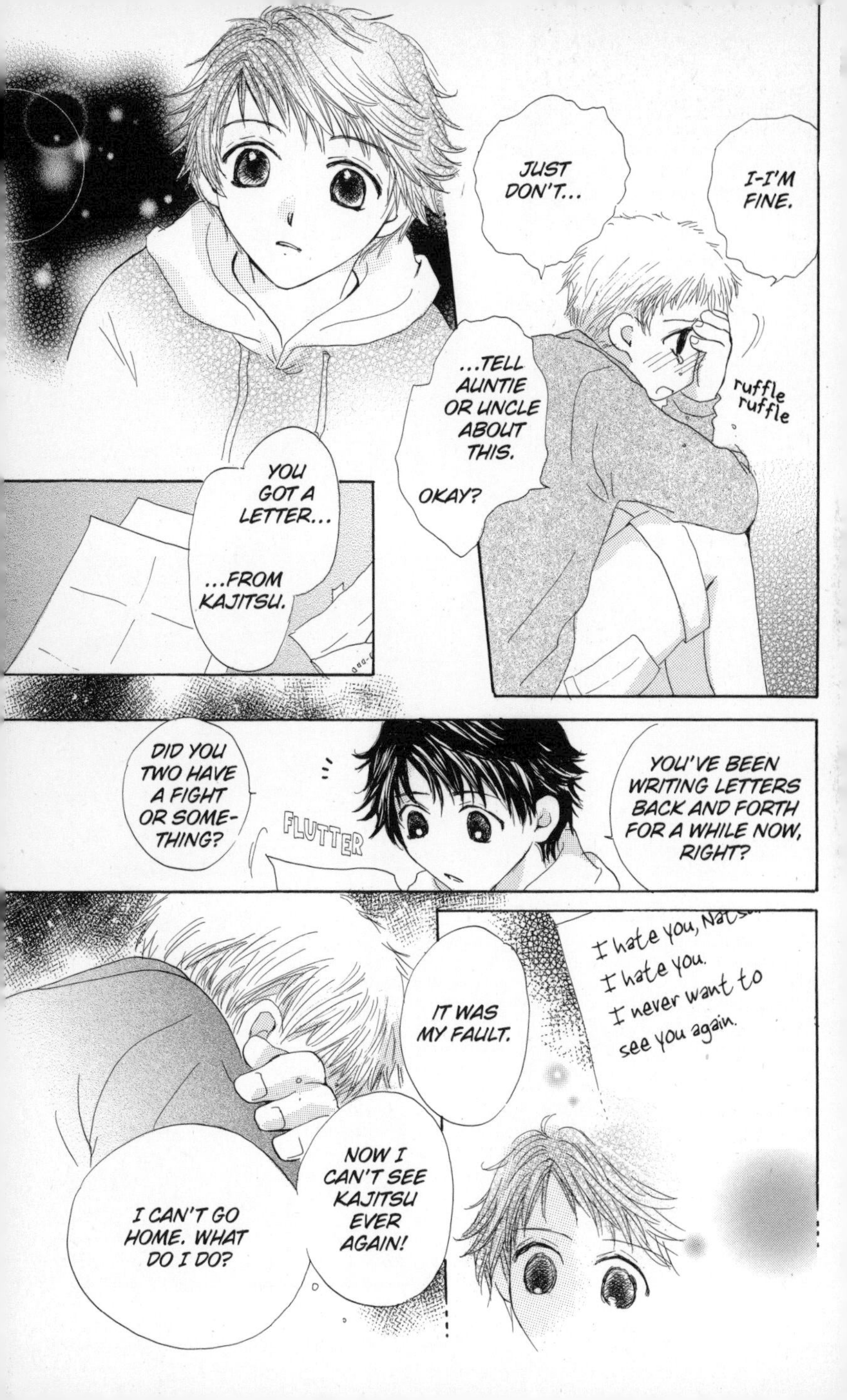
I-I'M FINE.
JUST DON'T...
...TELL AUNTIE OR UNCLE ABOUT THIS.
OKAY?
ruffle ruffle
YOU GOT A LETTER...
...FROM KAJITSU.
YOU'VE BEEN WRITING LETTERS BACK AND FORTH FOR A WHILE NOW, RIGHT?
FLUTTER
DID YOU TWO HAVE A FIGHT OR SOME-THING?
I hate you, Nats
I hate you.
I never want to see you again.
IT WAS MY FAULT.
NOW I CAN'T SEE KAJITSU EVER AGAIN!
I CAN'T GO HOME. WHAT DO I DO?

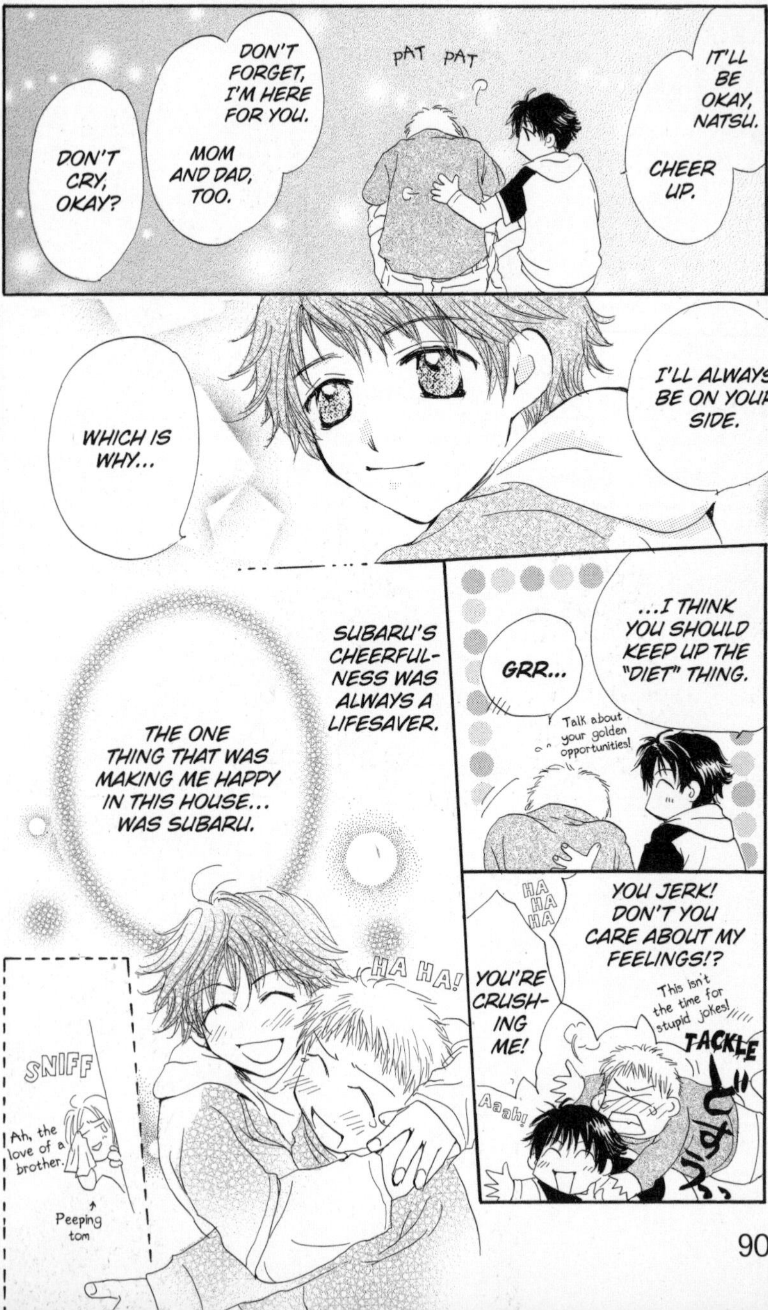
IT'LL BE OKAY, NATSU.
CHEER UP.
PAT PAT
DON'T FORGET, I'M HERE FOR YOU.
MOM AND DAD, TOO.
DON'T CRY, OKAY?
I'LL ALWAYS BE ON YOUR SIDE.
WHICH IS WHY...
...I THINK YOU SHOULD KEEP UP THE "DIET" THING.
GRR...
Talk about your golden opportunities!
YOU JERK! DON'T YOU CARE ABOUT MY FEELINGS!?
HA HA HA
YOU'RE CRUSHING ME!
This isn't the time for stupid jokes!
TACKLE
Aaah!
SUBARU'S CHEERFUL-NESS WAS ALWAYS A LIFESAVER.
THE ONE THING THAT WAS MAKING ME HAPPY IN THIS HOUSE... WAS SUBARU.
HA HA!
SNIFF
Ah, the love of a brother.
Peeping tom

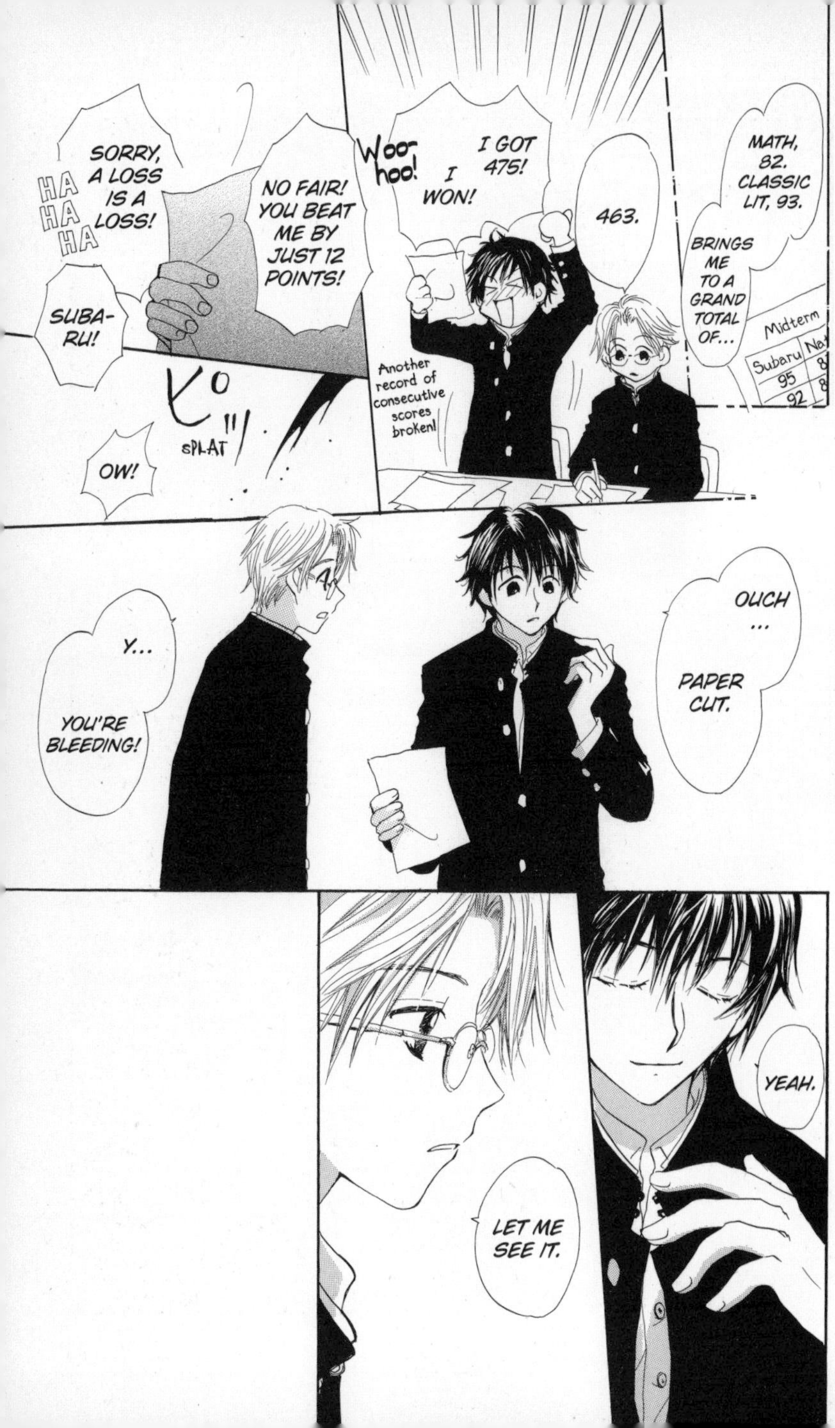
MATH, 82. CLASSIC LIT, 93.
BRINGS ME TO A GRAND TOTAL OF...
Midterm
Subaru
95
92
463.
I GOT 475!
Woo-hoo!
I WON!
Another record of consecutive scores broken!
NO FAIR! YOU BEAT ME BY JUST 12 POINTS!
SORRY, A LOSS IS A LOSS!
HA HA HA
SUBA-RU!
SPLAT
OW!
OUCH ... PAPER CUT.
Y...
YOU'RE BLEEDING!
YEAH.
LET ME SEE IT.

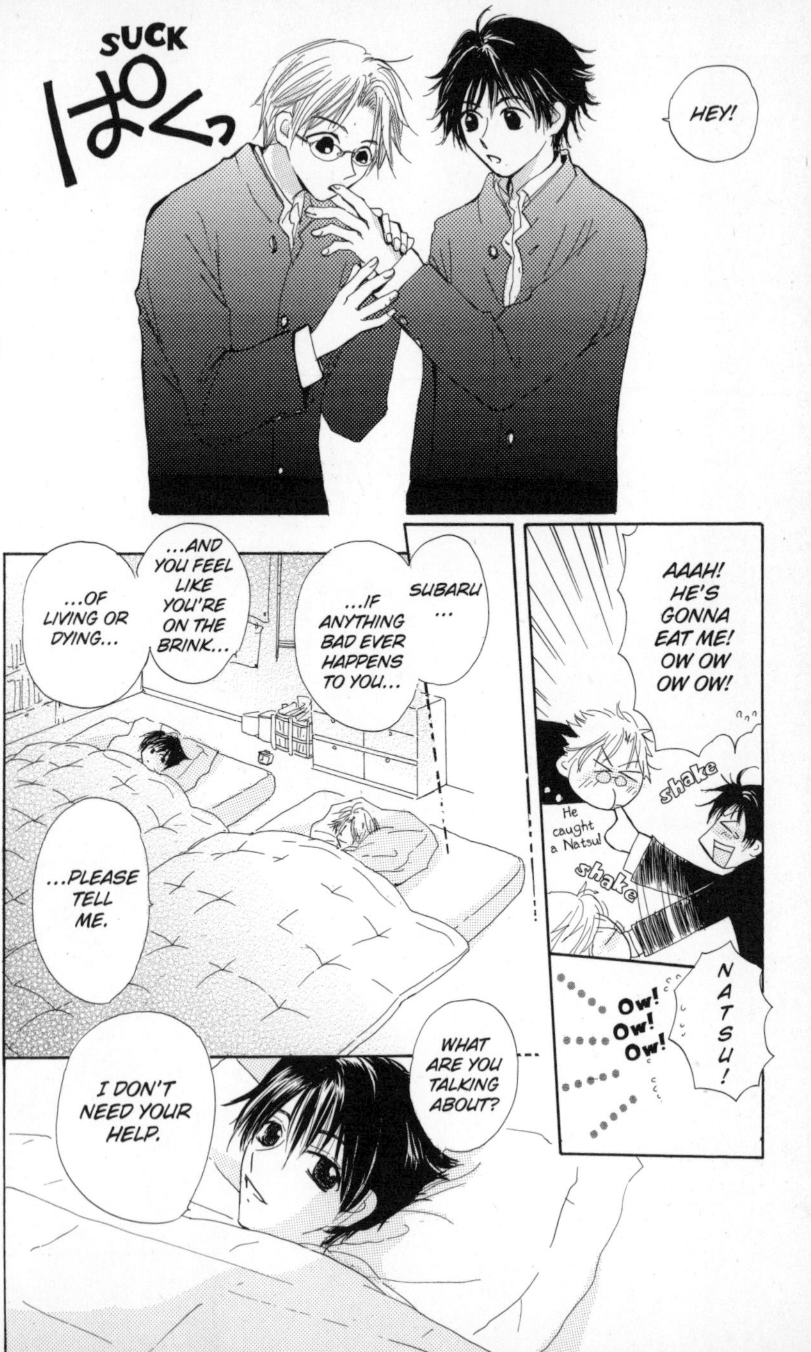
HEY!
SUCK
ぱくっ
AAAH! HE'S GONNA EAT ME! OW OW OW OW!
shake
He caught a Natsu!
shake
NATSU!
Ow! Ow! Ow!
SUBARU...
...IF ANYTHING BAD EVER HAPPENS TO YOU...
...AND YOU FEEL LIKE YOU'RE ON THE BRINK...
...OF LIVING OR DYING...
...PLEASE TELL ME.
WHAT ARE YOU TALKING ABOUT?
I DON'T NEED YOUR HELP.

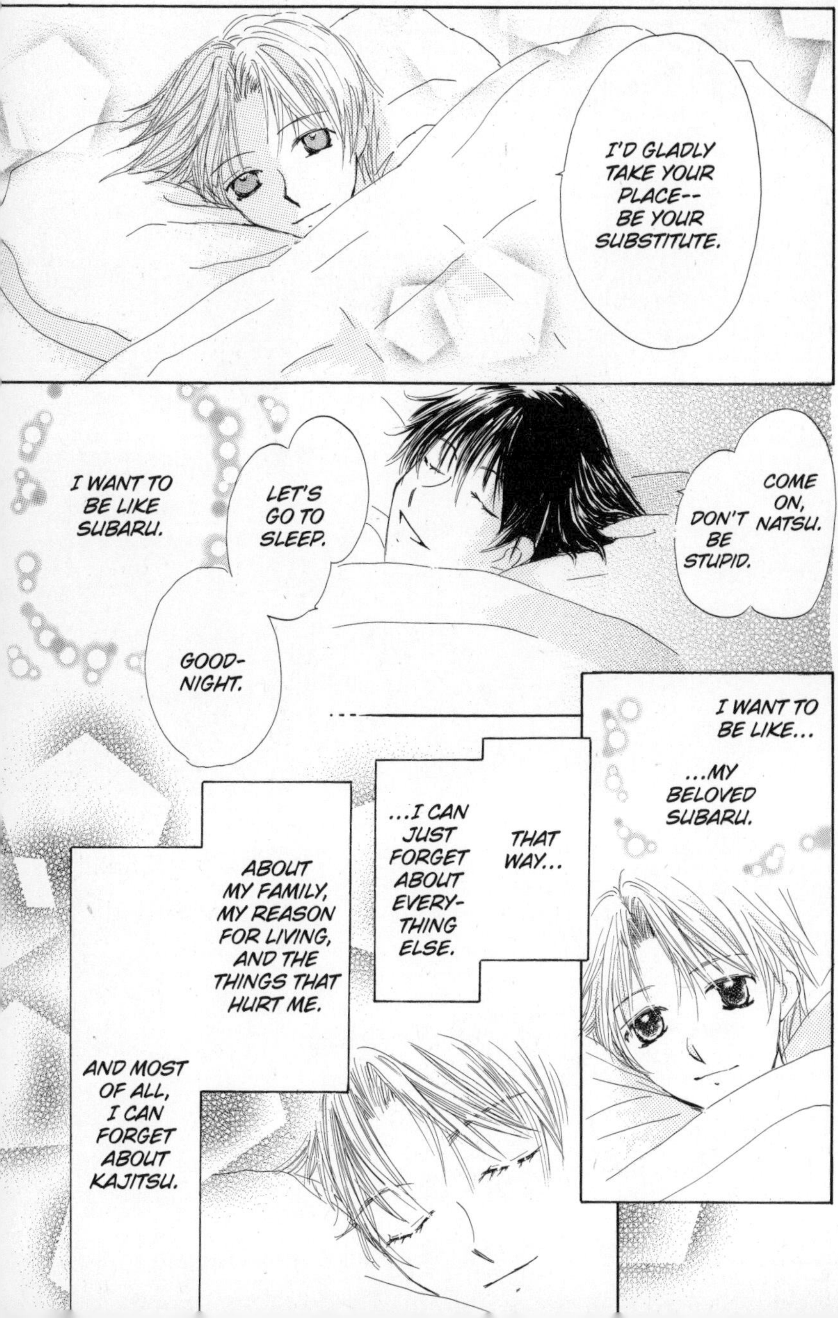
I'D GLADLY TAKE YOUR PLACE-- BE YOUR SUBSTITUTE.
COME ON, NATSU.
DON'T BE STUPID.
LET'S GO TO SLEEP.
GOOD-NIGHT.
I WANT TO BE LIKE SUBARU.
I WANT TO BE LIKE...
...MY BELOVED SUBARU.
THAT WAY...
...I CAN JUST FORGET ABOUT EVERY-THING ELSE.
ABOUT MY FAMILY, MY REASON FOR LIVING, AND THE THINGS THAT HURT ME.
AND MOST OF ALL, I CAN FORGET ABOUT KAJITSU.

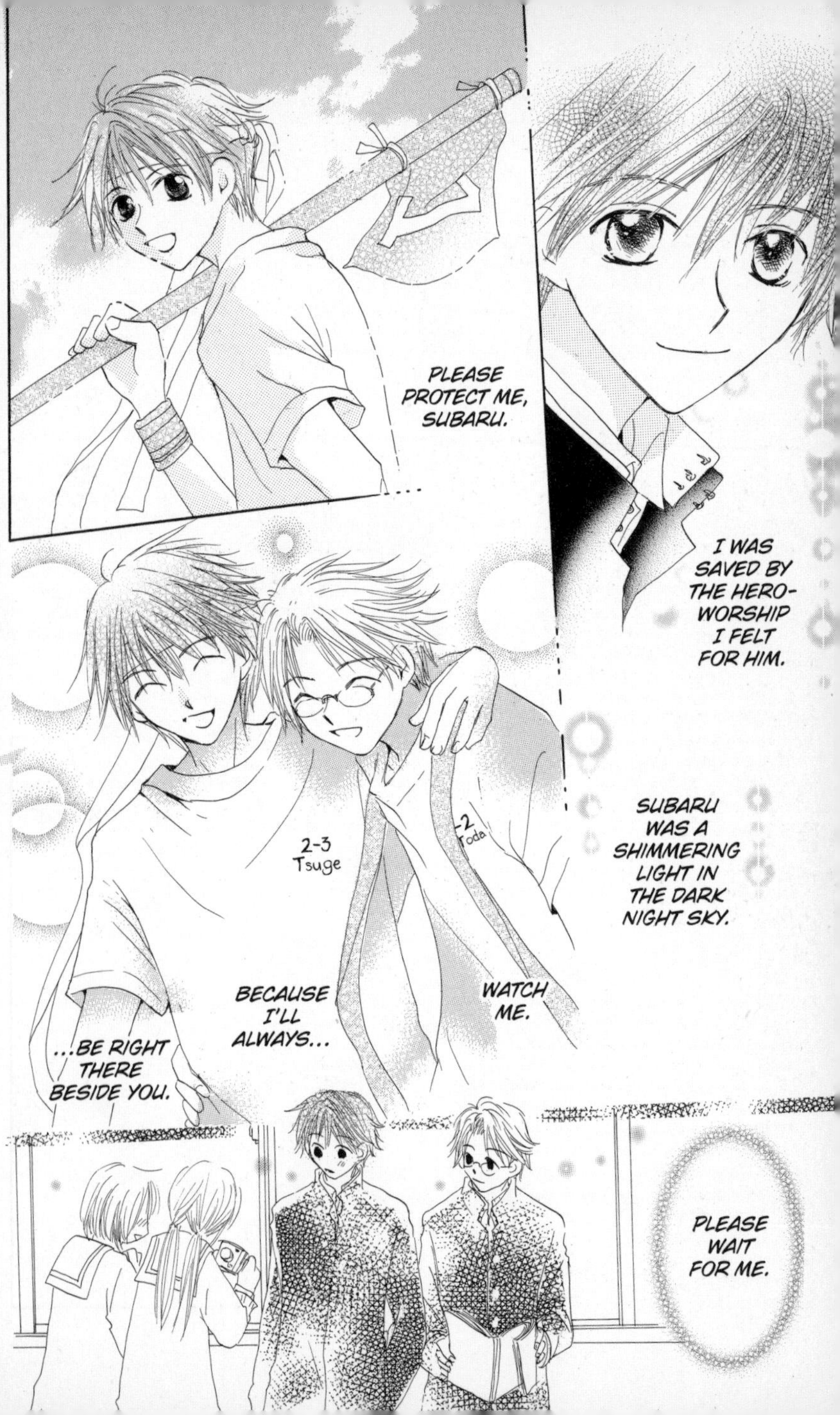
I WAS SAVED BY THE HERO-WORSHIP I FELT FOR HIM.
SUBARU WAS A SHIMMERING LIGHT IN THE DARK NIGHT SKY.
PLEASE PROTECT ME, SUBARU.
WATCH ME.
-2 Toda
2-3 Tsuge
BECAUSE I'LL ALWAYS...
...BE RIGHT THERE BESIDE YOU.
PLEASE WAIT FOR ME.

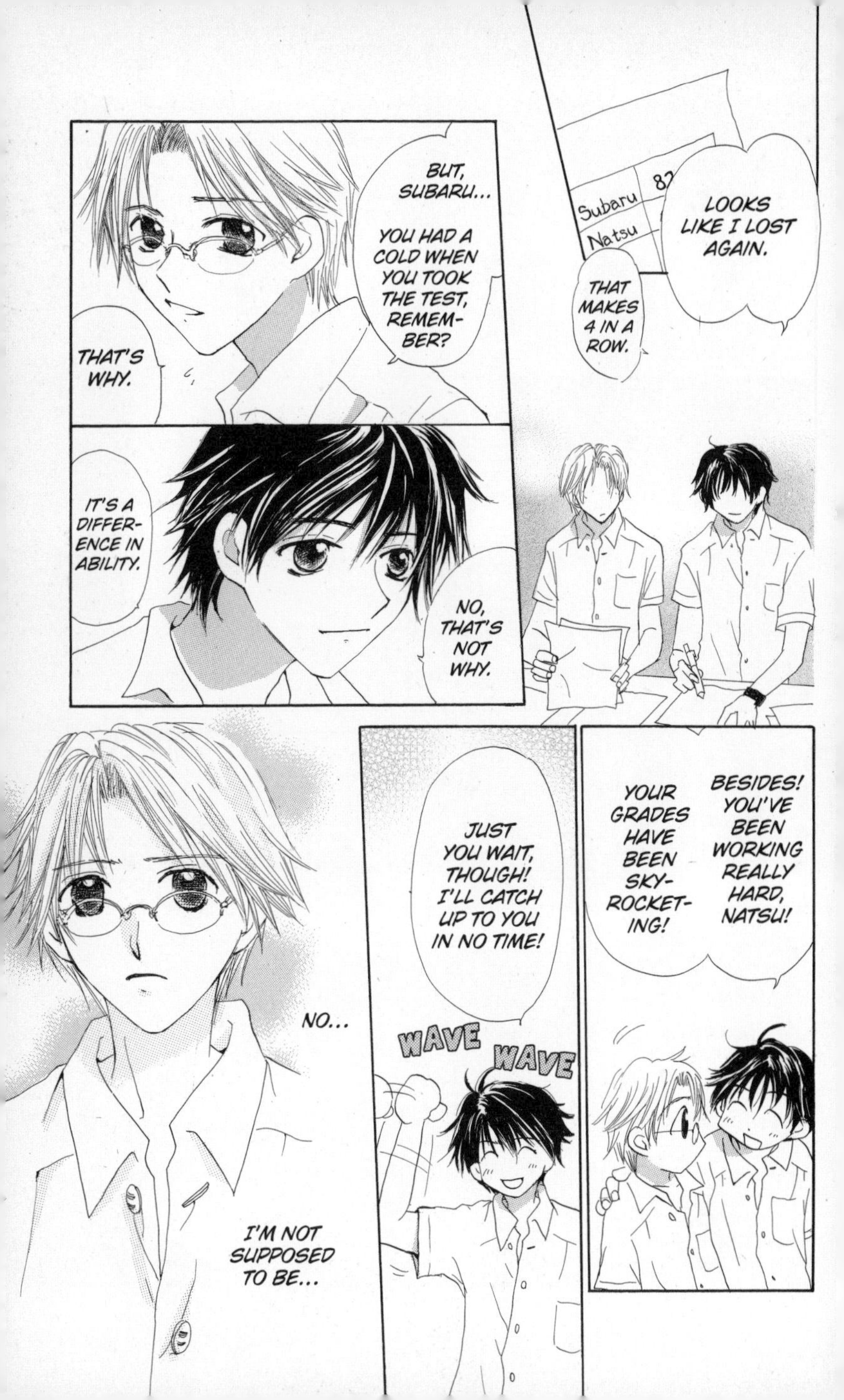
Subaru
Natsu
LOOKS LIKE I LOST AGAIN.
THAT MAKES 4 IN A ROW.
BUT, SUBARU...
YOU HAD A COLD WHEN YOU TOOK THE TEST, REMEMBER?
THAT'S WHY.
NO, THAT'S NOT WHY.
IT'S A DIFFERENCE IN ABILITY.
BESIDES! YOU'VE BEEN WORKING REALLY HARD, NATSU!
YOUR GRADES HAVE BEEN SKY-ROCKETING!
JUST YOU WAIT, THOUGH! I'LL CATCH UP TO YOU IN NO TIME!
WAVE
WAVE
NO...
I'M NOT SUPPOSED TO BE...

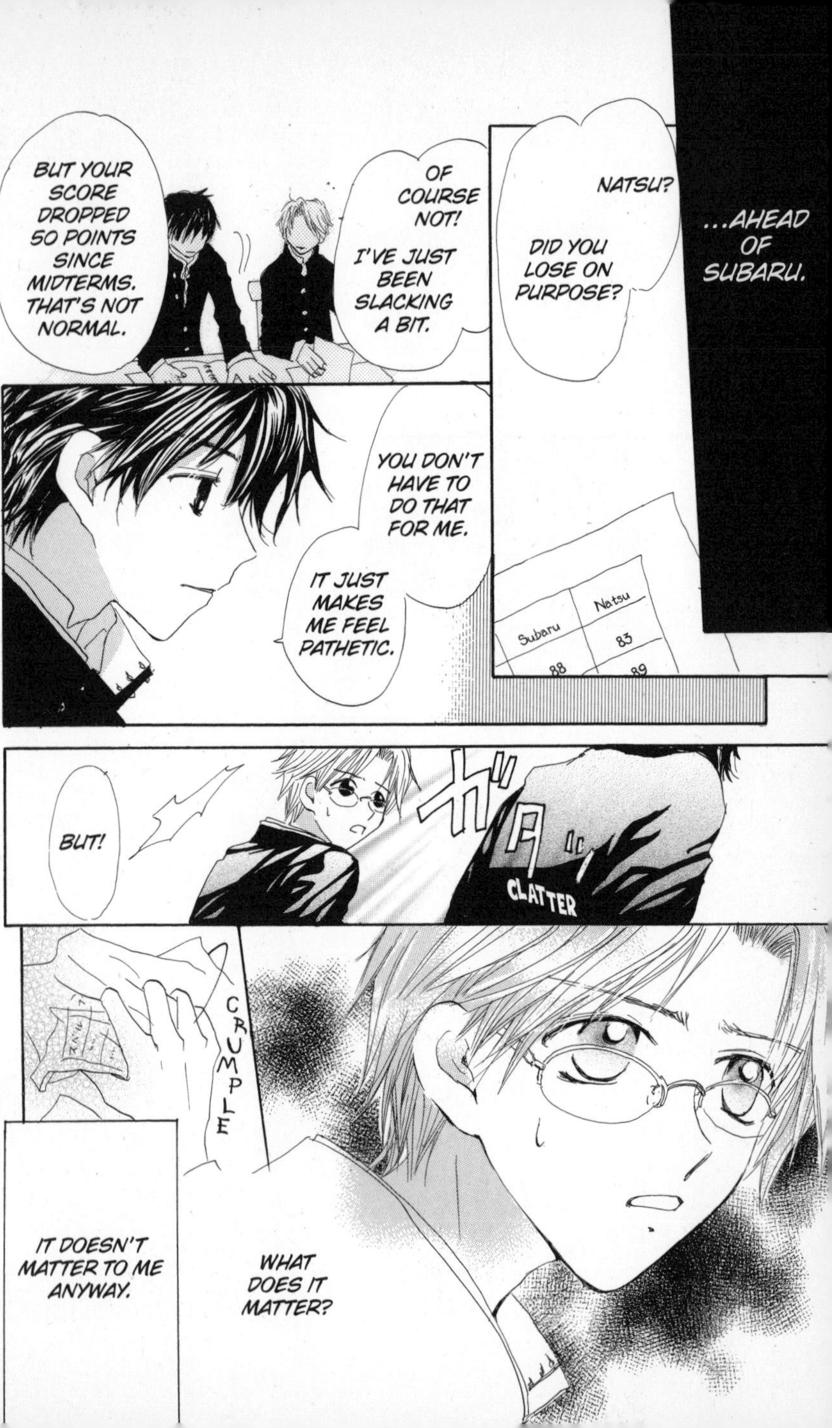
...AHEAD OF SUBARU.
NATSU?
DID YOU LOSE ON PURPOSE?
Natsu
Subaru
83
88
89
OF COURSE NOT!
I'VE JUST BEEN SLACKING A BIT.
BUT YOUR SCORE DROPPED 50 POINTS SINCE MIDTERMS. THAT'S NOT NORMAL.
YOU DON'T HAVE TO DO THAT FOR ME.
IT JUST MAKES ME FEEL PATHETIC.
ガタ
CLATTER
BUT!
CRUMPLE
WHAT DOES IT MATTER?
IT DOESN'T MATTER TO ME ANYWAY.

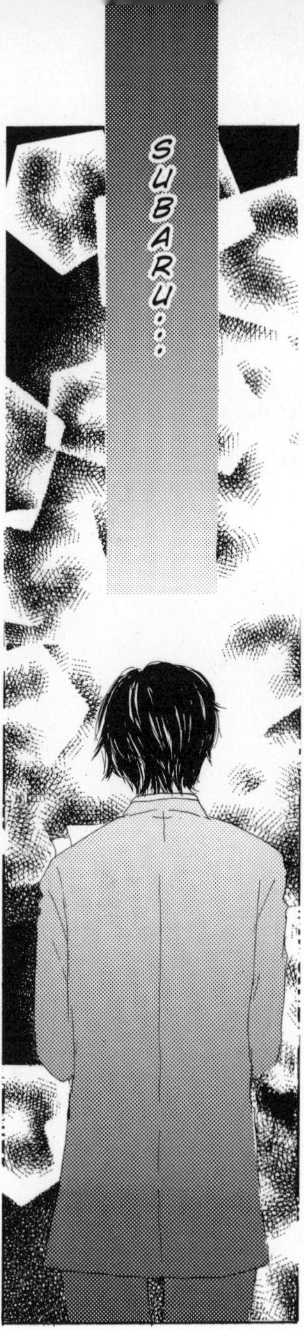
SUBARU...

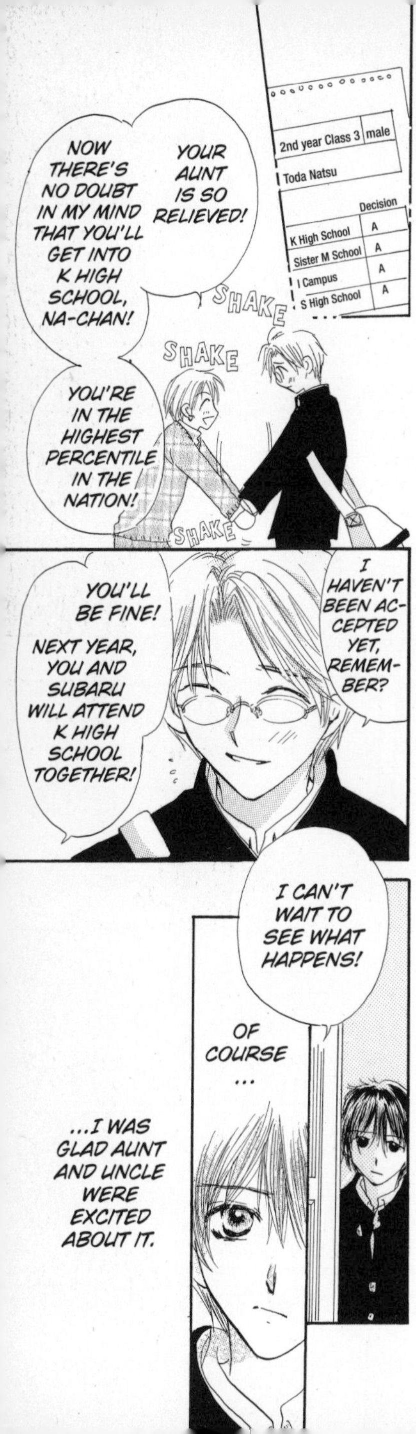
2nd year Class 3 male
Toda Natsu
Decision
K High School A
Sister M School A
I Campus A
S High School A
YOUR AUNT IS SO RELIEVED!
NOW THERE'S NO DOUBT IN MY MIND THAT YOU'LL GET INTO K HIGH SCHOOL, NA-CHAN!
SHAKE
SHAKE
YOU'RE IN THE HIGHEST PERCENTILE IN THE NATION!
SHAKE
I HAVEN'T BEEN AC-CEPTED YET, REMEM-BER?
YOU'LL BE FINE!
NEXT YEAR, YOU AND SUBARU WILL ATTEND K HIGH SCHOOL TOGETHER!
I CAN'T WAIT TO SEE WHAT HAPPENS!
OF COURSE...
...I WAS GLAD AUNT AND UNCLE WERE EXCITED ABOUT IT.

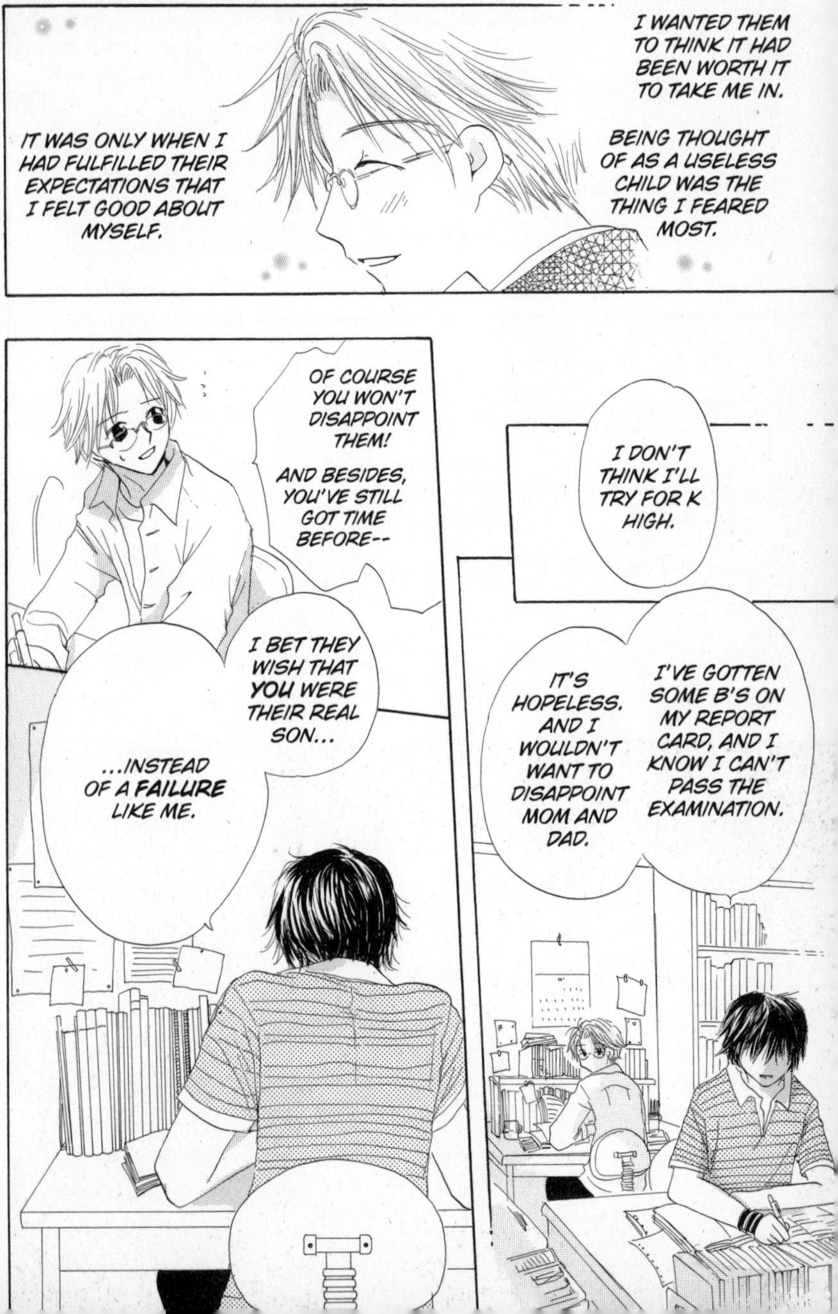
I WANTED THEM TO THINK IT HAD BEEN WORTH IT TO TAKE ME IN.
BEING THOUGHT OF AS A USELESS CHILD WAS THE THING I FEARED MOST.
IT WAS ONLY WHEN I HAD FULFILLED THEIR EXPECTATIONS THAT I FELT GOOD ABOUT MYSELF.
I DON'T THINK I'LL TRY FOR K HIGH.
I'VE GOTTEN SOME B'S ON MY REPORT CARD, AND I KNOW I CAN'T PASS THE EXAMINATION.
IT'S HOPELESS. AND I WOULDN'T WANT TO DISAPPOINT MOM AND DAD.
OF COURSE YOU WON'T DISAPPOINT THEM!
AND BESIDES, YOU'VE STILL GOT TIME BEFORE--
I BET THEY WISH THAT YOU WERE THEIR REAL SON...
...INSTEAD OF A FAILURE LIKE ME.

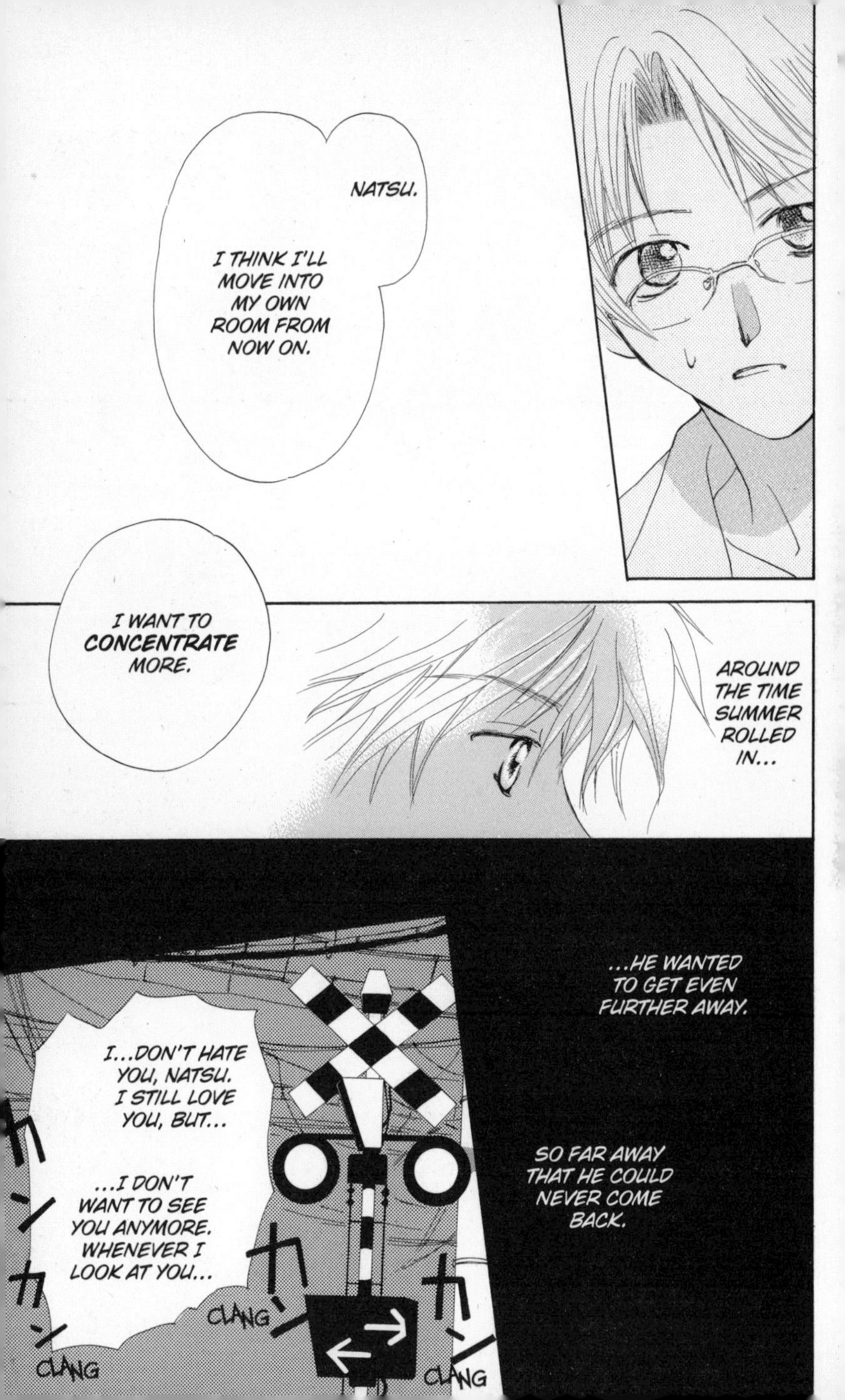
NATSU.
I THINK I'LL MOVE INTO MY OWN ROOM FROM NOW ON.
I WANT TO **CONCENTRATE** MORE.
AROUND THE TIME SUMMER ROLLED IN...
...HE WANTED TO GET EVEN FURTHER AWAY.
SO FAR AWAY THAT HE COULD NEVER COME BACK.
I...DON'T HATE YOU, NATSU. I STILL LOVE YOU, BUT...
...I DON'T WANT TO SEE YOU ANYMORE. WHENEVER I LOOK AT YOU...
CLANG
CLANG
CLANG

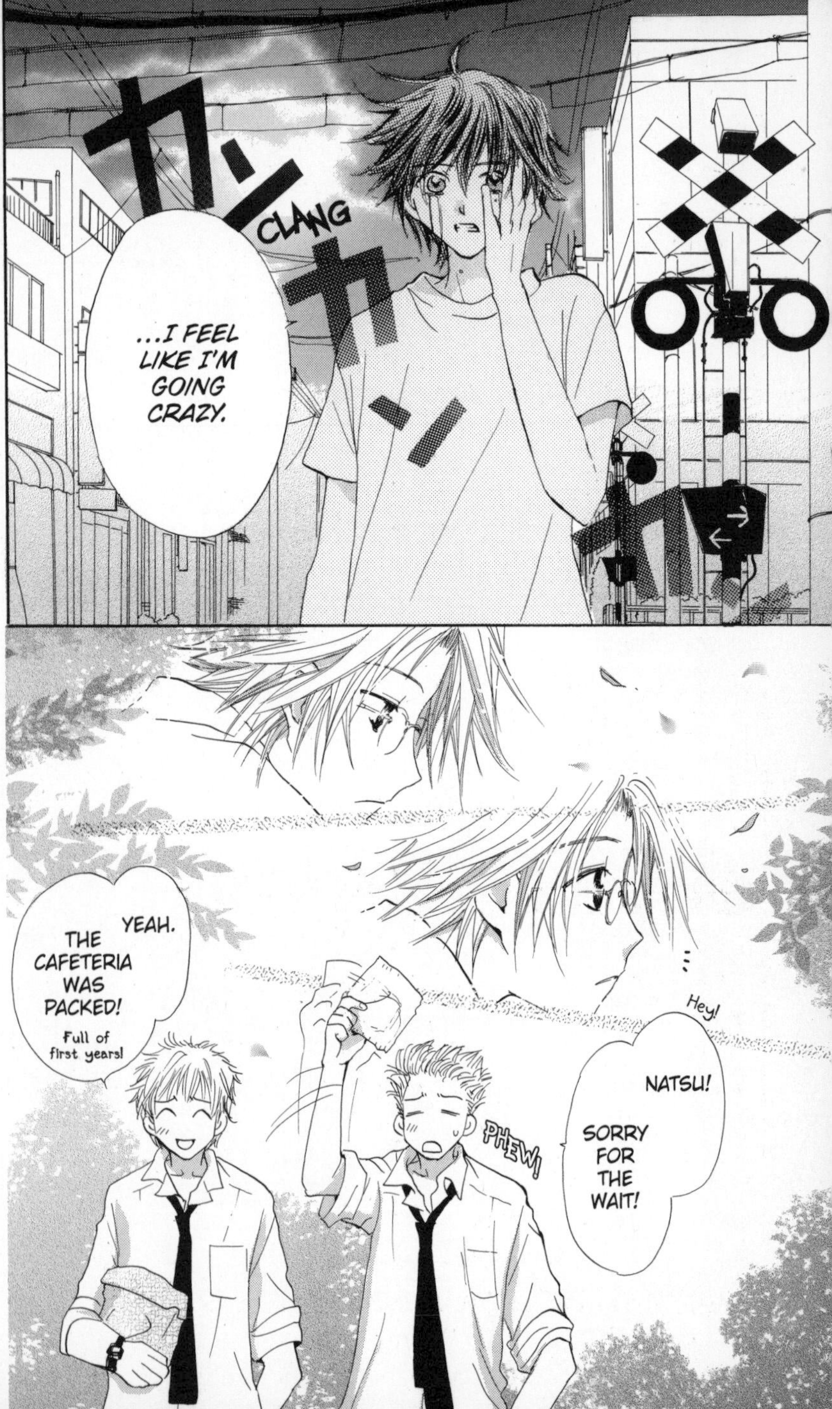
CLANG
...I FEEL LIKE I'M GOING CRAZY.
Hey!
NATSU!
SORRY FOR THE WAIT!
PHEW!
YEAH. THE CAFETERIA WAS PACKED!
Full of first years!

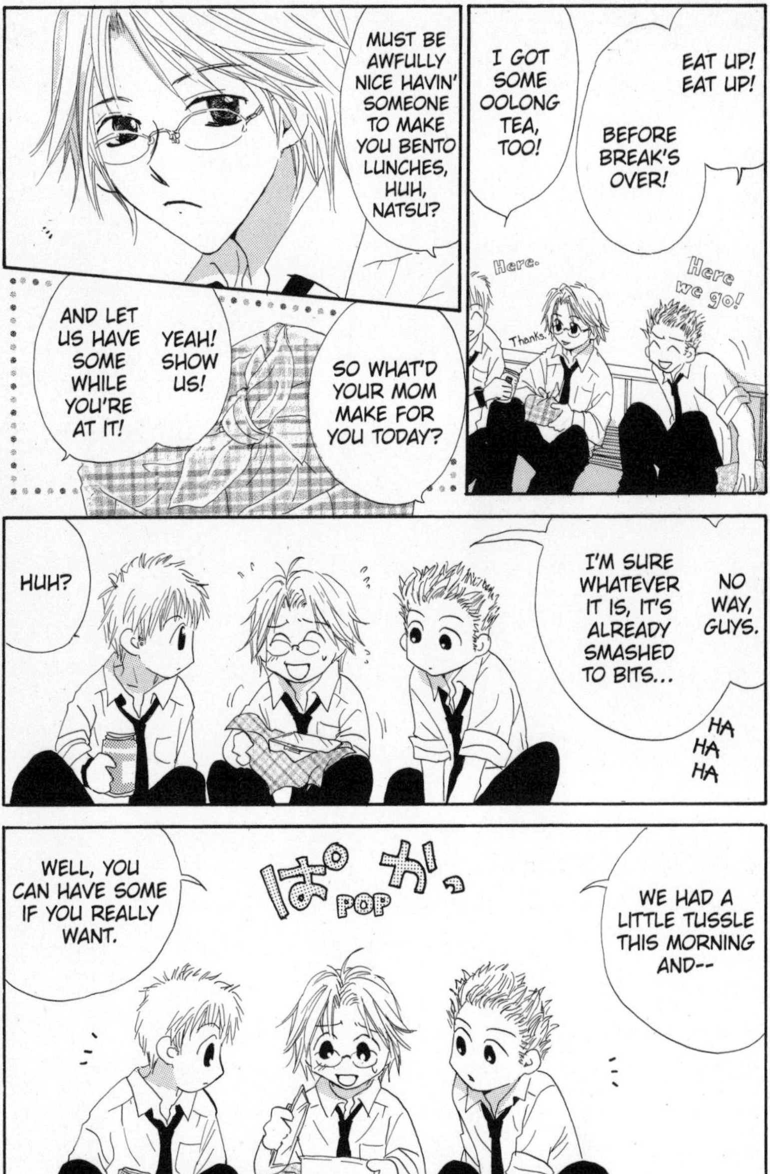
EAT UP! EAT UP!
BEFORE BREAK'S OVER!
I GOT SOME OOLONG TEA, TOO!
Here we go!
Here.
Thanks.
MUST BE AWFULLY NICE HAVIN' SOMEONE TO MAKE YOU BENTO LUNCHES, HUH, NATSU?
SO WHAT'D YOUR MOM MAKE FOR YOU TODAY?
YEAH! SHOW US!
AND LET US HAVE SOME WHILE YOU'RE AT IT!
NO WAY, GUYS.
I'M SURE WHATEVER IT IS, IT'S ALREADY SMASHED TO BITS...
HA HA HA
HUH?
WE HAD A LITTLE TUSSLE THIS MORNING AND--
ぱかっ
POP
WELL, YOU CAN HAVE SOME IF YOU REALLY WANT.

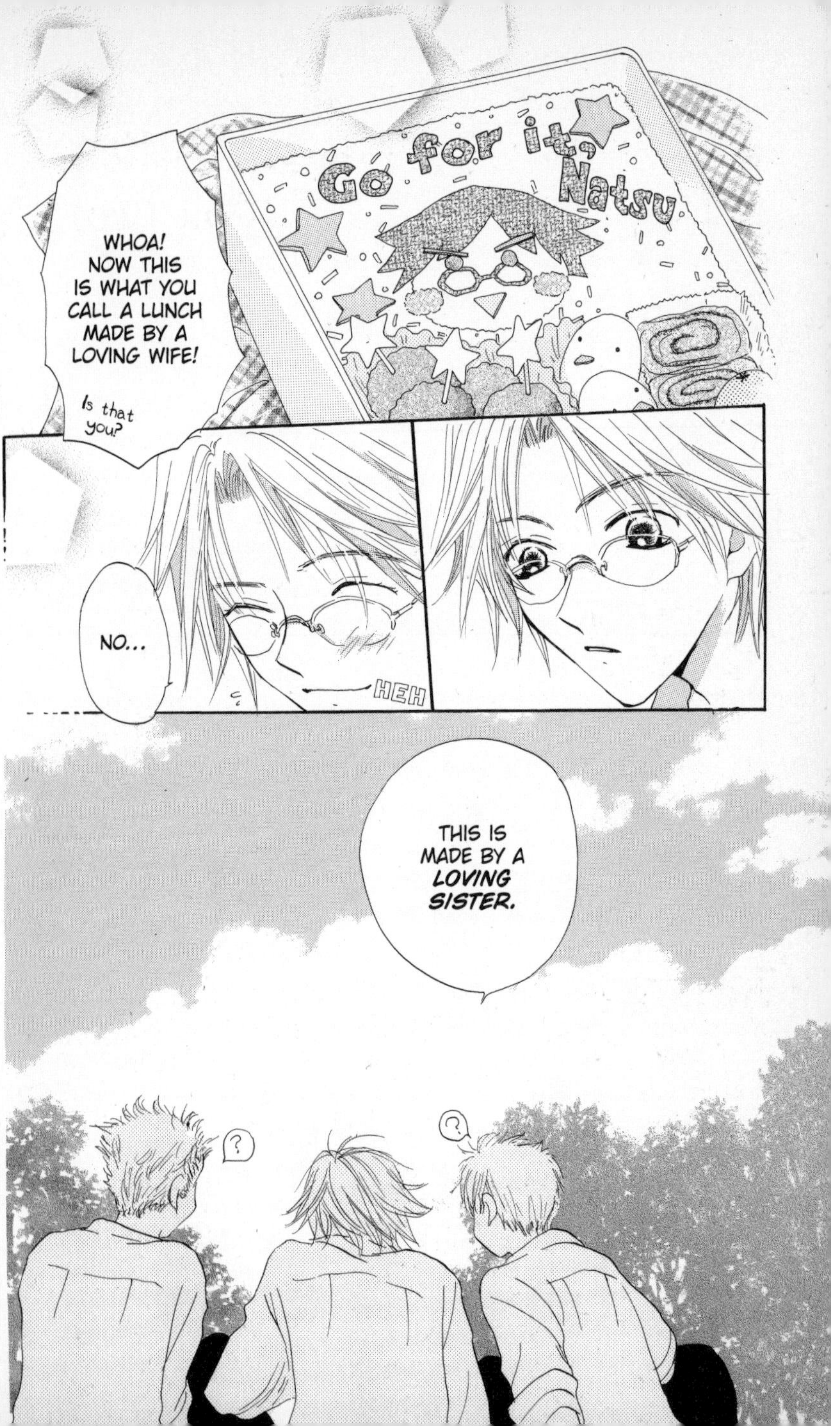
Go for it, Natsu
WHOA! NOW THIS IS WHAT YOU CALL A LUNCH MADE BY A LOVING WIFE!
Is that you?
NO...
HEH
THIS IS MADE BY A *LOVING SISTER.*
?
?

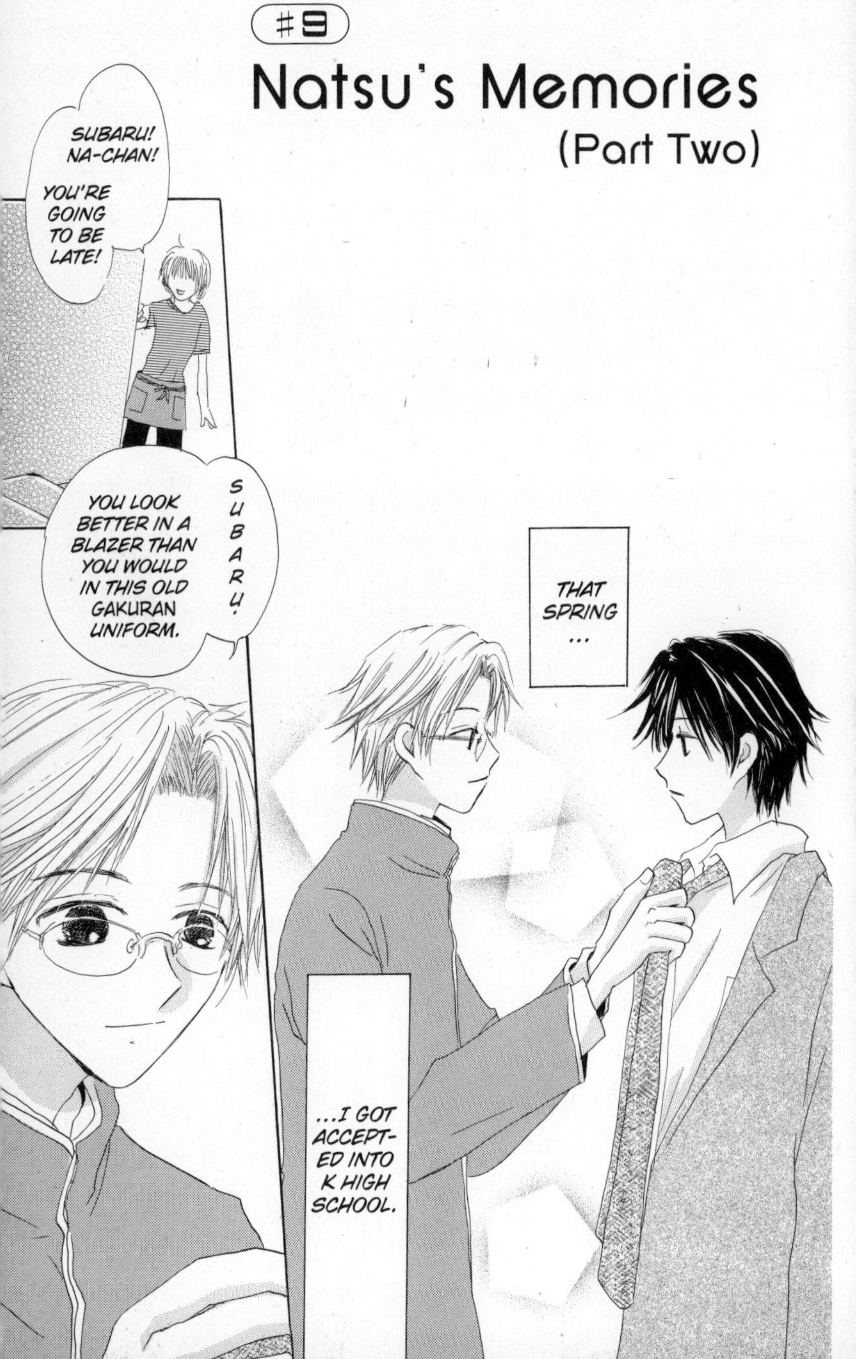
#9
Natsu's Memories (Part Two)
THAT SPRING ...
...I GOT ACCEPTED INTO K HIGH SCHOOL.
SUBARU! NA-CHAN!
YOU'RE GOING TO BE LATE!
SUBARU!
YOU LOOK BETTER IN A BLAZER THAN YOU WOULD IN THIS OLD GAKURAN UNIFORM.

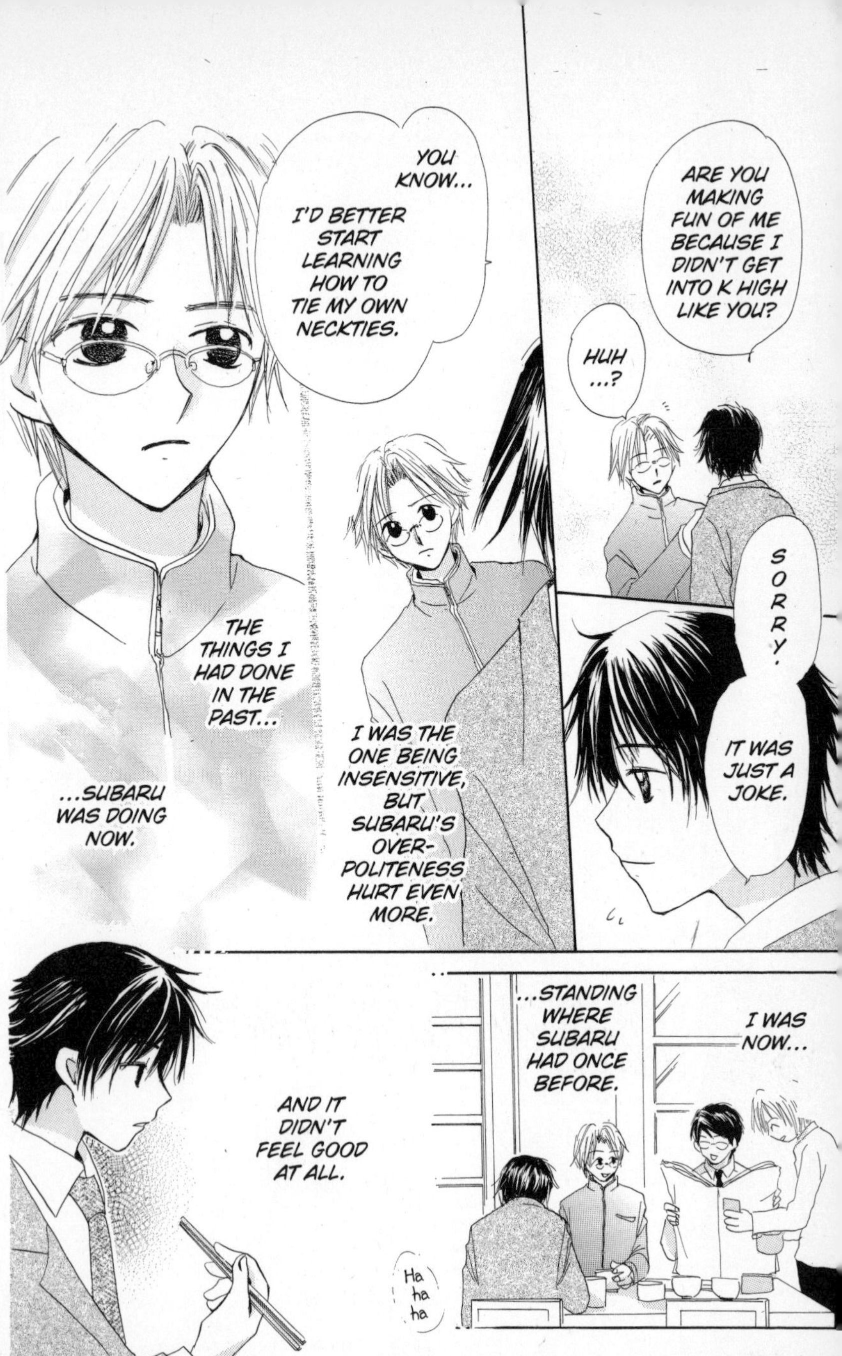
ARE YOU MAKING FUN OF ME BECAUSE I DIDN'T GET INTO K HIGH LIKE YOU?
HUH ...?
SORRY.
IT WAS JUST A JOKE.
YOU KNOW...
I'D BETTER START LEARNING HOW TO TIE MY OWN NECKTIES.
I WAS THE ONE BEING INSENSITIVE, BUT SUBARU'S OVER-POLITENESS HURT EVEN MORE.
THE THINGS I HAD DONE IN THE PAST...
...SUBARU WAS DOING NOW.
I WAS NOW...
...STANDING WHERE SUBARU HAD ONCE BEFORE.
Ha ha ha
AND IT DIDN'T FEEL GOOD AT ALL.

crossroad Chapter 8: Natsu's Memories (Part 2)

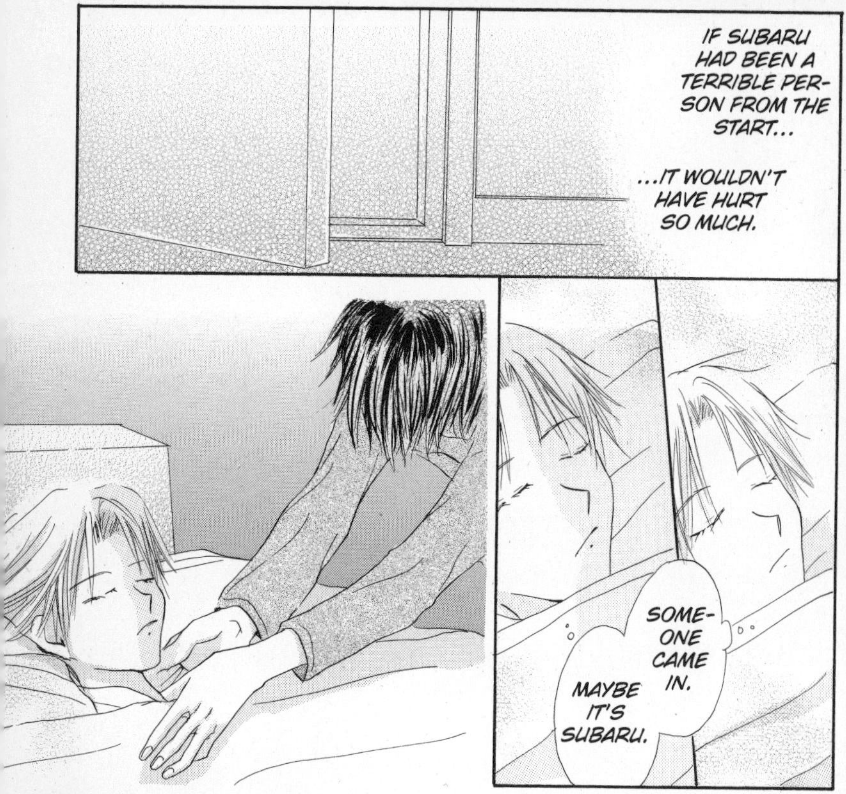
IF SUBARU HAD BEEN A TERRIBLE PERSON FROM THE START...
...IT WOULDN'T HAVE HURT SO MUCH.
SOME-ONE CAME IN.
MAYBE IT'S SUBARU.

Ninjas...Again

Now I wouldn't exactly call myself a Gamer, but I do own a PlayStation 2. For no reason at all, I bought the family set and had loads of fun with games like "Xevious" and "Itadaki Street" (a game that combines characters from DragonQuest and Final Fantasy). I really wanted to play "Ninja Hattori-Kun" so I borrowed it from Kise-san. I think the original version is really amazing. For one, the player can die SO EASILY! Not only do you have no "continues," but you can't even SAVE the game, so once it's over, it's over. I don't think the games in the family set make "clearing the stage" the goal. And I don't think machines are trying to kill humans "like bugs." But playing "Ninja Hattori-Kun" made me really, really hate machines for the first time in my life. They are the enemy. I will not forgive them. Chuckle chuckle... (4)

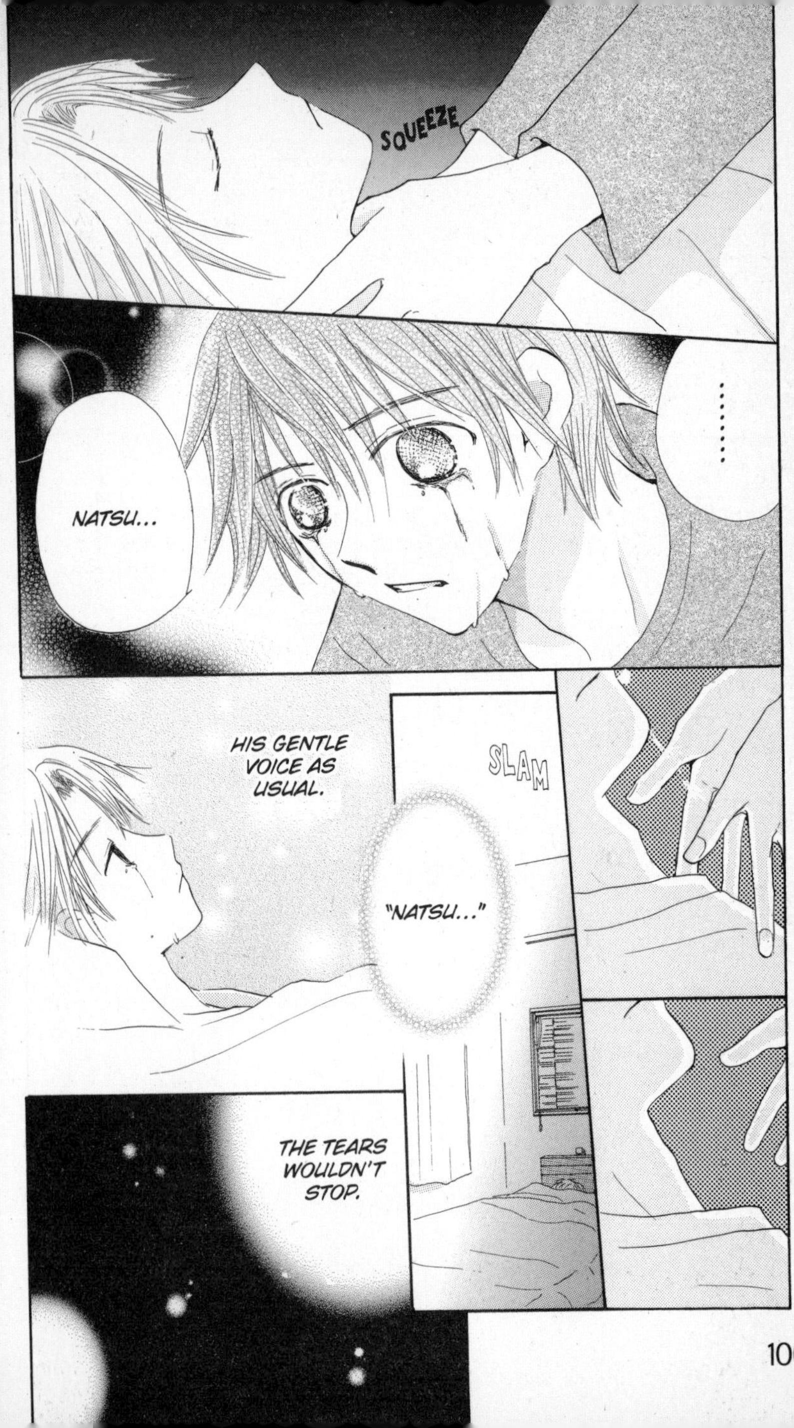
SQUEEZE
......
NATSU...
SLAM
"NATSU..."
HIS GENTLE VOICE AS USUAL.
THE TEARS WOULDN'T STOP.

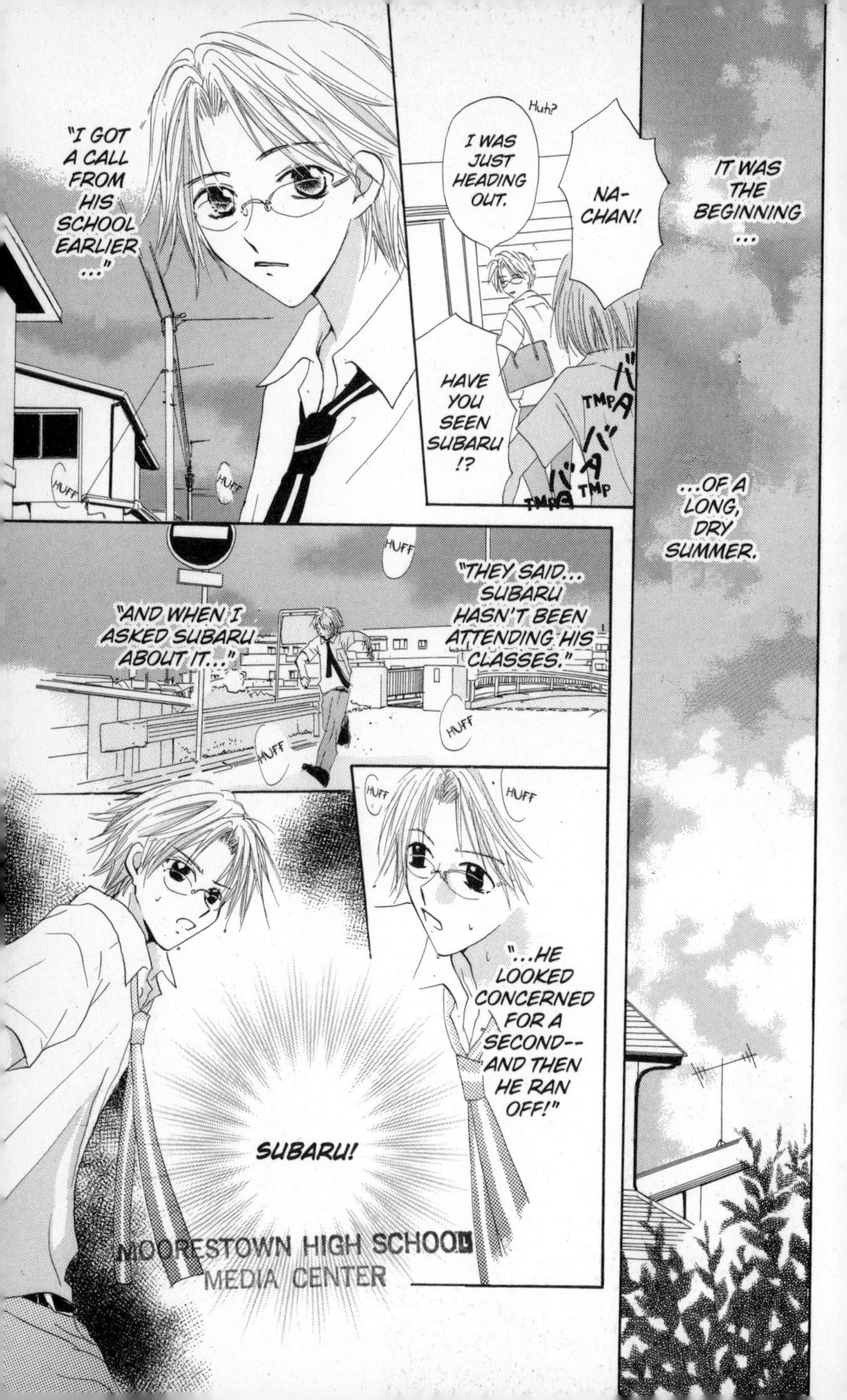
IT WAS THE BEGINNING...
...OF A LONG, DRY SUMMER.
NA-CHAN!
Huh?
I WAS JUST HEADING OUT.
HAVE YOU SEEN SUBARU!?
バ TMP
バ TMP
バ TMP
"I GOT A CALL FROM HIS SCHOOL EARLIER..."
HUFF
HUFF
HUFF
"THEY SAID... SUBARU HASN'T BEEN ATTENDING HIS CLASSES."
"AND WHEN I ASKED SUBARU ABOUT IT..."
HUFF
HUFF
HUFF
HUFF
"...HE LOOKED CONCERNED FOR A SECOND-- AND THEN HE RAN OFF!"
SUBARU!

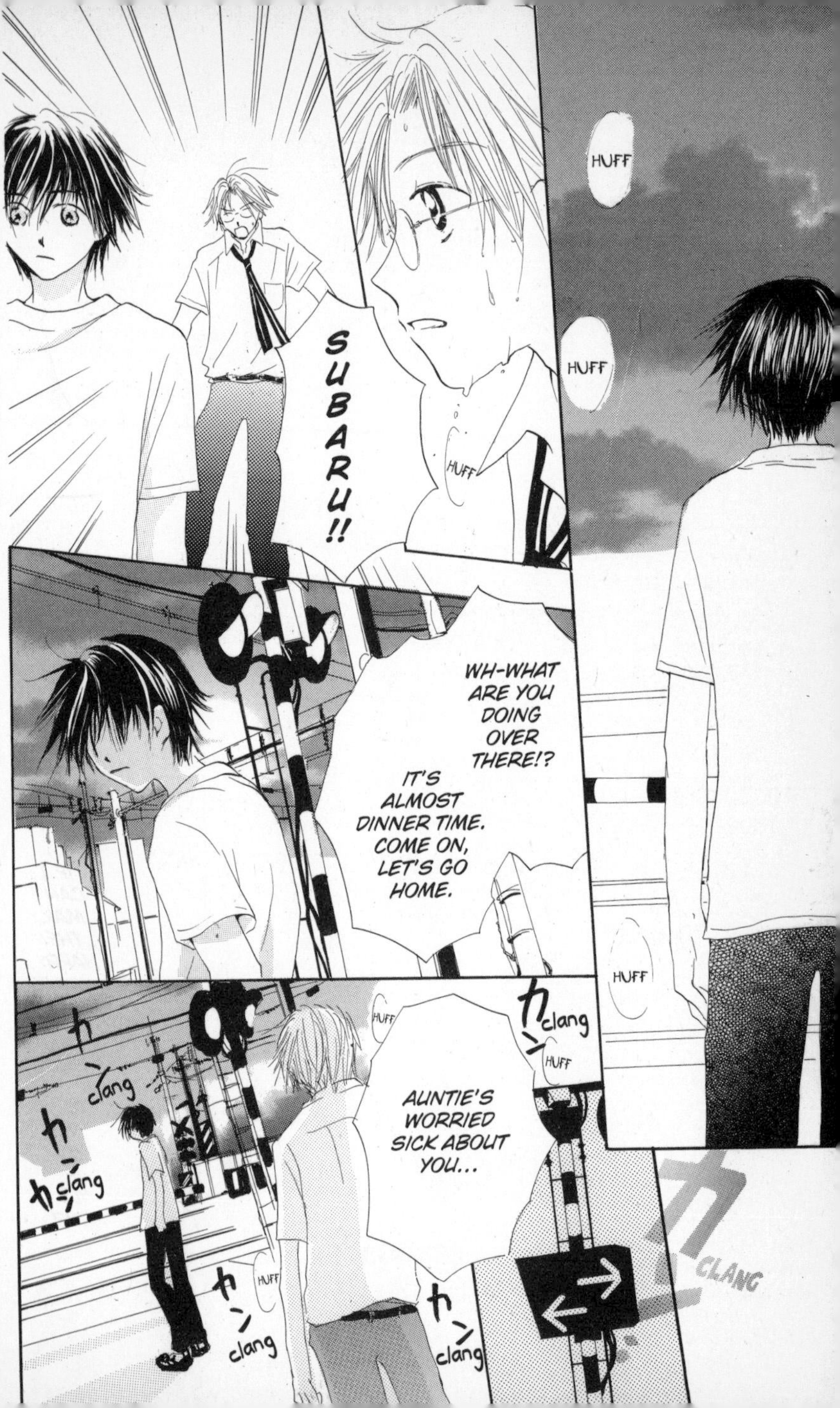
HUFF
HUFF
HUFF
HUFF
SUBARU!!
WH-WHAT ARE YOU DOING OVER THERE!?
IT'S ALMOST DINNER TIME. COME ON, LET'S GO HOME.
CLANG
clang
HUFF
HUFF
AUNTIE'S WORRIED SICK ABOUT YOU...
clang
clang
HUFF
clang
clang
clang

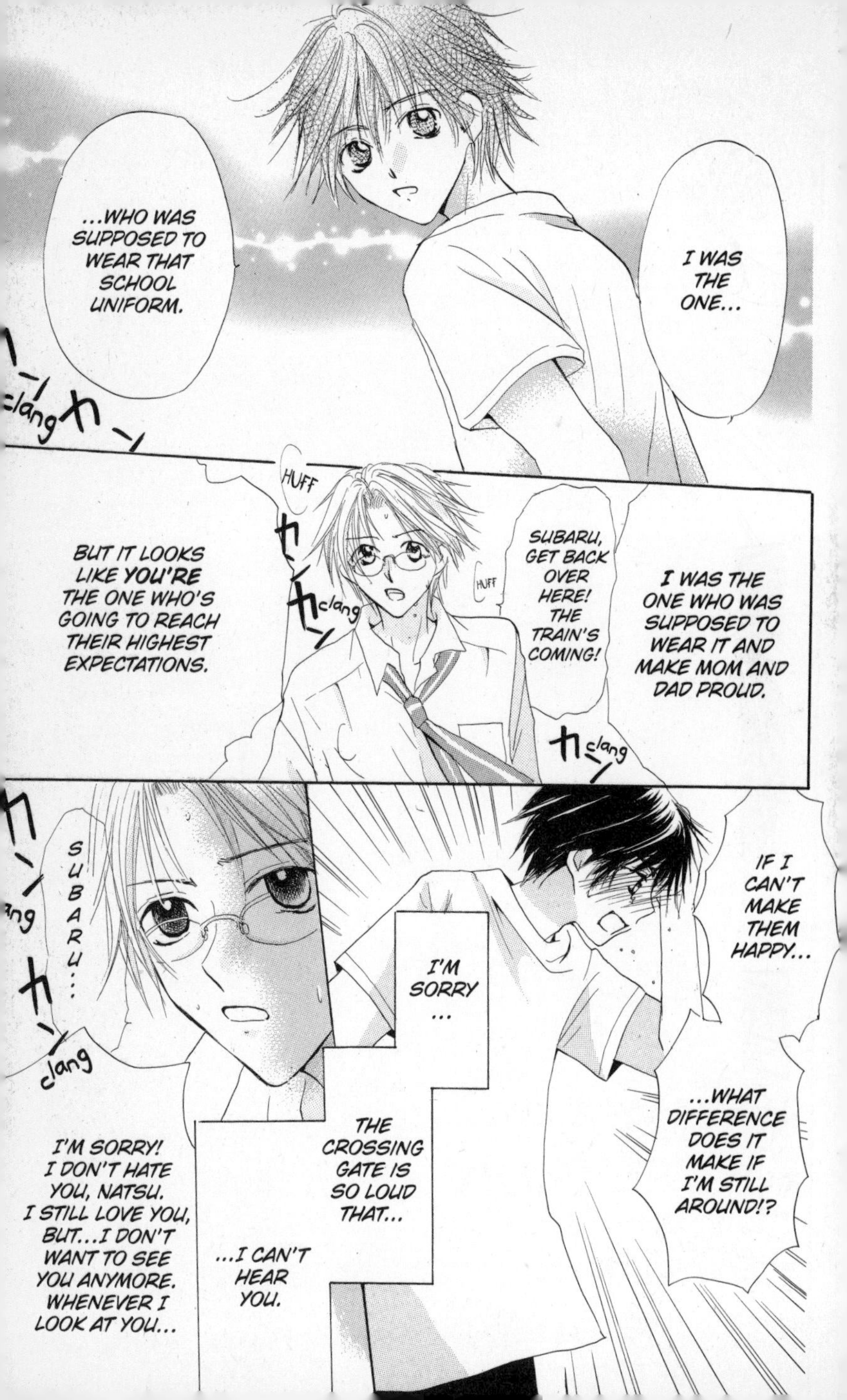
I WAS THE ONE...
...WHO WAS SUPPOSED TO WEAR THAT SCHOOL UNIFORM.
clang
I WAS THE ONE WHO WAS SUPPOSED TO WEAR IT AND MAKE MOM AND DAD PROUD.
SUBARU, GET BACK OVER HERE! THE TRAIN'S COMING!
HUFF
clang
HUFF
clang
BUT IT LOOKS LIKE YOU'RE THE ONE WHO'S GOING TO REACH THEIR HIGHEST EXPECTATIONS.
IF I CAN'T MAKE THEM HAPPY...
...WHAT DIFFERENCE DOES IT MAKE IF I'M STILL AROUND!?
I'M SORRY...
THE CROSSING GATE IS SO LOUD THAT...
...I CAN'T HEAR YOU.
SUBARU...
I'M SORRY! I DON'T HATE YOU, NATSU. I STILL LOVE YOU, BUT...I DON'T WANT TO SEE YOU ANYMORE. WHENEVER I LOOK AT YOU...
clang

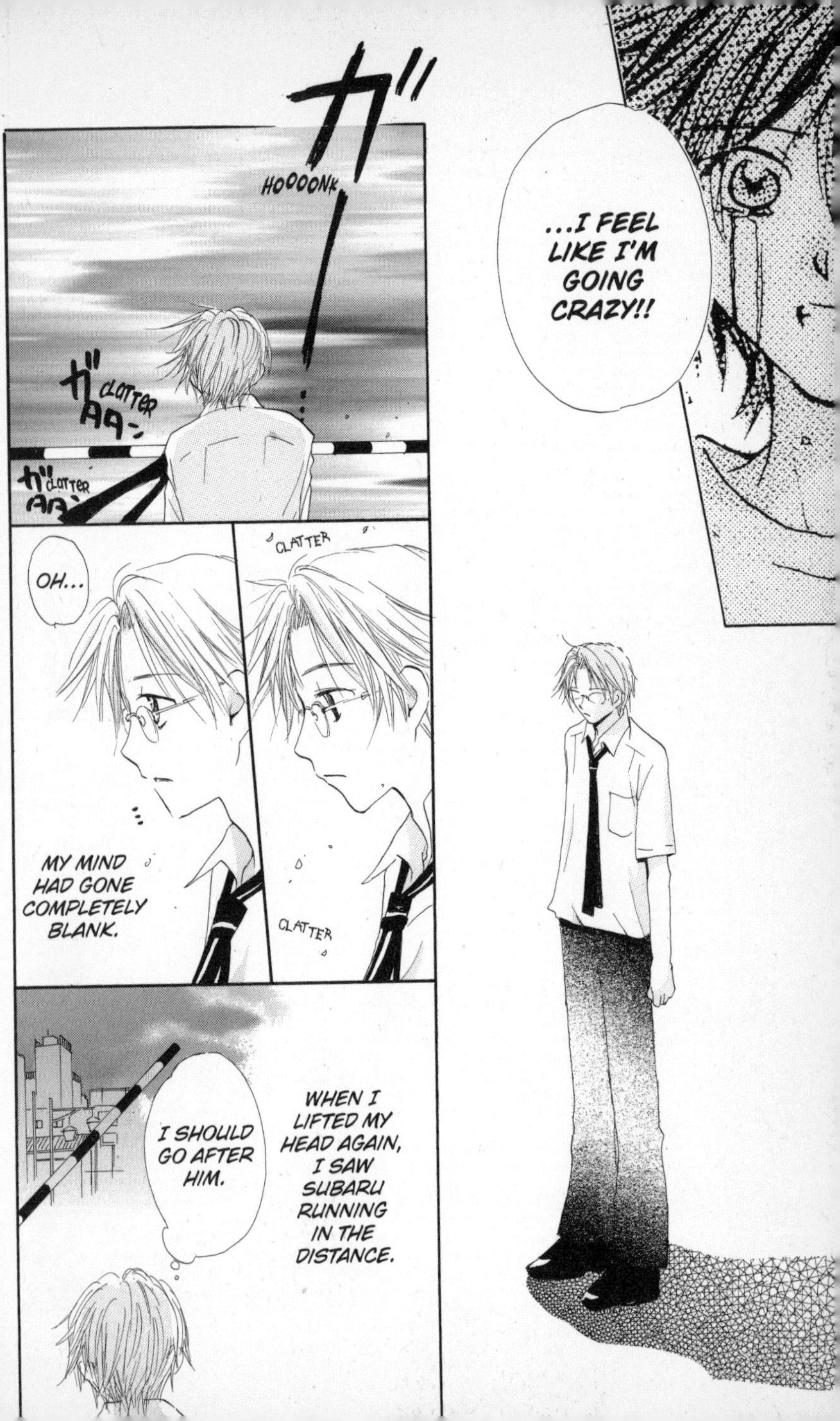
...I FEEL LIKE I'M GOING CRAZY!!
HOOOONK
CLATTER
CLATTER
CLATTER
CLATTER
OH...
MY MIND HAD GONE COMPLETELY BLANK.
WHEN I LIFTED MY HEAD AGAIN, I SAW SUBARU RUNNING IN THE DISTANCE.
I SHOULD GO AFTER HIM.

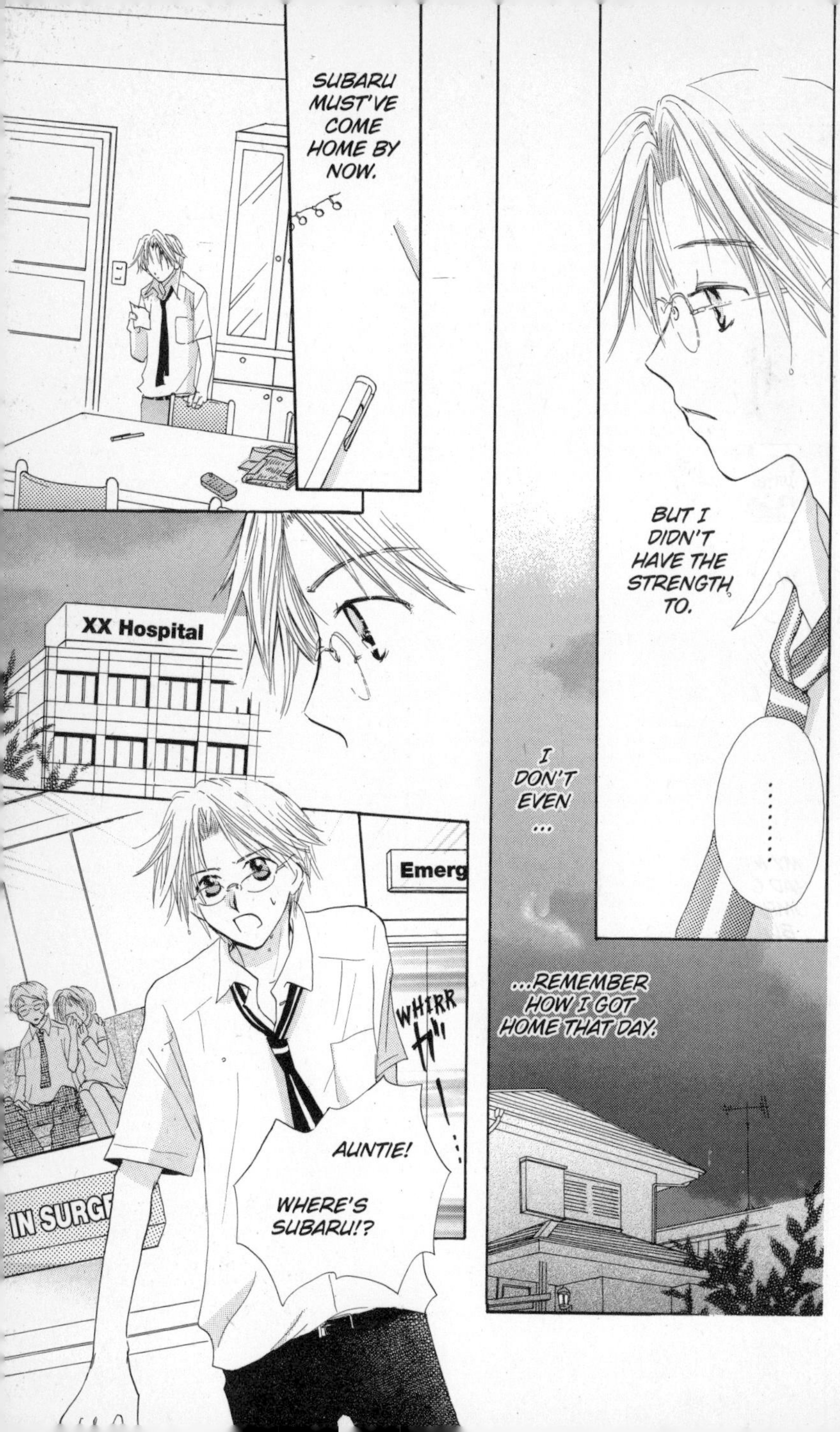
BUT I DIDN'T HAVE THE STRENGTH TO.
......
SUBARU MUST'VE COME HOME BY NOW.
XX Hospital
Emerg
IN SURGE
AUNTIE!
WHERE'S SUBARU!?
WHIRR
I DON'T EVEN ...
...REMEMBER HOW I GOT HOME THAT DAY.

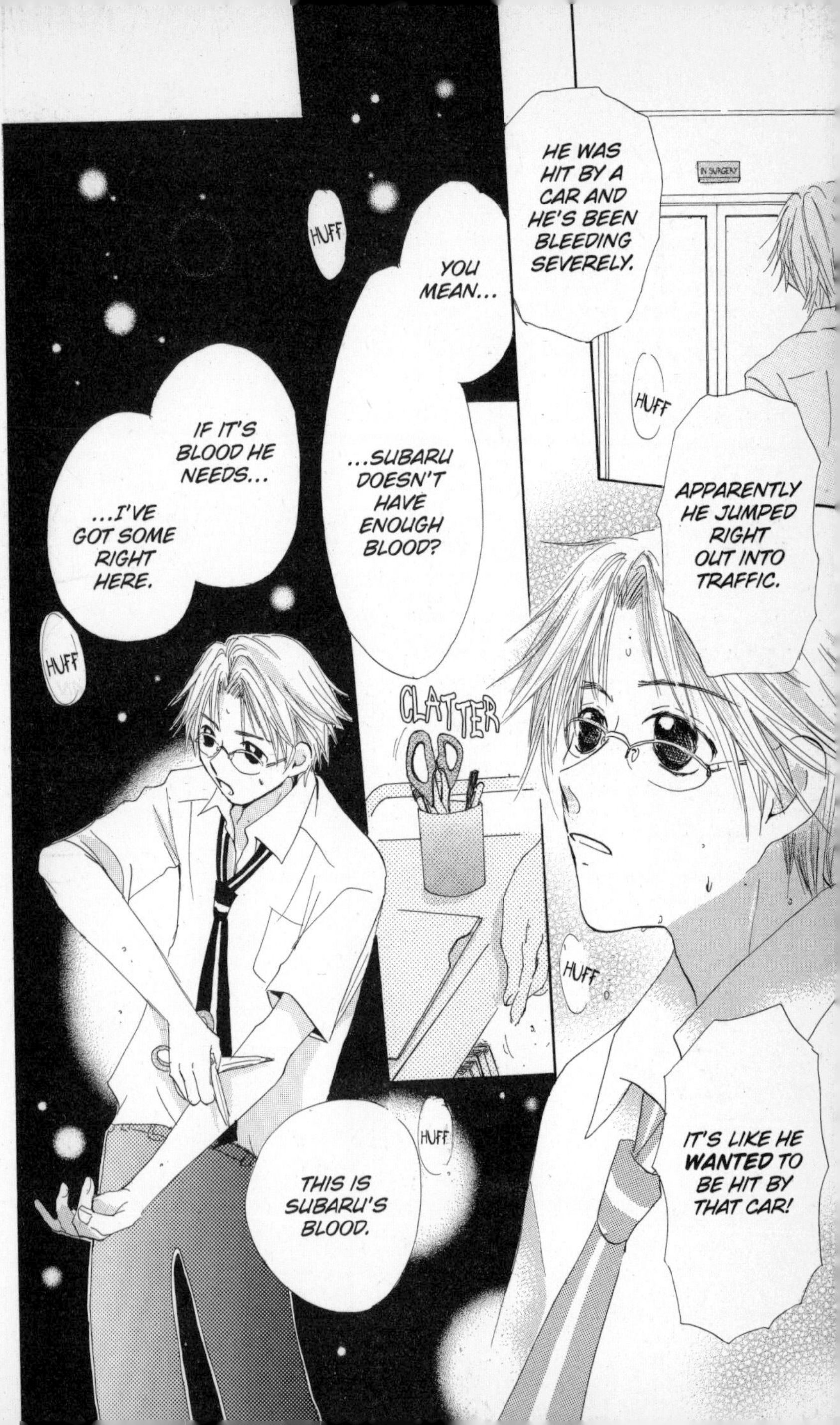
HE WAS HIT BY A CAR AND HE'S BEEN BLEEDING SEVERELY.
IN SURGERY
HUFF
APPARENTLY HE JUMPED RIGHT OUT INTO TRAFFIC.
HUFF
IT'S LIKE HE **WANTED** TO BE HIT BY THAT CAR!
HUFF
YOU MEAN...
...SUBARU DOESN'T HAVE ENOUGH BLOOD?
CLATTER
IF IT'S BLOOD HE NEEDS...
...I'VE GOT SOME RIGHT HERE.
HUFF
HUFF
THIS IS SUBARU'S BLOOD.

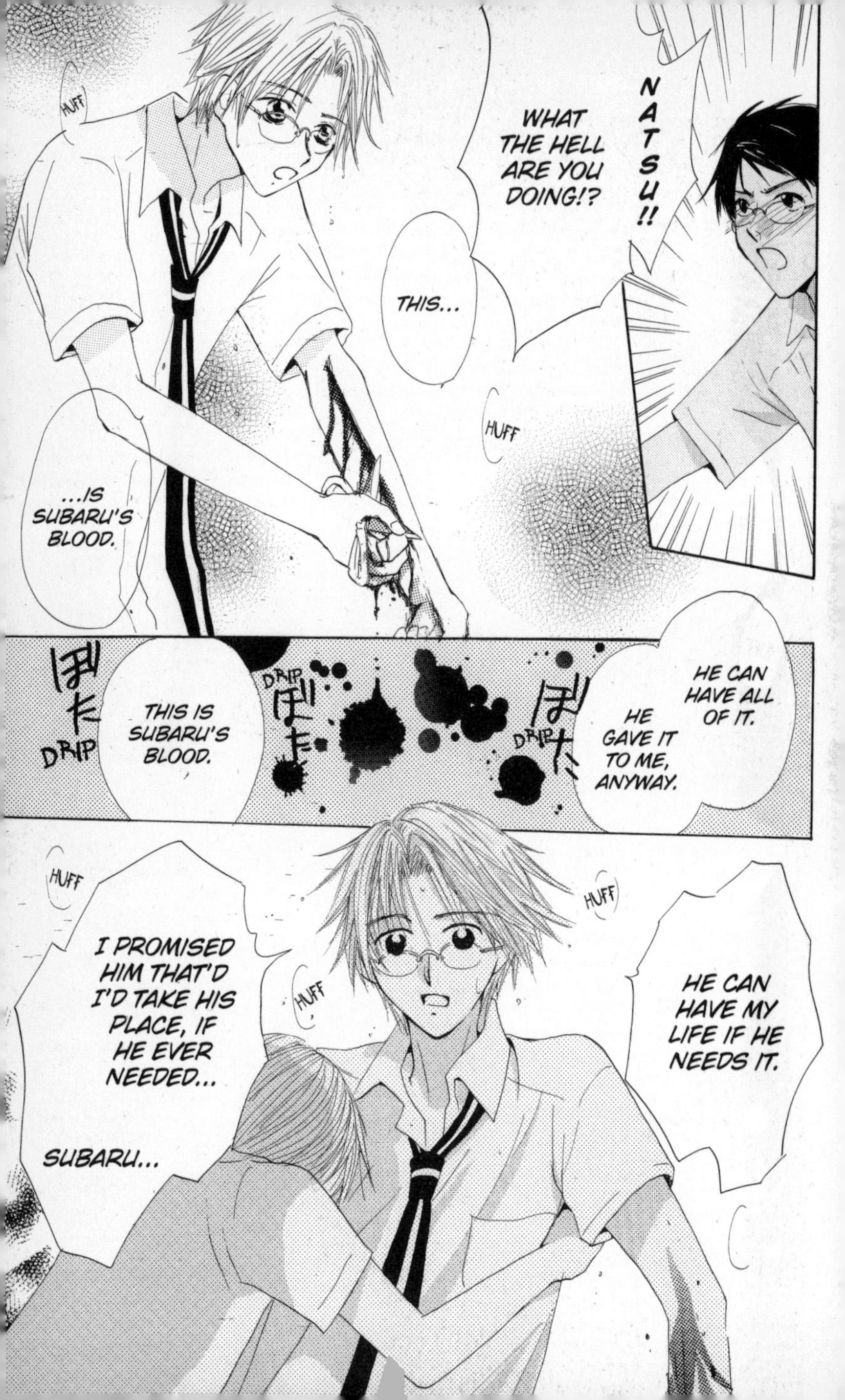
NATSU!!
WHAT THE HELL ARE YOU DOING!?
HUFF
THIS...
HUFF
...IS SUBARU'S BLOOD.
HE CAN HAVE ALL OF IT.
HE GAVE IT TO ME, ANYWAY.
ぽた DRIP
ぽた DRIP
THIS IS SUBARU'S BLOOD.
ぽた DRIP
HUFF
HE CAN HAVE MY LIFE IF HE NEEDS IT.
HUFF
I PROMISED HIM THAT'D I'D TAKE HIS PLACE, IF HE EVER NEEDED...
HUFF
SUBARU...

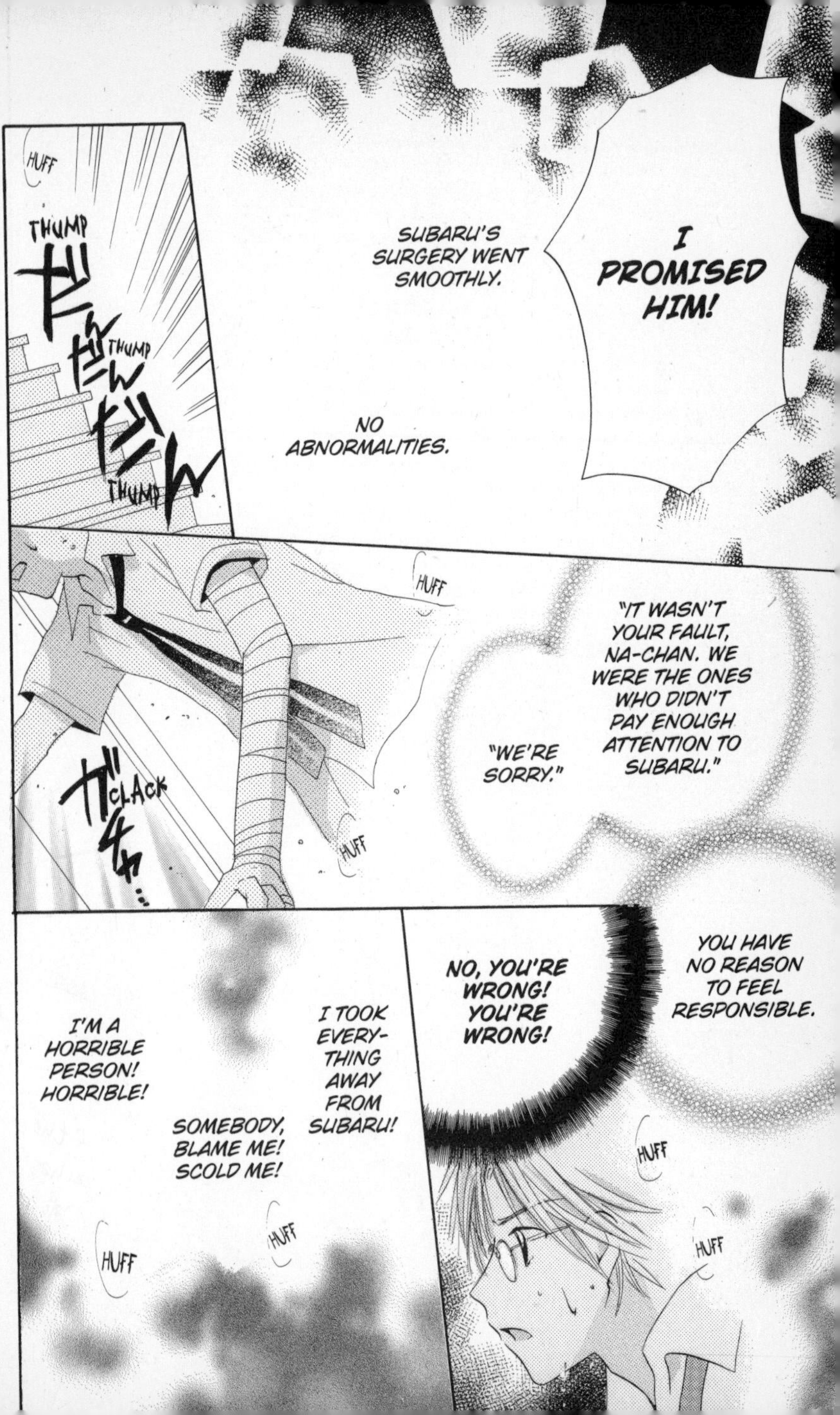
I PROMISED HIM!
SUBARU'S SURGERY WENT SMOOTHLY.
NO ABNORMALITIES.
HUFF
THUMP
THUMP
THUMP
"IT WASN'T YOUR FAULT, NA-CHAN. WE WERE THE ONES WHO DIDN'T PAY ENOUGH ATTENTION TO SUBARU."
"WE'RE SORRY."
HUFF
HUFF
CLACK
YOU HAVE NO REASON TO FEEL RESPONSIBLE.
NO, YOU'RE WRONG! YOU'RE WRONG!
HUFF
HUFF
I TOOK EVERY-THING AWAY FROM SUBARU!
I'M A HORRIBLE PERSON! HORRIBLE!
SOMEBODY, BLAME ME! SCOLD ME!
HUFF
HUFF

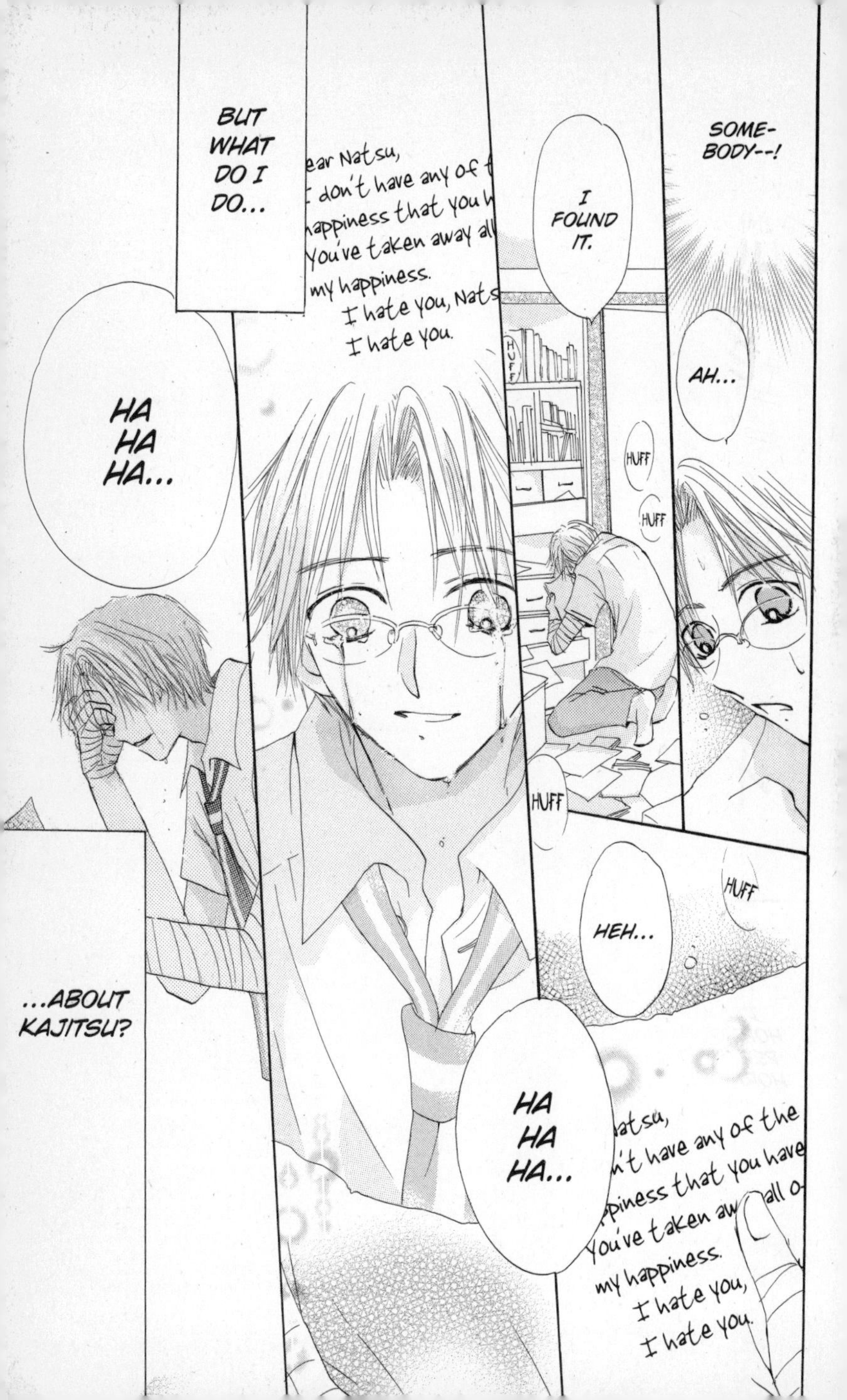
SOME-BODY--!
AH...
I FOUND IT.
HUFF
HUFF
HUFF
HUFF
HUFF
HEH...
HA HA HA...
atsu,
n't have any of the
ppiness that you have
You've taken aw all o
my happiness.
I hate you,
I hate you.
ear Natsu,
don't have any of
happiness that you h
You've taken away al
my happiness.
I hate you, Nats
I hate you.
BUT WHAT DO I DO...
HA HA HA...
...ABOUT KAJITSU?

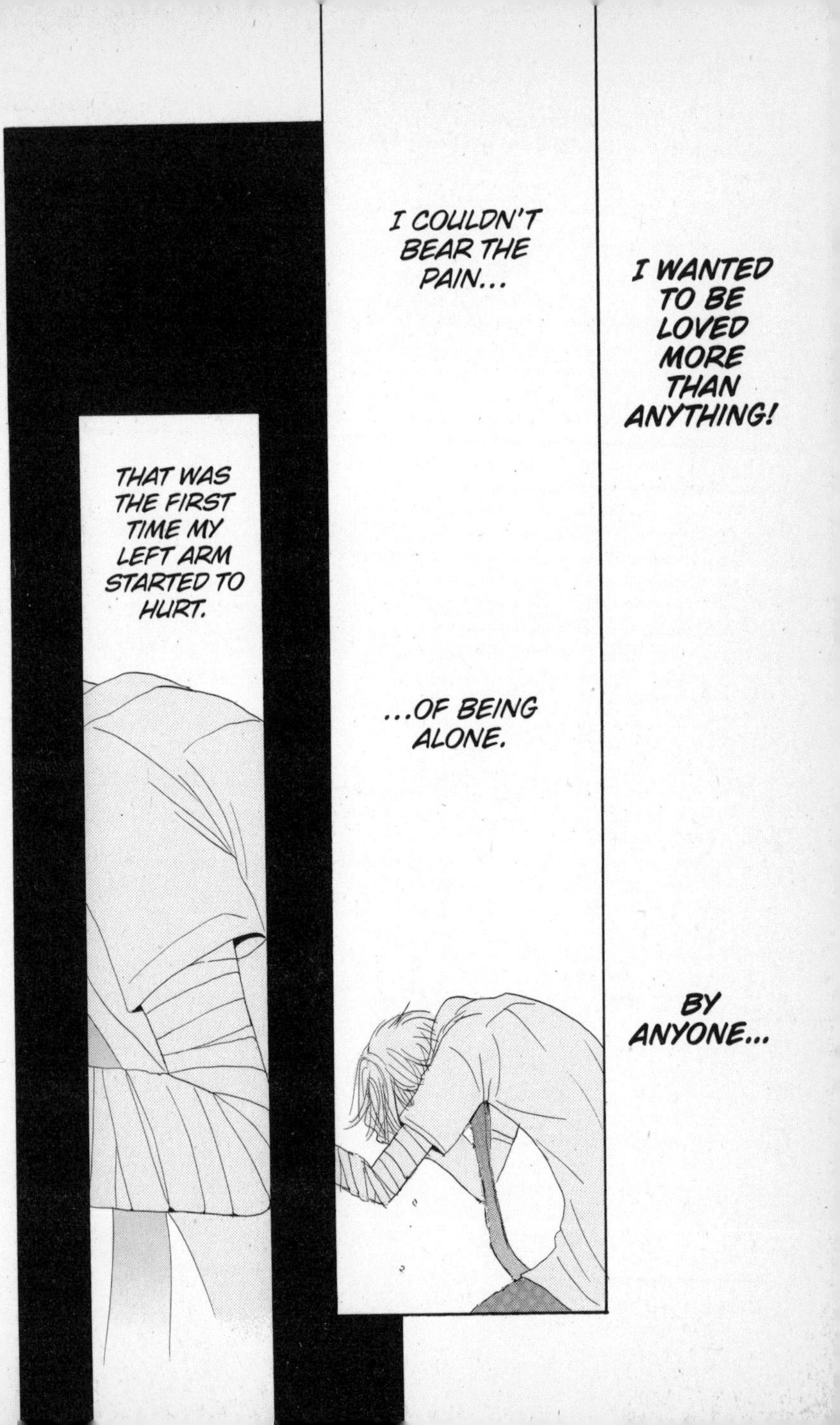
I WANTED TO BE LOVED MORE THAN ANYTHING!
BY ANYONE...
I COULDN'T BEAR THE PAIN...
...OF BEING ALONE.
THAT WAS THE FIRST TIME MY LEFT ARM STARTED TO HURT.

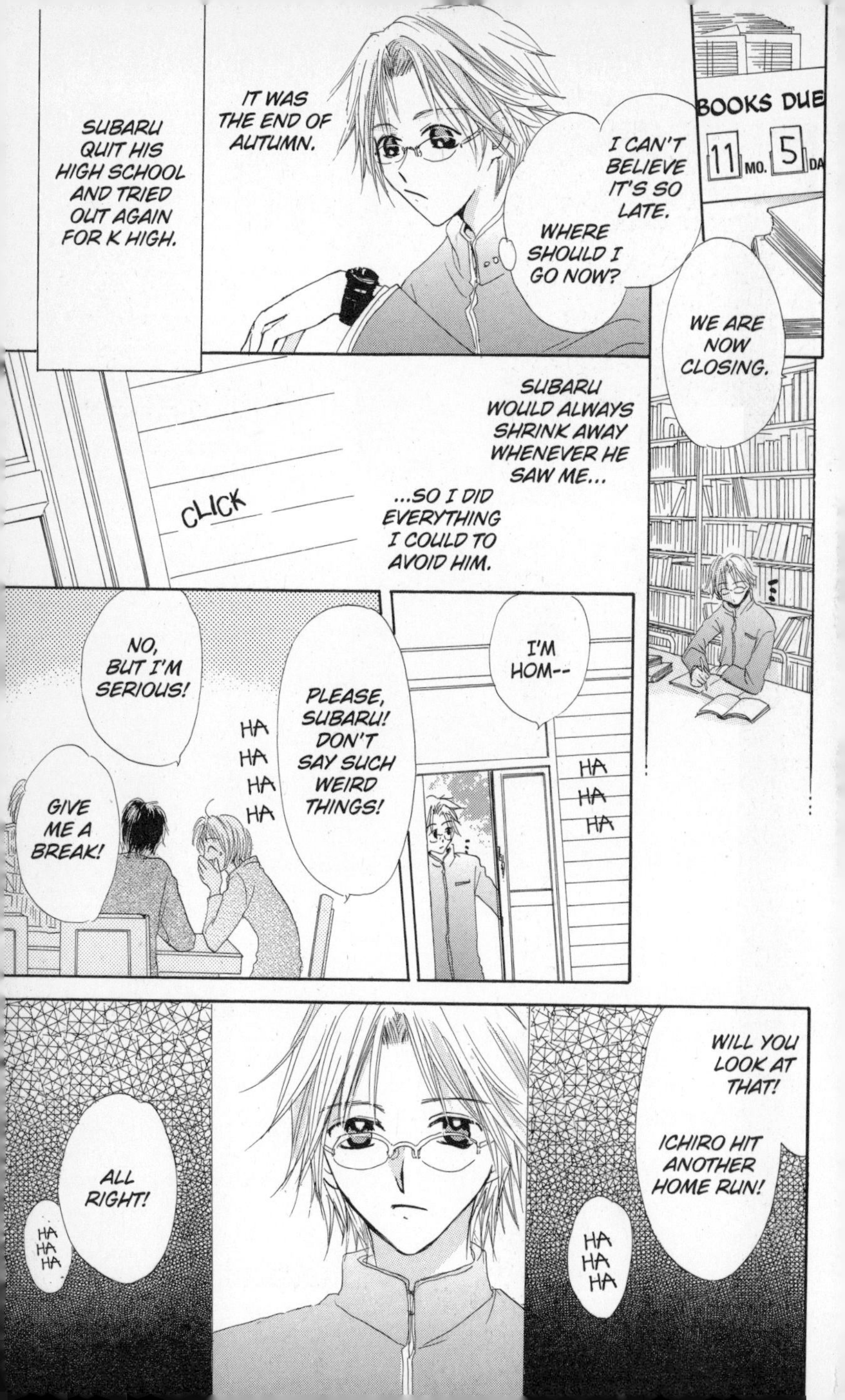
BOOKS DUE
11 MO. 5 DA
I CAN'T BELIEVE IT'S SO LATE.
WHERE SHOULD I GO NOW?
IT WAS THE END OF AUTUMN.
SUBARU QUIT HIS HIGH SCHOOL AND TRIED OUT AGAIN FOR K HIGH.
WE ARE NOW CLOSING.
SUBARU WOULD ALWAYS SHRINK AWAY WHENEVER HE SAW ME...
...SO I DID EVERYTHING I COULD TO AVOID HIM.
CLICK
I'M HOM--
HA HA HA
PLEASE, SUBARU! DON'T SAY SUCH WEIRD THINGS!
HA HA HA HA
NO, BUT I'M SERIOUS!
GIVE ME A BREAK!
WILL YOU LOOK AT THAT!
ICHIRO HIT ANOTHER HOME RUN!
HA HA HA
ALL RIGHT!
HA HA HA

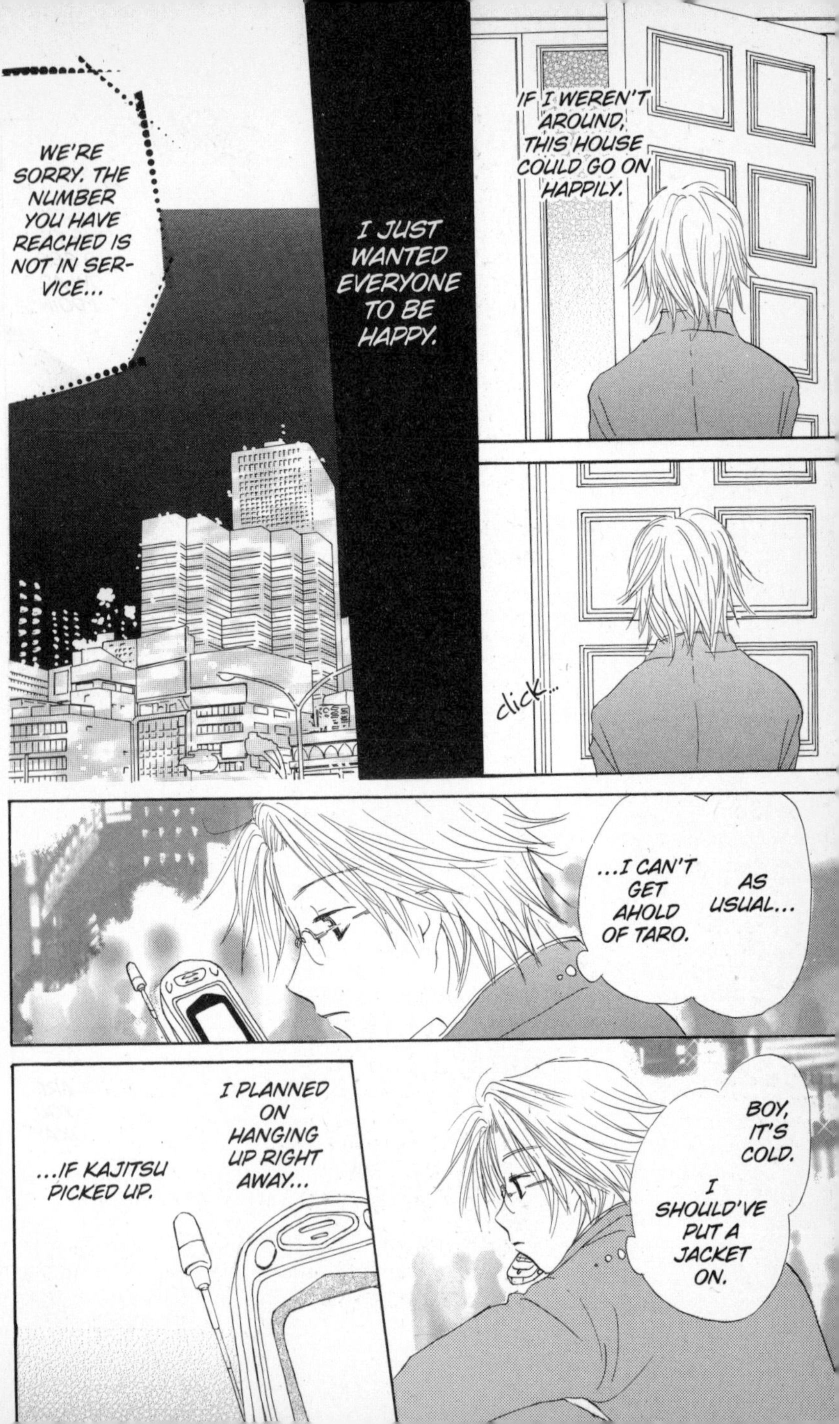
IF I WEREN'T AROUND, THIS HOUSE COULD GO ON HAPPILY.
click...
I JUST WANTED EVERYONE TO BE HAPPY.
WE'RE SORRY. THE NUMBER YOU HAVE REACHED IS NOT IN SER-VICE...
AS USUAL...
...I CAN'T GET AHOLD OF TARO.
BOY, IT'S COLD.
I SHOULD'VE PUT A JACKET ON.
I PLANNED ON HANGING UP RIGHT AWAY...
...IF KAJITSU PICKED UP.

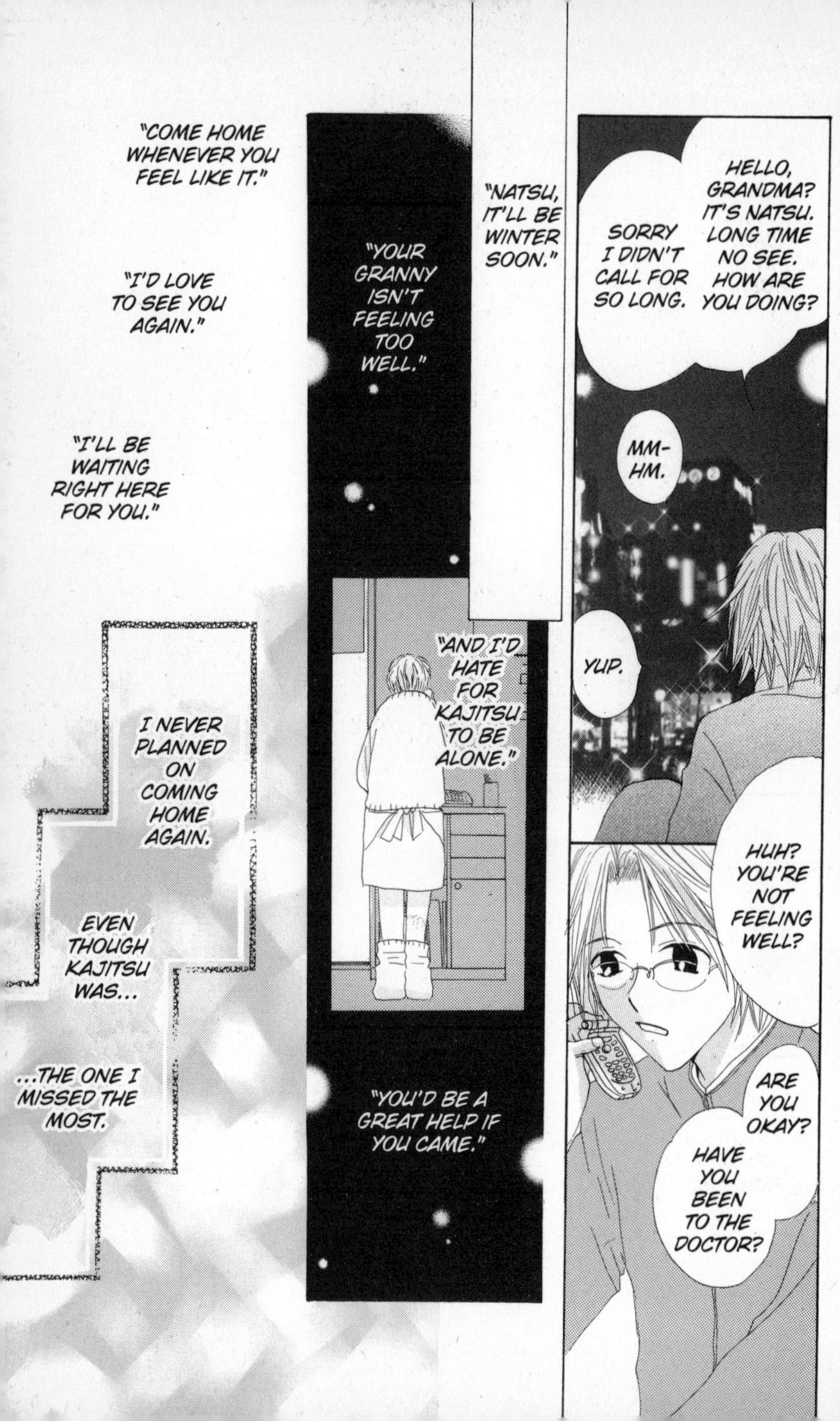
HELLO, GRANDMA? IT'S NATSU. LONG TIME NO SEE. HOW ARE YOU DOING?
SORRY I DIDN'T CALL FOR SO LONG.
MM-HM.
YUP.
HUH? YOU'RE NOT FEELING WELL?
ARE YOU OKAY?
HAVE YOU BEEN TO THE DOCTOR?
"NATSU, IT'LL BE WINTER SOON."
"YOUR GRANNY ISN'T FEELING TOO WELL."
"AND I'D HATE FOR KAJITSU TO BE ALONE."
"YOU'D BE A GREAT HELP IF YOU CAME."
"COME HOME WHENEVER YOU FEEL LIKE IT."
"I'D LOVE TO SEE YOU AGAIN."
"I'LL BE WAITING RIGHT HERE FOR YOU."
I NEVER PLANNED ON COMING HOME AGAIN.
EVEN THOUGH KAJITSU WAS...
...THE ONE I MISSED THE MOST.

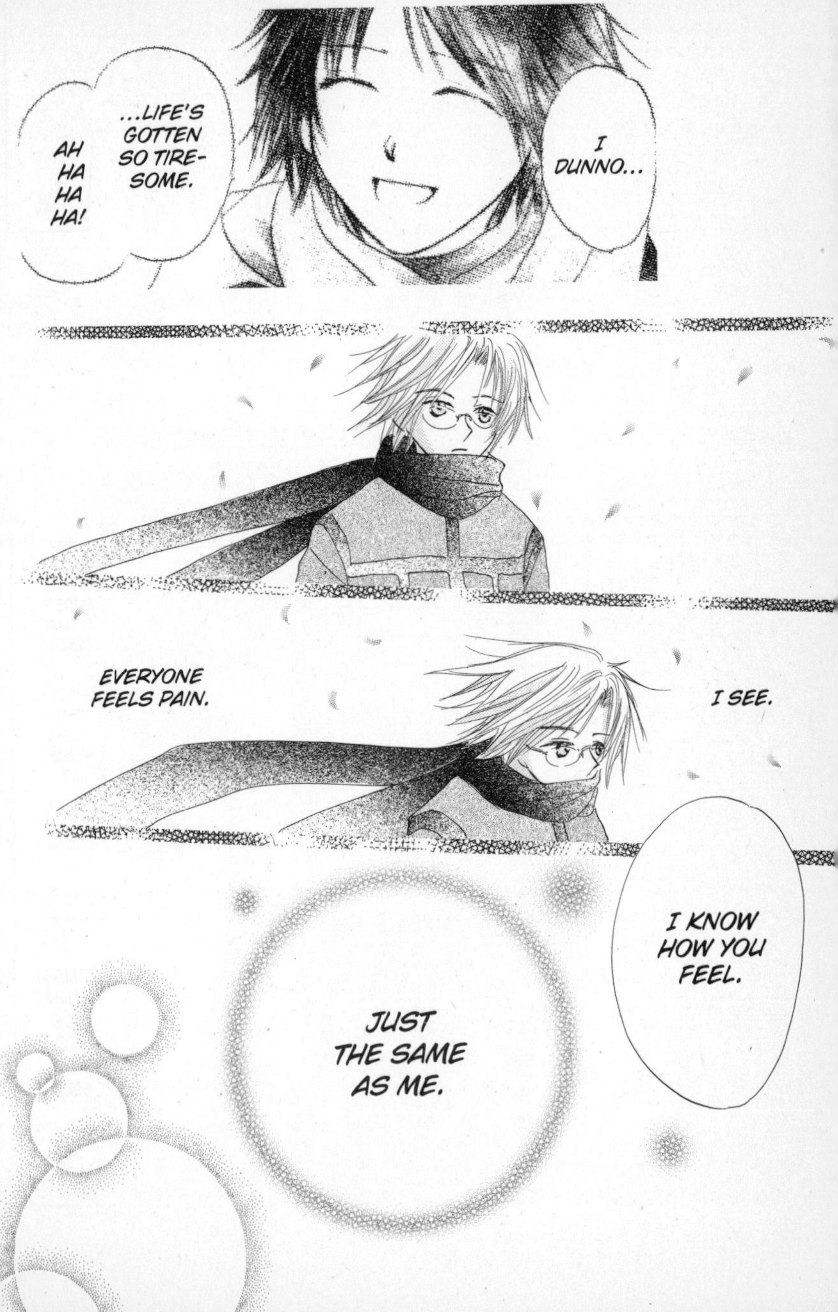
I DUNNO...
...LIFE'S GOTTEN SO TIRE-SOME.
AH HA HA HA!
I SEE.
EVERYONE FEELS PAIN.
I KNOW HOW YOU FEEL.
JUST THE SAME AS ME.

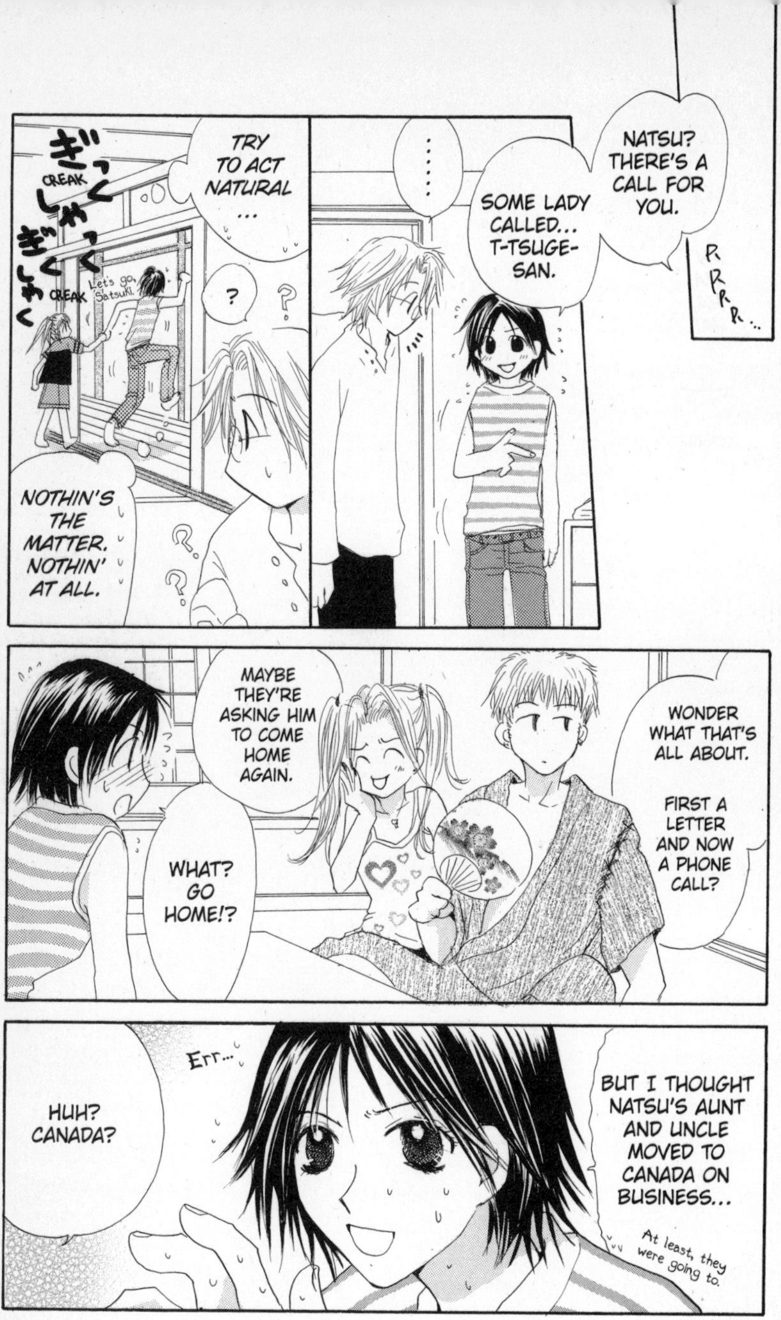
NATSU? THERE'S A CALL FOR YOU.
Pr Pr Pr Pr...
......
SOME LADY CALLED... T-TSUGE-SAN.
TRY TO ACT NATURAL...
?
ぎっくしゃっく
CREAK
ぎくしゃく
CREAK
Let's go, Satsuki.
NOTHIN'S THE MATTER. NOTHIN' AT ALL.
WONDER WHAT THAT'S ALL ABOUT.
FIRST A LETTER AND NOW A PHONE CALL?
MAYBE THEY'RE ASKING HIM TO COME HOME AGAIN.
WHAT? GO HOME!?
BUT I THOUGHT NATSU'S AUNT AND UNCLE MOVED TO CANADA ON BUSINESS...
At least, they were going to.
Err...
HUH? CANADA?

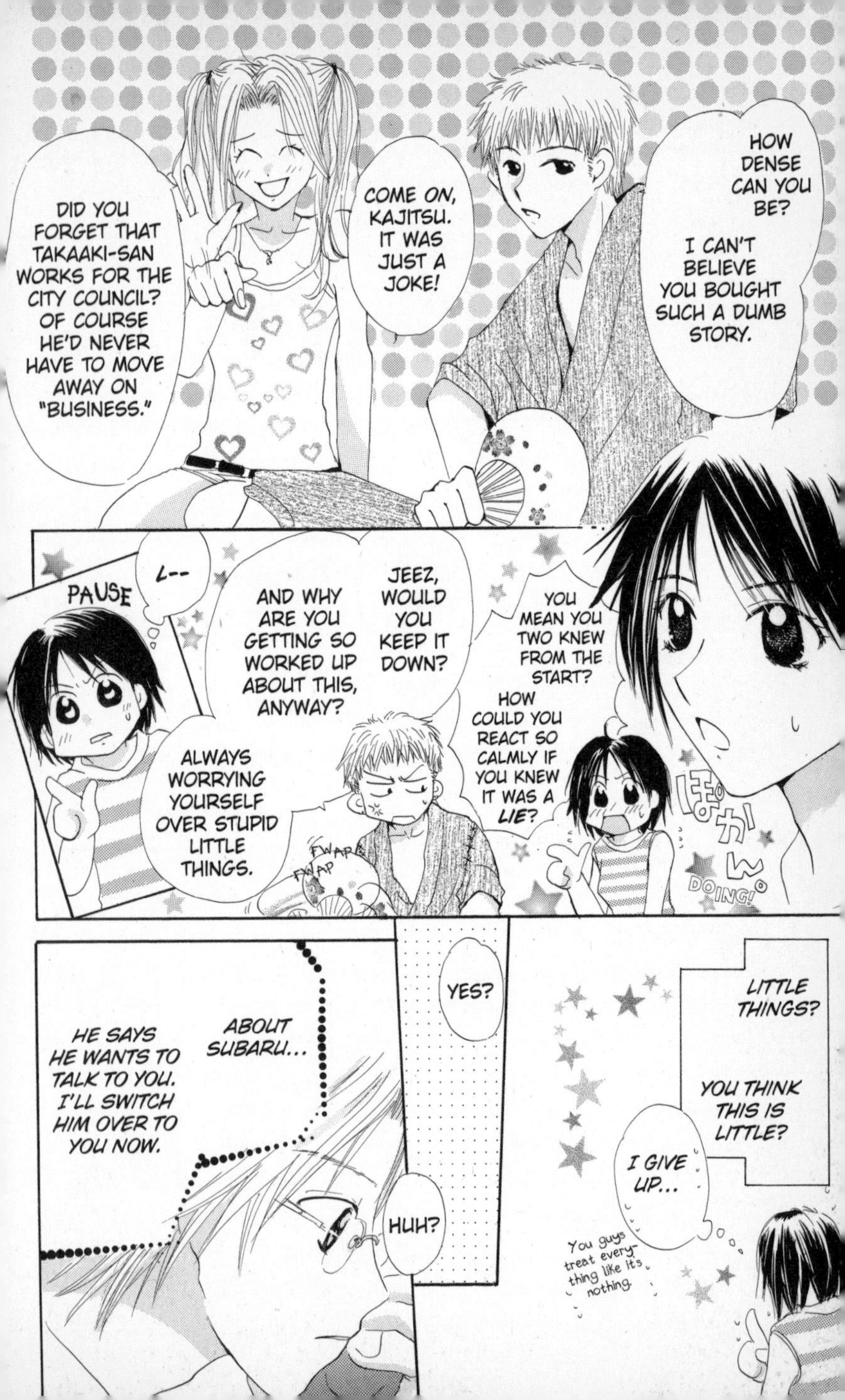
HOW DENSE CAN YOU BE?
I CAN'T BELIEVE YOU BOUGHT SUCH A DUMB STORY.
COME ON, KAJITSU. IT WAS JUST A JOKE!
DID YOU FORGET THAT TAKAAKI-SAN WORKS FOR THE CITY COUNCIL? OF COURSE HE'D NEVER HAVE TO MOVE AWAY ON "BUSINESS."
YOU MEAN YOU TWO KNEW FROM THE START?
DOING!
HOW COULD YOU REACT SO CALMLY IF YOU KNEW IT WAS A LIE?
JEEZ, WOULD YOU KEEP IT DOWN?
AND WHY ARE YOU GETTING SO WORKED UP ABOUT THIS, ANYWAY?
FWAP FWAP
ALWAYS WORRYING YOURSELF OVER STUPID LITTLE THINGS.
I--
PAUSE
LITTLE THINGS?
YOU THINK THIS IS LITTLE?
I GIVE UP...
You guys treat every-thing like it's nothing.
YES?
HUH?
ABOUT SUBARU...
HE SAYS HE WANTS TO TALK TO YOU. I'LL SWITCH HIM OVER TO YOU NOW.

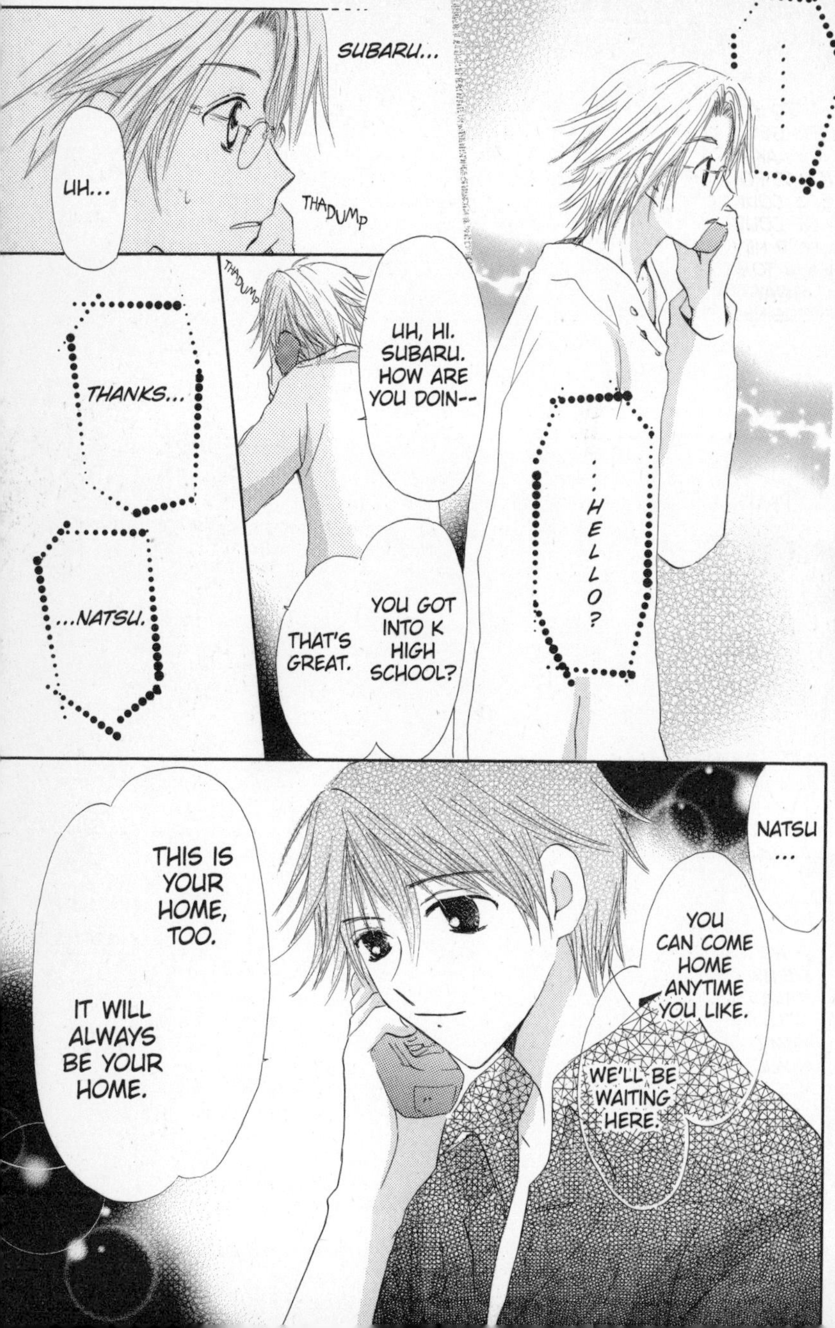

......
...HELLO?
SUBARU...
UH...
THADUMP
THADUMP
UH, HI. SUBARU. HOW ARE YOU DOIN--
YOU GOT INTO K HIGH SCHOOL?
THAT'S GREAT.
THANKS...
...NATSU.
NATSU...
YOU CAN COME HOME ANYTIME YOU LIKE.
WE'LL BE WAITING HERE.
THIS IS YOUR HOME, TOO.
IT WILL ALWAYS BE YOUR HOME.

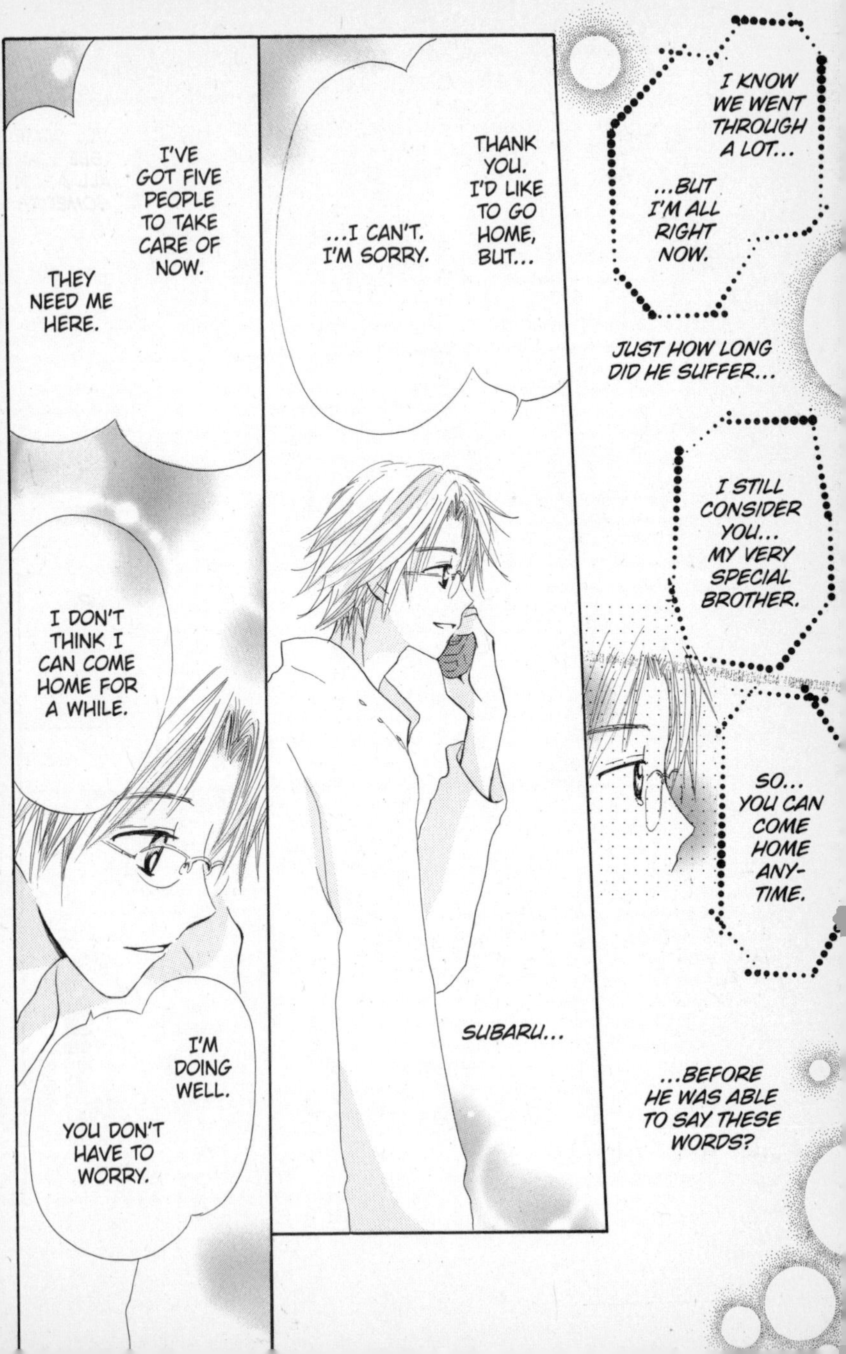
I KNOW WE WENT THROUGH A LOT...
...BUT I'M ALL RIGHT NOW.
JUST HOW LONG DID HE SUFFER...
I STILL CONSIDER YOU... MY VERY SPECIAL BROTHER.
SO... YOU CAN COME HOME ANY-TIME.
...BEFORE HE WAS ABLE TO SAY THESE WORDS?
THANK YOU. I'D LIKE TO GO HOME, BUT...
...I CAN'T. I'M SORRY.
SUBARU...
I'VE GOT FIVE PEOPLE TO TAKE CARE OF NOW.
THEY NEED ME HERE.
I DON'T THINK I CAN COME HOME FOR A WHILE.
I'M DOING WELL.
YOU DON'T HAVE TO WORRY.

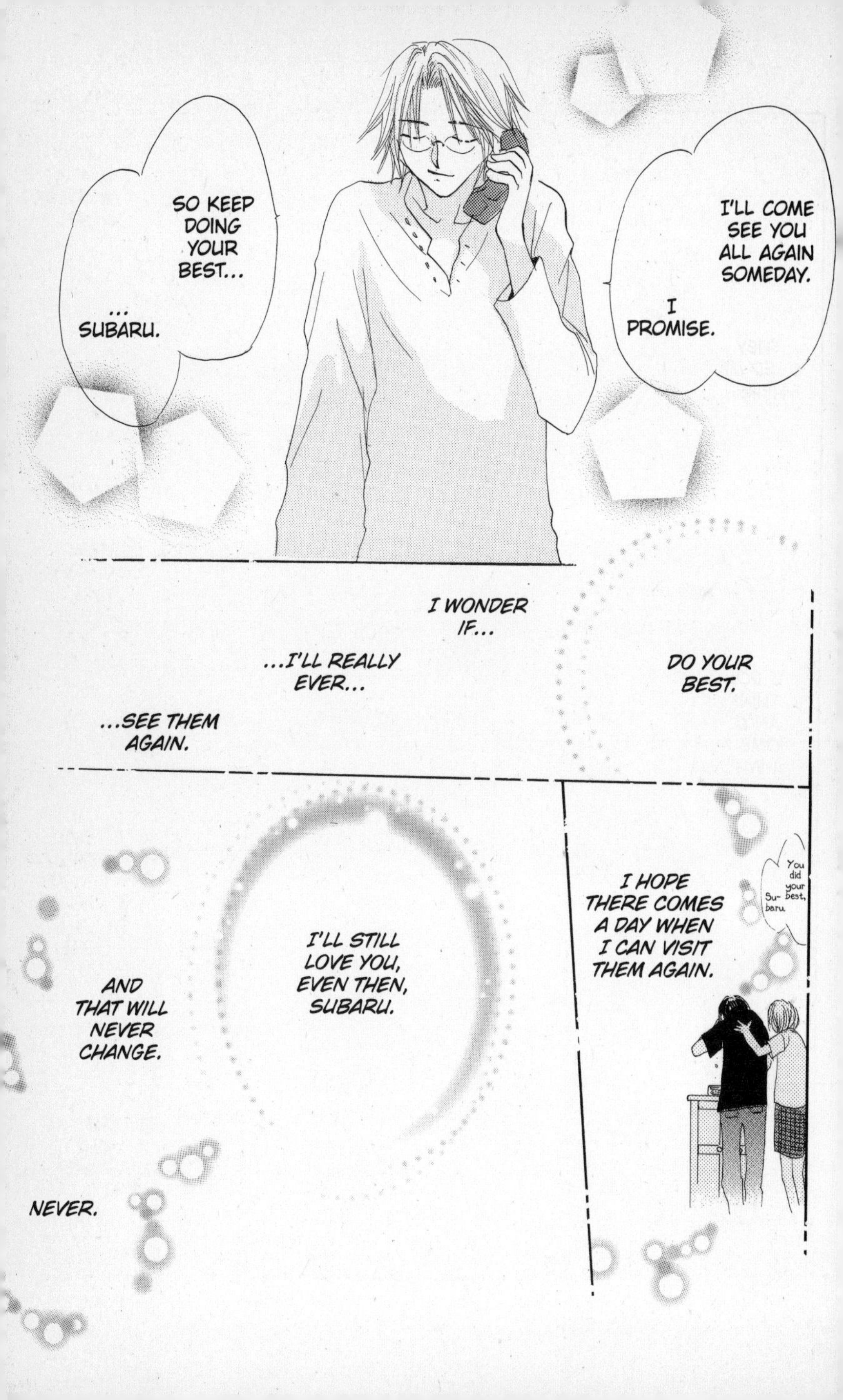
I'LL COME SEE YOU ALL AGAIN SOMEDAY.
I PROMISE.
SO KEEP DOING YOUR BEST...
...SUBARU.
DO YOUR BEST.
I WONDER IF...
...I'LL REALLY EVER...
...SEE THEM AGAIN.
You did your best, Su-baru.
I HOPE THERE COMES A DAY WHEN I CAN VISIT THEM AGAIN.
I'LL STILL LOVE YOU, EVEN THEN, SUBARU.
AND THAT WILL NEVER CHANGE.
NEVER.

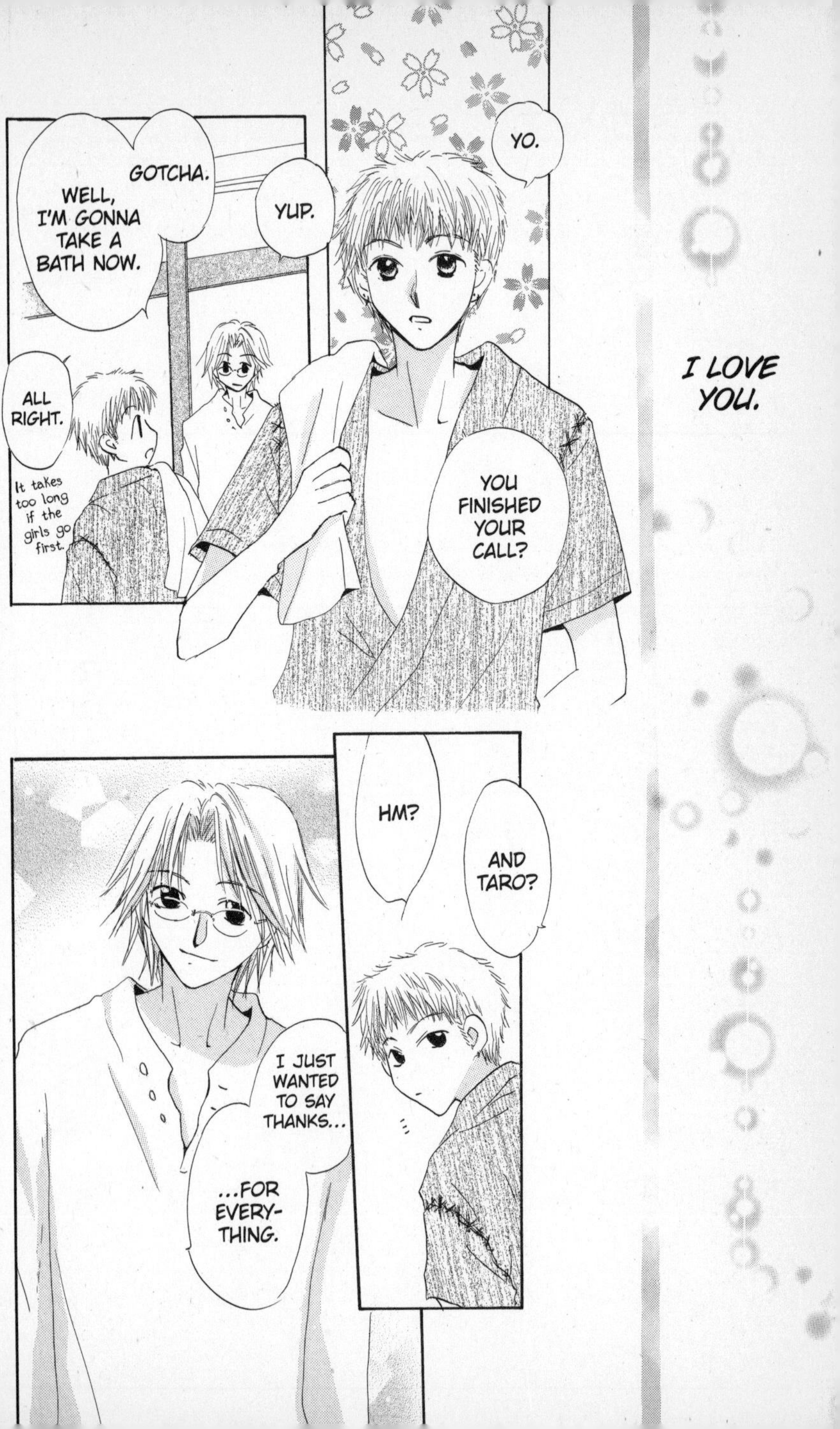
I LOVE YOU.
YO.
YOU FINISHED YOUR CALL?
YUP.
GOTCHA.
WELL, I'M GONNA TAKE A BATH NOW.
ALL RIGHT.
It takes too long if the girls go first.
AND TARO?
HM?
I JUST WANTED TO SAY THANKS...
...FOR EVERY-THING.

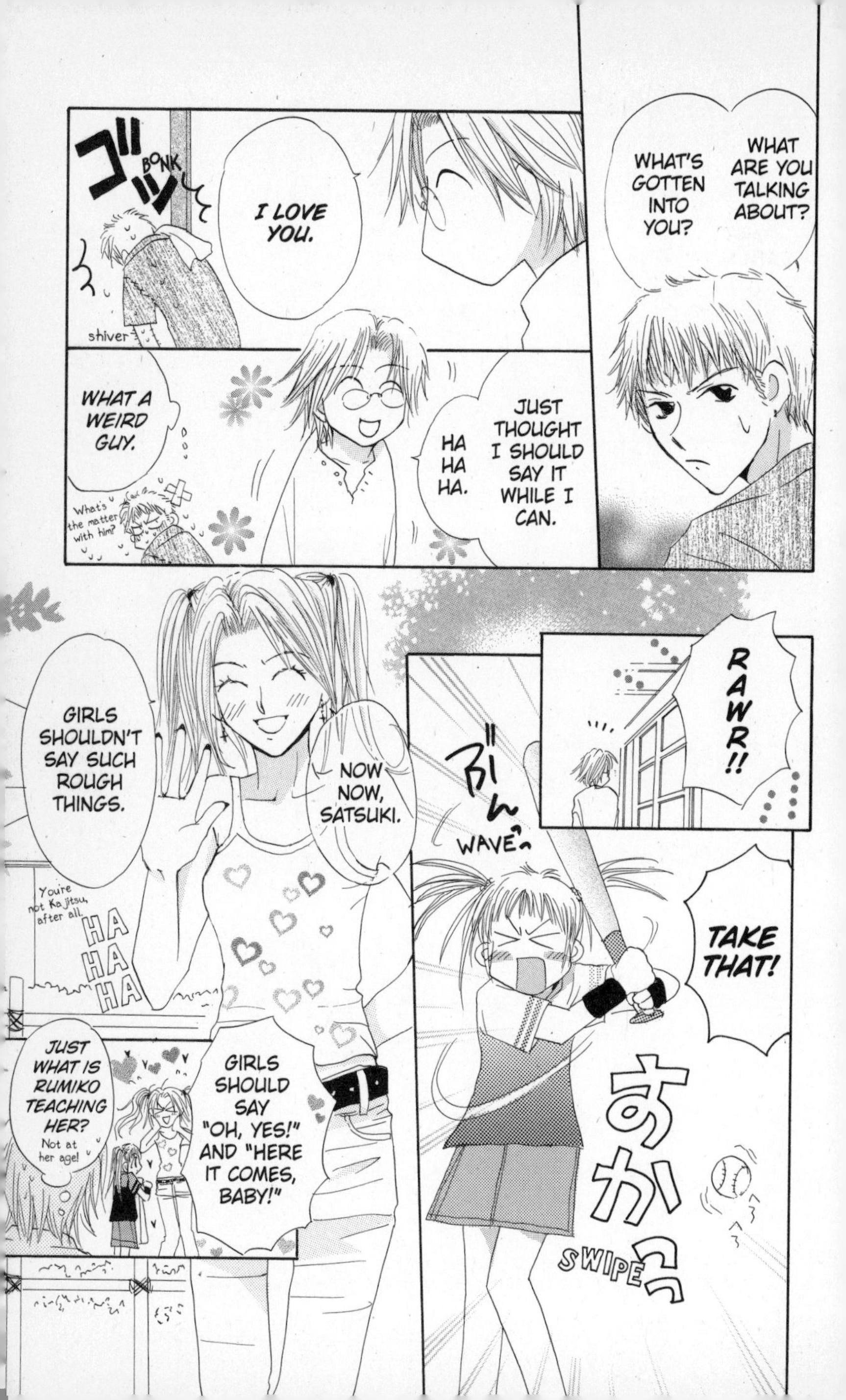
WHAT ARE YOU TALKING ABOUT?
WHAT'S GOTTEN INTO YOU?
I LOVE YOU.
BONK
shiver
JUST THOUGHT I SHOULD SAY IT WHILE I CAN.
HA HA HA.
WHAT A WEIRD GUY.
What's the matter with him?
RAWR!!
TAKE THAT!
SWIPE
WAVE
NOW NOW, SATSUKI.
GIRLS SHOULDN'T SAY SUCH ROUGH THINGS.
You're not Kajitsu, after all.
HA HA HA
GIRLS SHOULD SAY "OH, YES!" AND "HERE IT COMES, BABY!"
JUST WHAT IS RUMIKO TEACHING HER?
Not at her age!

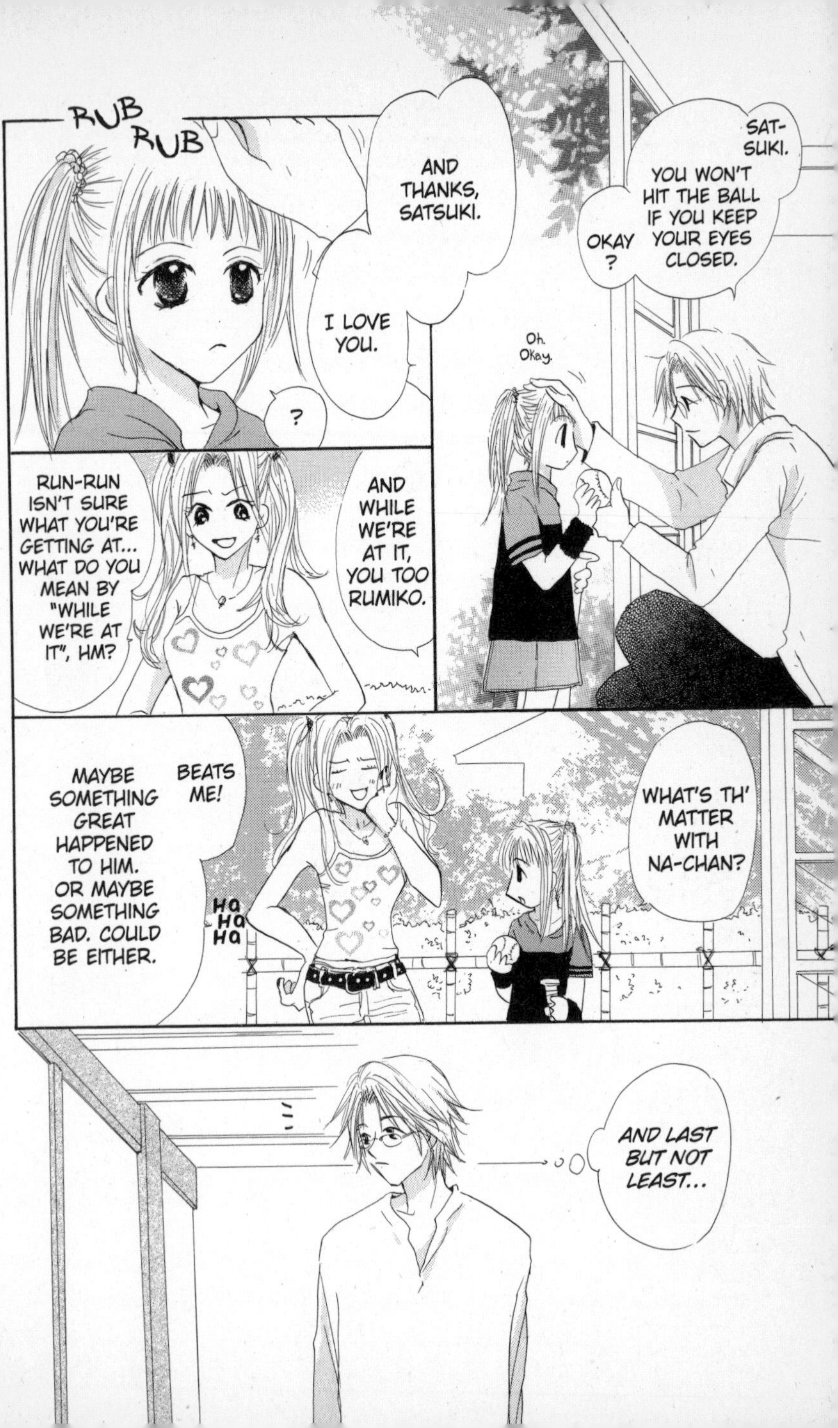
SAT-SUKI.
YOU WON'T HIT THE BALL IF YOU KEEP YOUR EYES CLOSED.
OKAY?
Oh. Okay.
RUB RUB
AND THANKS, SATSUKI.
I LOVE YOU.
?
AND WHILE WE'RE AT IT, YOU TOO RUMIKO.
RUN-RUN ISN'T SURE WHAT YOU'RE GETTING AT... WHAT DO YOU MEAN BY "WHILE WE'RE AT IT", HM?
WHAT'S TH' MATTER WITH NA-CHAN?
BEATS ME!
MAYBE SOMETHING GREAT HAPPENED TO HIM. OR MAYBE SOMETHING BAD. COULD BE EITHER.
Ha Ha Ha
AND LAST BUT NOT LEAST...

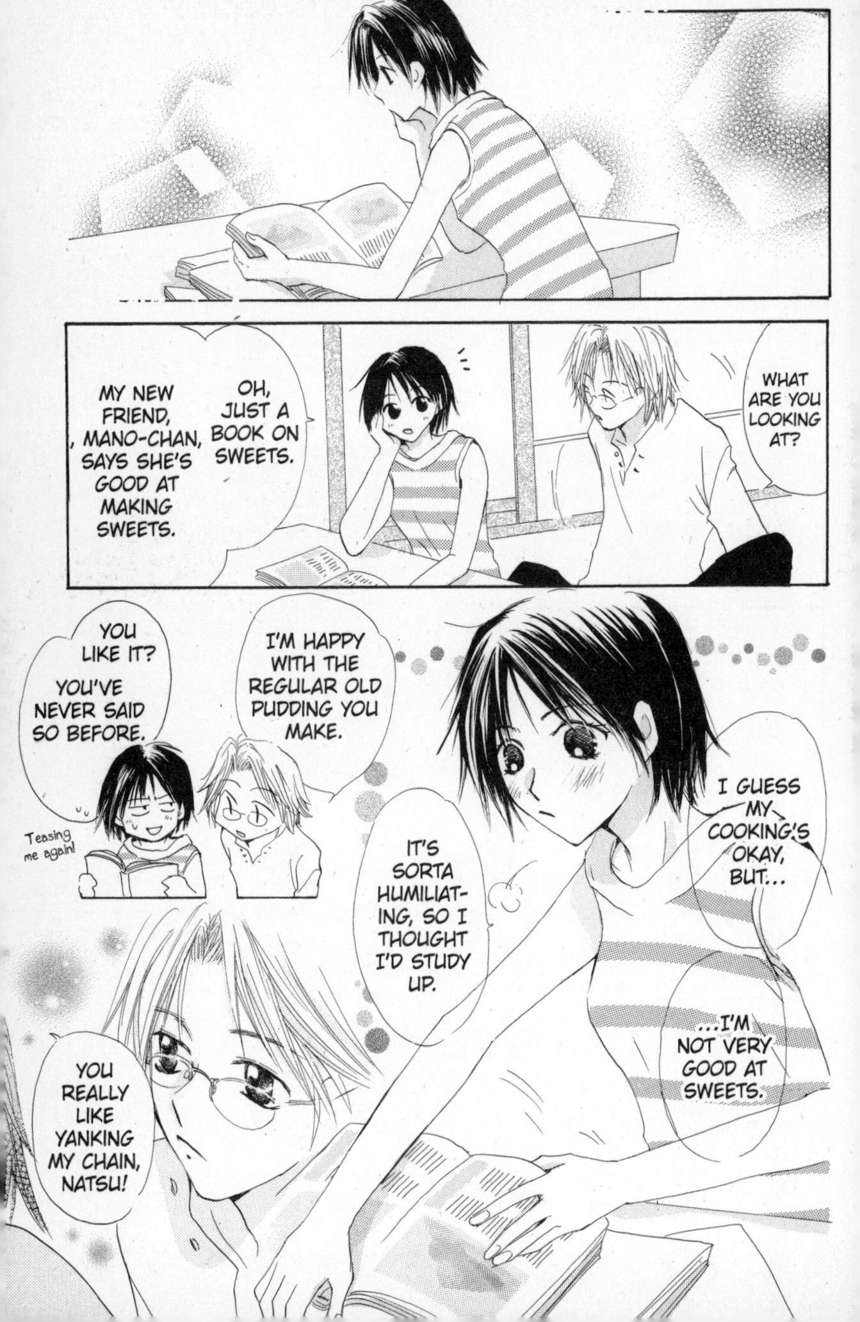
WHAT ARE YOU LOOKING AT?
OH, JUST A BOOK ON SWEETS.
MY NEW FRIEND, MANO-CHAN, SAYS SHE'S GOOD AT MAKING SWEETS.
I GUESS MY COOKING'S OKAY, BUT...
...I'M NOT VERY GOOD AT SWEETS.
IT'S SORTA HUMILIAT-ING, SO I THOUGHT I'D STUDY UP.
I'M HAPPY WITH THE REGULAR OLD PUDDING YOU MAKE.
YOU LIKE IT? YOU'VE NEVER SAID SO BEFORE.
Teasing me again!
YOU REALLY LIKE YANKING MY CHAIN, NATSU!

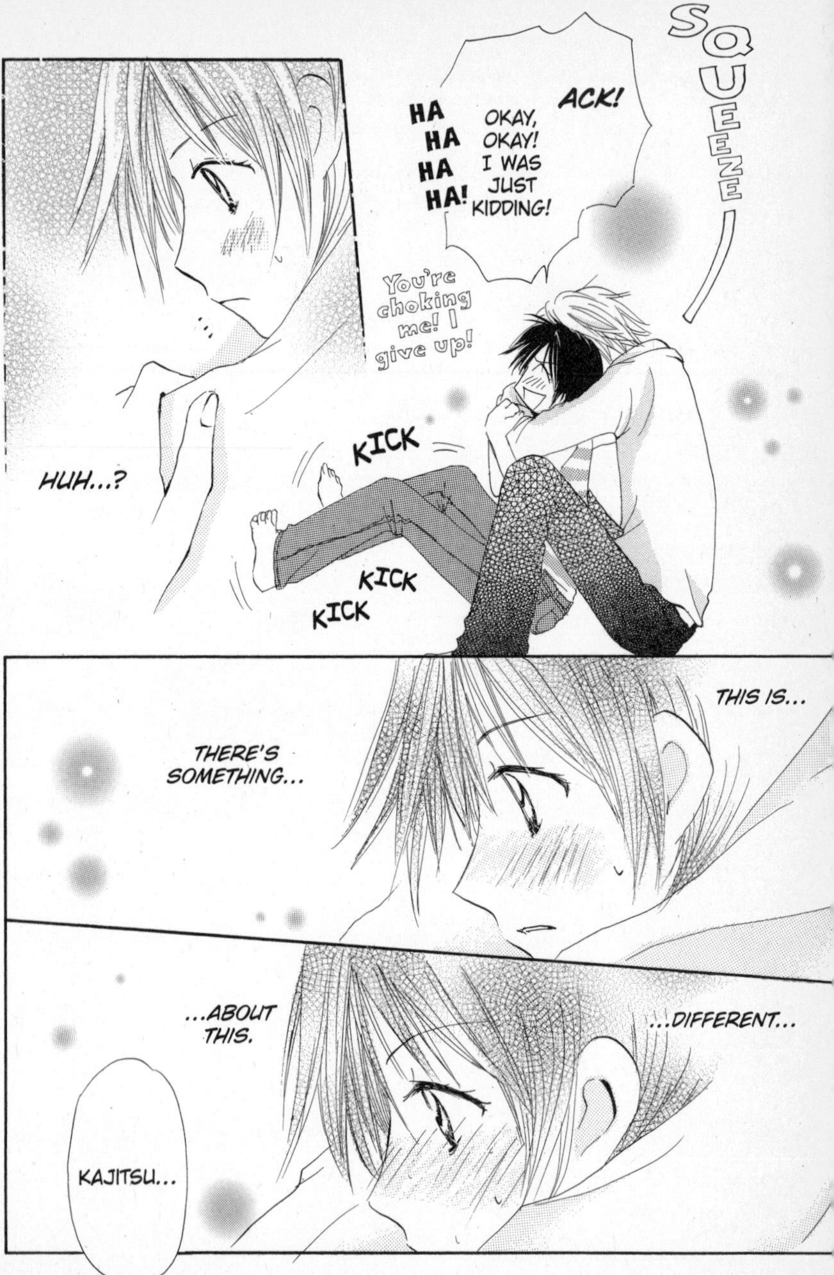
SQUEEZE
ACK!
OKAY, OKAY! I WAS JUST KIDDING!
HA HA HA HA!
You're choking me! I give up!
KICK
KICK
KICK
HUH...?
THIS IS...
THERE'S SOMETHING...
...DIFFERENT...
...ABOUT THIS.
KAJITSU...

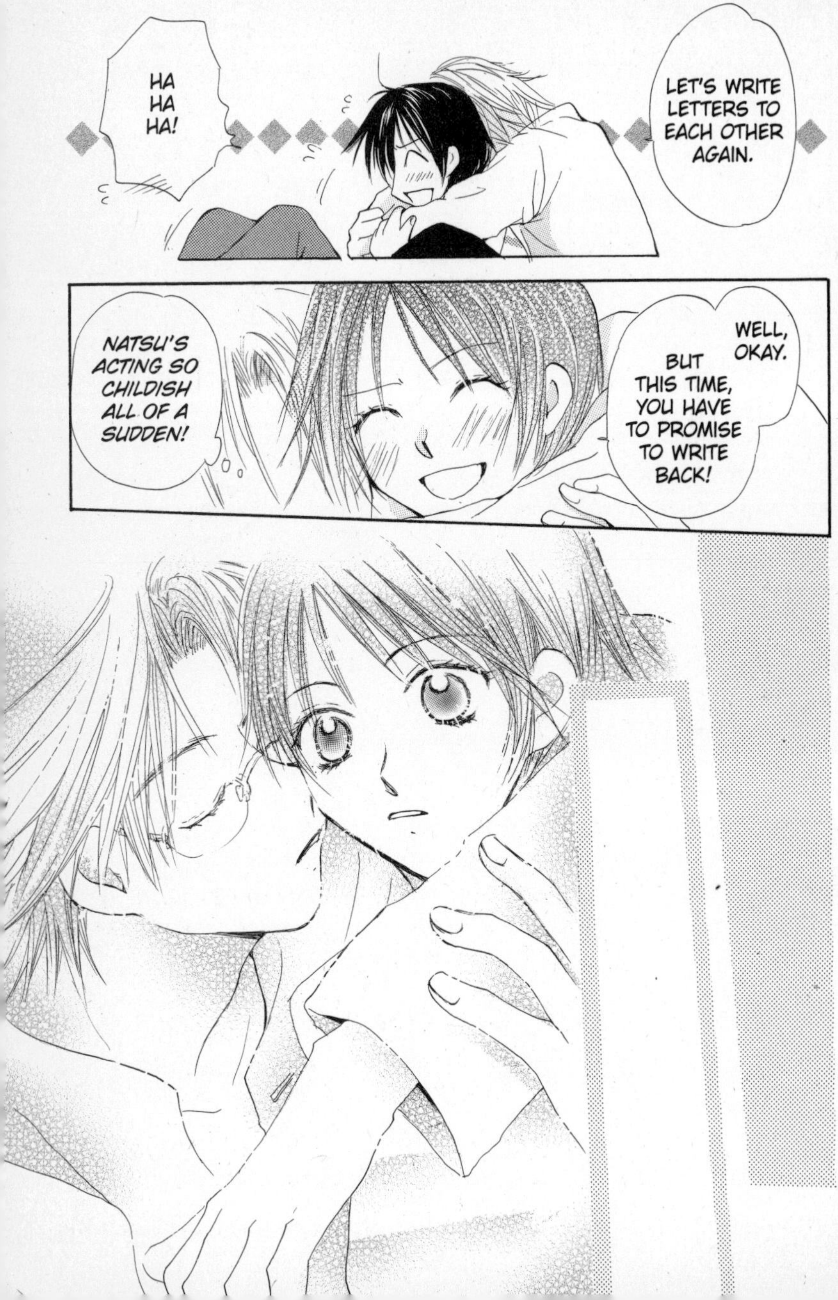
LET'S WRITE LETTERS TO EACH OTHER AGAIN.
HA HA HA!
WELL, OKAY.
BUT THIS TIME, YOU HAVE TO PROMISE TO WRITE BACK!
NATSU'S ACTING SO CHILDISH ALL OF A SUDDEN!

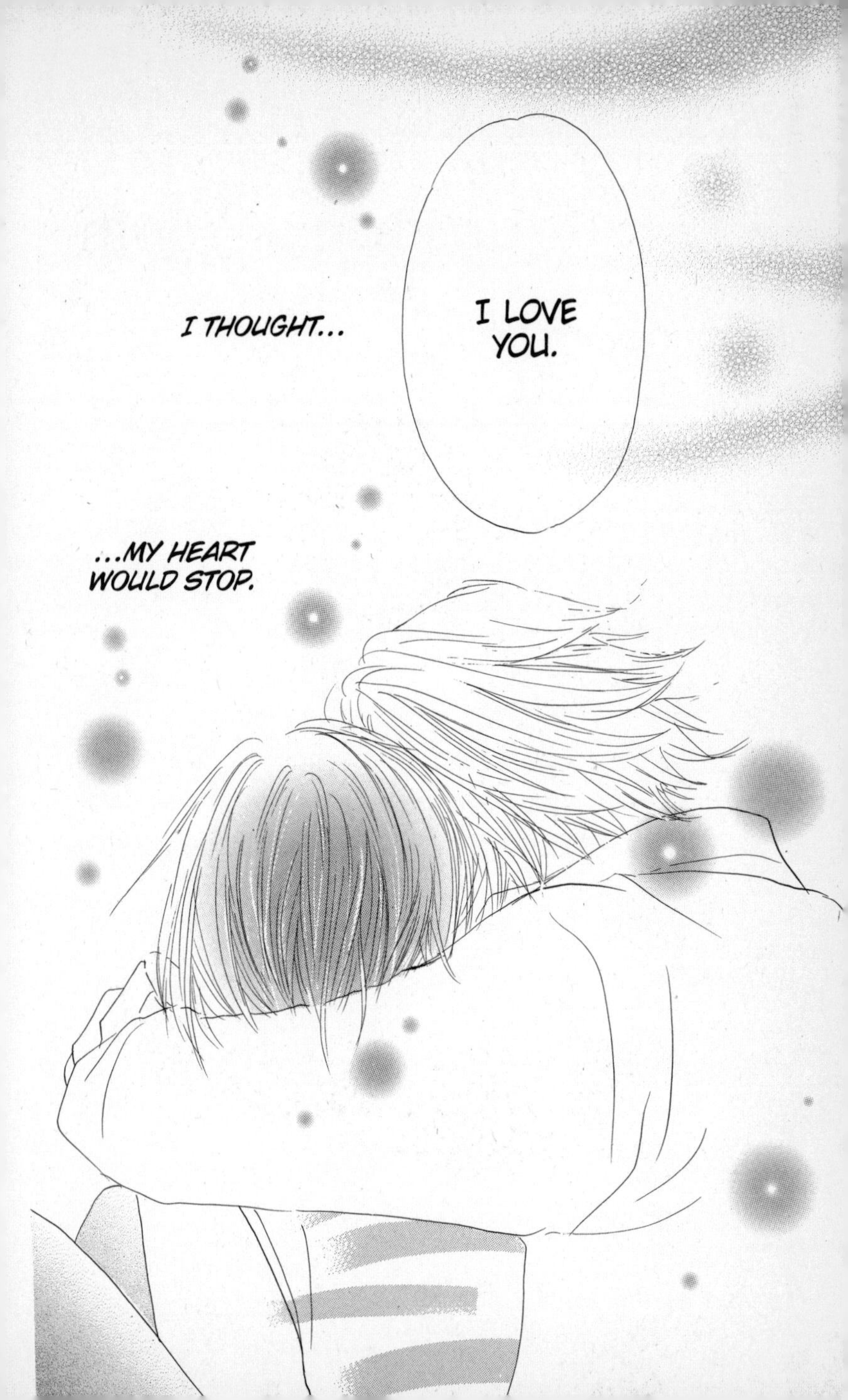
I LOVE YOU.
I THOUGHT...
...MY HEART WOULD STOP.

#10 Rhapsody of Youth

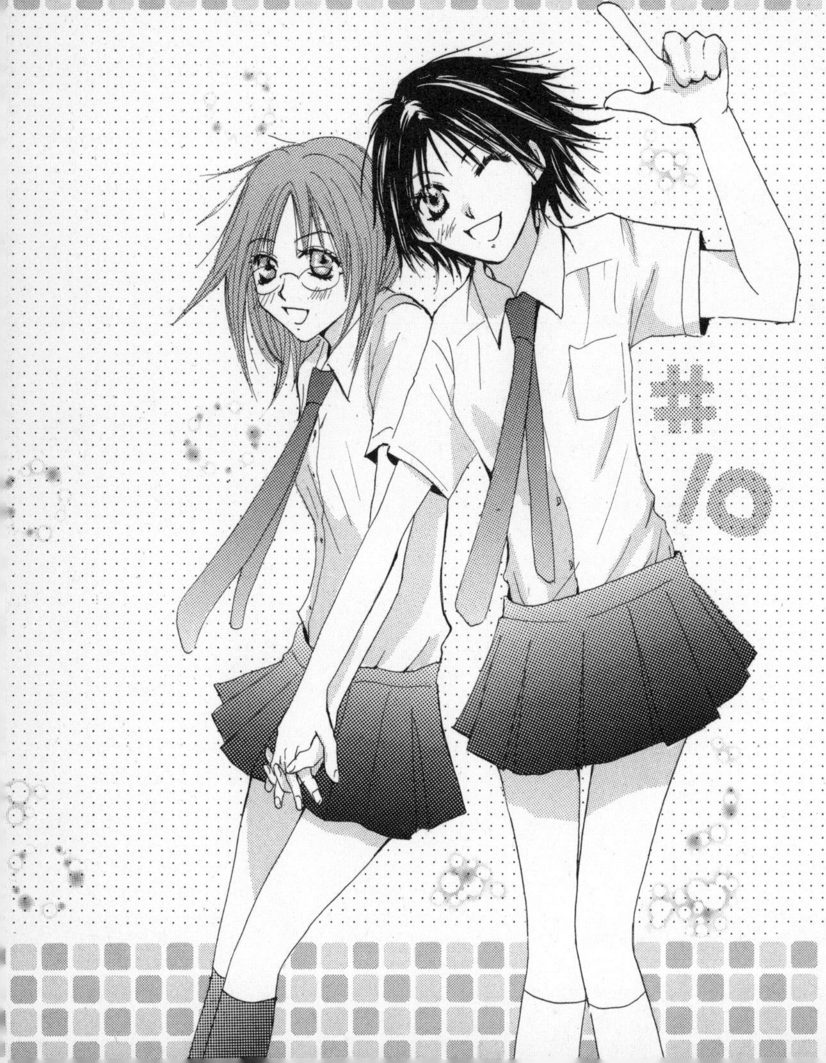
#10

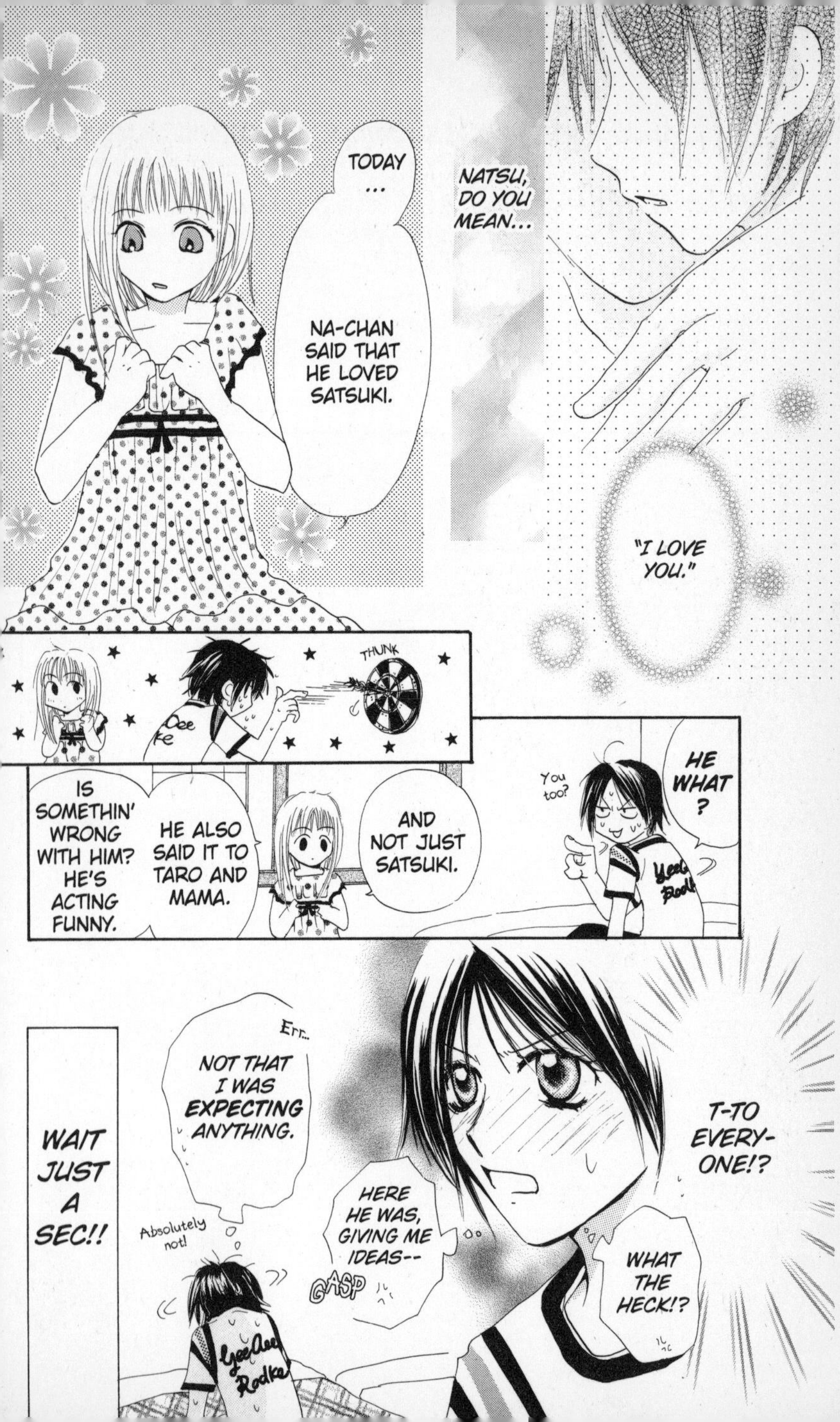
NATSU, DO YOU MEAN...
"I LOVE YOU."
TODAY ...
NA-CHAN SAID THAT HE LOVED SATSUKI.
THUNK
HE WHAT?
You too?
AND NOT JUST SATSUKI.
HE ALSO SAID IT TO TARO AND MAMA.
IS SOMETHIN' WRONG WITH HIM? HE'S ACTING FUNNY.
T-TO EVERY-ONE!?
WHAT THE HECK!?
HERE HE WAS, GIVING ME IDEAS--
GASP
Err...
NOT THAT I WAS EXPECTING ANYTHING.
Absolutely not!
WAIT JUST A SEC!!

crossroad Chapter 10: Rhapsody of Youth

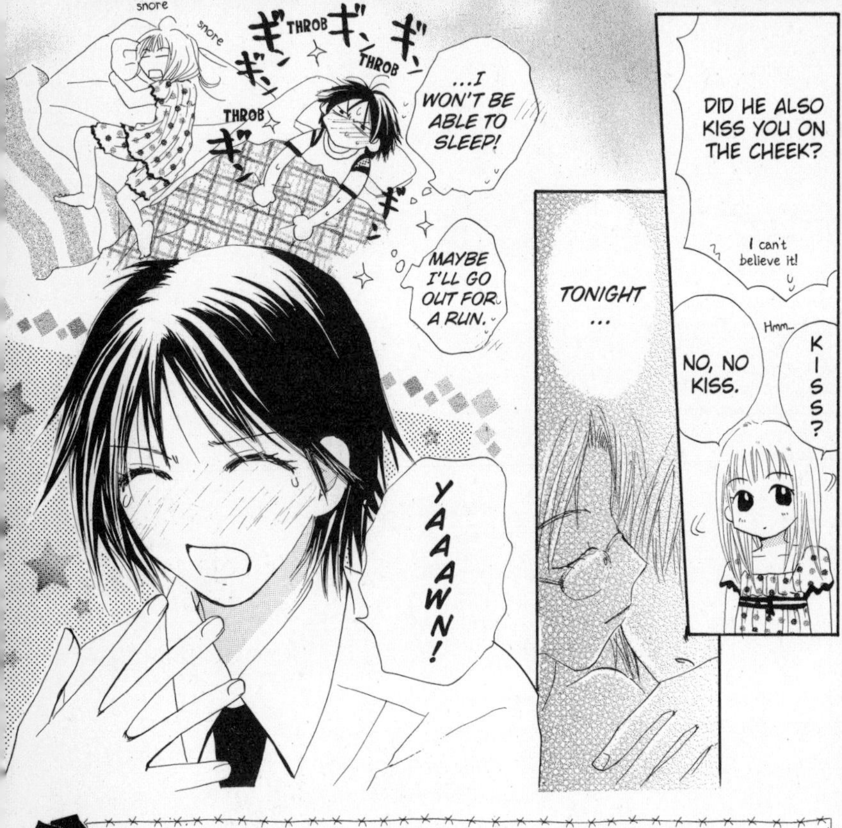
DID HE ALSO KISS YOU ON THE CHEEK?
I can't believe it!
KISS?
Hmm...
NO, NO KISS.
TONIGHT ...
THROB
THROB
THROB
...I WON'T BE ABLE TO SLEEP!
snore
snore
MAYBE I'LL GO OUT FOR A RUN.
YAAAAWN!

Every time I publish a manga, I wind up talking about some trip I went on. But ever since I started Crossroad, I haven't traveled anywhere at all. I don't really have the energy...or time or money anyway. I used to know exactly who I planned to travel with, but lately all my friends are into "going on an adventure that doesn't take money!" I'm still thinking, "As long as it's got a roof, I can sleep there," but my friends are like, "Even if doesn't have a roof, it's not a problem!" I think they've got a survival spirit watching over them. Speaking of which, I changed the location of my office. Guess that counts as traveling, if only a little. Now I don't have to listen to those damn temple drums every morning -- and all the dead bodies are gone! Banzai!!

Move on!! ⑤

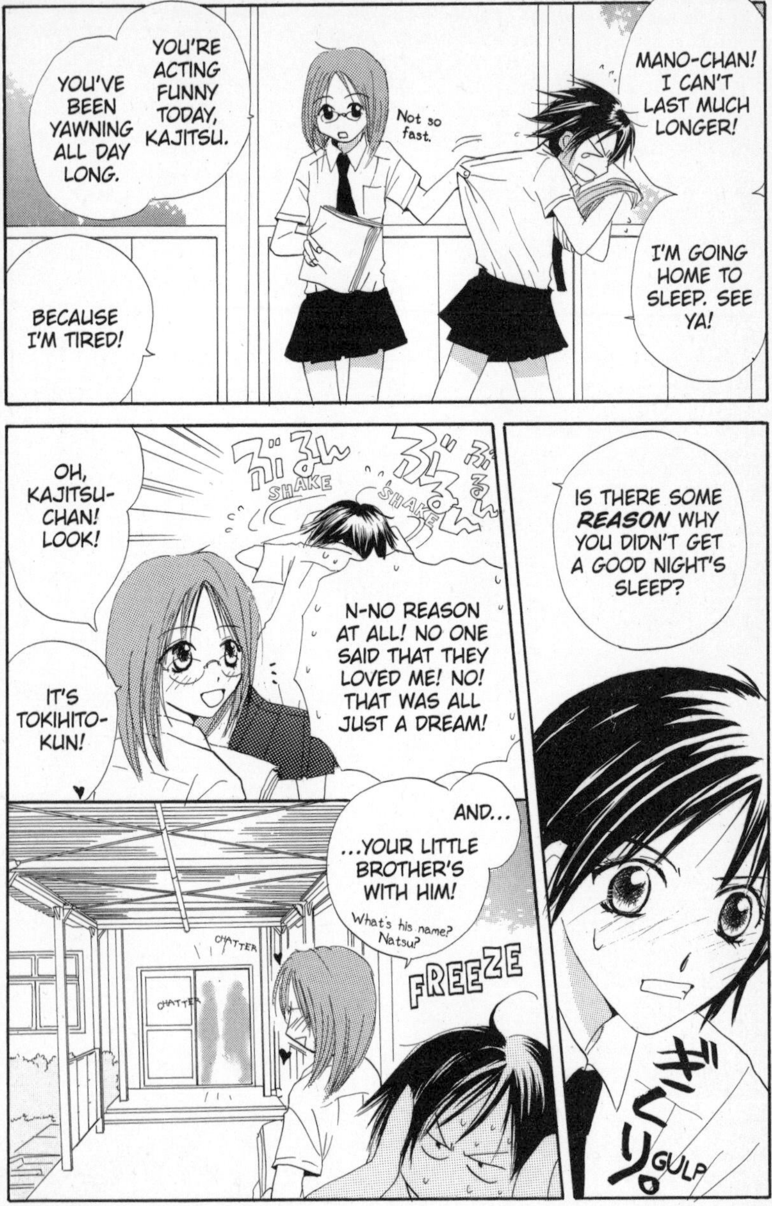
MANO-CHAN! I CAN'T LAST MUCH LONGER!
I'M GOING HOME TO SLEEP. SEE YA!
Not so fast.
YOU'RE ACTING FUNNY TODAY, KAJITSU.
YOU'VE BEEN YAWNING ALL DAY LONG.
BECAUSE I'M TIRED!
IS THERE SOME ***REASON*** WHY YOU DIDN'T GET A GOOD NIGHT'S SLEEP?
ぎくり。
GULP
ぶるん
SHAKE
ぶるん
ぶるん
SHAKE
N-NO REASON AT ALL! NO ONE SAID THAT THEY LOVED ME! NO! THAT WAS ALL JUST A DREAM!
OH, KAJITSU-CHAN! LOOK!
IT'S TOKIHITO-KUN!
AND...
...YOUR LITTLE BROTHER'S WITH HIM!
What's his name? Natsu?
FREEZE
CHATTER
CHATTER

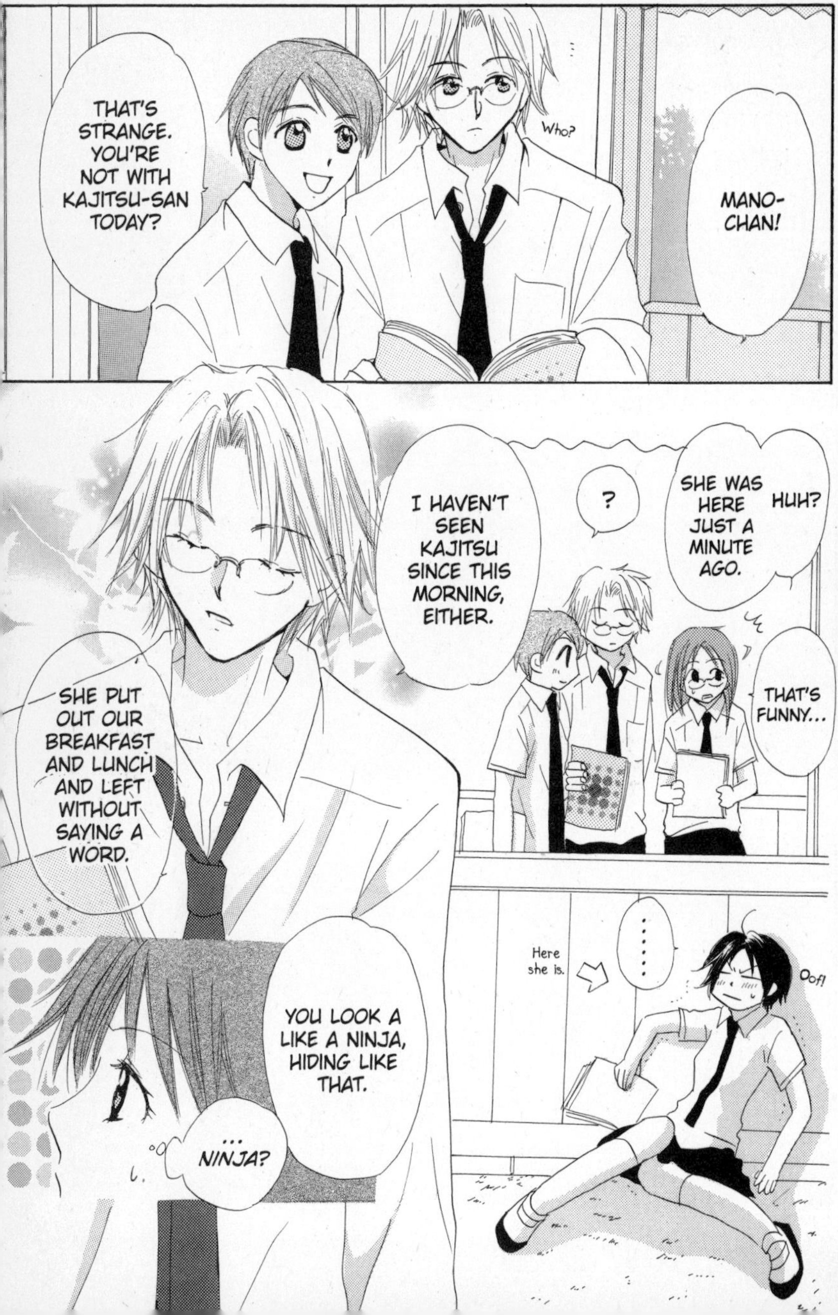
MANO-CHAN!
Who?
THAT'S STRANGE. YOU'RE NOT WITH KAJITSU-SAN TODAY?
HUH?
SHE WAS HERE JUST A MINUTE AGO.
?
THAT'S FUNNY...
I HAVEN'T SEEN KAJITSU SINCE THIS MORNING, EITHER.
SHE PUT OUT OUR BREAKFAST AND LUNCH AND LEFT WITHOUT SAYING A WORD.
Oof!
......
Here she is.
YOU LOOK A LIKE A NINJA, HIDING LIKE THAT.
...NINJA?

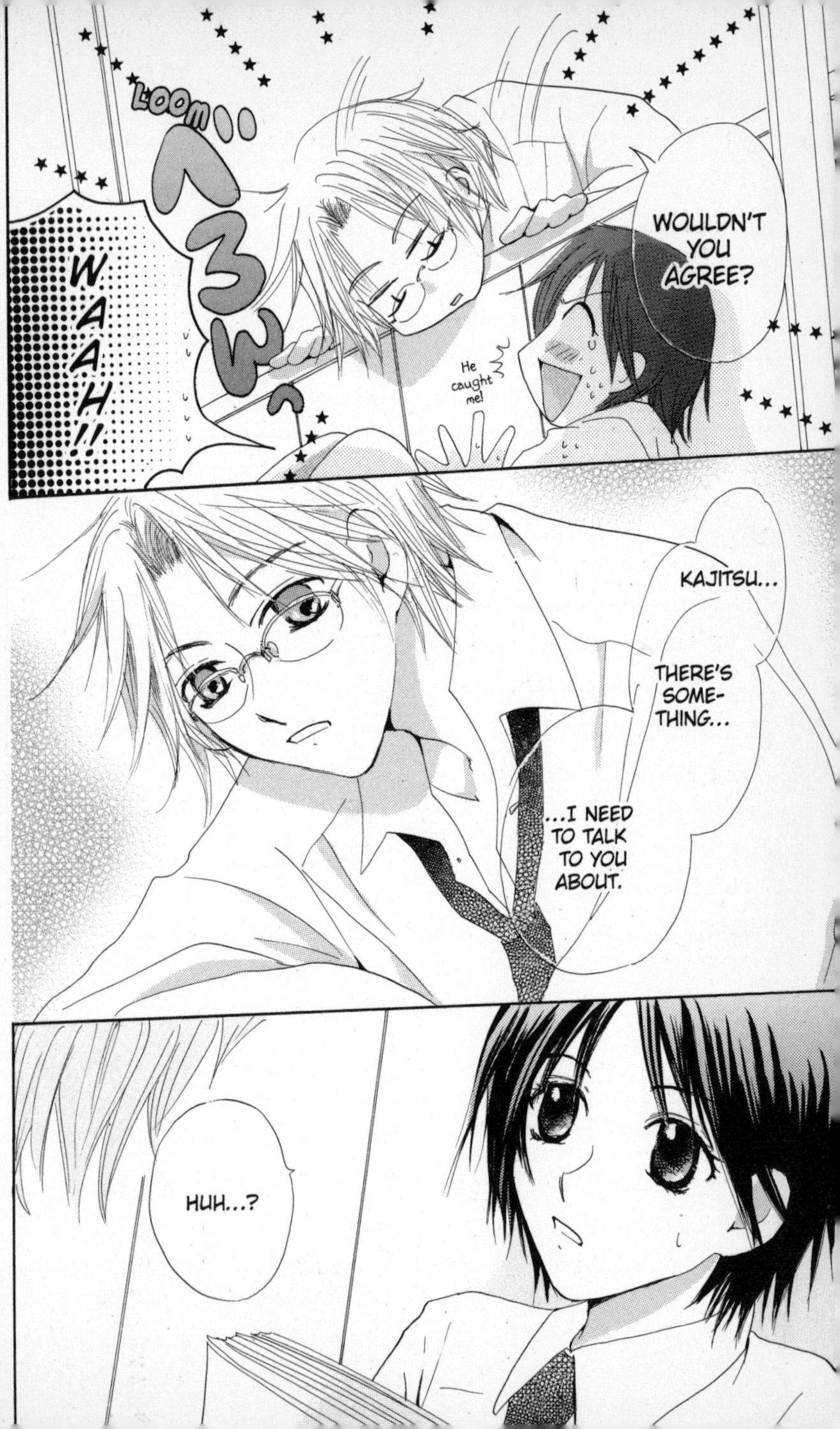
WOULDN'T YOU AGREE?
He caught me!
WAAH!!
KAJITSU...
THERE'S SOME-THING...
...I NEED TO TALK TO YOU ABOUT.
HUH...?

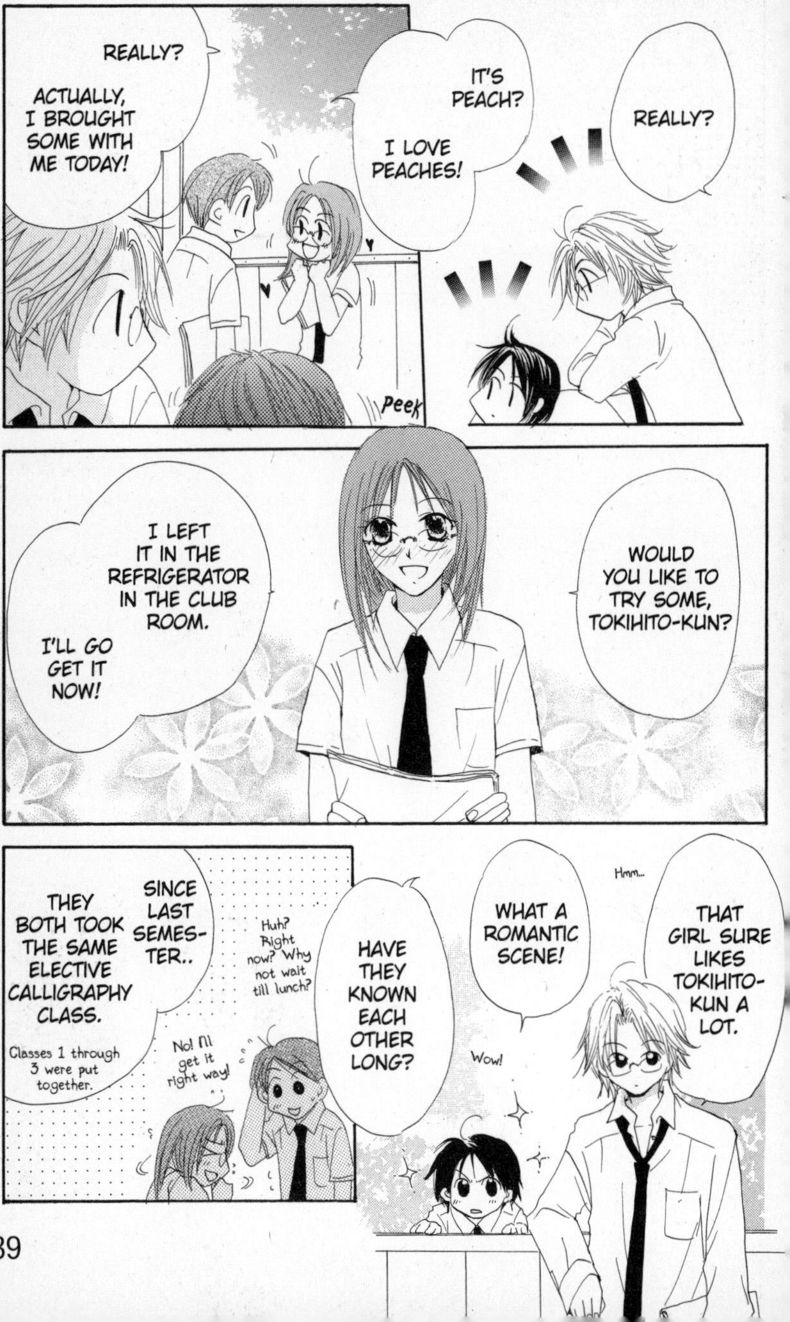
REALLY?
IT'S PEACH? I LOVE PEACHES!
REALLY? ACTUALLY, I BROUGHT SOME WITH ME TODAY!
Peek
WOULD YOU LIKE TO TRY SOME, TOKIHITO-KUN?
I LEFT IT IN THE REFRIGERATOR IN THE CLUB ROOM. I'LL GO GET IT NOW!
Hmm...
THAT GIRL SURE LIKES TOKIHITO-KUN A LOT.
WHAT A ROMANTIC SCENE!
Wow!
HAVE THEY KNOWN EACH OTHER LONG?
SINCE LAST SEMES-TER..
THEY BOTH TOOK THE SAME ELECTIVE CALLIGRAPHY CLASS.
Classes 1 through 3 were put together.
Huh? Right now? Why not wait till lunch?
No! I'll get it right way!

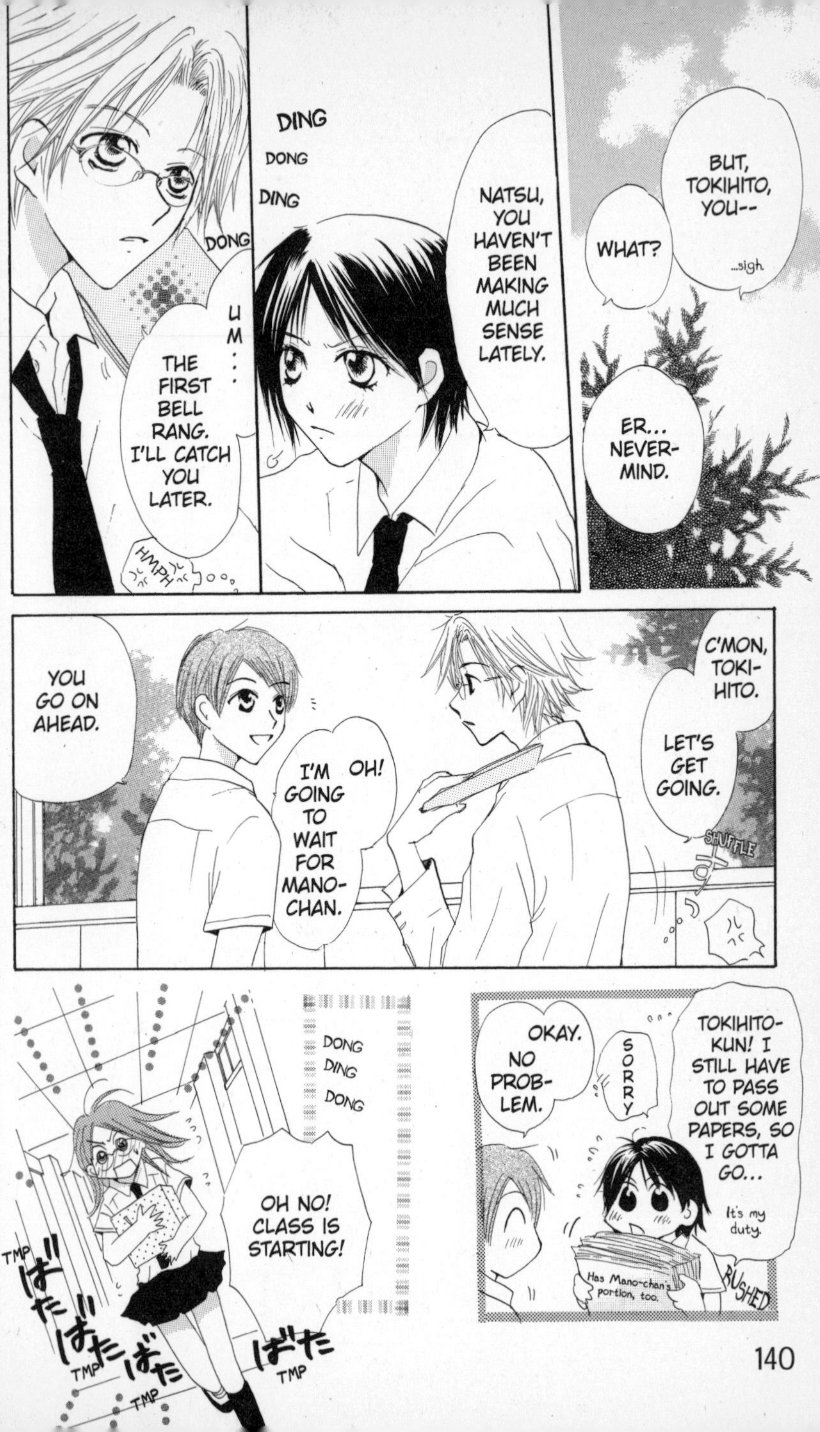
BUT, TOKIHITO, YOU--
WHAT?
...sigh.
ER... NEVER-MIND.
DING
DONG
DING
DONG
NATSU, YOU HAVEN'T BEEN MAKING MUCH SENSE LATELY.
UM...
THE FIRST BELL RANG. I'LL CATCH YOU LATER.
HMPH
C'MON, TOKI-HITO.
LET'S GET GOING.
SHUFFLE
OH!
I'M GOING TO WAIT FOR MANO-CHAN.
YOU GO ON AHEAD.
TOKIHITO-KUN! I STILL HAVE TO PASS OUT SOME PAPERS, SO I GOTTA GO...
It's my duty.
SORRY
OKAY. NO PROB-LEM.
Has Mano-chan's portion, too.
RUSHED
DONG
DING
DONG
OH NO! CLASS IS STARTING!
TMP ばた
TMP ばた
TMP ばた
TMP ばた

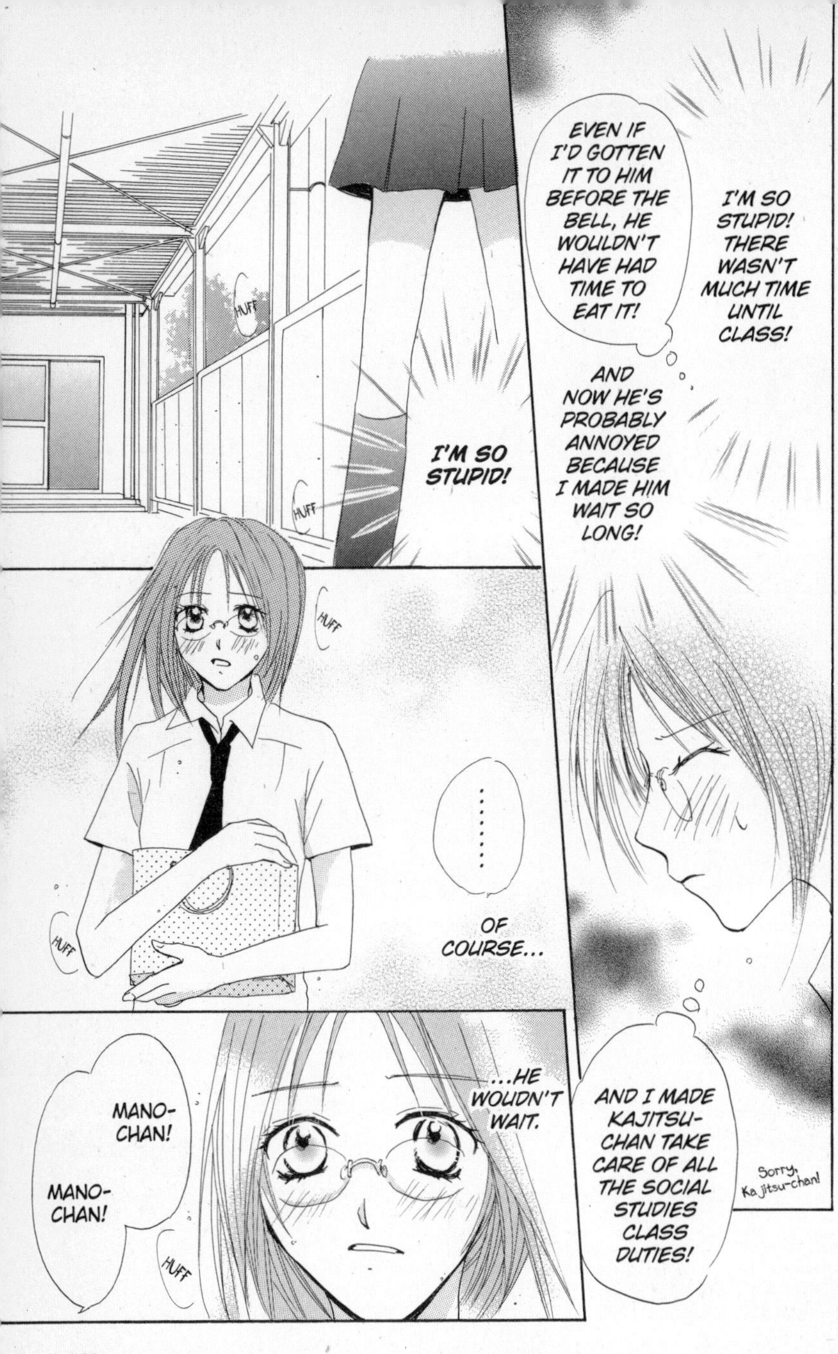
I'M SO STUPID! THERE WASN'T MUCH TIME UNTIL CLASS!
EVEN IF I'D GOTTEN IT TO HIM BEFORE THE BELL, HE WOULDN'T HAVE HAD TIME TO EAT IT!
AND NOW HE'S PROBABLY ANNOYED BECAUSE I MADE HIM WAIT SO LONG!
AND I MADE KAJITSU-CHAN TAKE CARE OF ALL THE SOCIAL STUDIES CLASS DUTIES!
Sorry, Kajitsu-chan!
HUFF
I'M SO STUPID!
HUFF
HUFF
......
OF COURSE...
HUFF
...HE WOUDN'T WAIT.
MANO-CHAN!
MANO-CHAN!
HUFF

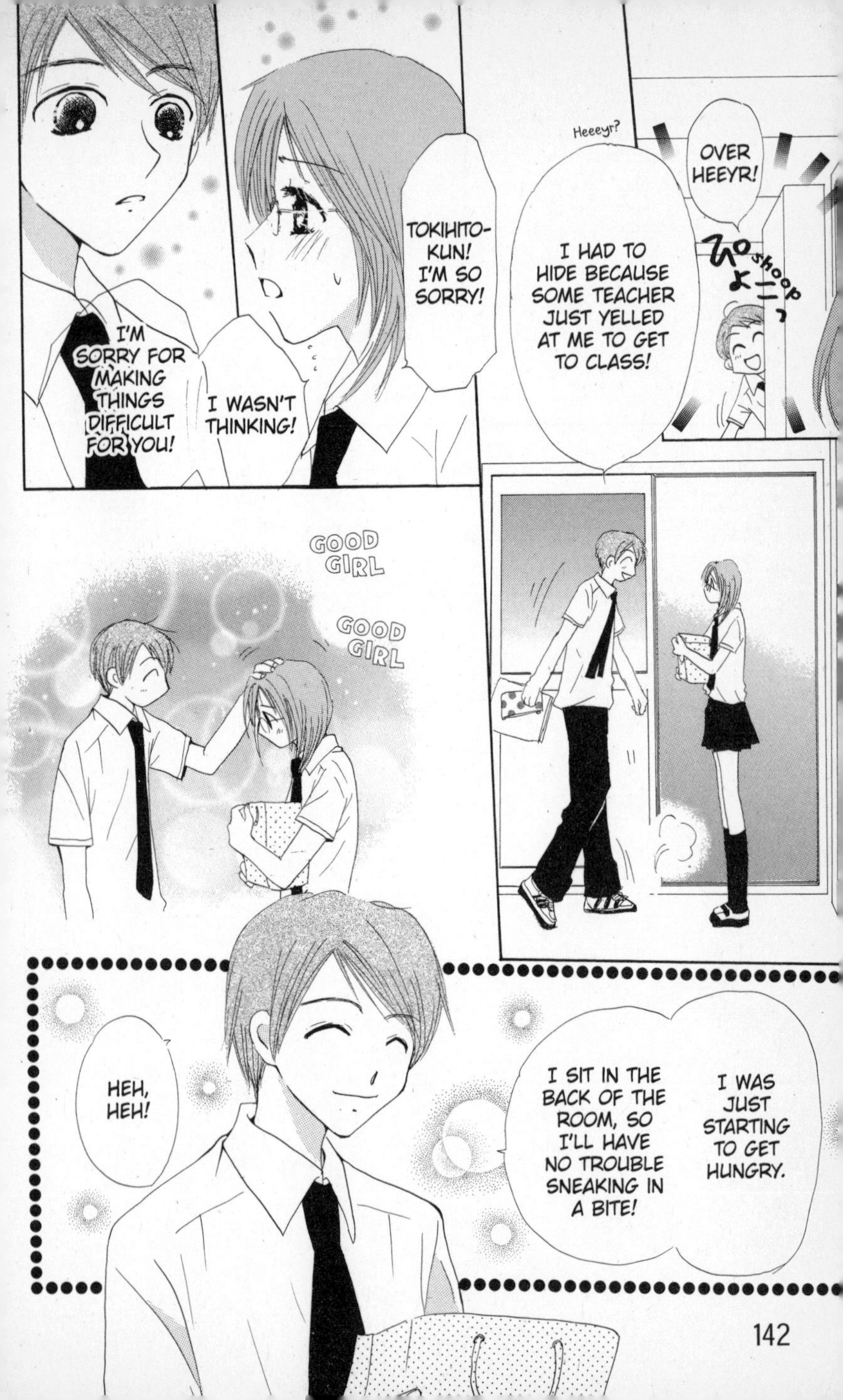
OVER HEEYR!
shoop
Heeeyr?
I HAD TO HIDE BECAUSE SOME TEACHER JUST YELLED AT ME TO GET TO CLASS!
TOKIHITO-KUN! I'M SO SORRY!
I WASN'T THINKING!
I'M SORRY FOR MAKING THINGS DIFFICULT FOR YOU!
GOOD GIRL
GOOD GIRL
I WAS JUST STARTING TO GET HUNGRY.
I SIT IN THE BACK OF THE ROOM, SO I'LL HAVE NO TROUBLE SNEAKING IN A BITE!
HEH, HEH!

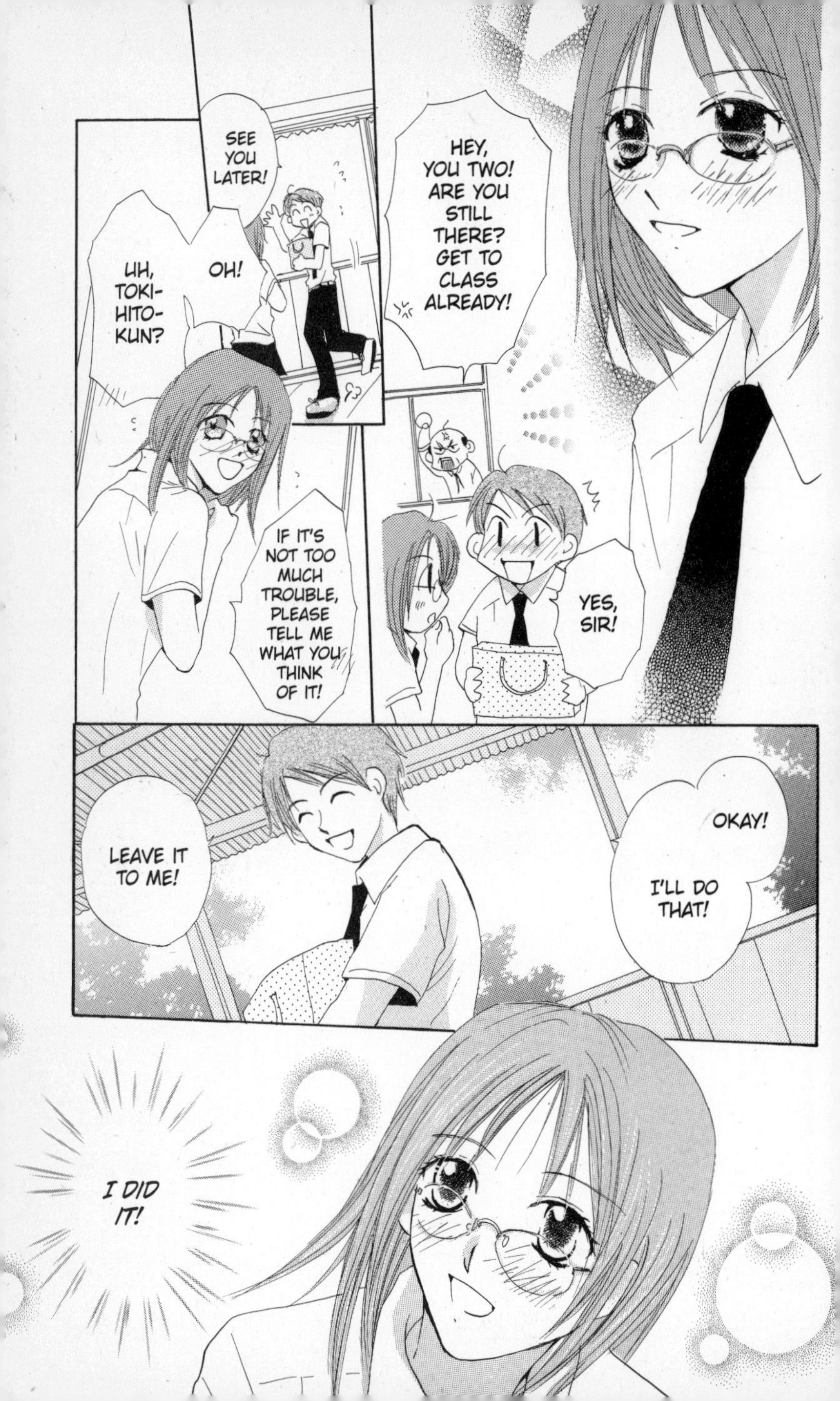
HEY, YOU TWO! ARE YOU STILL THERE? GET TO CLASS ALREADY!
YES, SIR!
SEE YOU LATER!
OH!
UH, TOKI-HITO-KUN?
IF IT'S NOT TOO MUCH TROUBLE, PLEASE TELL ME WHAT YOU THINK OF IT!
OKAY!
I'LL DO THAT!
LEAVE IT TO ME!
I DID IT!

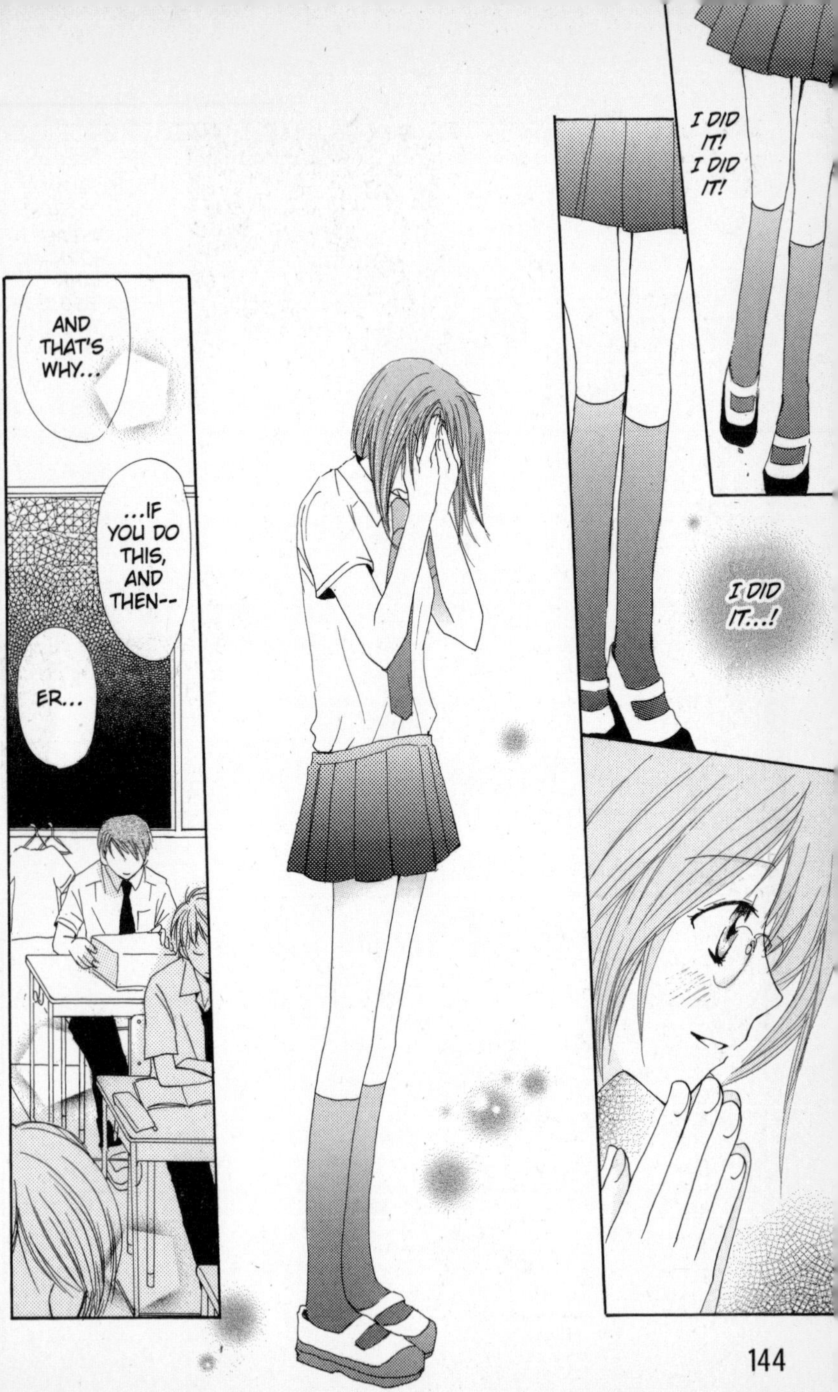
I DID IT! I DID IT!
I DID IT...!
AND THAT'S WHY...
...IF YOU DO THIS, AND THEN--
ER...

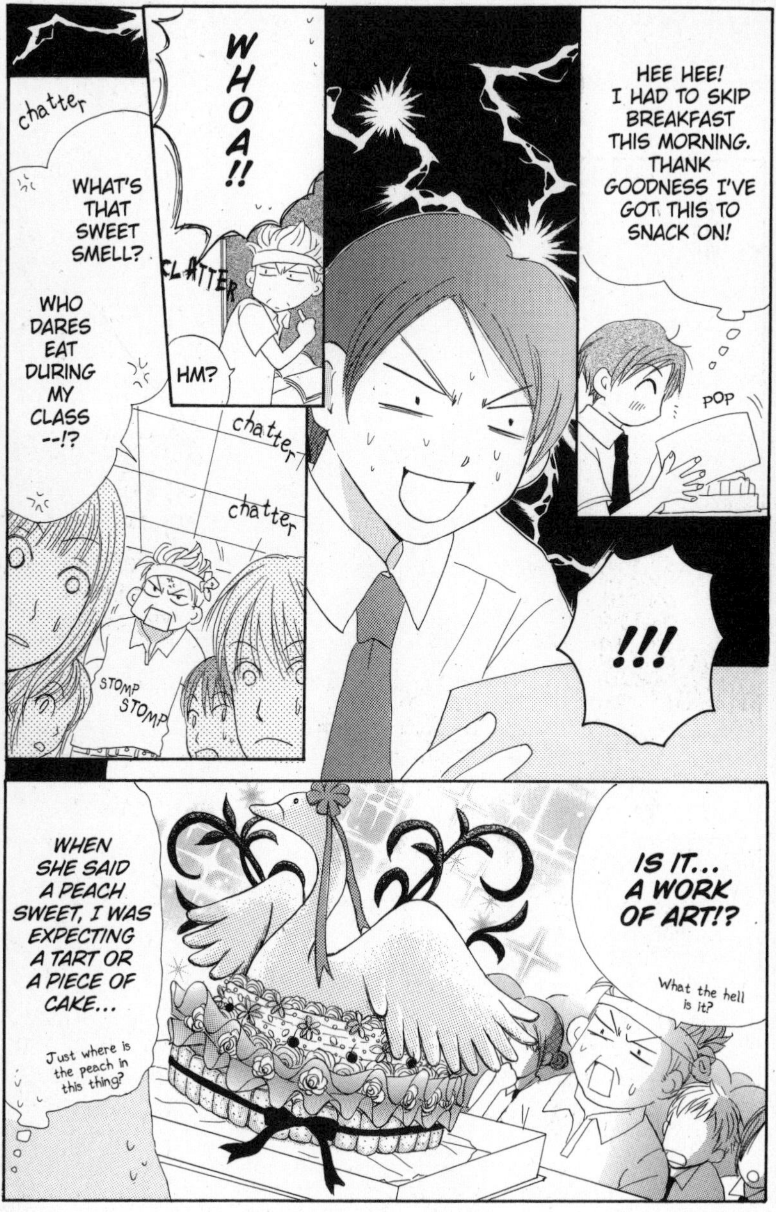
HEE HEE! I HAD TO SKIP BREAKFAST THIS MORNING. THANK GOODNESS I'VE GOT THIS TO SNACK ON!
POP
!!!
WHOA!!
CLATTER
HM?
chatter
WHAT'S THAT SWEET SMELL?
WHO DARES EAT DURING MY CLASS --!?
chatter
chatter
STOMP STOMP
IS IT... A WORK OF ART!?
What the hell is it?
WHEN SHE SAID A PEACH SWEET, I WAS EXPECTING A TART OR A PIECE OF CAKE...
Just where is the peach in this thing?

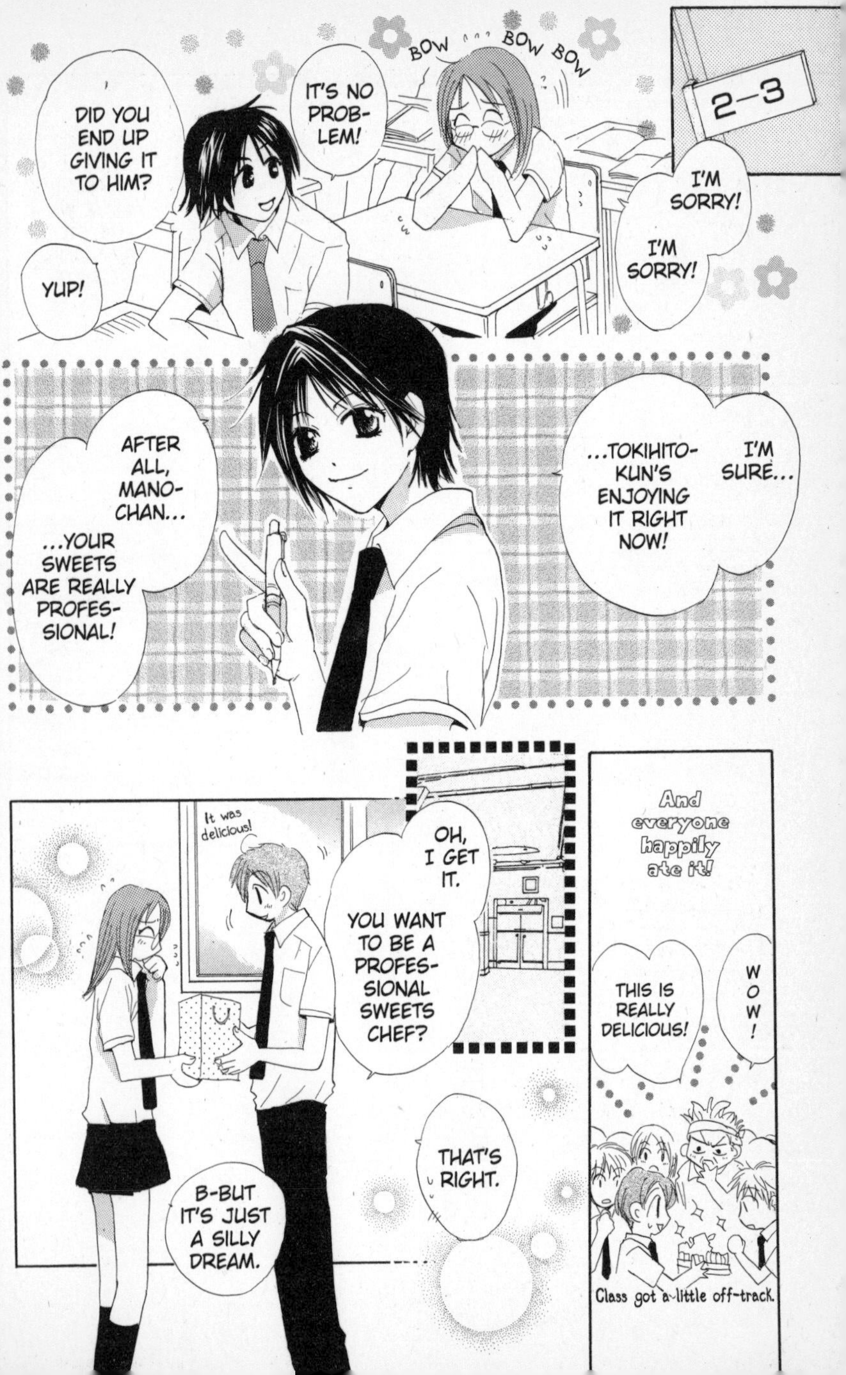
2-3
I'M SORRY!
I'M SORRY!
BOW BOW BOW
IT'S NO PROBLEM!
DID YOU END UP GIVING IT TO HIM?
YUP!
I'M SURE...
...TOKIHITO-KUN'S ENJOYING IT RIGHT NOW!
AFTER ALL, MANO-CHAN...
...YOUR SWEETS ARE REALLY PROFESSIONAL!
And everyone happily ate it!
WOW!
THIS IS REALLY DELICIOUS!
Class got a little off-track.
It was delicious!
OH, I GET IT.
YOU WANT TO BE A PROFESSIONAL SWEETS CHEF?
THAT'S RIGHT.
B-BUT IT'S JUST A SILLY DREAM.

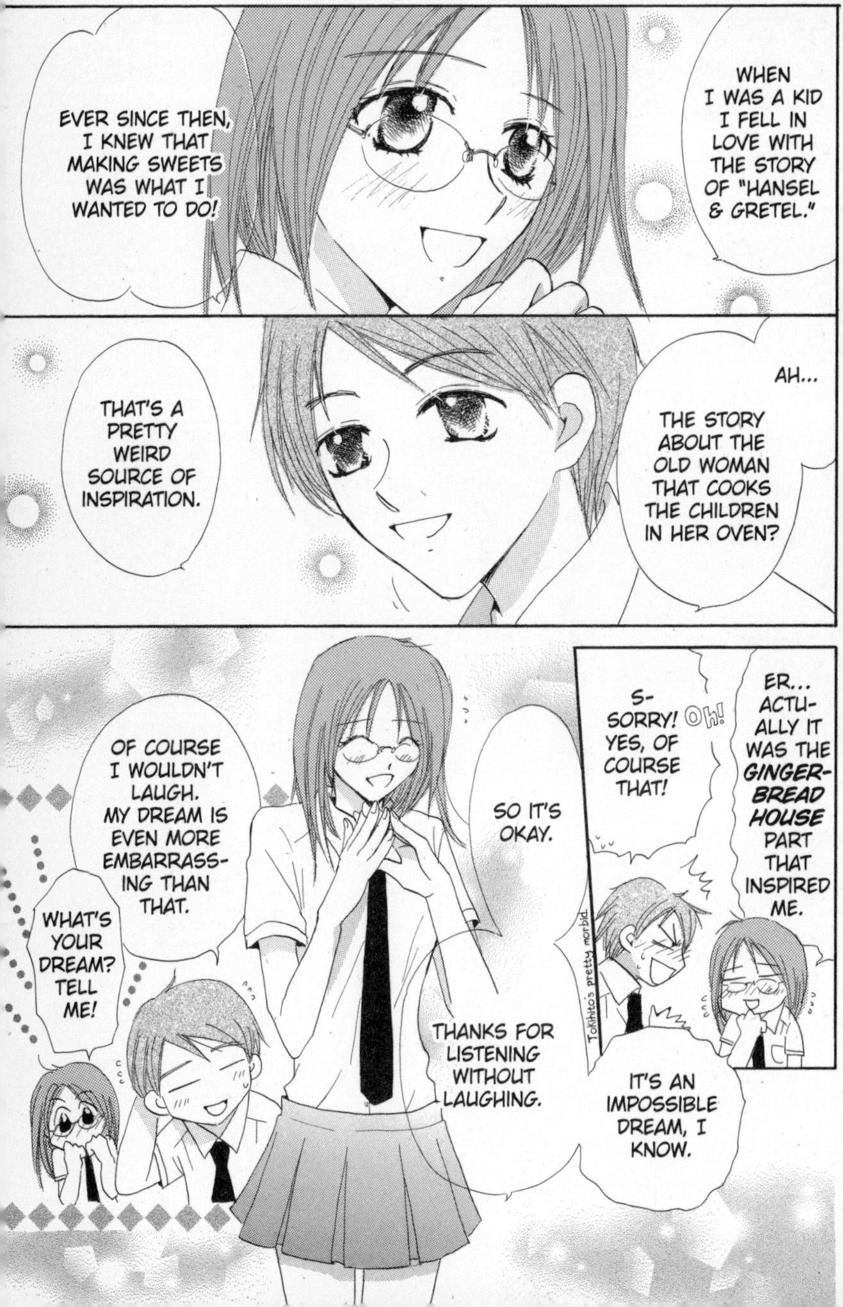
WHEN I WAS A KID I FELL IN LOVE WITH THE STORY OF "HANSEL & GRETEL."
EVER SINCE THEN, I KNEW THAT MAKING SWEETS WAS WHAT I WANTED TO DO!
AH...
THE STORY ABOUT THE OLD WOMAN THAT COOKS THE CHILDREN IN HER OVEN?
THAT'S A PRETTY WEIRD SOURCE OF INSPIRATION.
ER... ACTU-ALLY IT WAS THE *GINGER-BREAD HOUSE* PART THAT INSPIRED ME.
Oh!
S-SORRY! YES, OF COURSE THAT!
Tokihito's pretty morbid.
IT'S AN IMPOSSIBLE DREAM, I KNOW.
THANKS FOR LISTENING WITHOUT LAUGHING.
SO IT'S OKAY.
OF COURSE I WOULDN'T LAUGH. MY DREAM IS EVEN MORE EMBARRASS-ING THAN THAT.
WHAT'S YOUR DREAM? TELL ME!

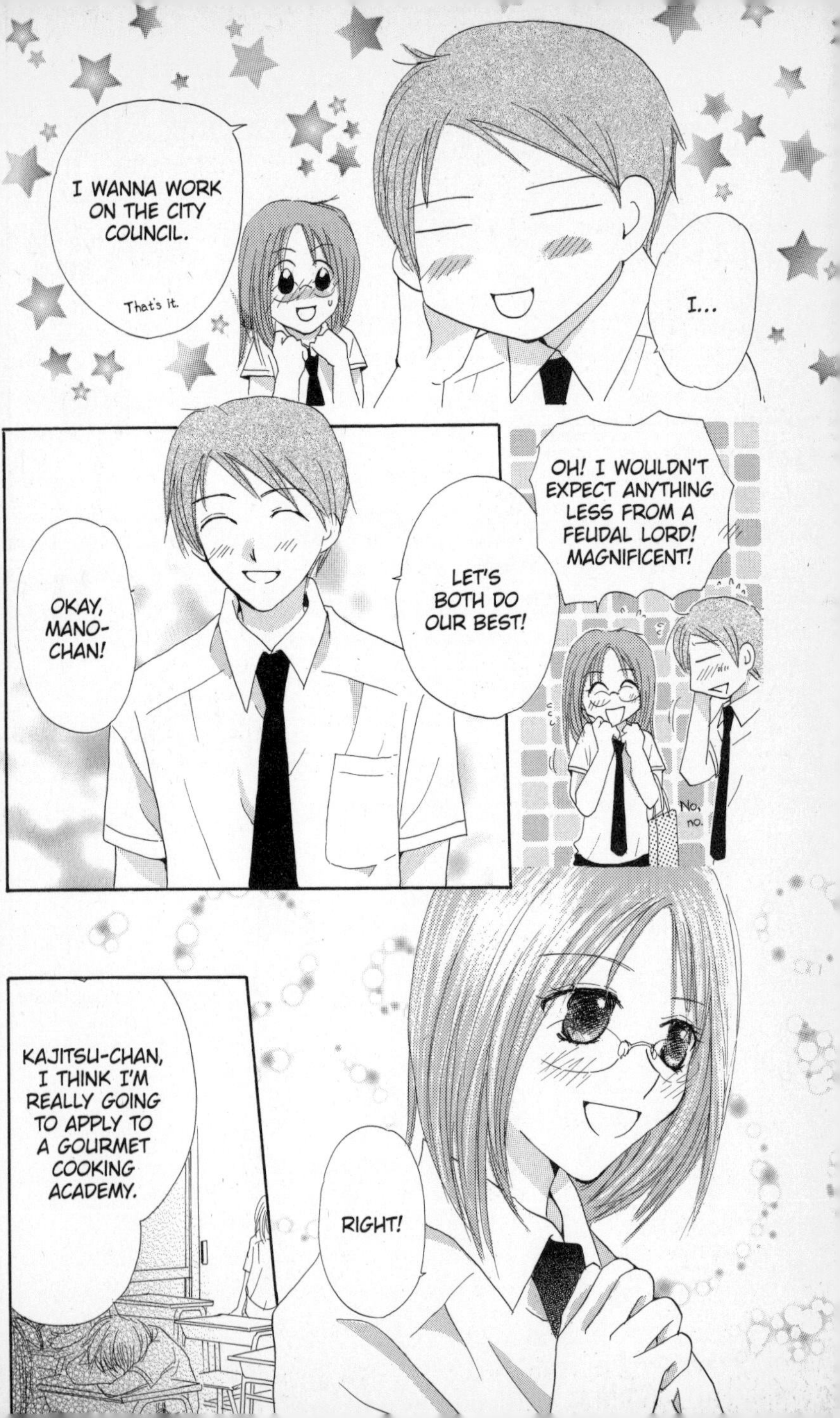
I...
I WANNA WORK ON THE CITY COUNCIL.
That's it.
OH! I WOULDN'T EXPECT ANYTHING LESS FROM A FEUDAL LORD! MAGNIFICENT!
No, no.
LET'S BOTH DO OUR BEST!
OKAY, MANO-CHAN!
KAJITSU-CHAN, I THINK I'M REALLY GOING TO APPLY TO A GOURMET COOKING ACADEMY.
RIGHT!

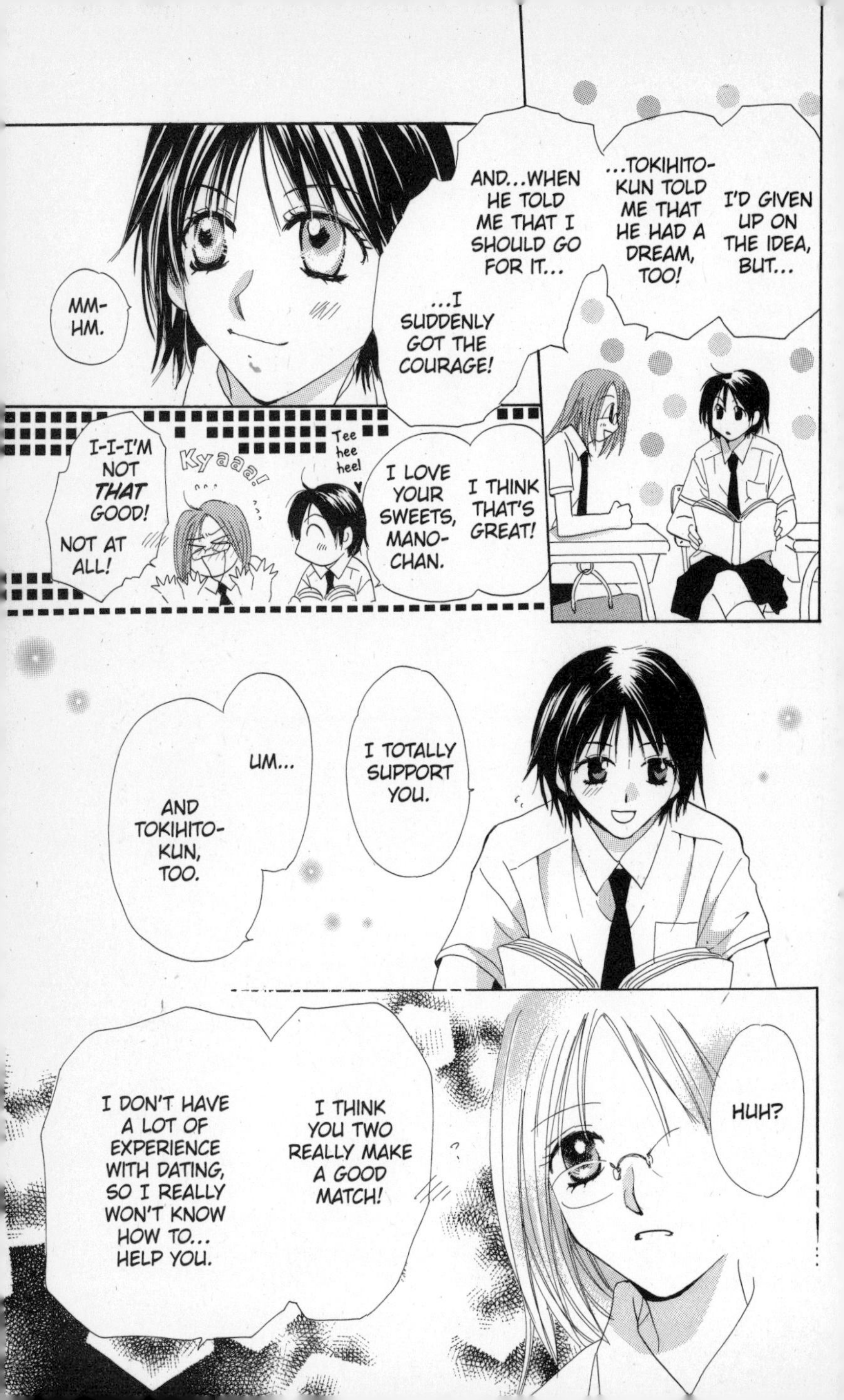
I'D GIVEN UP ON THE IDEA, BUT...
...TOKIHITO-KUN TOLD ME THAT HE HAD A DREAM, TOO!
AND...WHEN HE TOLD ME THAT I SHOULD GO FOR IT...
...I SUDDENLY GOT THE COURAGE!
MM-HM.
I THINK THAT'S GREAT!
I LOVE YOUR SWEETS, MANO-CHAN.
Tee hee hee!
Kyaaa!
I-I-I'M NOT *THAT* GOOD!
NOT AT ALL!
I TOTALLY SUPPORT YOU.
UM...
AND TOKIHITO-KUN, TOO.
HUH?
I THINK YOU TWO REALLY MAKE A GOOD MATCH!
I DON'T HAVE A LOT OF EXPERIENCE WITH DATING, SO I REALLY WON'T KNOW HOW TO... HELP YOU.

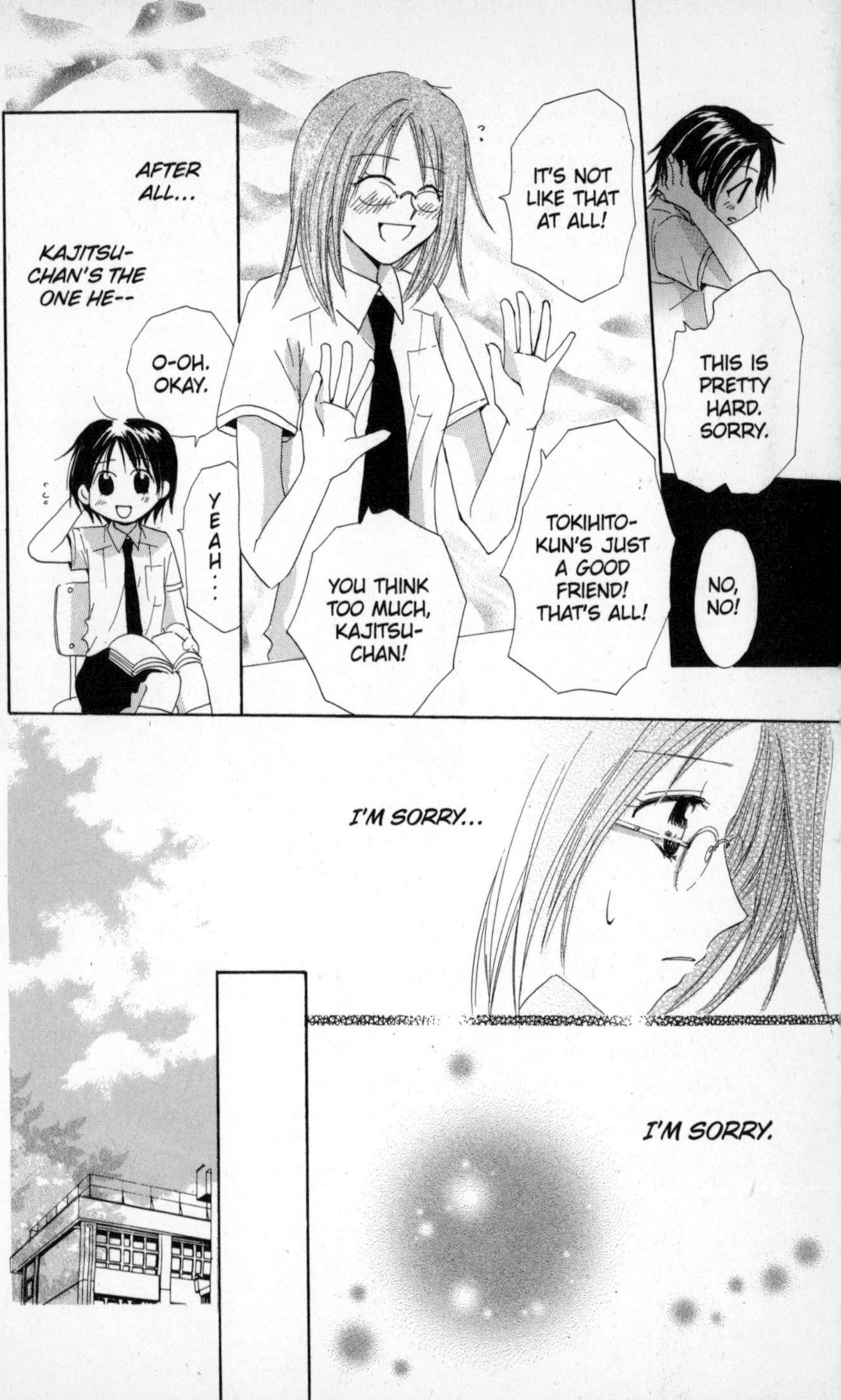
THIS IS PRETTY HARD. SORRY.
NO, NO!
IT'S NOT LIKE THAT AT ALL!
TOKIHITO-KUN'S JUST A GOOD FRIEND! THAT'S ALL!
YOU THINK TOO MUCH, KAJITSU-CHAN!
AFTER ALL...
KAJITSU-CHAN'S THE ONE HE--
O-OH. OKAY.
YEAH...
I'M SORRY...
I'M SORRY.

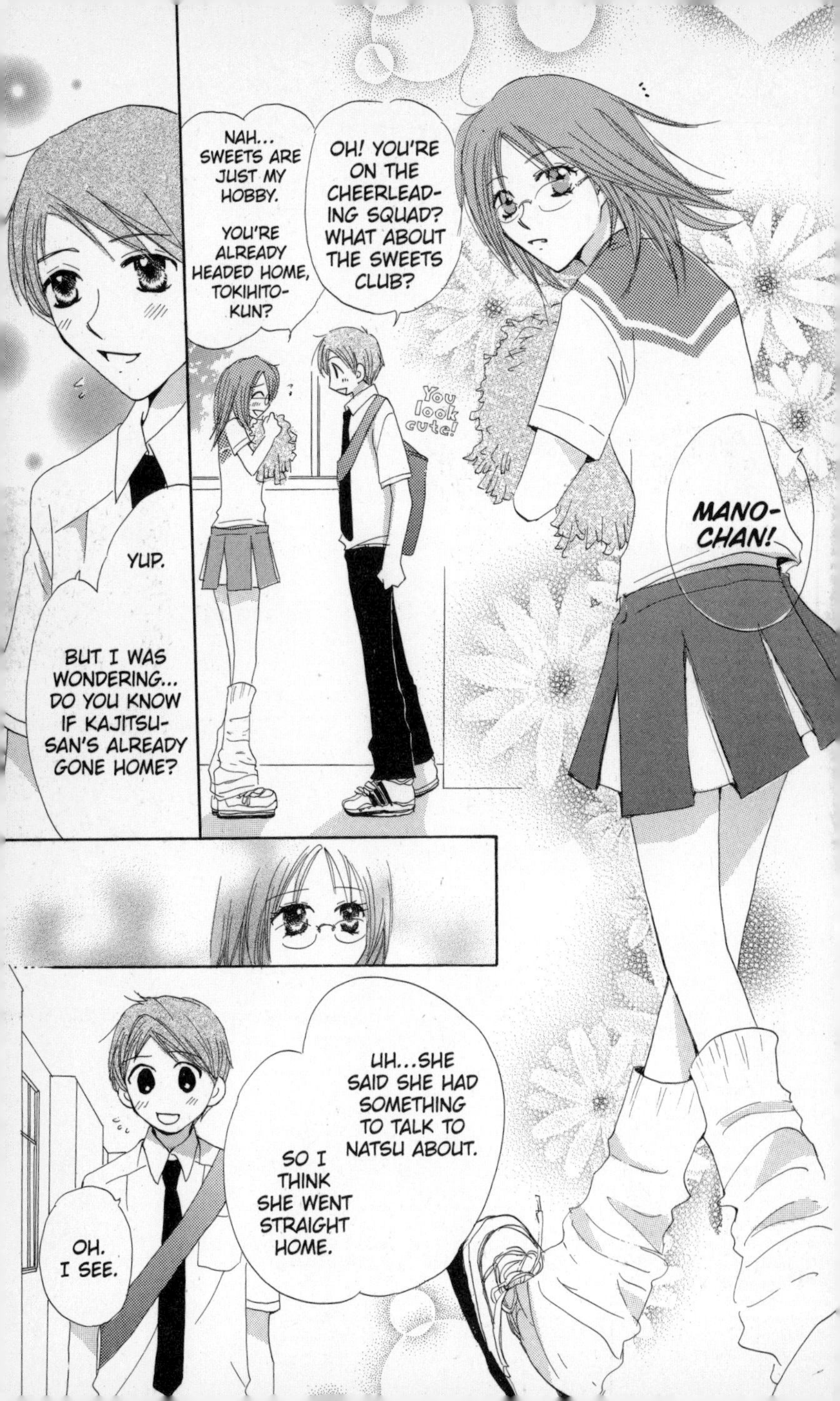
MANO-CHAN!
OH! YOU'RE ON THE CHEERLEAD-ING SQUAD? WHAT ABOUT THE SWEETS CLUB?
NAH... SWEETS ARE JUST MY HOBBY.
YOU'RE ALREADY HEADED HOME, TOKIHITO-KUN?
You look cute!
YUP.
BUT I WAS WONDERING... DO YOU KNOW IF KAJITSU-SAN'S ALREADY GONE HOME?
UH...SHE SAID SHE HAD SOMETHING TO TALK TO NATSU ABOUT.
SO I THINK SHE WENT STRAIGHT HOME.
OH. I SEE.

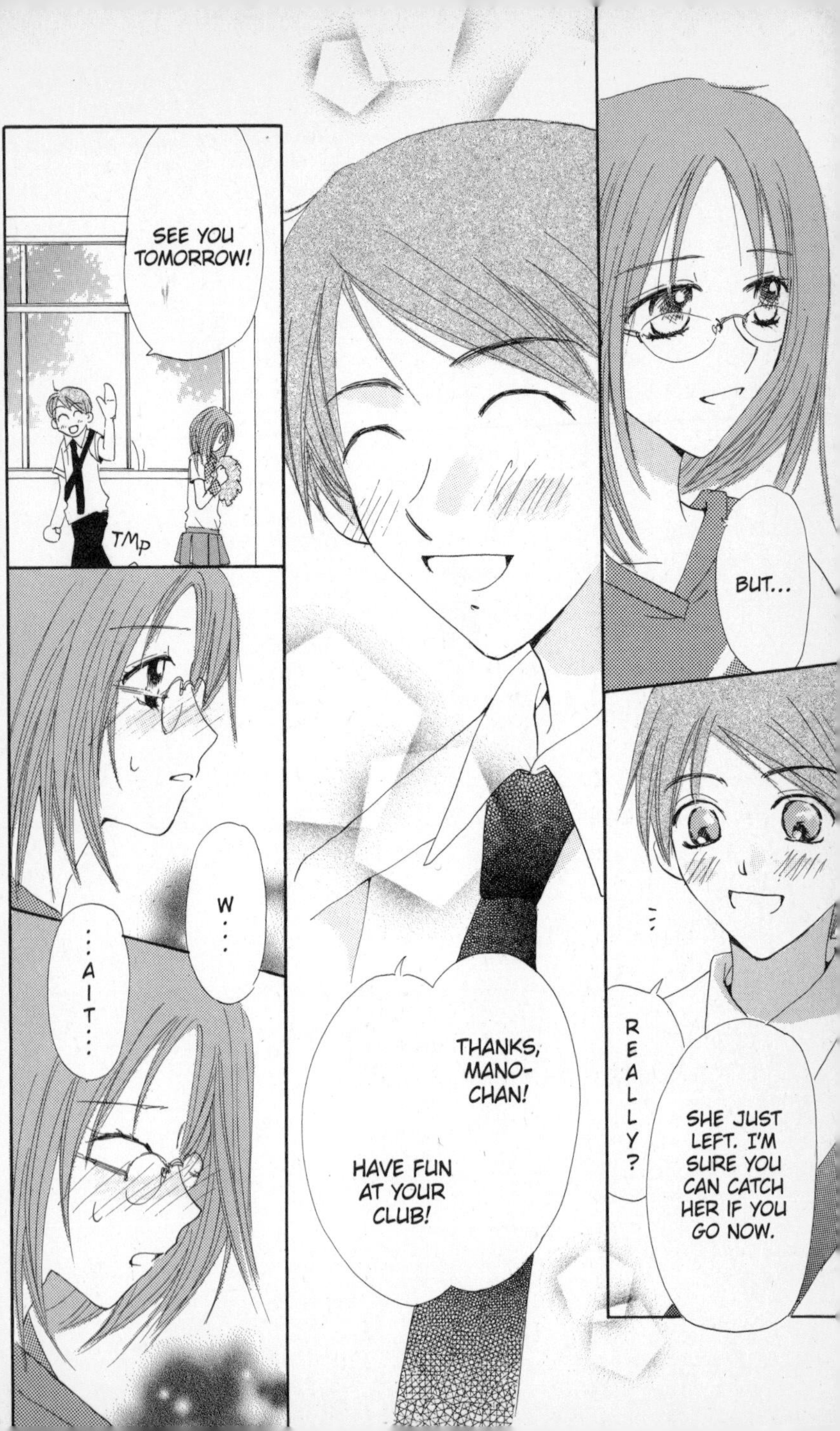
BUT...
...!
REALLY?
SHE JUST LEFT. I'M SURE YOU CAN CATCH HER IF YOU GO NOW.
THANKS, MANO-CHAN!
HAVE FUN AT YOUR CLUB!
SEE YOU TOMORROW!
TMP
W...
...AIT...

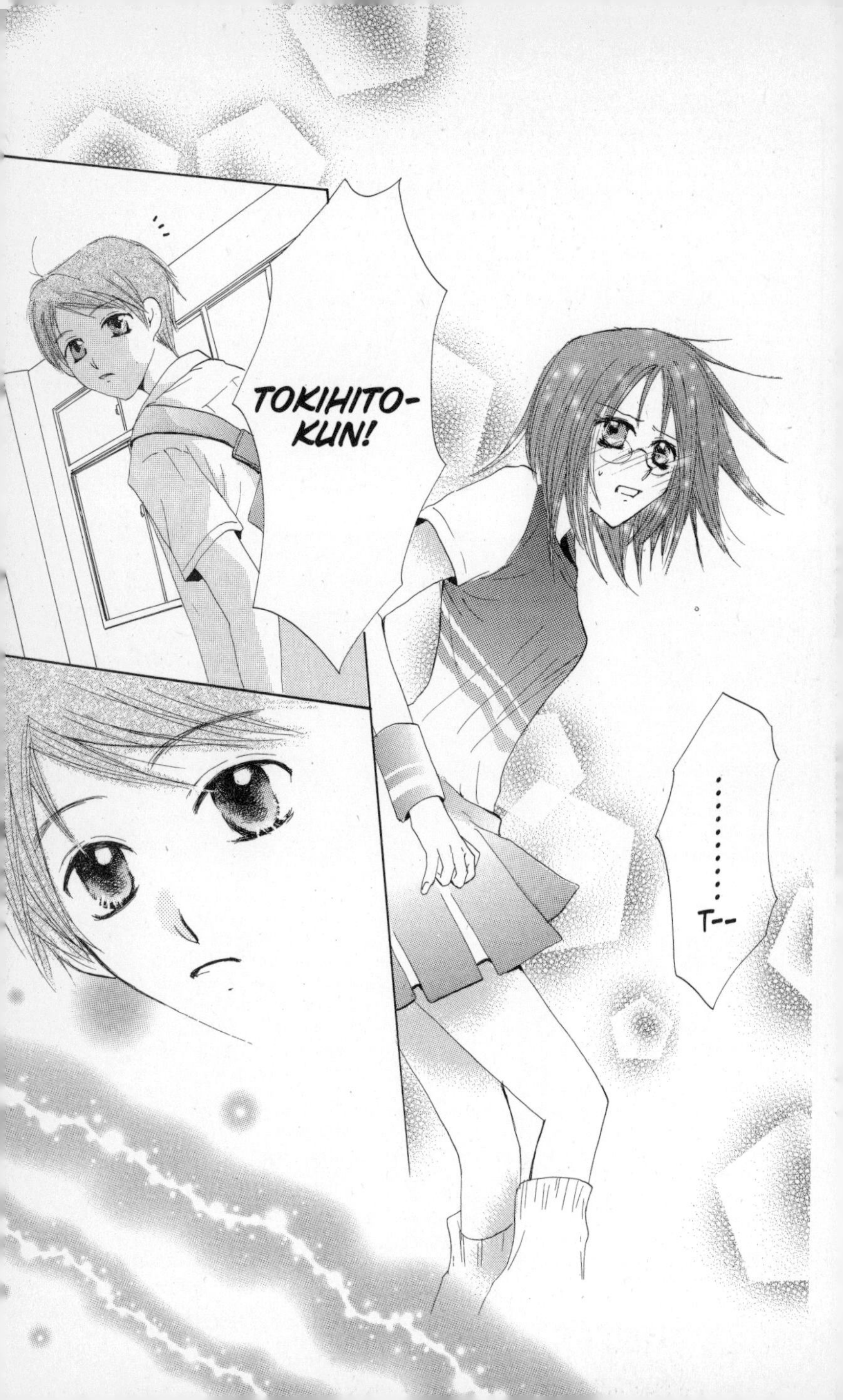
TOKIHITO-KUN!
!!
..........T--

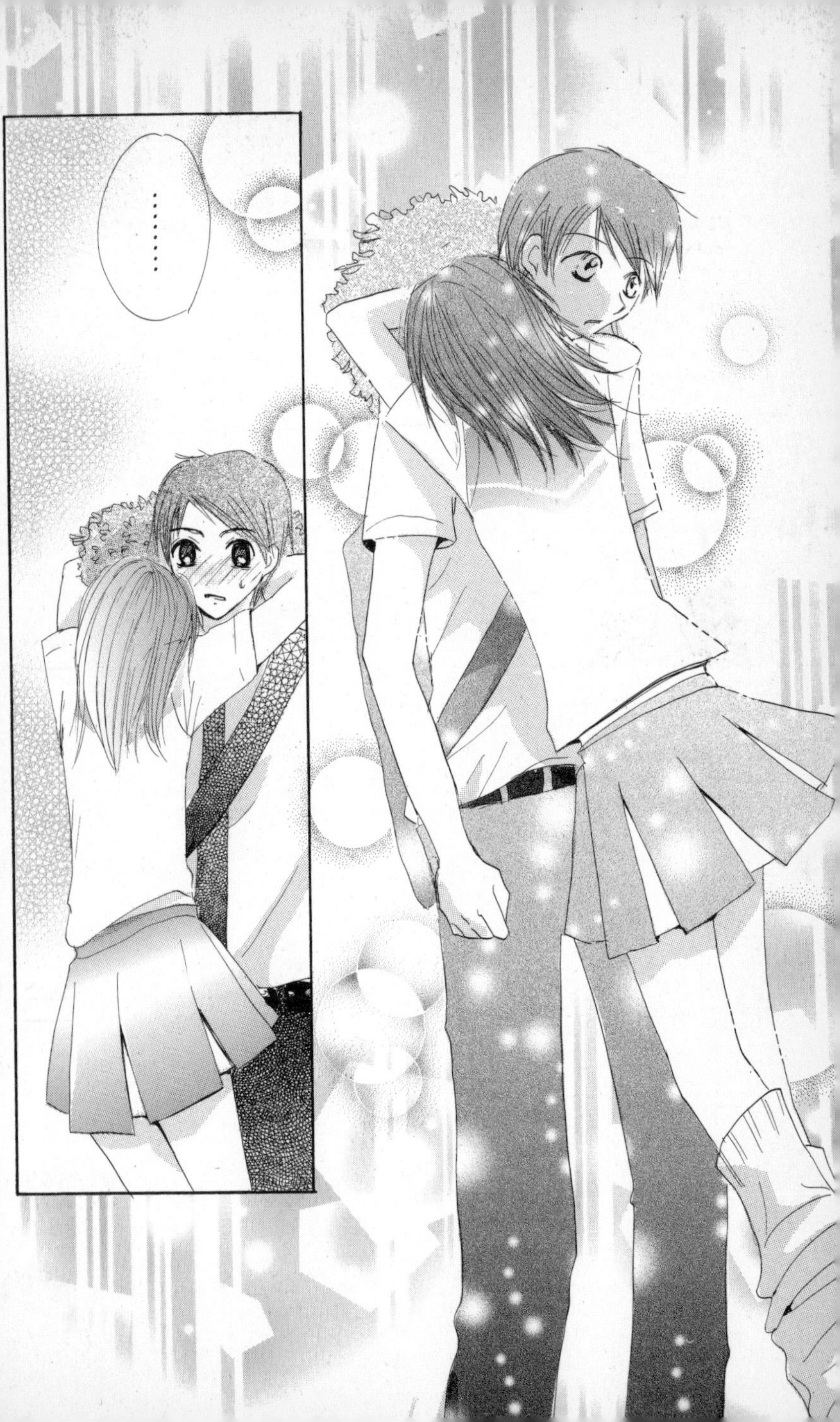
……

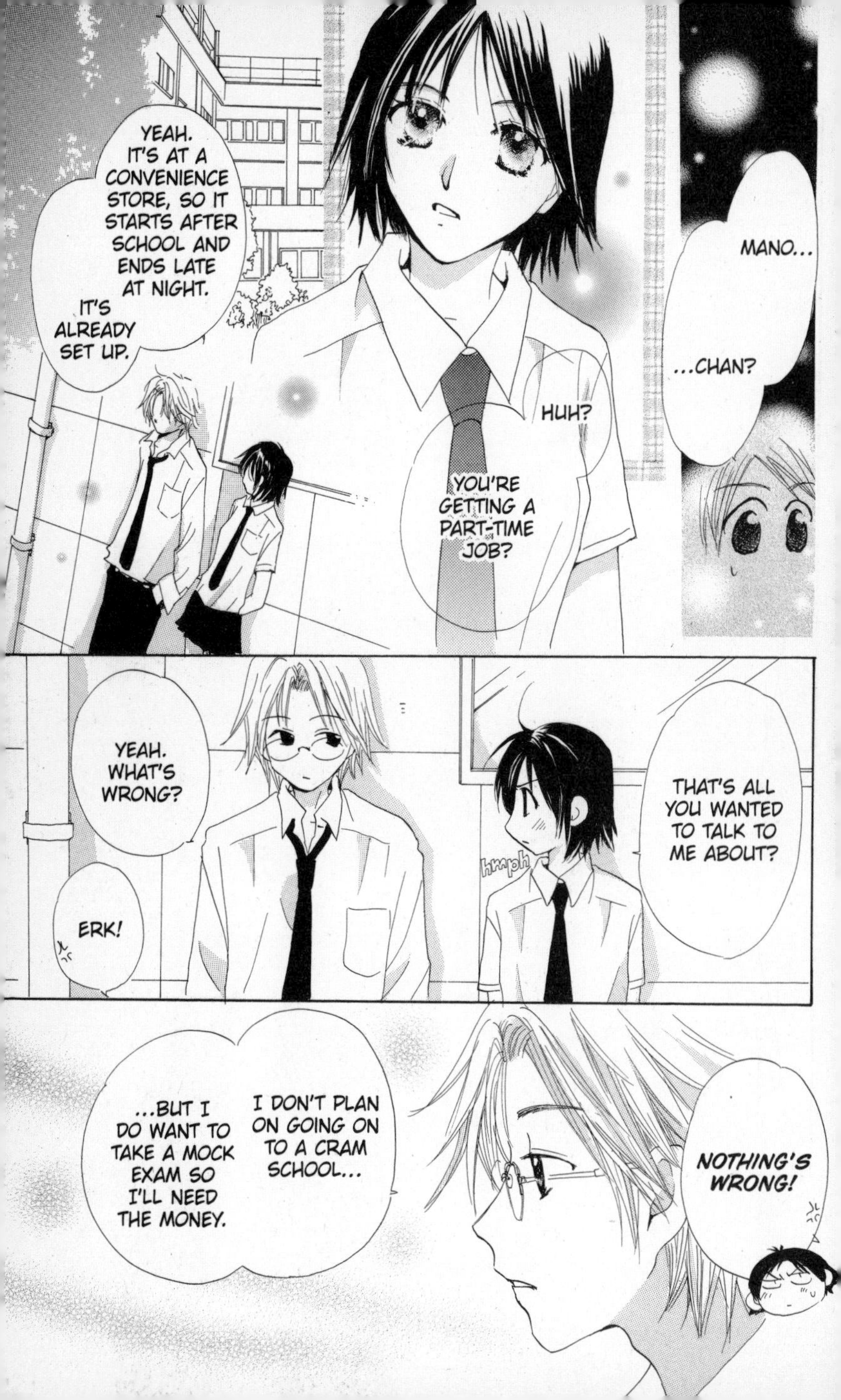
MANO...
...CHAN?
HUH?
YOU'RE GETTING A PART-TIME JOB?
YEAH. IT'S AT A CONVENIENCE STORE, SO IT STARTS AFTER SCHOOL AND ENDS LATE AT NIGHT.
IT'S ALREADY SET UP.
THAT'S ALL YOU WANTED TO TALK TO ME ABOUT?
hmph
YEAH. WHAT'S WRONG?
ERK!
NOTHING'S WRONG!
I DON'T PLAN ON GOING ON TO A CRAM SCHOOL...
...BUT I DO WANT TO TAKE A MOCK EXAM SO I'LL NEED THE MONEY.

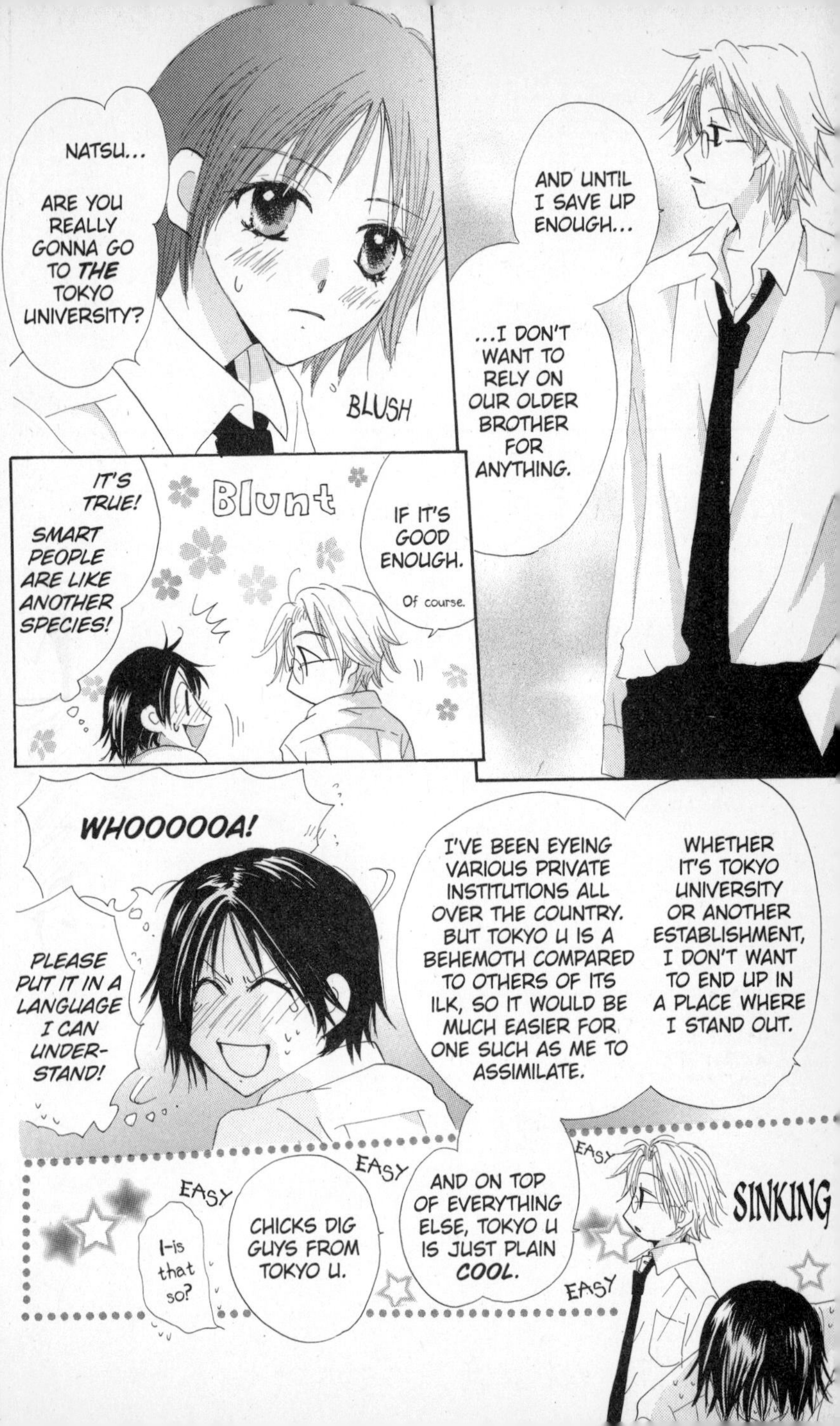
AND UNTIL I SAVE UP ENOUGH...
...I DON'T WANT TO RELY ON OUR OLDER BROTHER FOR ANYTHING.
NATSU...
ARE YOU REALLY GONNA GO TO THE TOKYO UNIVERSITY?
BLUSH
IF IT'S GOOD ENOUGH.
Of course.
Blunt
IT'S TRUE!
SMART PEOPLE ARE LIKE ANOTHER SPECIES!
WHETHER IT'S TOKYO UNIVERSITY OR ANOTHER ESTABLISHMENT, I DON'T WANT TO END UP IN A PLACE WHERE I STAND OUT.
I'VE BEEN EYEING VARIOUS PRIVATE INSTITUTIONS ALL OVER THE COUNTRY. BUT TOKYO U IS A BEHEMOTH COMPARED TO OTHERS OF ITS ILK, SO IT WOULD BE MUCH EASIER FOR ONE SUCH AS ME TO ASSIMILATE.
WHOOOOOA!
PLEASE PUT IT IN A LANGUAGE I CAN UNDER-STAND!
SINKING
EASY
EASY
AND ON TOP OF EVERYTHING ELSE, TOKYO U IS JUST PLAIN COOL.
EASY
CHICKS DIG GUYS FROM TOKYO U.
EASY
I-is that so?

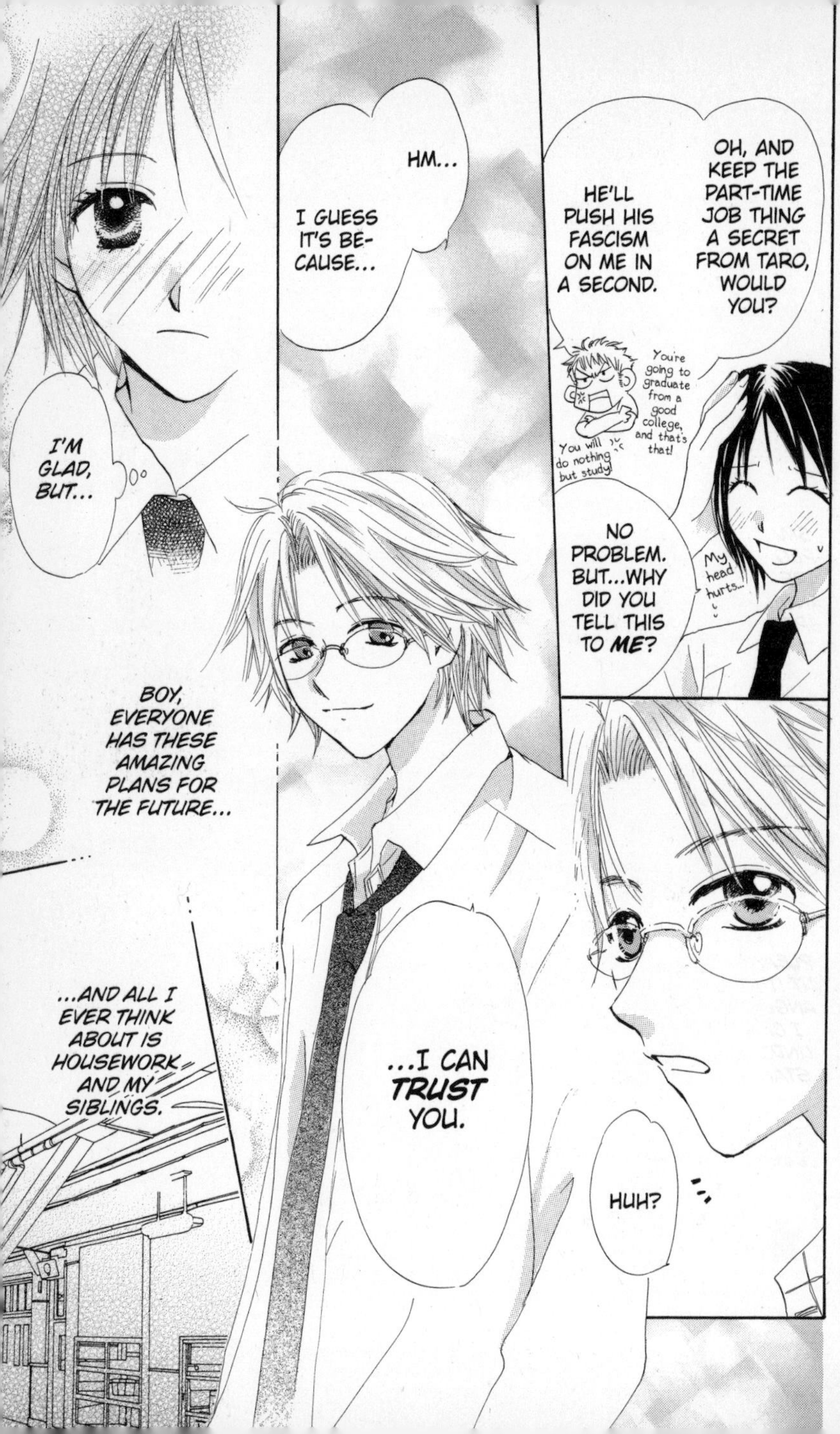
OH, AND KEEP THE PART-TIME JOB THING A SECRET FROM TARO, WOULD YOU?
HE'LL PUSH HIS FASCISM ON ME IN A SECOND.
You're going to graduate from a good college, and that's that!
You will do nothing but study!
My head hurts...
NO PROBLEM. BUT...WHY DID YOU TELL THIS TO ME?
HM...
I GUESS IT'S BE-CAUSE...
...I CAN TRUST YOU.
HUH?
I'M GLAD, BUT...
BOY, EVERYONE HAS THESE AMAZING PLANS FOR THE FUTURE...
...AND ALL I EVER THINK ABOUT IS HOUSEWORK AND MY SIBLINGS.

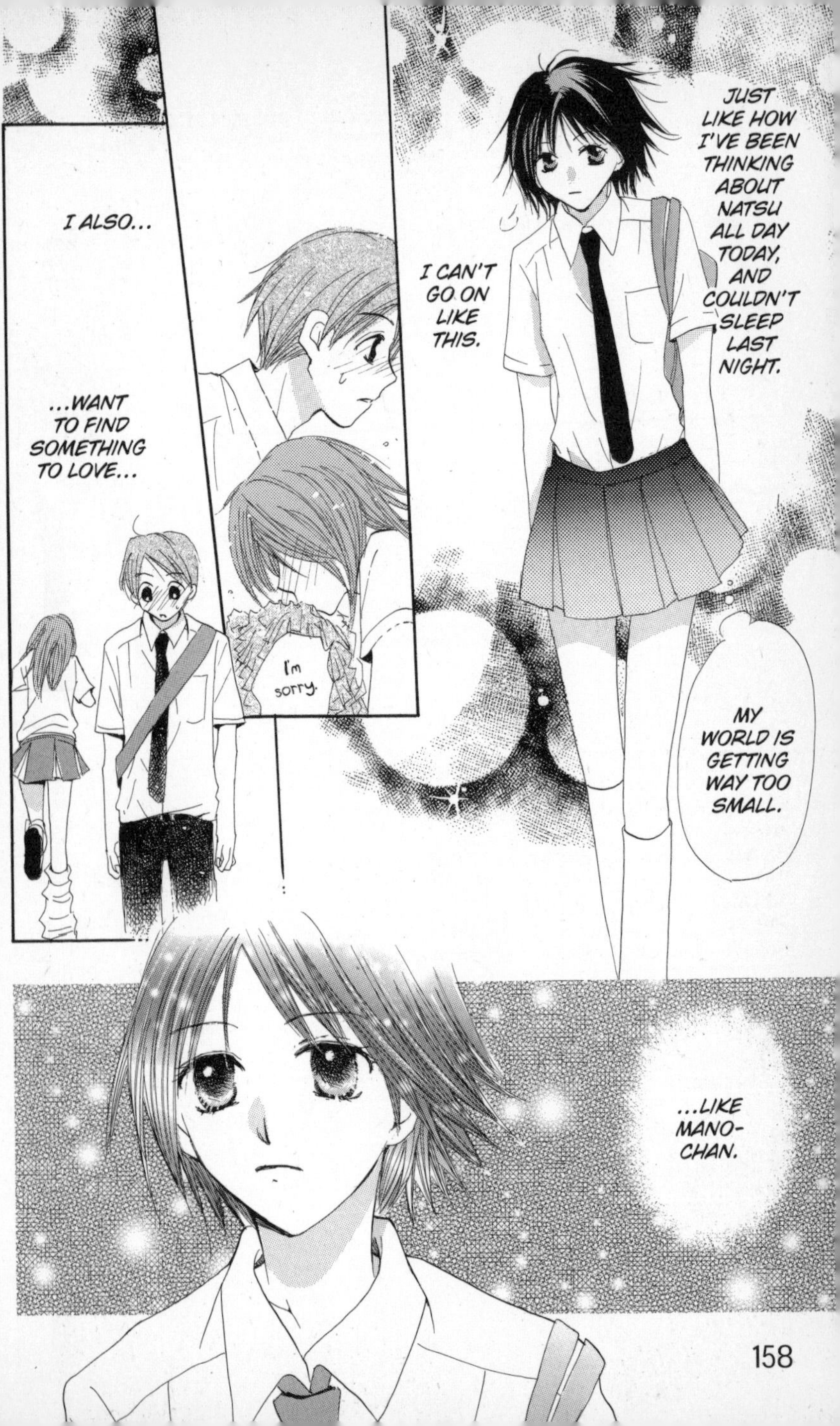
JUST LIKE HOW I'VE BEEN THINKING ABOUT NATSU ALL DAY TODAY, AND COULDN'T SLEEP LAST NIGHT.
I CAN'T GO ON LIKE THIS.
MY WORLD IS GETTING WAY TOO SMALL.
I'm sorry.
I ALSO...
...WANT TO FIND SOMETHING TO LOVE...
...LIKE MANO-CHAN.

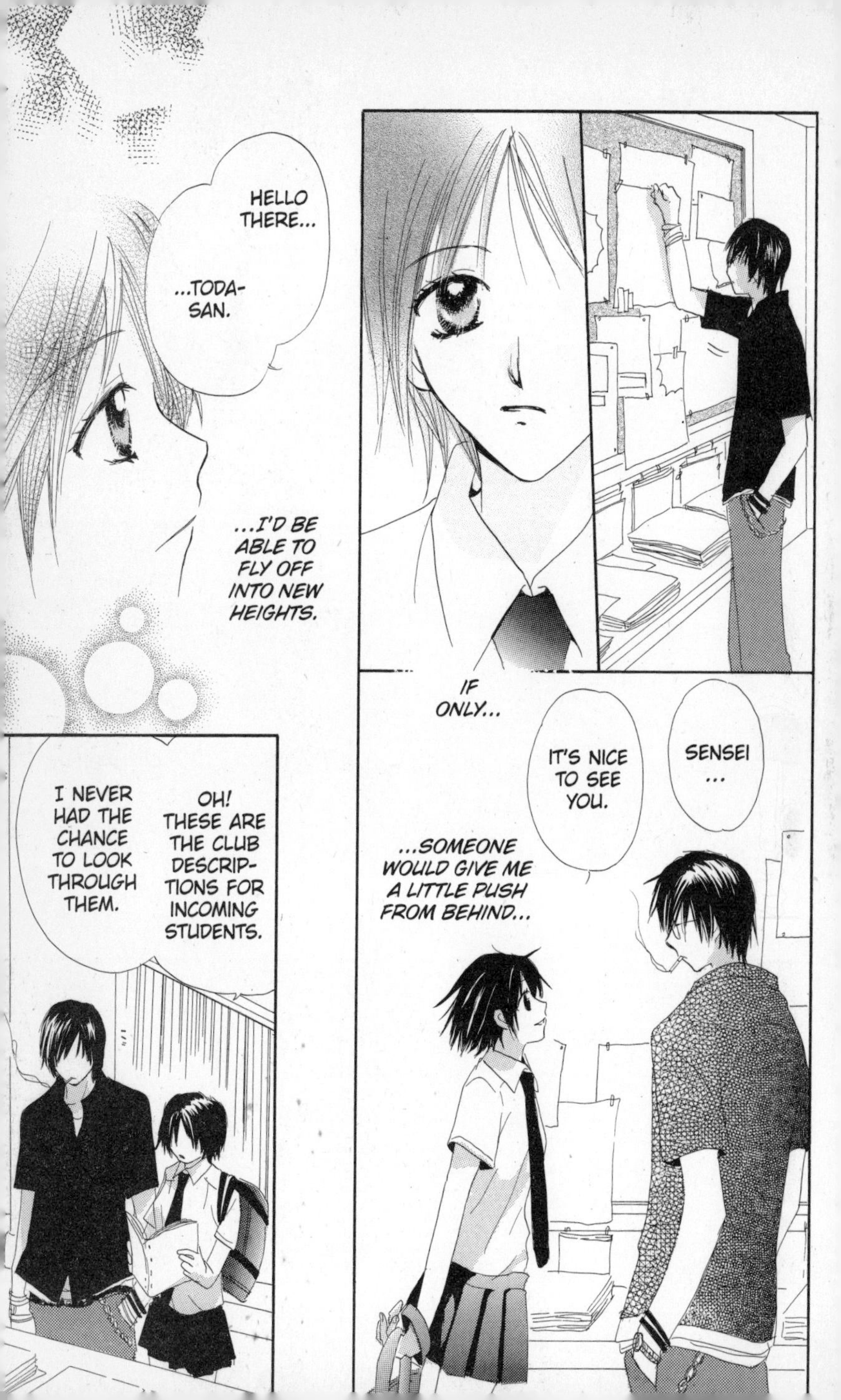
IF ONLY...
SENSEI ...
IT'S NICE TO SEE YOU.
...SOMEONE WOULD GIVE ME A LITTLE PUSH FROM BEHIND...
...I'D BE ABLE TO FLY OFF INTO NEW HEIGHTS.
HELLO THERE... ...TODA-SAN.
OH! THESE ARE THE CLUB DESCRIPTIONS FOR INCOMING STUDENTS.
I NEVER HAD THE CHANCE TO LOOK THROUGH THEM.

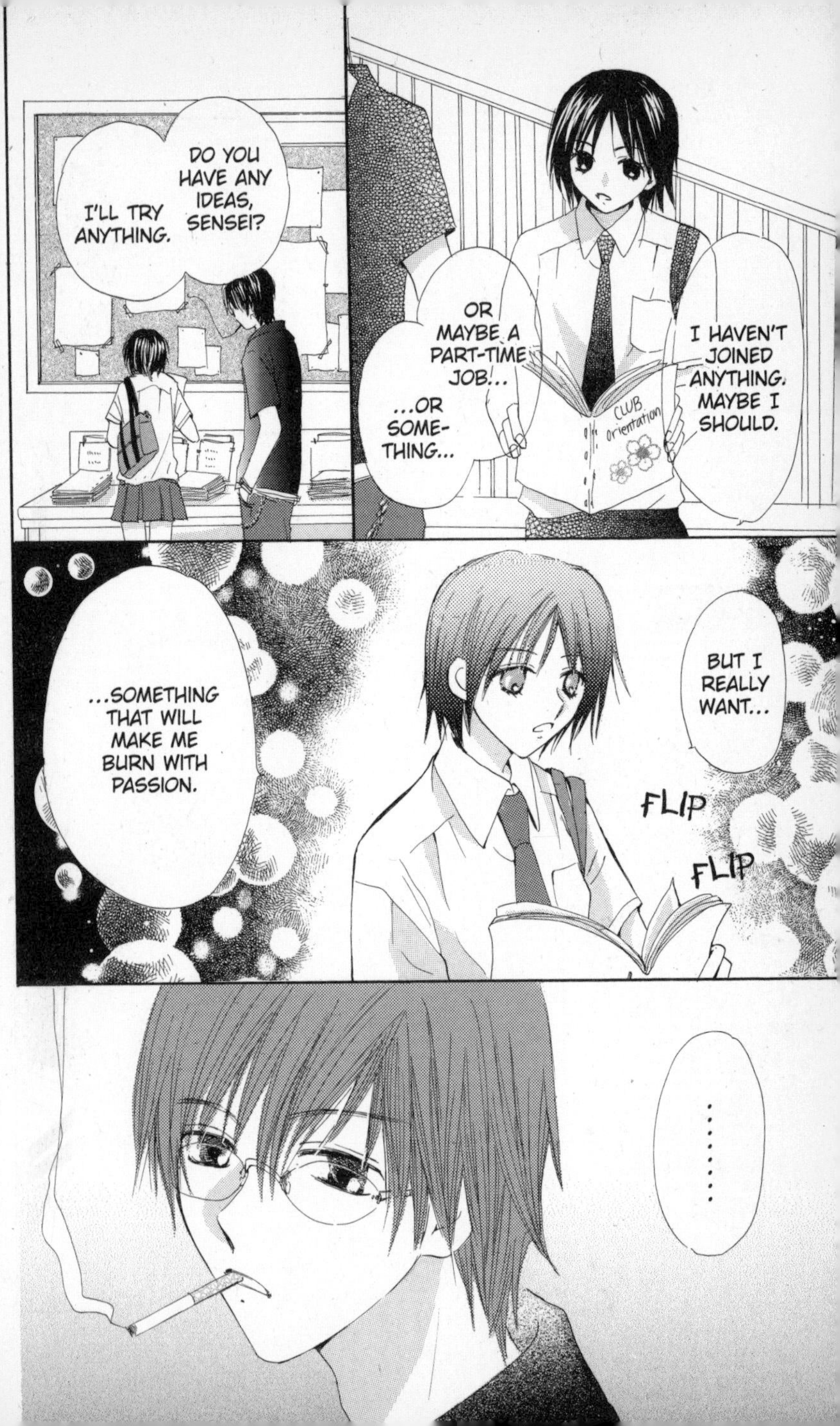

I HAVEN'T JOINED ANYTHING. MAYBE I SHOULD.
CLUB Orientation
OR MAYBE A PART-TIME JOB...
...OR SOMETHING...
DO YOU HAVE ANY IDEAS, SENSEI?
I'LL TRY ANYTHING.
BUT I REALLY WANT...
FLIP
FLIP
...SOMETHING THAT WILL MAKE ME BURN WITH PASSION.
......

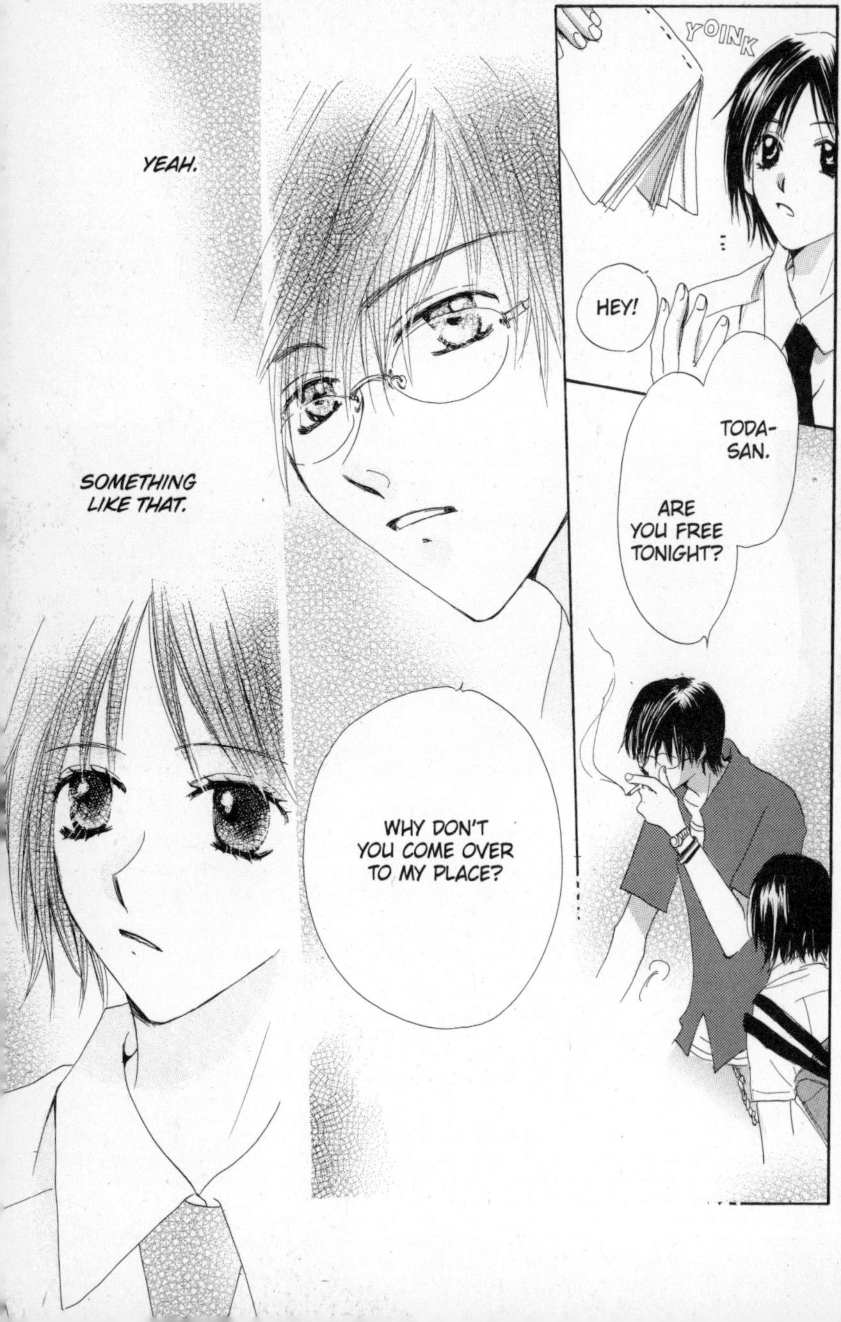

YOINK
...
HEY!
TODA-SAN.
ARE YOU FREE TONIGHT?
WHY DON'T YOU COME OVER TO MY PLACE?
YEAH.
SOMETHING LIKE THAT.

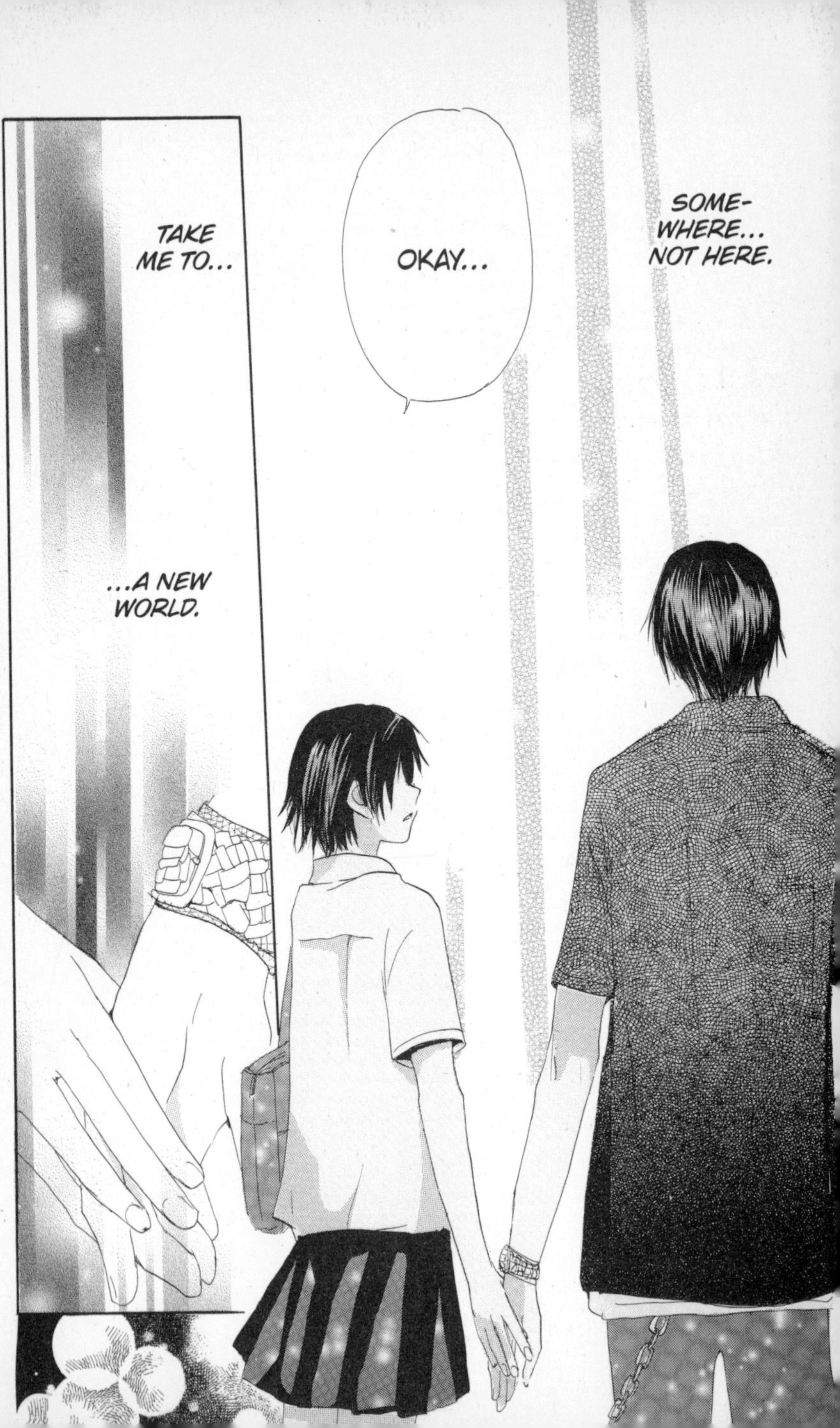
SOME-WHERE... NOT HERE.
OKAY...
TAKE ME TO...
...A NEW WORLD.

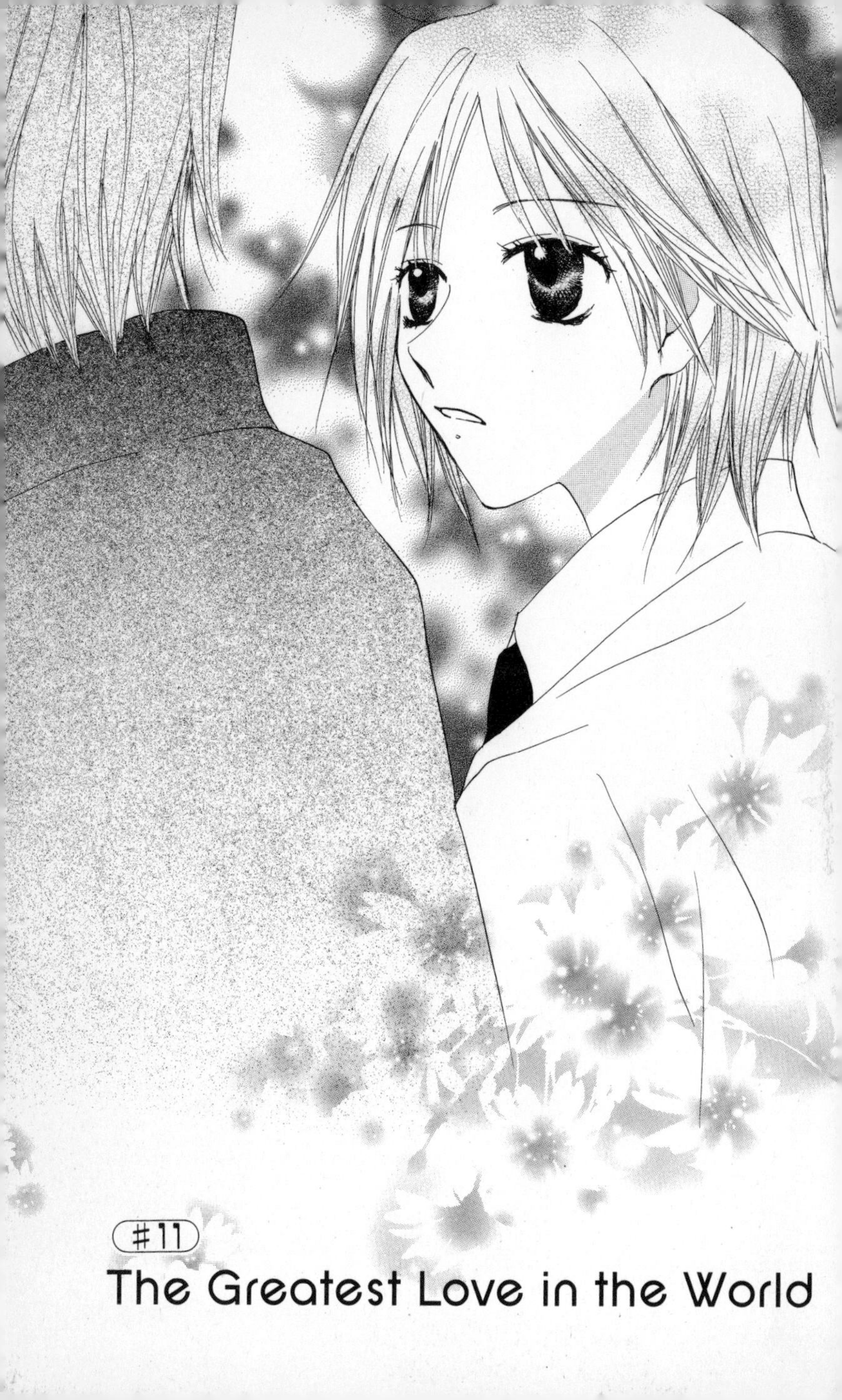

#11 The Greatest Love in the World

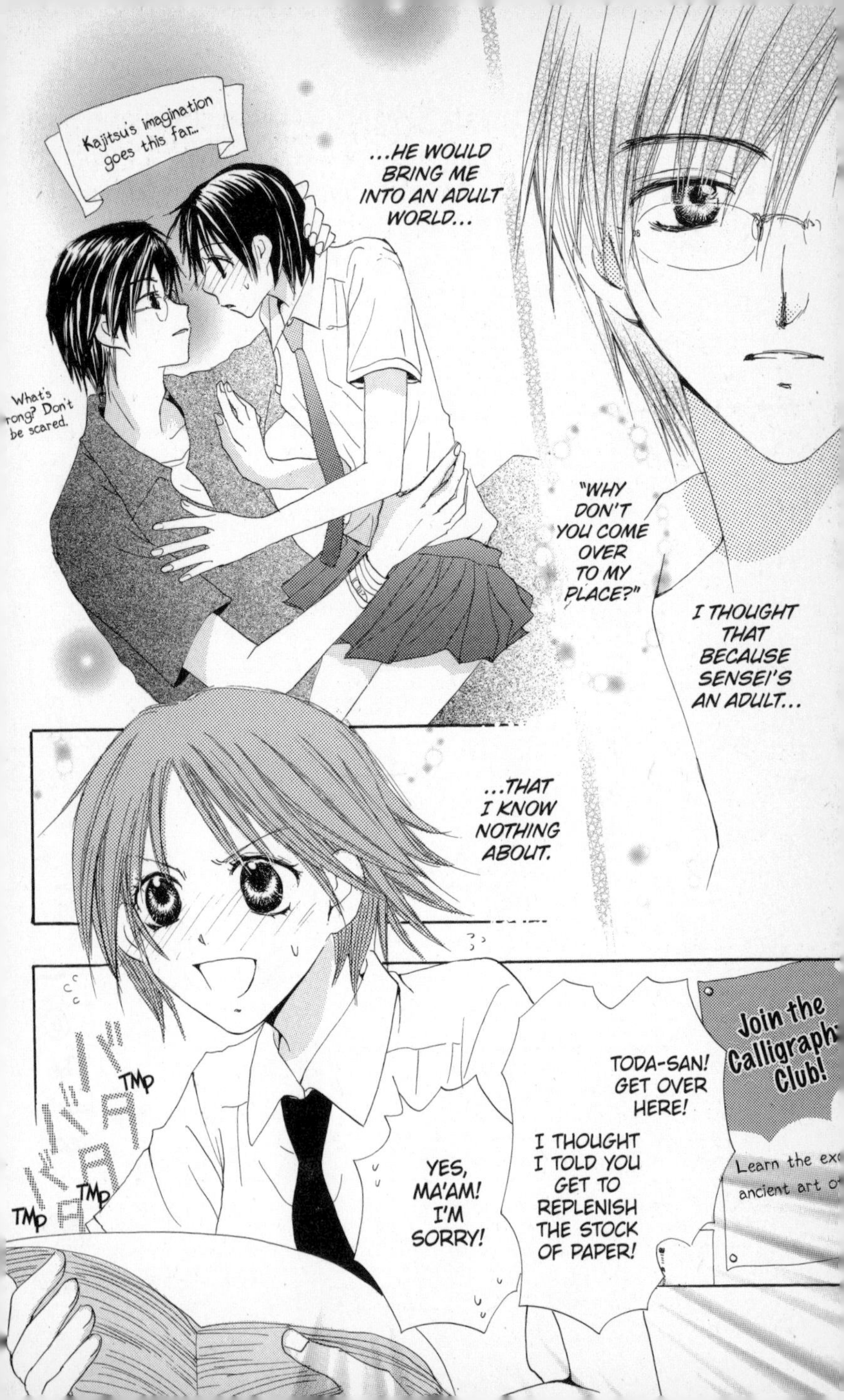
"WHY DON'T YOU COME OVER TO MY PLACE?"
I THOUGHT THAT BECAUSE SENSEI'S AN ADULT...
Kajitsu's imagination goes this far...
...HE WOULD BRING ME INTO AN ADULT WORLD...
What's rong? Don't be scared.
...THAT I KNOW NOTHING ABOUT.
Join the Calligraph Club!
Learn the ex ancient art o
TODA-SAN! GET OVER HERE!
I THOUGHT I TOLD YOU GET TO REPLENISH THE STOCK OF PAPER!
YES, MA'AM! I'M SORRY!
TMP
バタバタ
TMP
TMP

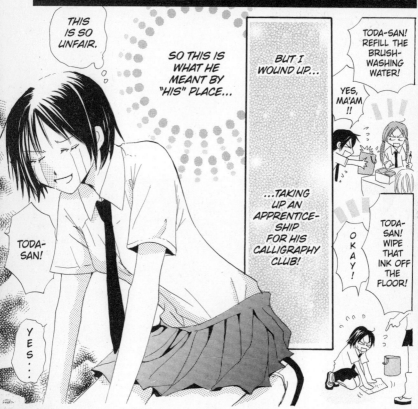

crossroad Chapter 11: The Greatest Love in the World

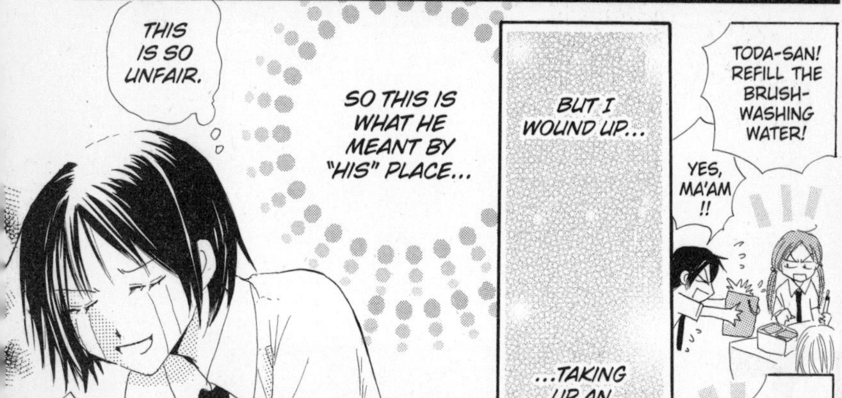
TODA-SAN! REFILL THE BRUSH-WASHING WATER!
YES, MA'AM !!
TODA-SAN! WIPE THAT INK OFF THE FLOOR!
OKAY!
BUT I WOUND UP...
...TAKING UP AN APPRENTICE-SHIP FOR HIS CALLIGRAPHY CLUB!
SO THIS IS WHAT HE MEANT BY "HIS" PLACE...
THIS IS SO UNFAIR.
TODA-SAN!
YES...

The Last Space! ⑥

Compared to the really popular manga creators, I don't get that much fan mail, but when letters do come, they're always very nice, telling me to keep doing my best. Thank you very much for those! In volume one, I wrote that this might be the last series I'd ever do, which may have caused some of you to worry -- but really, I intend to keep writing passionately every day. It's just that sometimes I think I shouldn't write such weird things anymore. Sorry if I made you worry. But thanks for caring! You know, when I have time to respond to my fanmail, I don't know what to write besides a polite reply. I finally updated my webpage a bit, so there's some new information you can check out. Also, I've had my flyers sent to book stores all over Japan, and I'm in Pop magazine. There's information on that too on the website. Be sure to check in at least seven times a month!

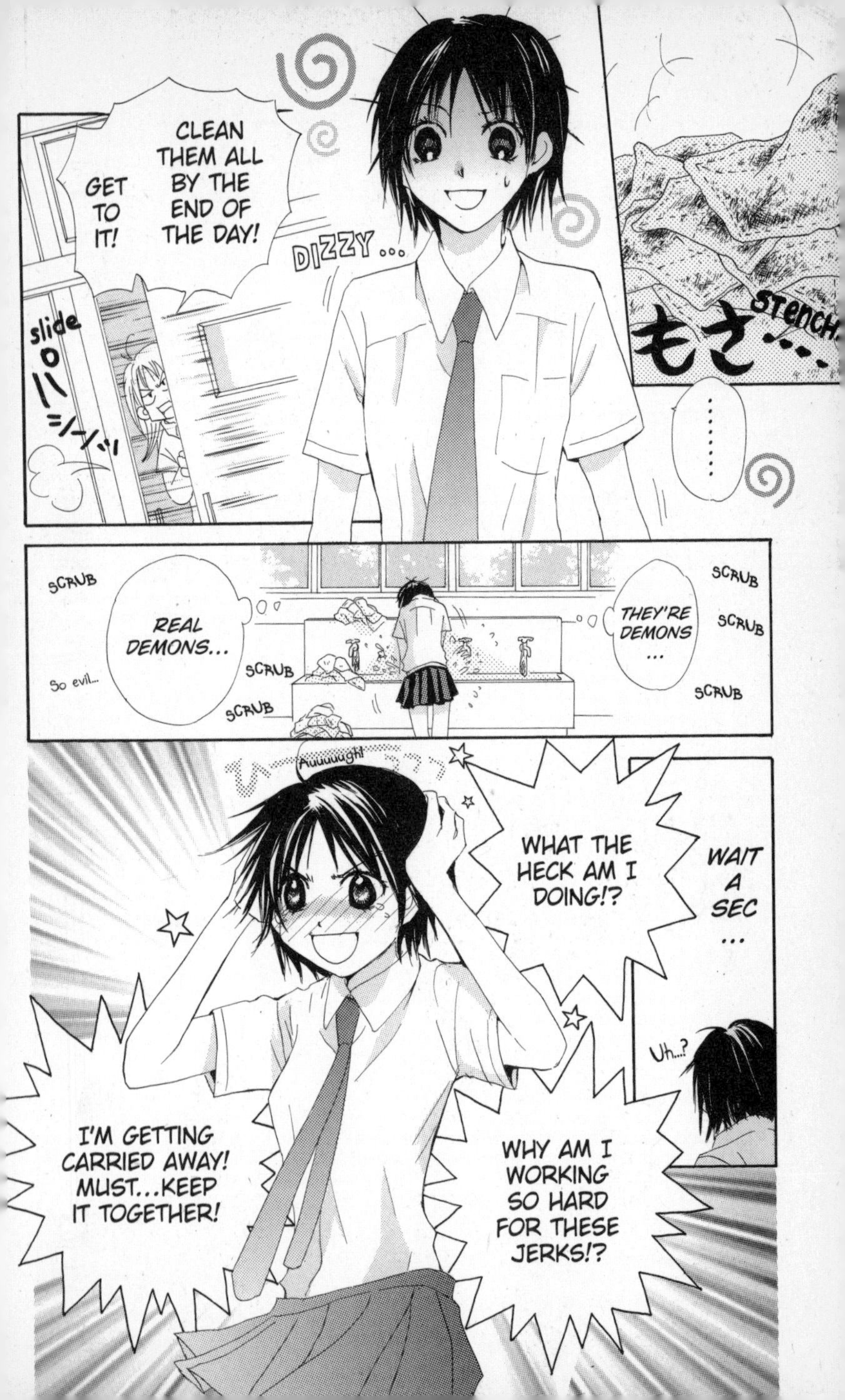
stench
もさ…
……
CLEAN THEM ALL BY THE END OF THE DAY!
GET TO IT!
slide
DIZZY...
SCRUB
THEY'RE DEMONS...
SCRUB
SCRUB
SCRUB
REAL DEMONS...
SCRUB
SCRUB
So evil...
Uh...?
WAIT A SEC...
Auuuuugh!
WHAT THE HECK AM I DOING!?
WHY AM I WORKING SO HARD FOR THESE JERKS!?
I'M GETTING CARRIED AWAY! MUST...KEEP IT TOGETHER!

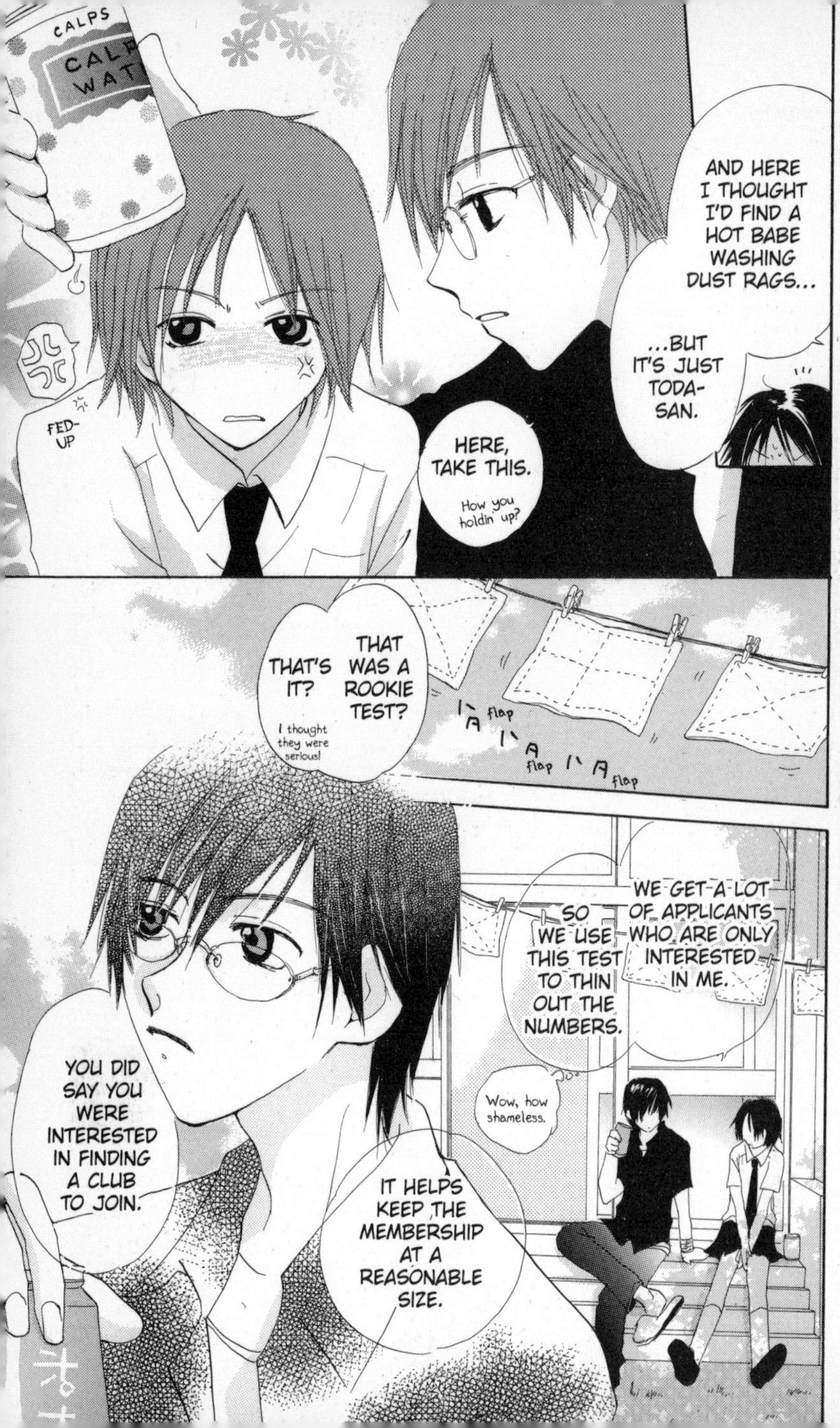

CALPS
AND HERE I THOUGHT I'D FIND A HOT BABE WASHING DUST RAGS...
...BUT IT'S JUST TODA-SAN.
HERE, TAKE THIS.
How you holdin up?
FED-UP
THAT WAS A ROOKIE TEST?
THAT'S IT?
I thought they were serious!
flap
flap
flap
WE GET A LOT OF APPLICANTS WHO ARE ONLY INTERESTED IN ME.
SO WE USE THIS TEST TO THIN OUT THE NUMBERS.
Wow, how shameless.
IT HELPS KEEP THE MEMBERSHIP AT A REASONABLE SIZE.
YOU DID SAY YOU WERE INTERESTED IN FINDING A CLUB TO JOIN.

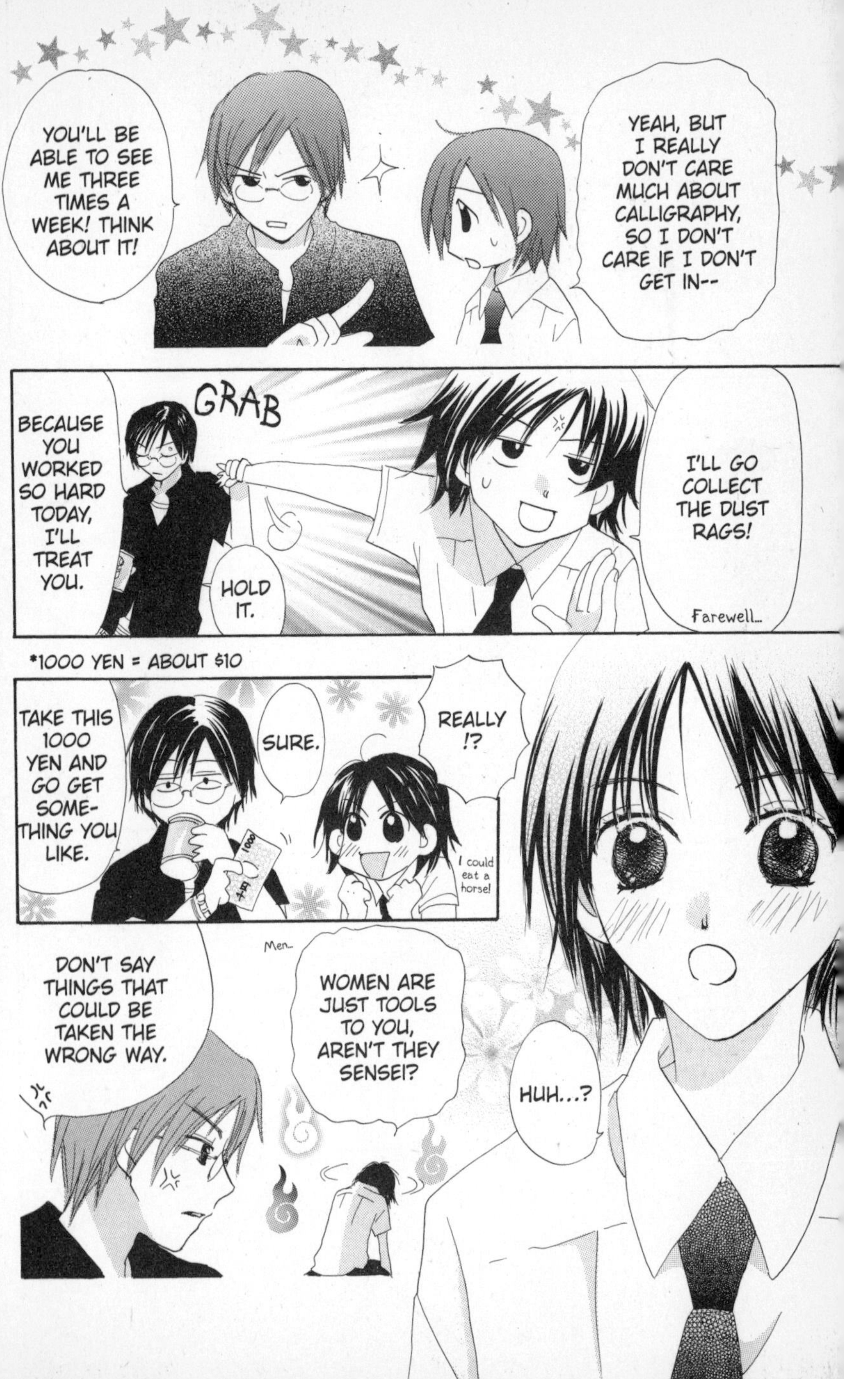
YEAH, BUT I REALLY DON'T CARE MUCH ABOUT CALLIGRAPHY, SO I DON'T CARE IF I DON'T GET IN--
YOU'LL BE ABLE TO SEE ME THREE TIMES A WEEK! THINK ABOUT IT!
I'LL GO COLLECT THE DUST RAGS!
Farewell...
GRAB
HOLD IT.
BECAUSE YOU WORKED SO HARD TODAY, I'LL TREAT YOU.
*1000 YEN = ABOUT $10
HUH...?
REALLY !?
SURE.
TAKE THIS 1000 YEN AND GO GET SOME-THING YOU LIKE.
I could eat a horse!
WOMEN ARE JUST TOOLS TO YOU, AREN'T THEY SENSEI?
Men...
DON'T SAY THINGS THAT COULD BE TAKEN THE WRONG WAY.

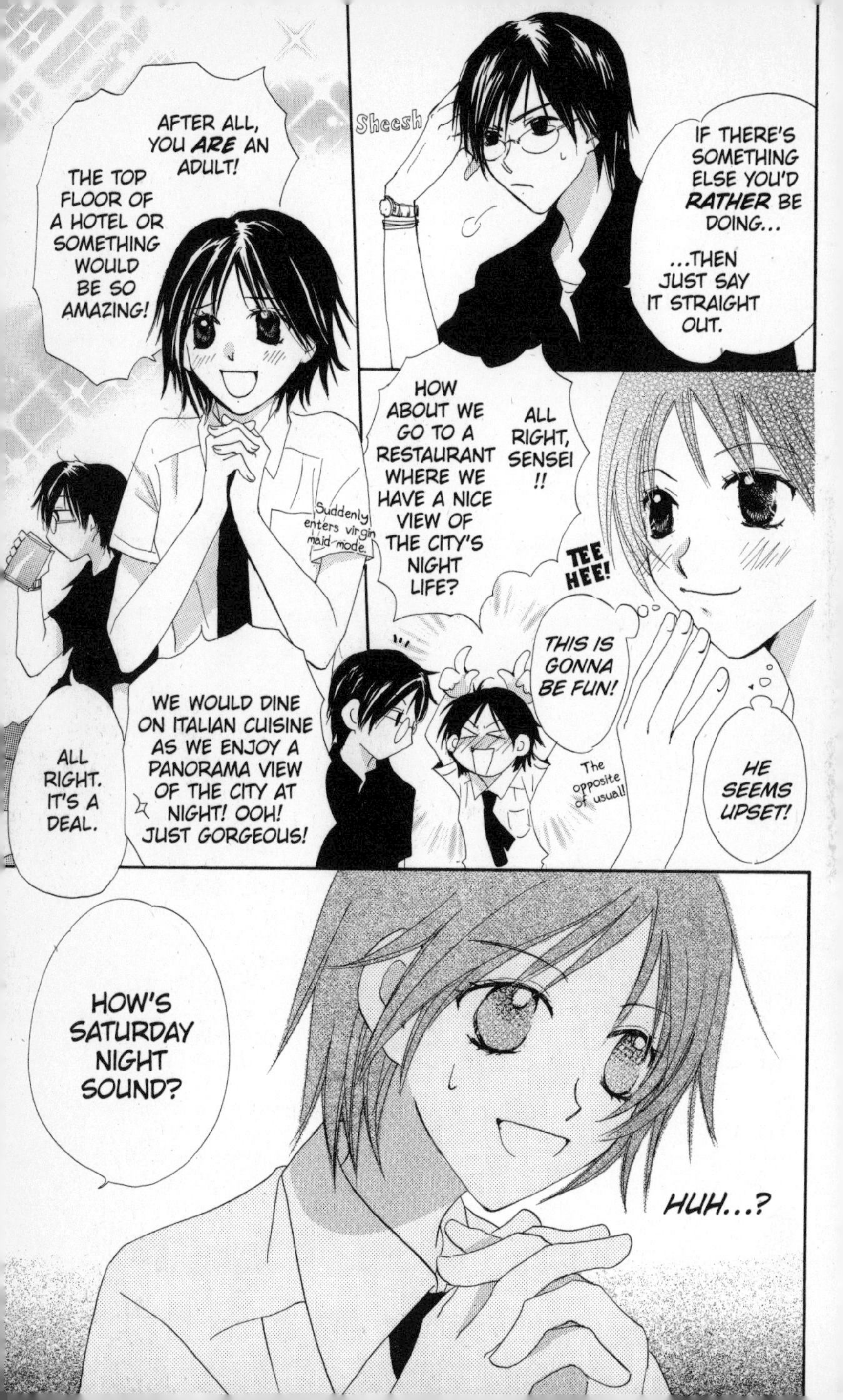
Sheesh
IF THERE'S SOMETHING ELSE YOU'D ***RATHER*** BE DOING...
...THEN JUST SAY IT STRAIGHT OUT.
ALL RIGHT, SENSEI !!
HOW ABOUT WE GO TO A RESTAURANT WHERE WE HAVE A NICE VIEW OF THE CITY'S NIGHT LIFE?
TEE HEE!
HE SEEMS UPSET!
THIS IS GONNA BE FUN!
The opposite of usual!
AFTER ALL, YOU ***ARE*** AN ADULT!
THE TOP FLOOR OF A HOTEL OR SOMETHING WOULD BE SO AMAZING!
Suddenly enters virgin maid mode.
WE WOULD DINE ON ITALIAN CUISINE AS WE ENJOY A PANORAMA VIEW OF THE CITY AT NIGHT! OOH! JUST GORGEOUS!
ALL RIGHT. IT'S A DEAL.
HOW'S SATURDAY NIGHT SOUND?
HUH...?

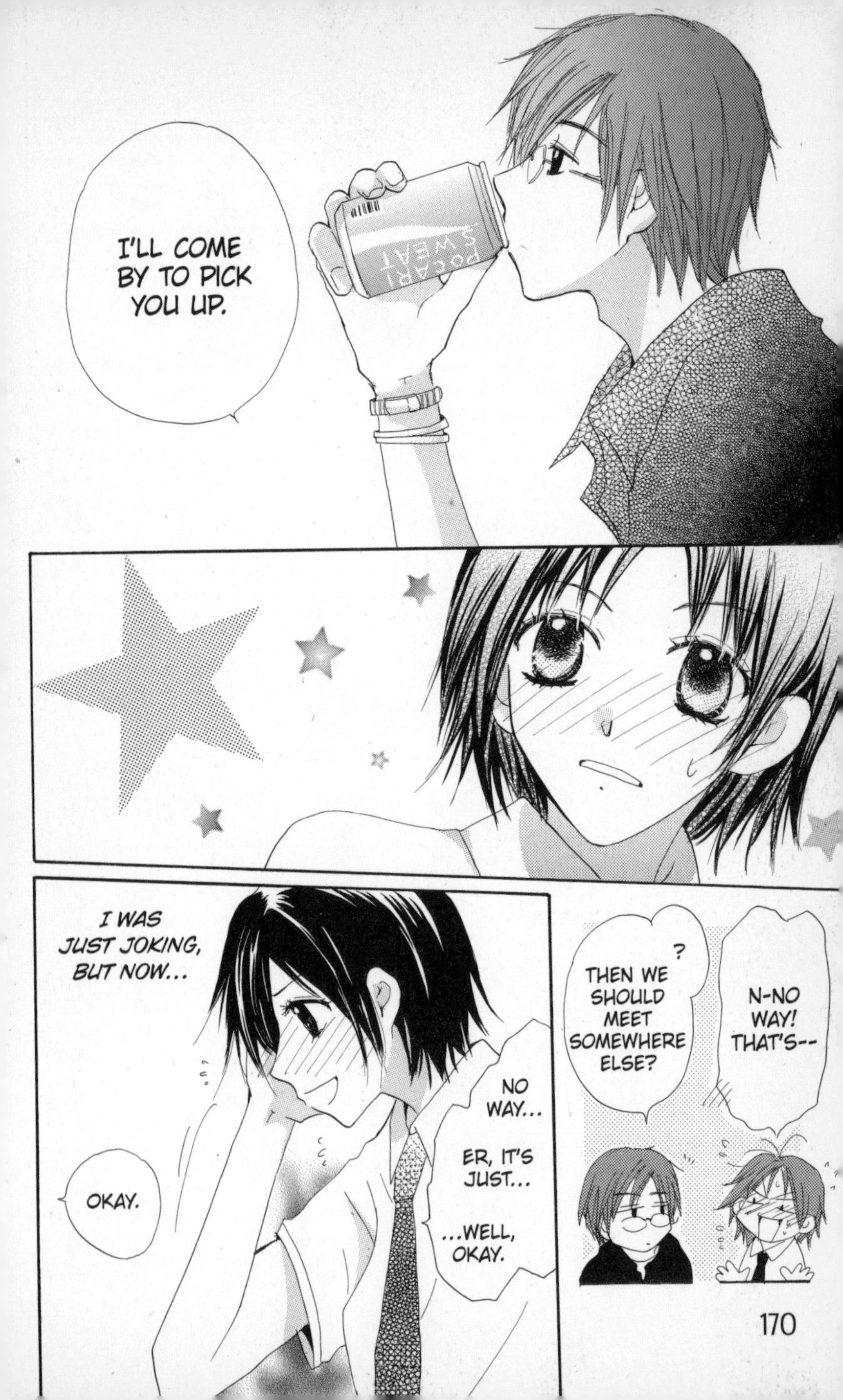
I'LL COME BY TO PICK YOU UP.
N-NO WAY! THAT'S--
THEN WE SHOULD MEET SOMEWHERE ELSE?
NO WAY...
ER, IT'S JUST...
...WELL, OKAY.
I WAS JUST JOKING, BUT NOW...
OKAY.

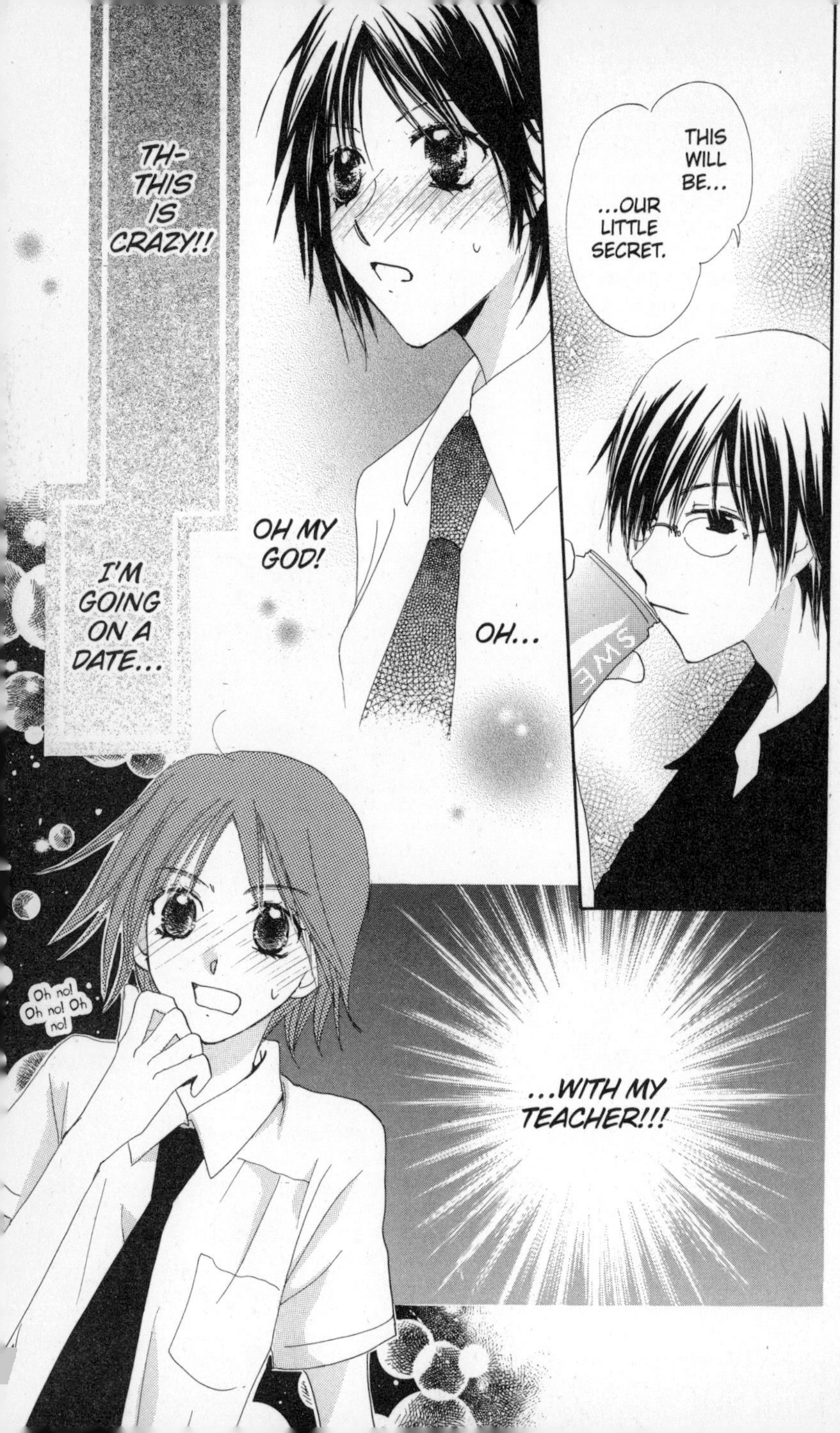
THIS WILL BE...
...OUR LITTLE SECRET.
OH...
OH MY GOD!
TH- THIS IS CRAZY!!
I'M GOING ON A DATE...
...WITH MY TEACHER!!!
Oh no! Oh no! Oh no!

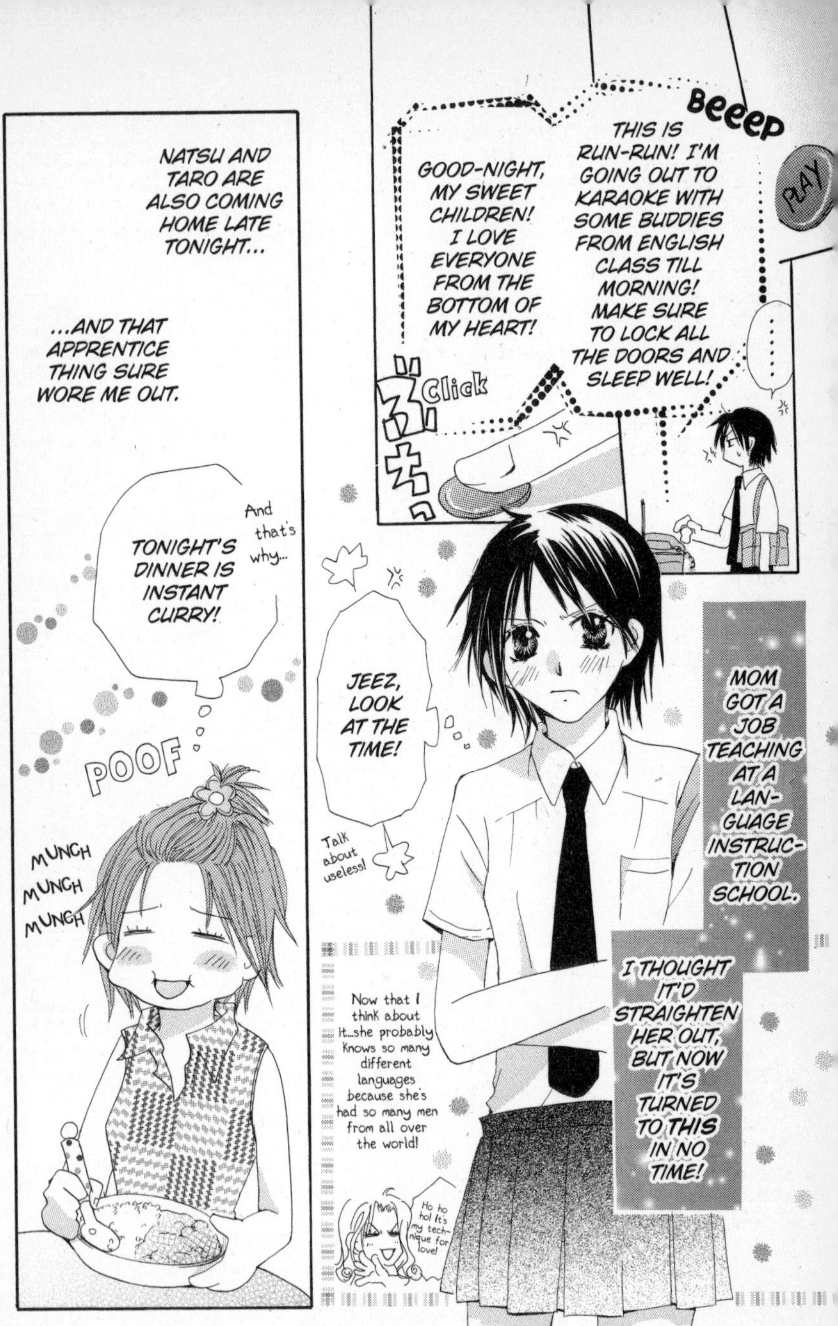

Beeep
PLAY
THIS IS RUN-RUN! I'M GOING OUT TO KARAOKE WITH SOME BUDDIES FROM ENGLISH CLASS TILL MORNING! MAKE SURE TO LOCK ALL THE DOORS AND SLEEP WELL!
GOOD-NIGHT, MY SWEET CHILDREN! I LOVE EVERYONE FROM THE BOTTOM OF MY HEART!
Click
...
MOM GOT A JOB TEACHING AT A LAN-GUAGE INSTRUC-TION SCHOOL.
I THOUGHT IT'D STRAIGHTEN HER OUT, BUT NOW IT'S TURNED TO THIS IN NO TIME!
JEEZ, LOOK AT THE TIME!
Talk about useless!
Now that I think about it...she probably knows so many different languages because she's had so many men from all over the world!
Ho ho ho! It's my tech-nique for love!
NATSU AND TARO ARE ALSO COMING HOME LATE TONIGHT...
...AND THAT APPRENTICE THING SURE WORE ME OUT.
TONIGHT'S DINNER IS INSTANT CURRY!
And that's why...
POOF
MUNCH MUNCH MUNCH

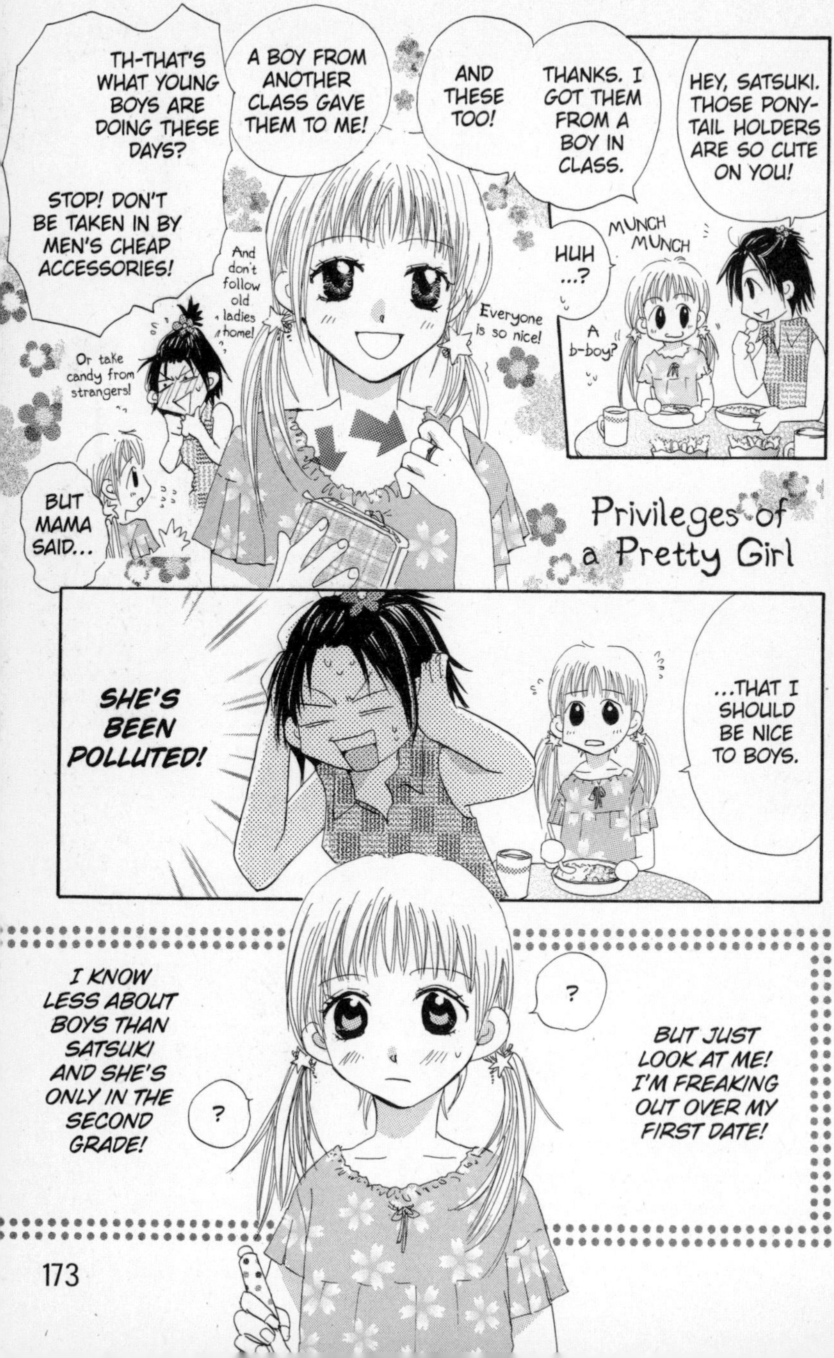
HEY, SATSUKI. THOSE PONY-TAIL HOLDERS ARE SO CUTE ON YOU!
THANKS. I GOT THEM FROM A BOY IN CLASS.
MUNCH MUNCH
HUH ...?
A b-boy?
AND THESE TOO!
A BOY FROM ANOTHER CLASS GAVE THEM TO ME!
Everyone is so nice!
TH-THAT'S WHAT YOUNG BOYS ARE DOING THESE DAYS?
STOP! DON'T BE TAKEN IN BY MEN'S CHEAP ACCESSORIES!
And don't follow old ladies home!
Or take candy from strangers!
BUT MAMA SAID...
Privileges of a Pretty Girl
...THAT I SHOULD BE NICE TO BOYS.
SHE'S BEEN POLLUTED!
?
BUT JUST LOOK AT ME! I'M FREAKING OUT OVER MY FIRST DATE!
I KNOW LESS ABOUT BOYS THAN SATSUKI AND SHE'S ONLY IN THE SECOND GRADE!
?

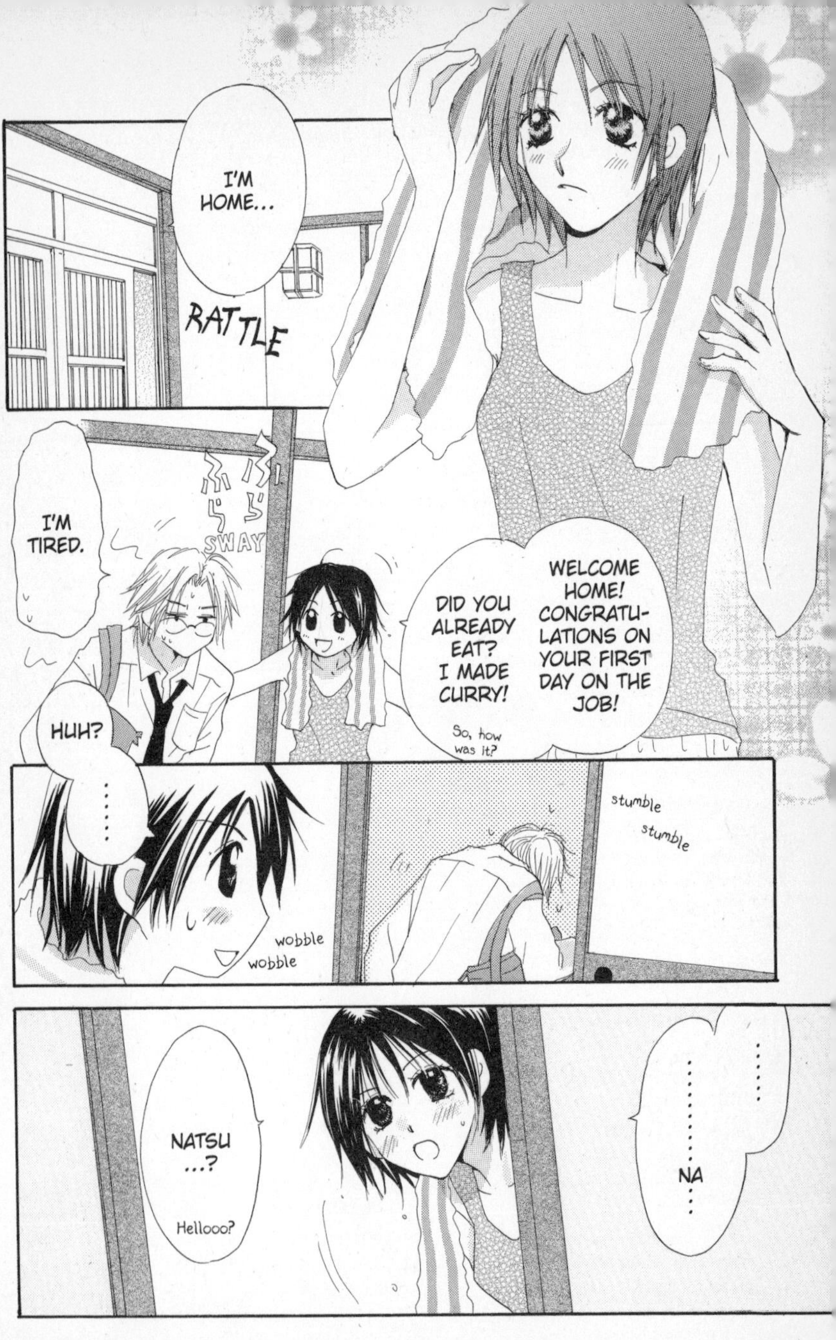
I'M HOME...
RATTLE
WELCOME HOME! CONGRATULATIONS ON YOUR FIRST DAY ON THE JOB!
DID YOU ALREADY EAT? I MADE CURRY!
So, how was it?
I'M TIRED.
ふらふら
SWAY
HUH?
stumble stumble
......
wobble wobble
......NA......
NATSU ...?
Hellooo?

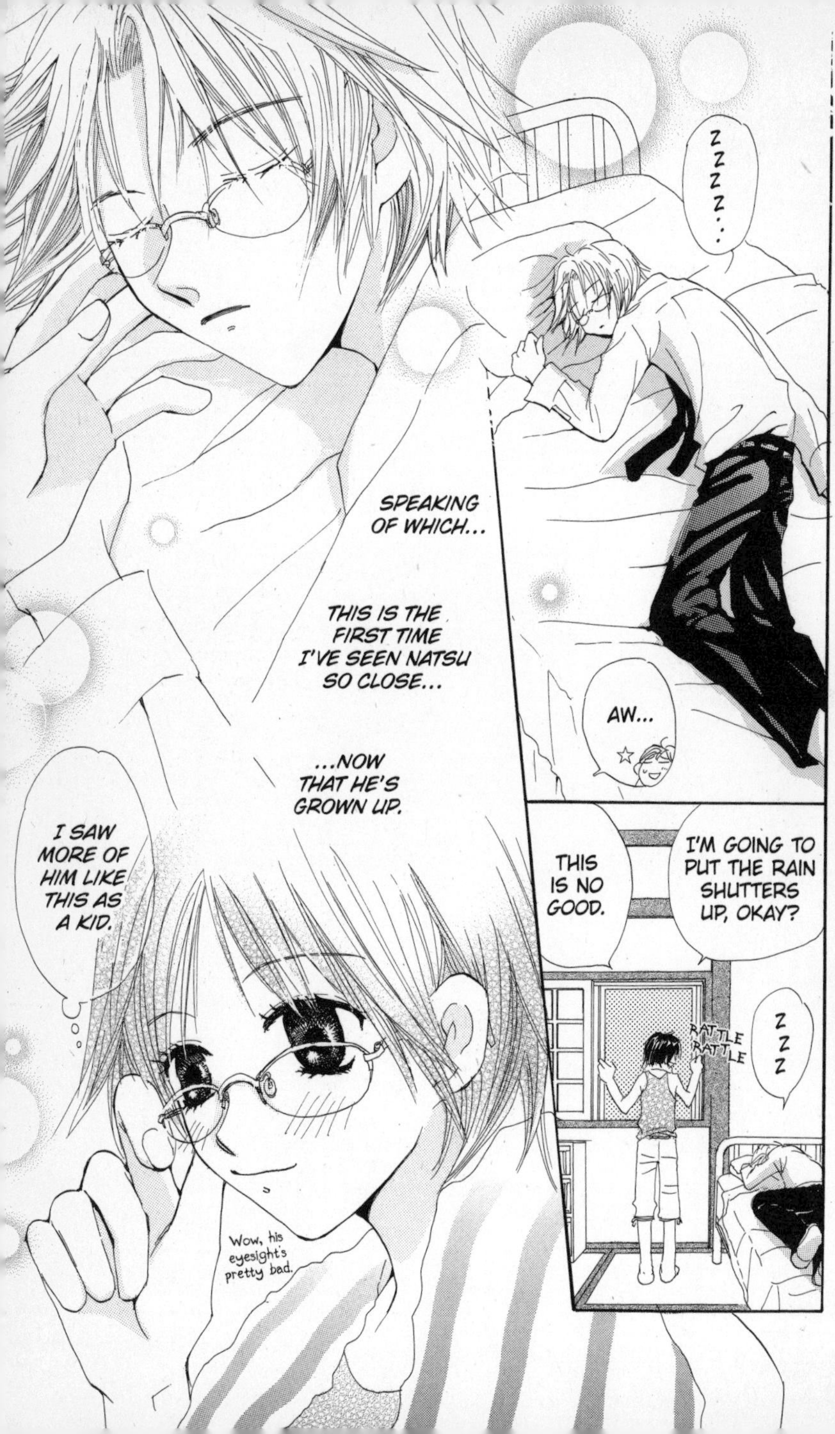
ZZZZ...
AW...
I'M GOING TO PUT THE RAIN SHUTTERS UP, OKAY?
THIS IS NO GOOD.
ZZZ
RATTLE RATTLE
SPEAKING OF WHICH...
THIS IS THE FIRST TIME I'VE SEEN NATSU SO CLOSE...
...NOW THAT HE'S GROWN UP.
I SAW MORE OF HIM LIKE THIS AS A KID.
Wow, his eyesight's pretty bad.

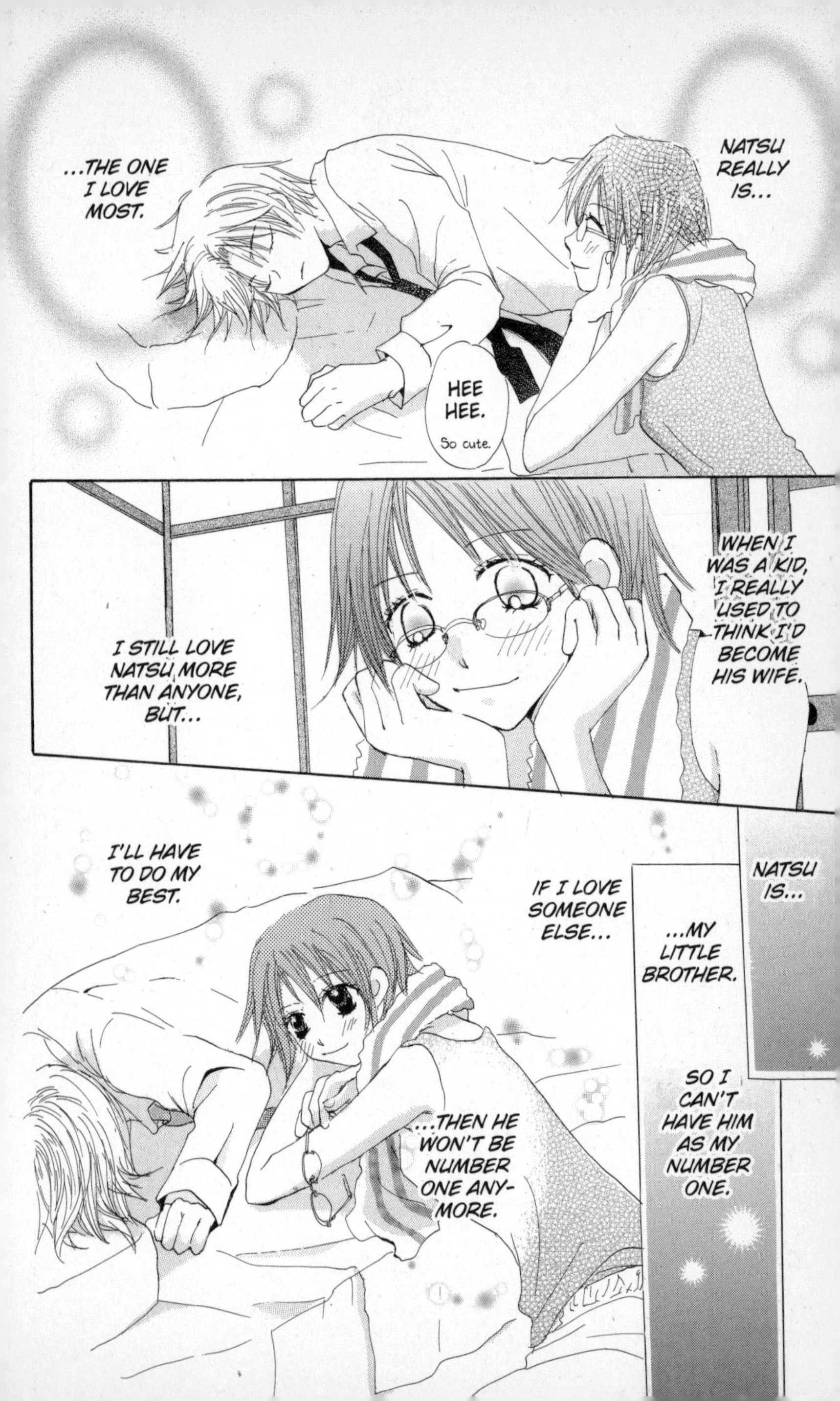
NATSU REALLY IS...
...THE ONE I LOVE MOST.
HEE HEE.
So cute.
WHEN I WAS A KID, I REALLY USED TO THINK I'D BECOME HIS WIFE.
I STILL LOVE NATSU MORE THAN ANYONE, BUT...
NATSU IS...
...MY LITTLE BROTHER.
SO I CAN'T HAVE HIM AS MY NUMBER ONE.
IF I LOVE SOMEONE ELSE...
...THEN HE WON'T BE NUMBER ONE ANY-MORE.
I'LL HAVE TO DO MY BEST.

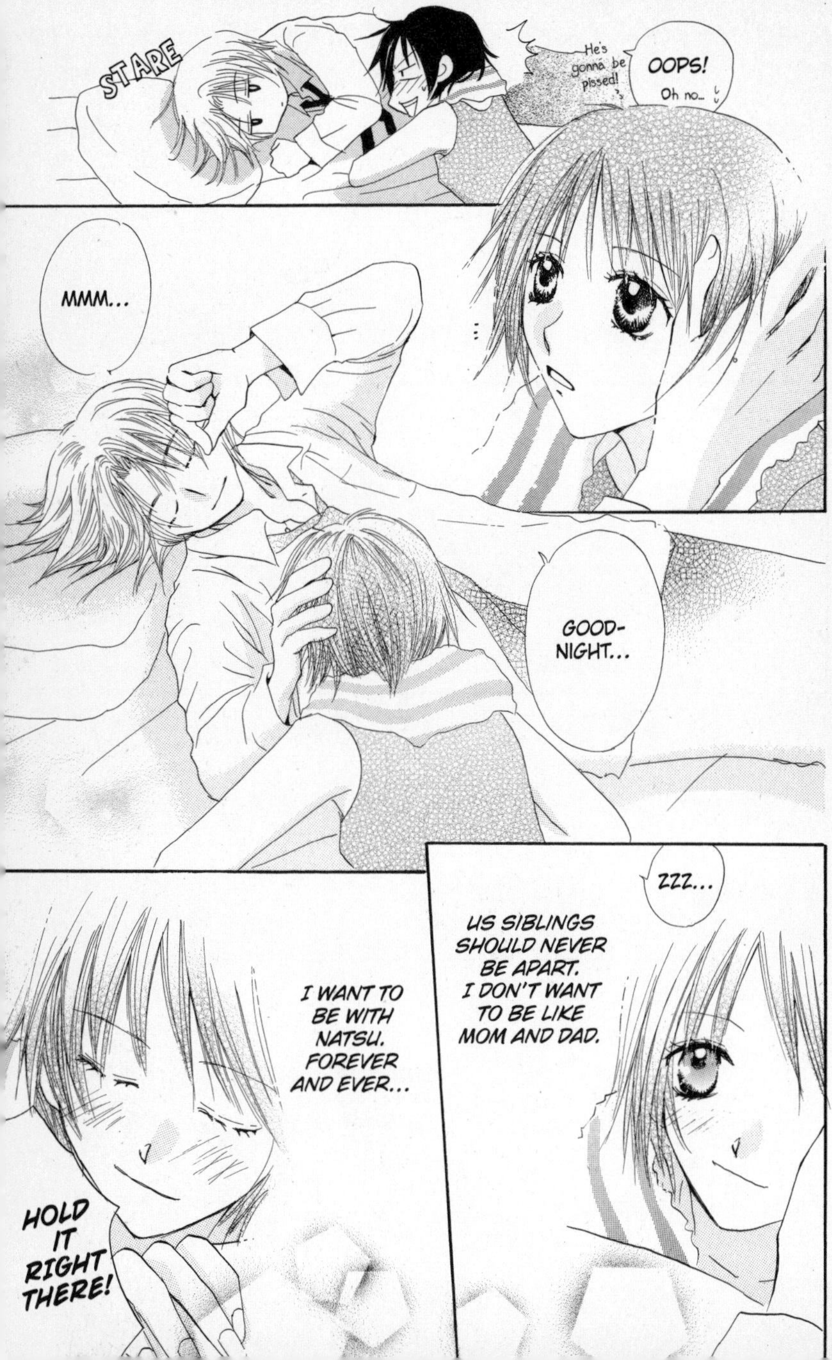
OOPS!
Oh no...
He's gonna be pissed!
STARE
MMM...
GOOD-NIGHT...
ZZZ...
US SIBLINGS SHOULD NEVER BE APART. I DON'T WANT TO BE LIKE MOM AND DAD.
I WANT TO BE WITH NATSU. FOREVER AND EVER...
HOLD IT RIGHT THERE!

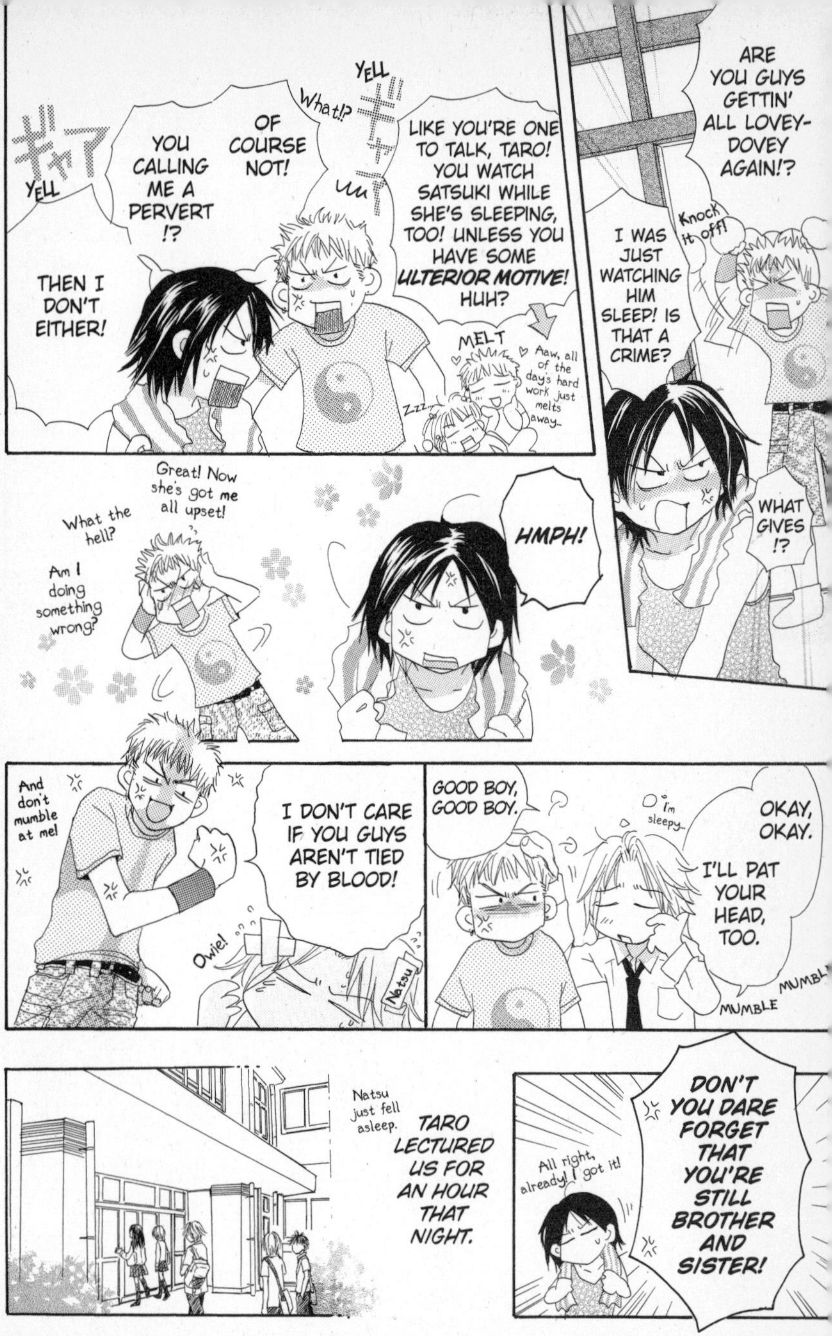
ARE YOU GUYS GETTIN' ALL LOVEY-DOVEY AGAIN!?
Knock it off!
I WAS JUST WATCHING HIM SLEEP! IS THAT A CRIME?
WHAT GIVES!?
LIKE YOU'RE ONE TO TALK, TARO! YOU WATCH SATSUKI WHILE SHE'S SLEEPING, TOO! UNLESS YOU HAVE SOME ULTERIOR MOTIVE! HUH?
YELL
What!?
OF COURSE NOT!
YOU CALLING ME A PERVERT!?
YELL
THEN I DON'T EITHER!
MELT
Aaw, all of the day's hard work just melts away...
Zzz...
HMPH!
Great! Now she's got me all upset!
What the hell?
Am I doing something wrong?
OKAY, OKAY.
I'm sleepy...
I'LL PAT YOUR HEAD, TOO.
GOOD BOY, GOOD BOY.
MUMBLE MUMBLE
I DON'T CARE IF YOU GUYS AREN'T TIED BY BLOOD!
Owie!
Natsu
And don't mumble at me!
DON'T YOU DARE FORGET THAT YOU'RE STILL BROTHER AND SISTER!
All right, already! I got it!
TARO LECTURED US FOR AN HOUR THAT NIGHT.
Natsu just fell asleep.

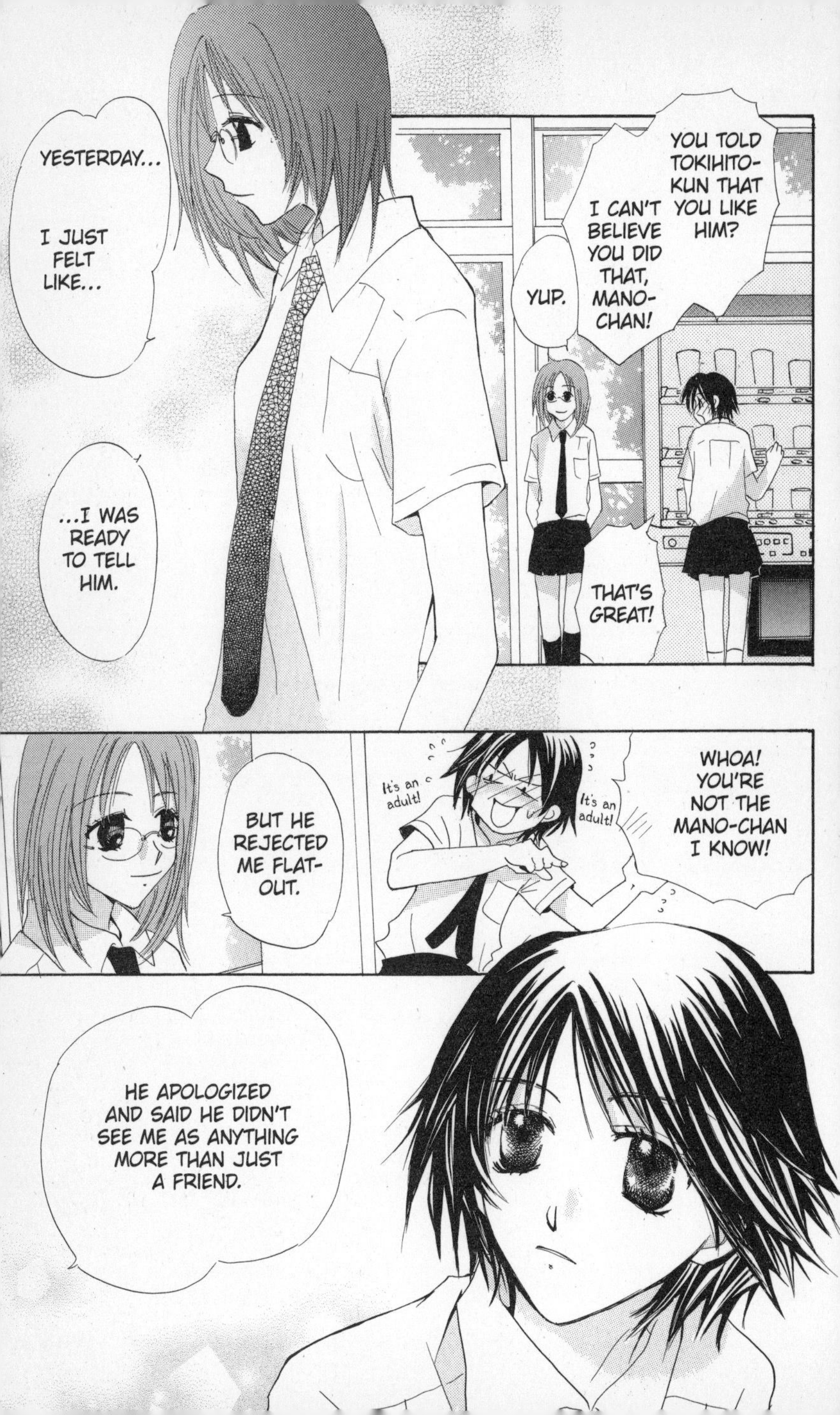
YOU TOLD TOKIHITO-KUN THAT YOU LIKE HIM?
I CAN'T BELIEVE YOU DID THAT, MANO-CHAN!
YUP.
THAT'S GREAT!
YESTERDAY...
I JUST FELT LIKE...
...I WAS READY TO TELL HIM.
WHOA! YOU'RE NOT THE MANO-CHAN I KNOW!
It's an adult!
It's an adult!
BUT HE REJECTED ME FLAT-OUT.
HE APOLOGIZED AND SAID HE DIDN'T SEE ME AS ANYTHING MORE THAN JUST A FRIEND.

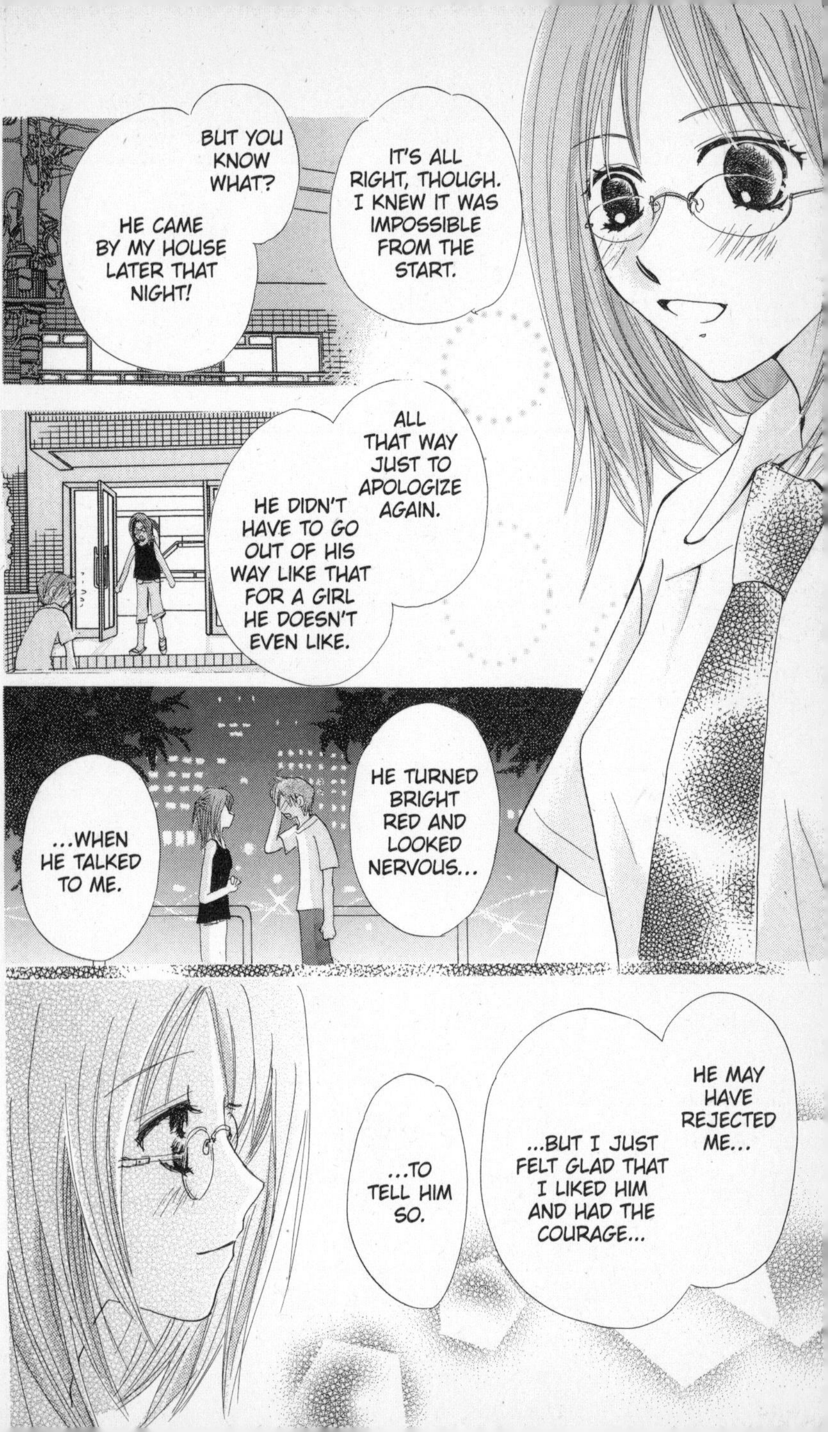
IT'S ALL RIGHT, THOUGH. I KNEW IT WAS IMPOSSIBLE FROM THE START.
BUT YOU KNOW WHAT?
HE CAME BY MY HOUSE LATER THAT NIGHT!
ALL THAT WAY JUST TO APOLOGIZE AGAIN.
HE DIDN'T HAVE TO GO OUT OF HIS WAY LIKE THAT FOR A GIRL HE DOESN'T EVEN LIKE.
HE TURNED BRIGHT RED AND LOOKED NERVOUS...
...WHEN HE TALKED TO ME.
HE MAY HAVE REJECTED ME...
...BUT I JUST FELT GLAD THAT I LIKED HIM AND HAD THE COURAGE...
...TO TELL HIM SO.

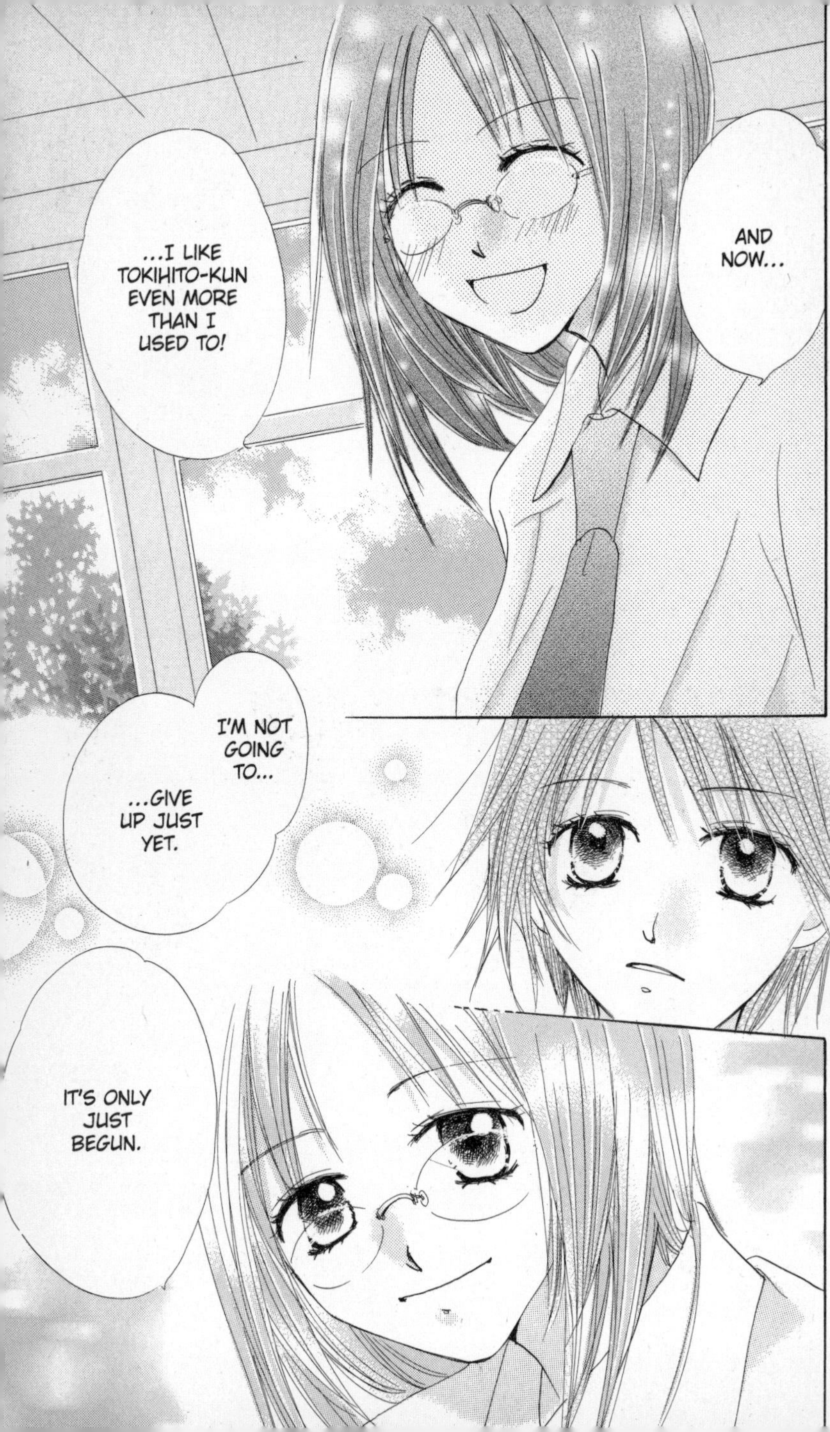
AND NOW...
...I LIKE TOKIHITO-KUN EVEN MORE THAN I USED TO!
I'M NOT GOING TO...
...GIVE UP JUST YET.
IT'S ONLY JUST BEGUN.

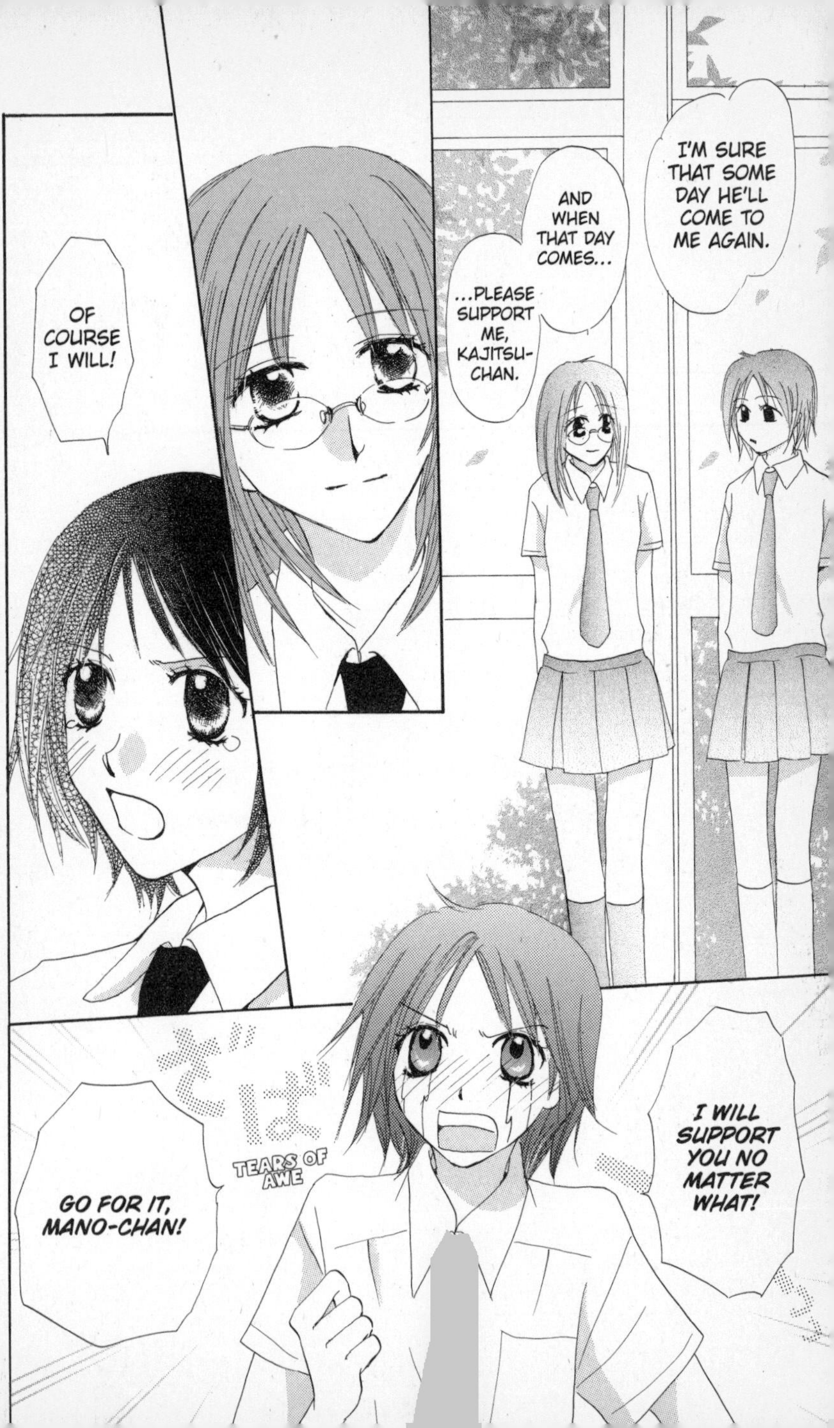
I'M SURE THAT SOME DAY HE'LL COME TO ME AGAIN.
AND WHEN THAT DAY COMES...
...PLEASE SUPPORT ME, KAJITSU-CHAN.
OF COURSE I WILL!
I WILL SUPPORT YOU NO MATTER WHAT!
TEARS OF AWE
GO FOR IT, MANO-CHAN!

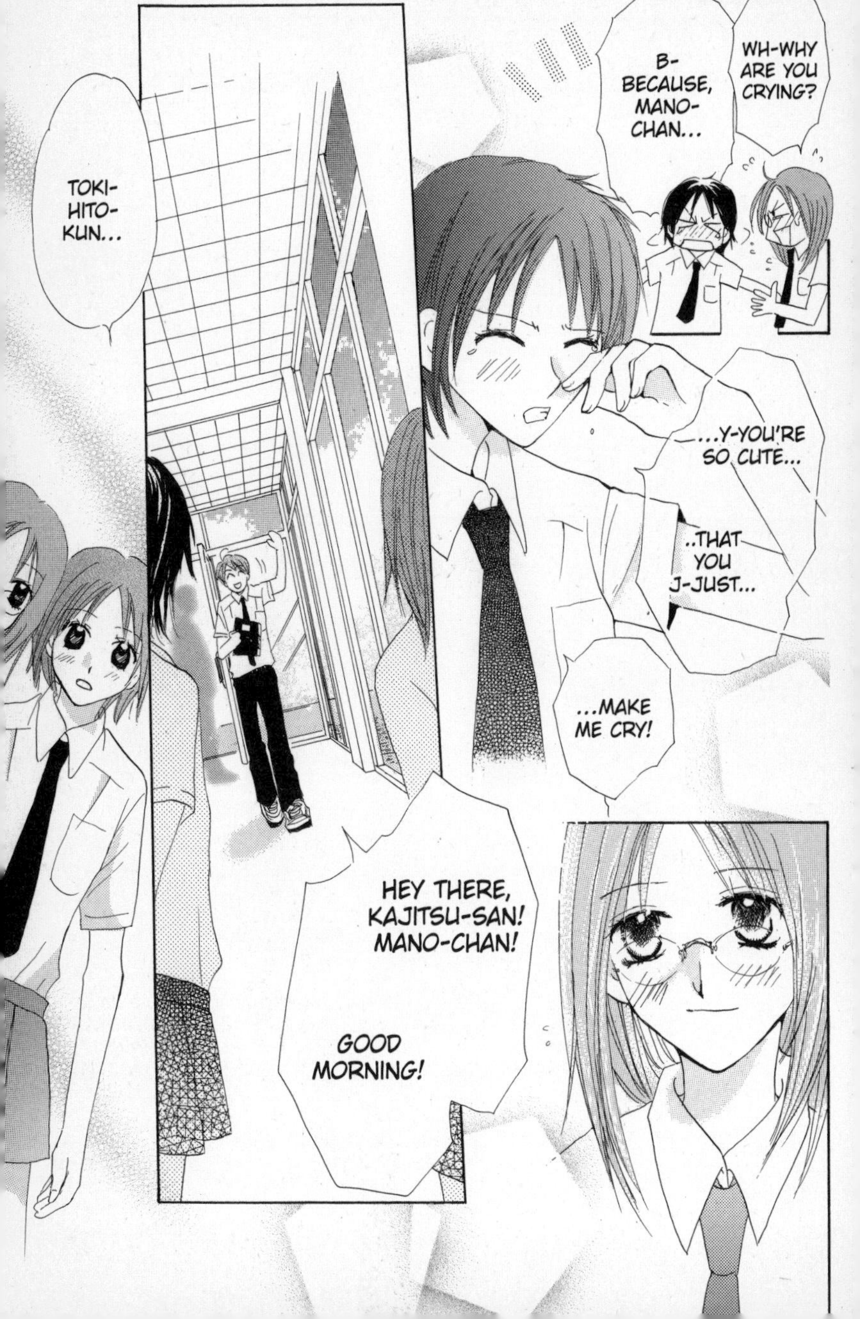
WH-WHY ARE YOU CRYING?
B-BECAUSE, MANO-CHAN...
...Y-YOU'RE SO CUTE...
..THAT YOU J-JUST...
...MAKE ME CRY!
HEY THERE, KAJITSU-SAN! MANO-CHAN!
GOOD MORNING!
TOKI-HITO-KUN...

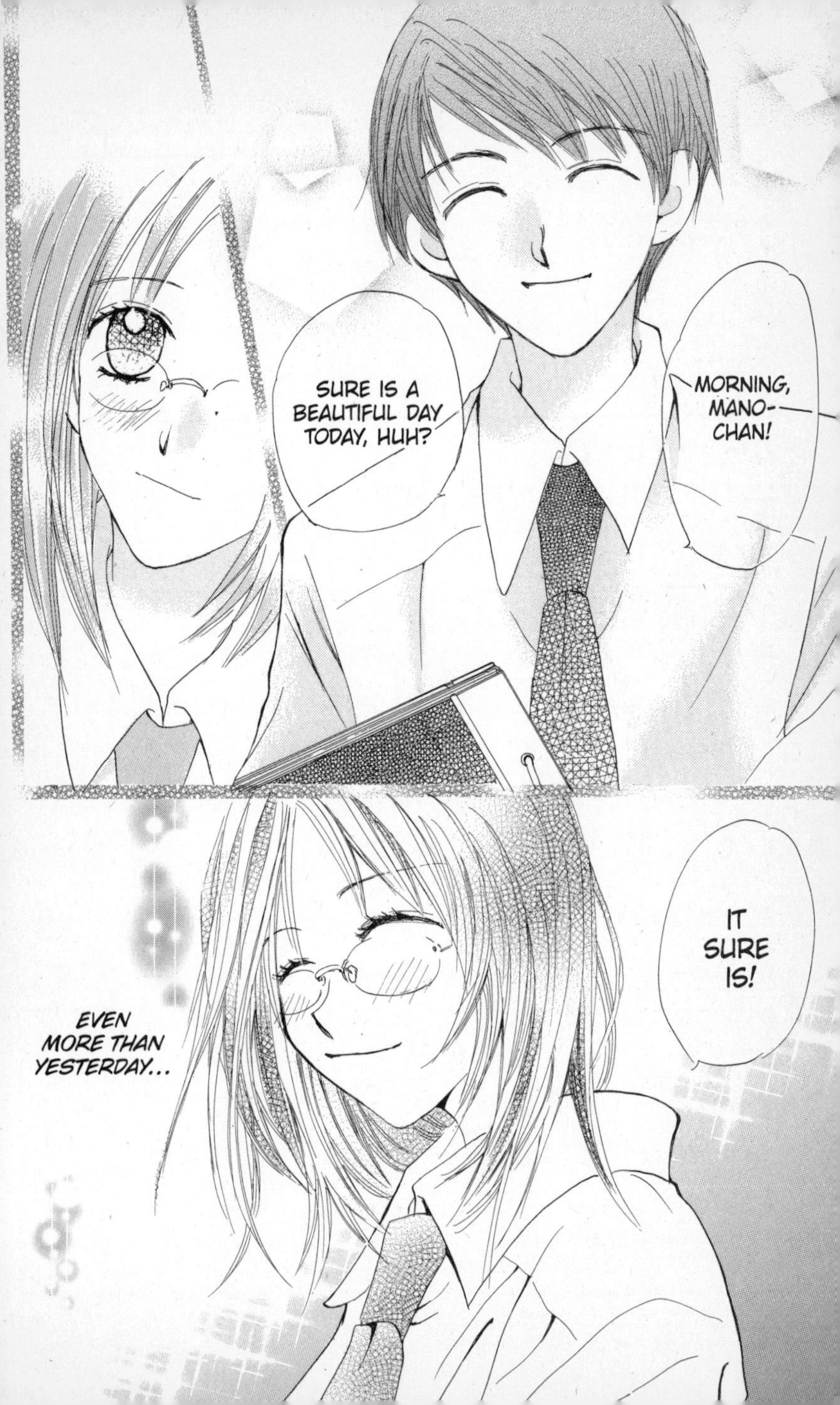
MORNING, MANO-CHAN!
SURE IS A BEAUTIFUL DAY TODAY, HUH?
IT SURE IS!
EVEN MORE THAN YESTERDAY...

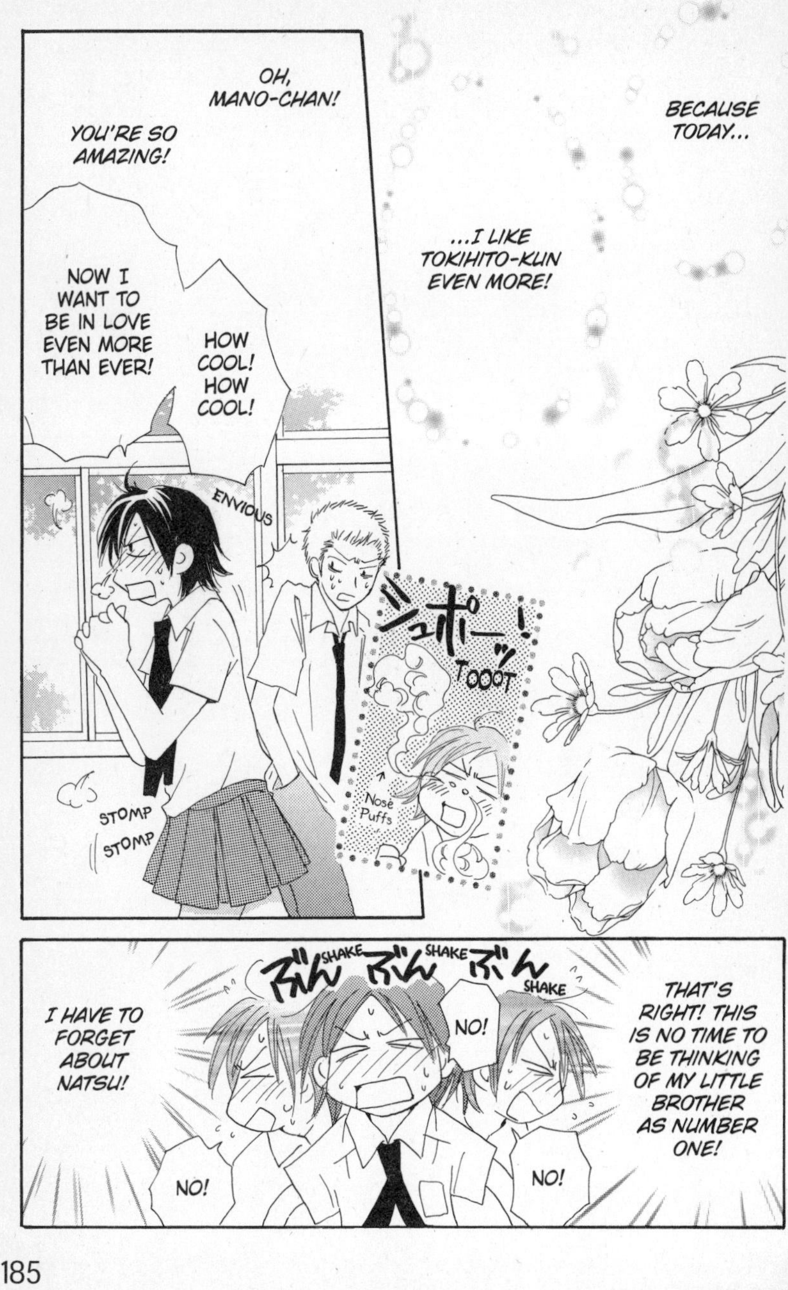
BECAUSE TODAY...
...I LIKE TOKIHITO-KUN EVEN MORE!
OH, MANO-CHAN!
YOU'RE SO AMAZING!
HOW COOL! HOW COOL!
NOW I WANT TO BE IN LOVE EVEN MORE THAN EVER!
ENVIOUS
ジュポー！
TOOOT
Nose Puffs
STOMP
STOMP
THAT'S RIGHT! THIS IS NO TIME TO BE THINKING OF MY LITTLE BROTHER AS NUMBER ONE!
ぶん
SHAKE
ぶん
SHAKE
ぶん
SHAKE
NO!
NO!
NO!
I HAVE TO FORGET ABOUT NATSU!

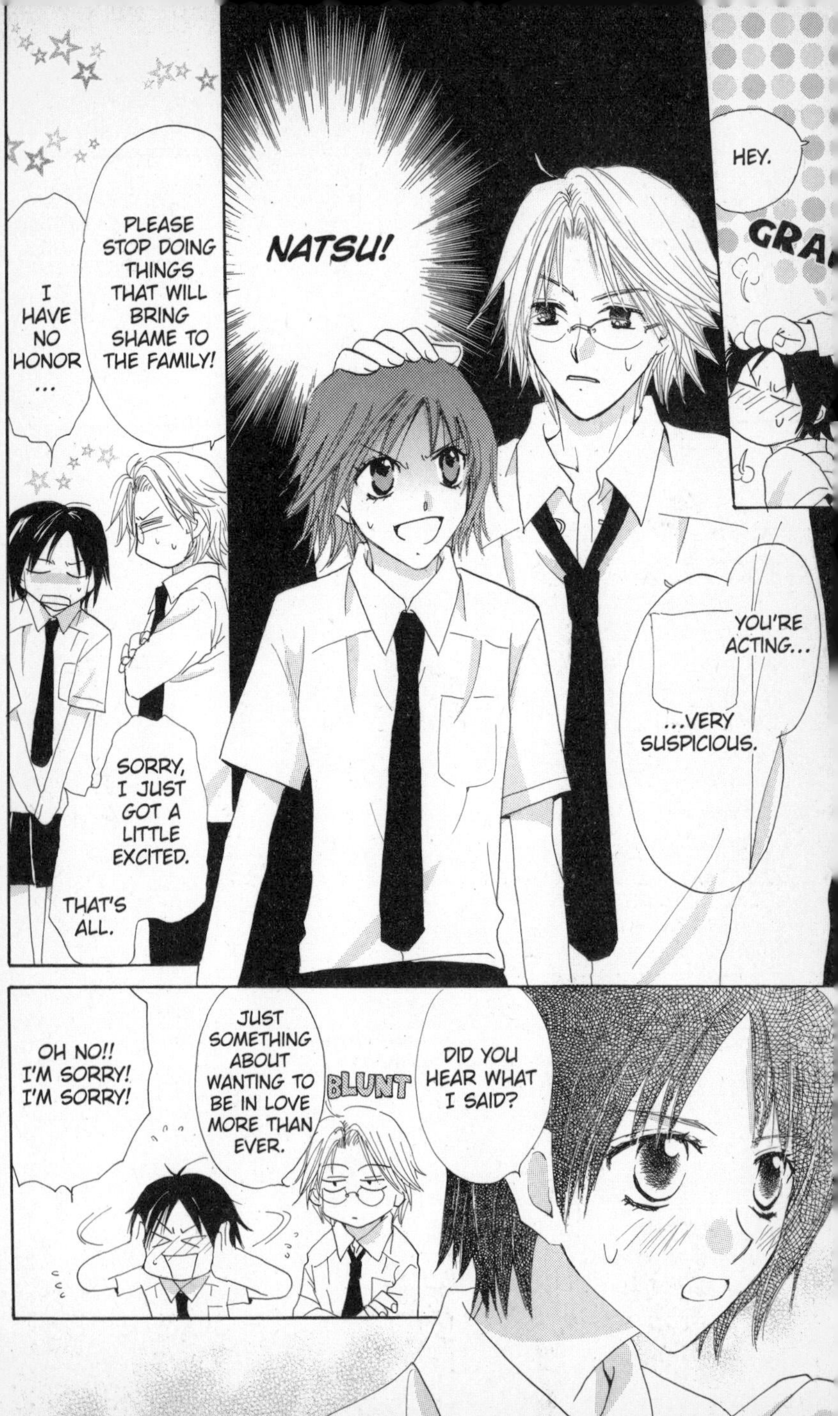
HEY.
GRA
NATSU!
YOU'RE ACTING...
...VERY SUSPICIOUS.
PLEASE STOP DOING THINGS THAT WILL BRING SHAME TO THE FAMILY!
I HAVE NO HONOR...
SORRY, I JUST GOT A LITTLE EXCITED.
THAT'S ALL.
DID YOU HEAR WHAT I SAID?
JUST SOMETHING ABOUT WANTING TO BE IN LOVE MORE THAN EVER.
BLUNT
OH NO!! I'M SORRY! I'M SORRY!

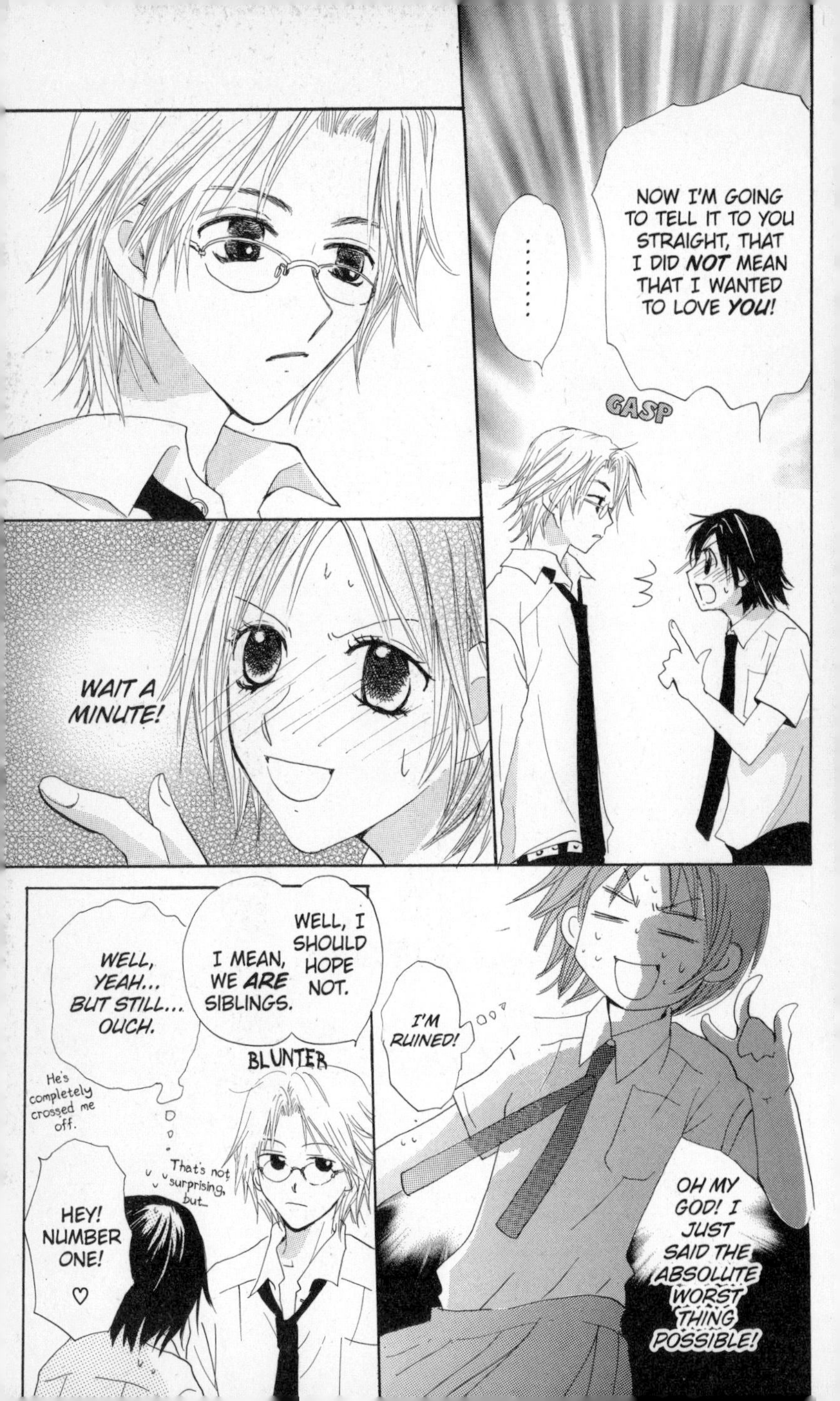
NOW I'M GOING TO TELL IT TO YOU STRAIGHT, THAT I DID ***NOT*** MEAN THAT I WANTED TO LOVE ***YOU!***
......
GASP
WAIT A MINUTE!
I'M RUINED!
OH MY GOD! I JUST SAID THE ABSOLUTE WORST THING POSSIBLE!
WELL, I SHOULD HOPE NOT.
I MEAN, WE ***ARE*** SIBLINGS.
BLUNTER
WELL, YEAH... BUT STILL... OUCH.
He's completely crossed me off.
That's not surprising, but...
HEY! NUMBER ONE! ♡

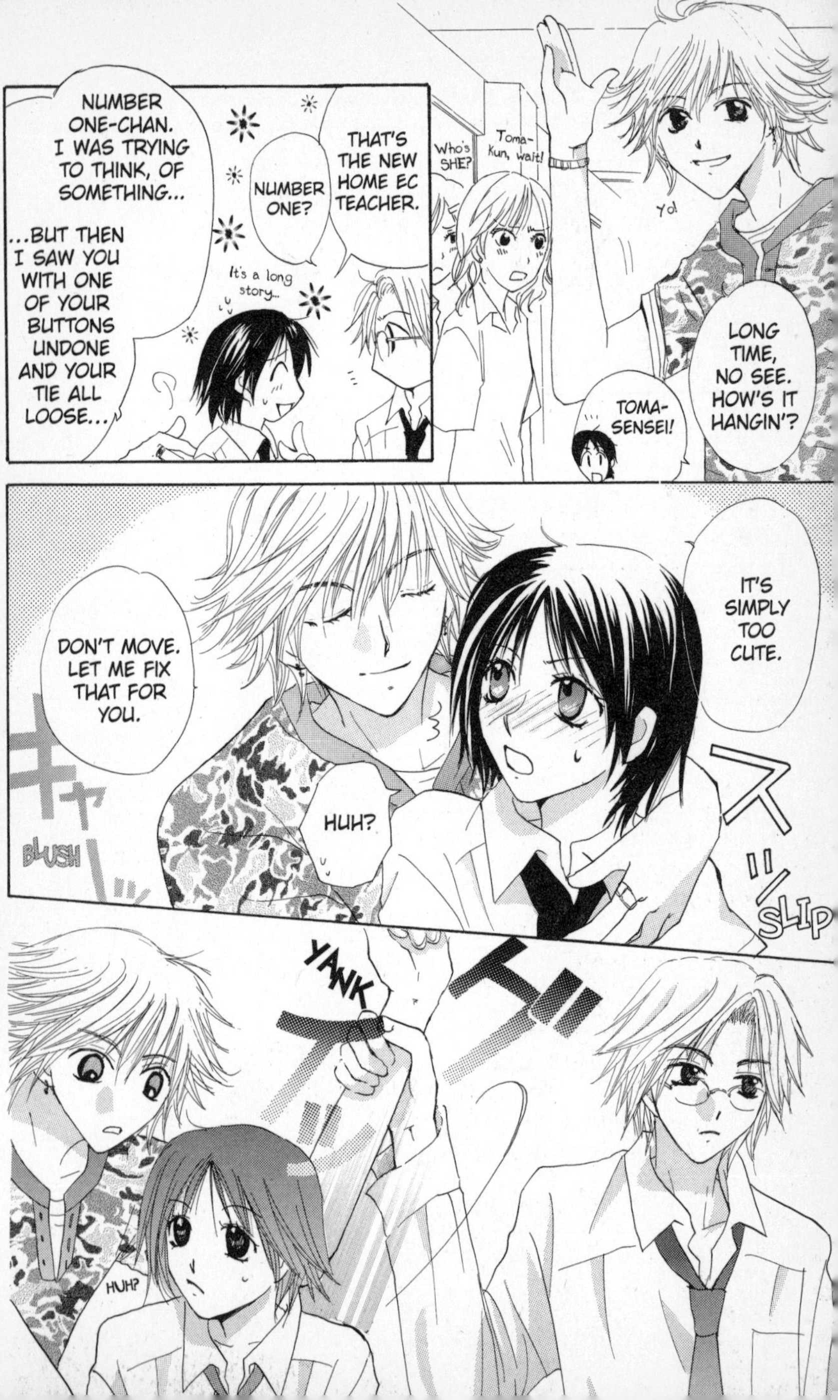

Yo!
LONG TIME, NO SEE. HOW'S IT HANGIN'?
Toma-kun, wait!
Who's SHE?
TOMA-SENSEI!
THAT'S THE NEW HOME EC TEACHER.
NUMBER ONE?
It's a long story...
NUMBER ONE-CHAN. I WAS TRYING TO THINK, OF SOMETHING...
...BUT THEN I SAW YOU WITH ONE OF YOUR BUTTONS UNDONE AND YOUR TIE ALL LOOSE...
IT'S SIMPLY TOO CUTE.
SLIP
DON'T MOVE. LET ME FIX THAT FOR YOU.
HUH?
BLUSH
YANK
HUH?

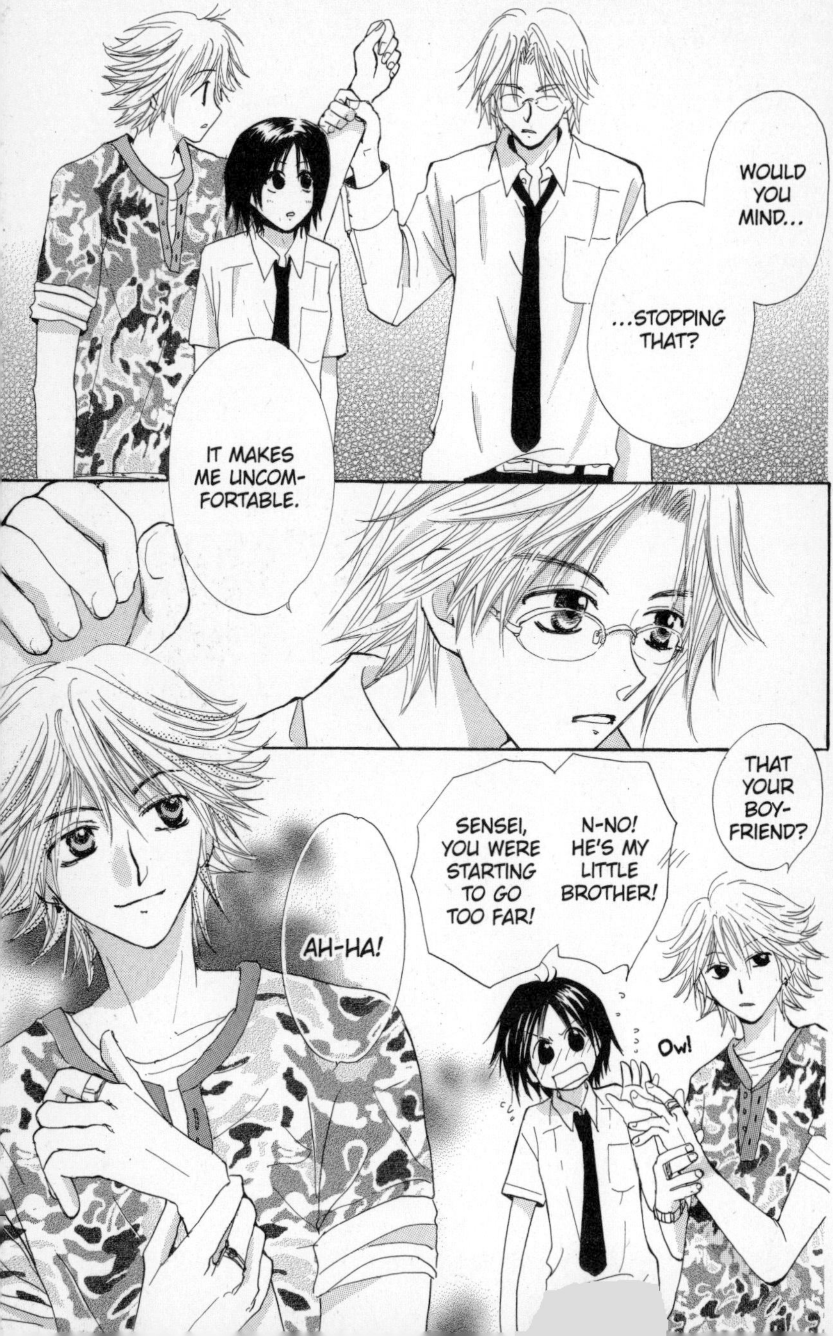
WOULD YOU MIND...
...STOPPING THAT?
IT MAKES ME UNCOM-FORTABLE.
THAT YOUR BOY-FRIEND?
N-NO! HE'S MY LITTLE BROTHER!
SENSEI, YOU WERE STARTING TO GO TOO FAR!
Ow!
AH-HA!

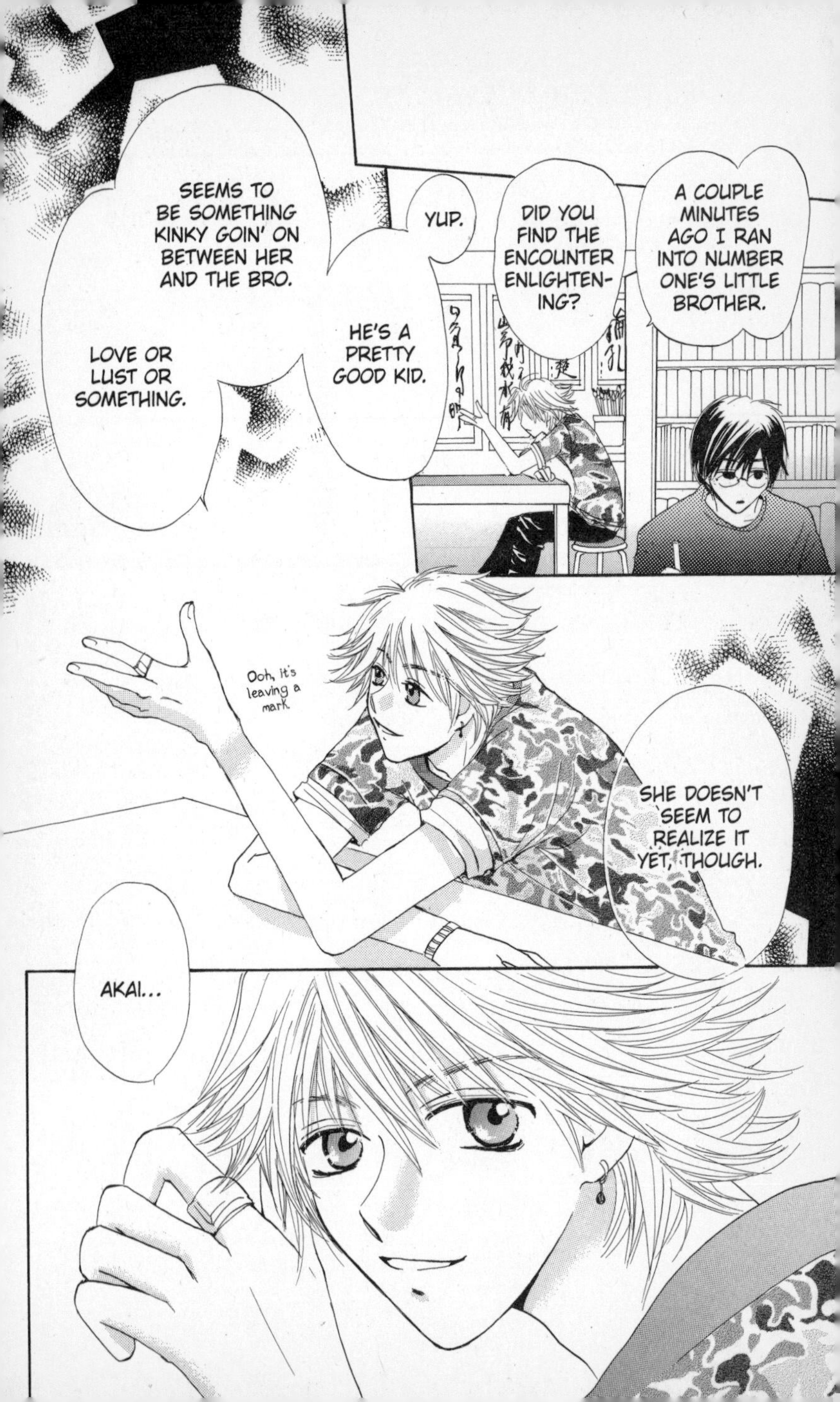

A COUPLE MINUTES AGO I RAN INTO NUMBER ONE'S LITTLE BROTHER.
DID YOU FIND THE ENCOUNTER ENLIGHTEN-ING?
YUP.
HE'S A PRETTY GOOD KID.
SEEMS TO BE SOMETHING KINKY GOIN' ON BETWEEN HER AND THE BRO.
LOVE OR LUST OR SOMETHING.
SHE DOESN'T SEEM TO REALIZE IT YET, THOUGH.
Ooh, it's leaving a mark.
AKAI...

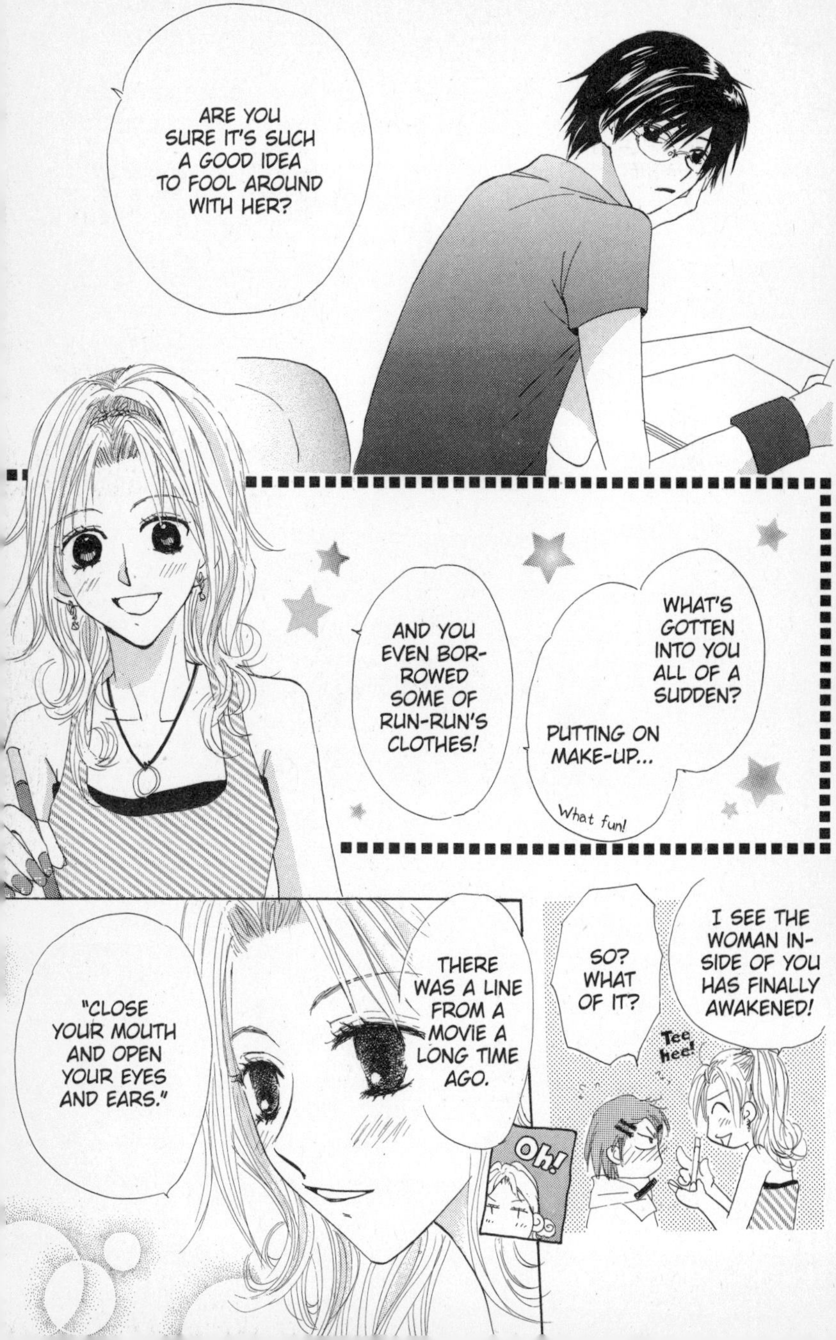
ARE YOU SURE IT'S SUCH A GOOD IDEA TO FOOL AROUND WITH HER?
WHAT'S GOTTEN INTO YOU ALL OF A SUDDEN?
PUTTING ON MAKE-UP...
What fun!
AND YOU EVEN BOR-ROWED SOME OF RUN-RUN'S CLOTHES!
I SEE THE WOMAN IN-SIDE OF YOU HAS FINALLY AWAKENED!
SO? WHAT OF IT?
Tee hee!
Oh!
THERE WAS A LINE FROM A MOVIE A LONG TIME AGO.
"CLOSE YOUR MOUTH AND OPEN YOUR EYES AND EARS."

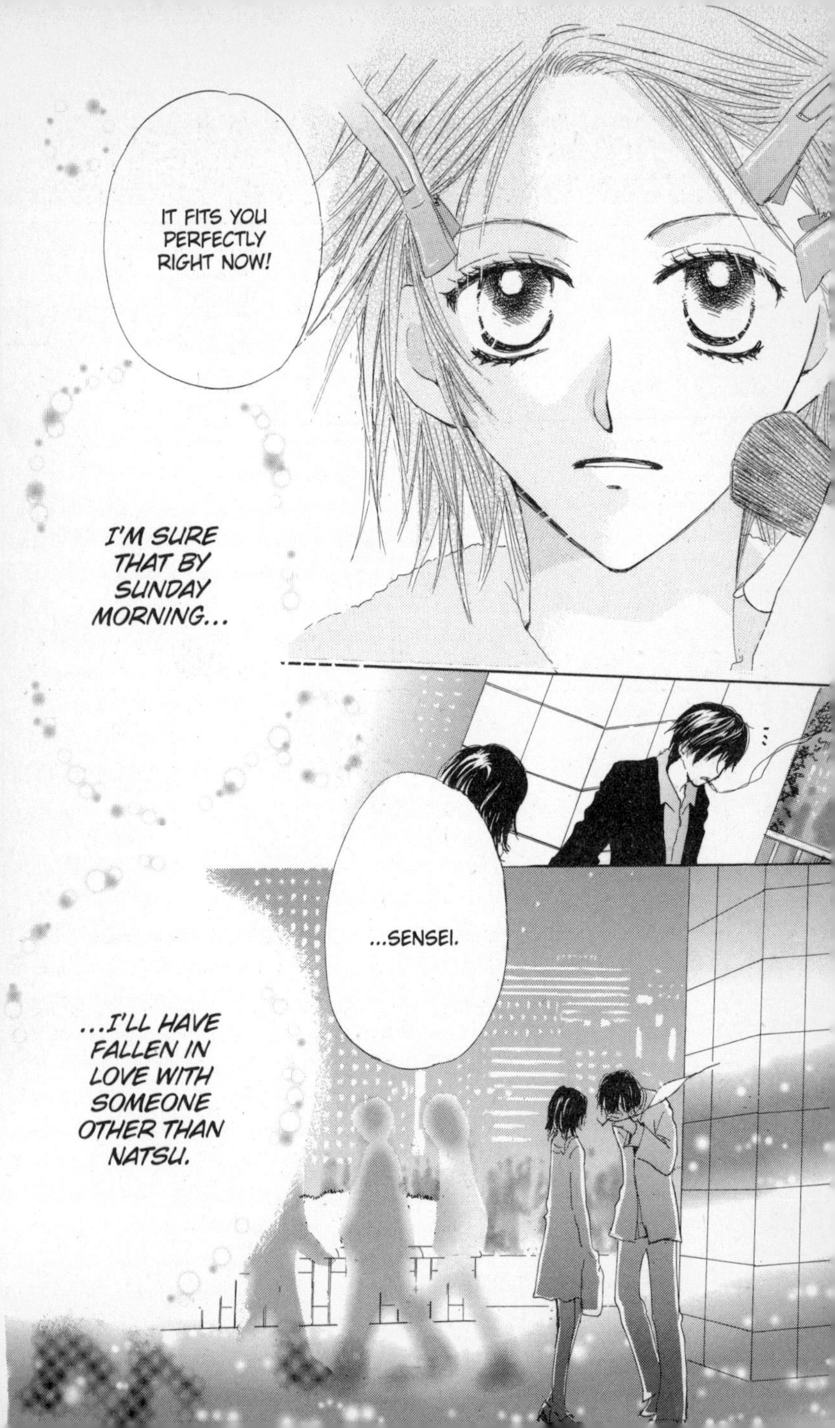
IT FITS YOU PERFECTLY RIGHT NOW!
I'M SURE THAT BY SUNDAY MORNING...
...SENSEI.
...I'LL HAVE FALLEN IN LOVE WITH SOMEONE OTHER THAN NATSU.

Bonus Comic 3: A Family Of Love

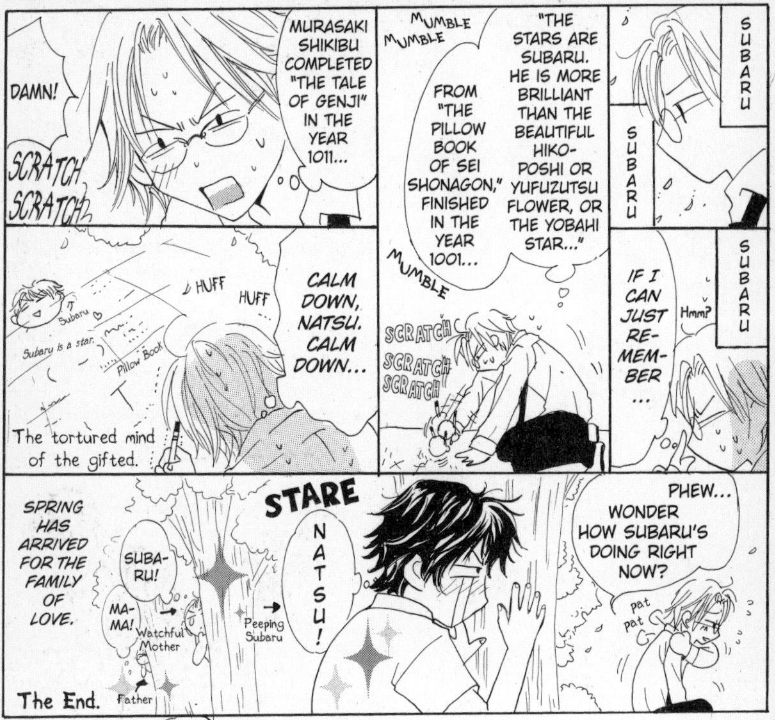

SUBARU
SUBARU
SUBARU
IF I CAN JUST RE-MEMBER...
Hmm?
MUMBLE MUMBLE
FROM "THE PILLOW BOOK OF SEI SHONAGON," FINISHED IN THE YEAR 1001...
"THE STARS ARE SUBARU. HE IS MORE BRILLIANT THAN THE BEAUTIFUL HIKO-POSHI OR YUFUZUTSU FLOWER, OR THE YOBAHI STAR..."
MUMBLE
SCRATCH SCRATCH SCRATCH
MURASAKI SHIKIBU COMPLETED "THE TALE OF GENJI" IN THE YEAR 1011...
DAMN!
SCRATCH SCRATCH
CALM DOWN, NATSU. CALM DOWN...
HUFF
HUFF
Subaru
Subaru is a star.
Pillow Book
The tortured mind of the gifted.
PHEW... WONDER HOW SUBARU'S DOING RIGHT NOW?
pat pat
STARE
NATSU!
Peeping Subaru
SUBA-RU!
MA-MA!
Watchful Mother
Father
SPRING HAS ARRIVED FOR THE FAMILY OF LOVE.
The End.

Plus **Postscript** Shioko Summary October, 2003

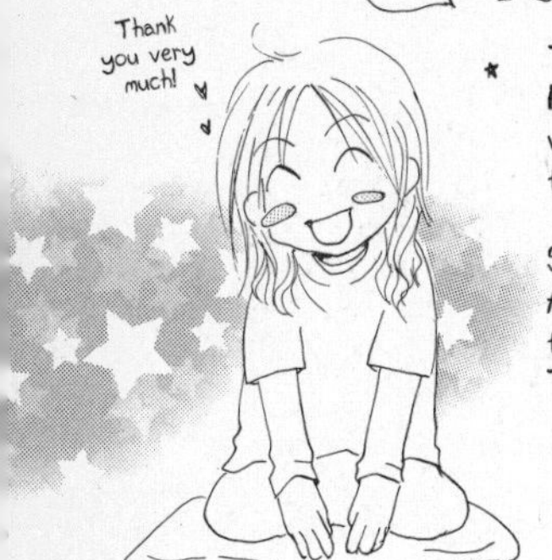

Thank you very much!

Thank you so much for reading until the very end! In Vol. 1, I said I was finished with half the plot, but now I'm not sure what's going to happen in the next chapter...though I do have the ending already figured out.

I'd like to thank everyone who helped me greatly: Kise-san, Sen-chan, Imuzo, Yamamoto-san, Miho-chan, and Ayu-chan. Also to Yamazaki-san, and my dear editor who saw me through the whole way. And last but not least, my readers! Thank you all so much!

Until next time!

Shioko Mizuki

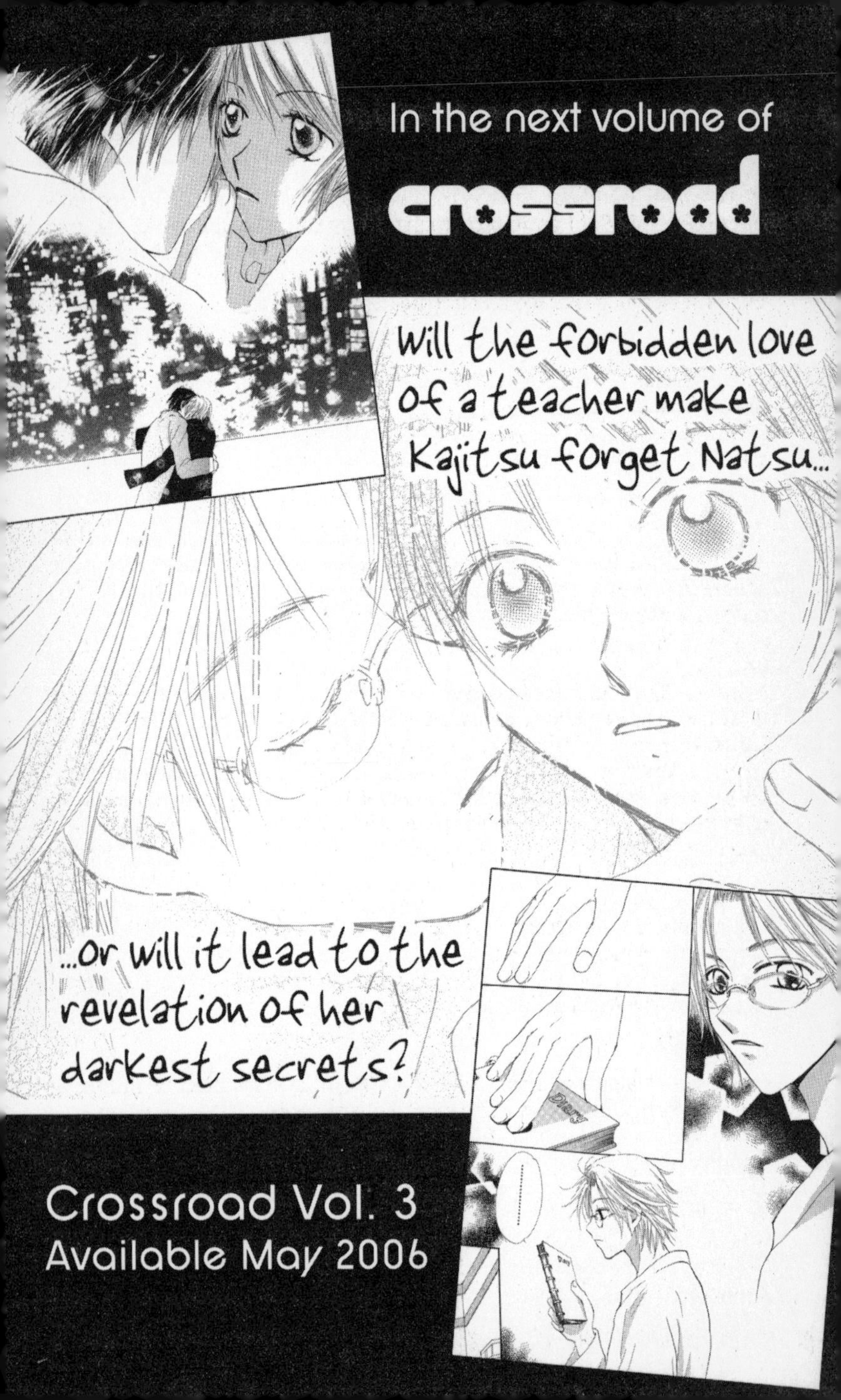
In the next volume of
crossroad
Will the forbidden love of a teacher make Kajitsu forget Natsu...
...or will it lead to the revelation of her darkest secrets?
Crossroad Vol. 3
Available May 2006

Translator's Notes

Pg. 11
Yaki-Imo—*Yaki-Imo*, or baked sweet potatoes, are a fall and winter comfort food. Sold from street carts or roaming trucks (like the one Tokihito-kun works in) the sweet potatoes are baked fresh in wood-fired ovens with long chimneys. Vendors play a Yaki-Imo song to attract customers, much like ice cream trucks in America.

Pg. 37
School terms – In Japanese high schools, the year is broken into three terms. School begins around April 1st, so now that Spring is here, a new school year begins! As second year students, Kajitsu and friends are entering the equivalent of 11th grade.

Pg. 38
The line, "What's that 'I got caught shoplifting in the Valley of the Hippos' look?" refers to the setting for a classic Japanese anime about the Muumin of Muumin Valley, which are creatures that look like hippos (just as Kajitsu's face does in the panel).

Pg. 74
Bento — *Bento*, or boxed lunches, are a traditional Japanese style of meal in which an assortment of foods are arranged in compartmentalized boxes. Often, *bento* presentations can be quite beautiful, featuring a variety of colors and textures and aesthetic flourishes. The boxes that Kajitsu prepares are the type that a doting mother might make for a child, with hot dogs cut to look like octopi and fish cake, *konnyaku* (starch cake) and veggies shaped into stars and hearts.

Pg. 80
Okonomiyaki – An Osaka regional specialty, *okonomiyaki* is a delicious mixture of eggs, veggies, meats, and just about anything else you want thrown together and cooked up on a grill right in front of you. It's sort of like a cross between an omelet and a pancake.

Pg. 103
Gakuran—Natsu's K High School uniform is a gakuran, a military-style uniform commonly worn in all-boys schools.

Pg. 193
The Pillow Book — The poem that Natsu is trying to remember was written by Sei Shonagon, a high-ranking lady-in-waiting from the Heian era who wrote one of Japan's most famous classics, *The Pillow Book of Sei Shonagon*. The subject of this particular poem is a cluster of bright stars known as "Subaru" in Japan (called "the Pleiades" by the Greeks).

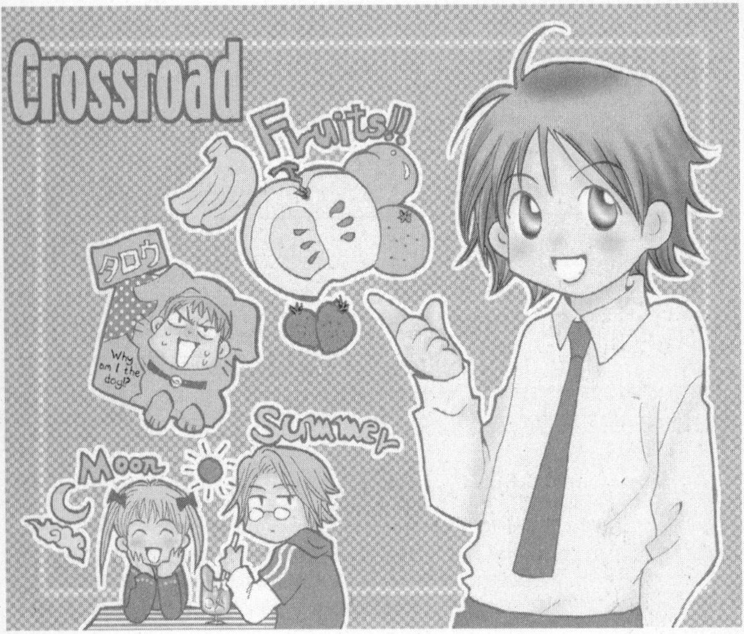
Crossroad
Fruits!!
タロウ
Why am I the dog!?
Summer
Moon

GO! COMI IS NOW TAKING FAN ART FOR FUTURE VOLUMES OF CROSSROAD! IF YOU'D LIKE TO TRY YOUR HAND AT DRAWING KAJITSU, NATSU OR ANYONE ELSE FROM (OR INSPIRED BY!) CROSSROAD, MAIL IT TO US AND YOU MIGHT JUST SEE IT IN PRINT! ALL ARTWORK SUBMITTED WILL NOT BE RETURNED, SO IF IT'S IMPORTANT TO YOU, MAKE SURE TO SEND A COPY. IF YOU'RE UNDER 18, PLEASE INCLUDE YOUR PARENT'S WRITTEN PERMISSION FOR US TO PUBLISH THE ART WITH YOUR SUBMISSION.

SEND YOUR FAN ART AND LETTERS TO:

GO! MEDIA ENTERTAINMENT
ATTN: CROSSROAD
5737 KANAN RD. #591
AGOURA HILLS, CA 91301

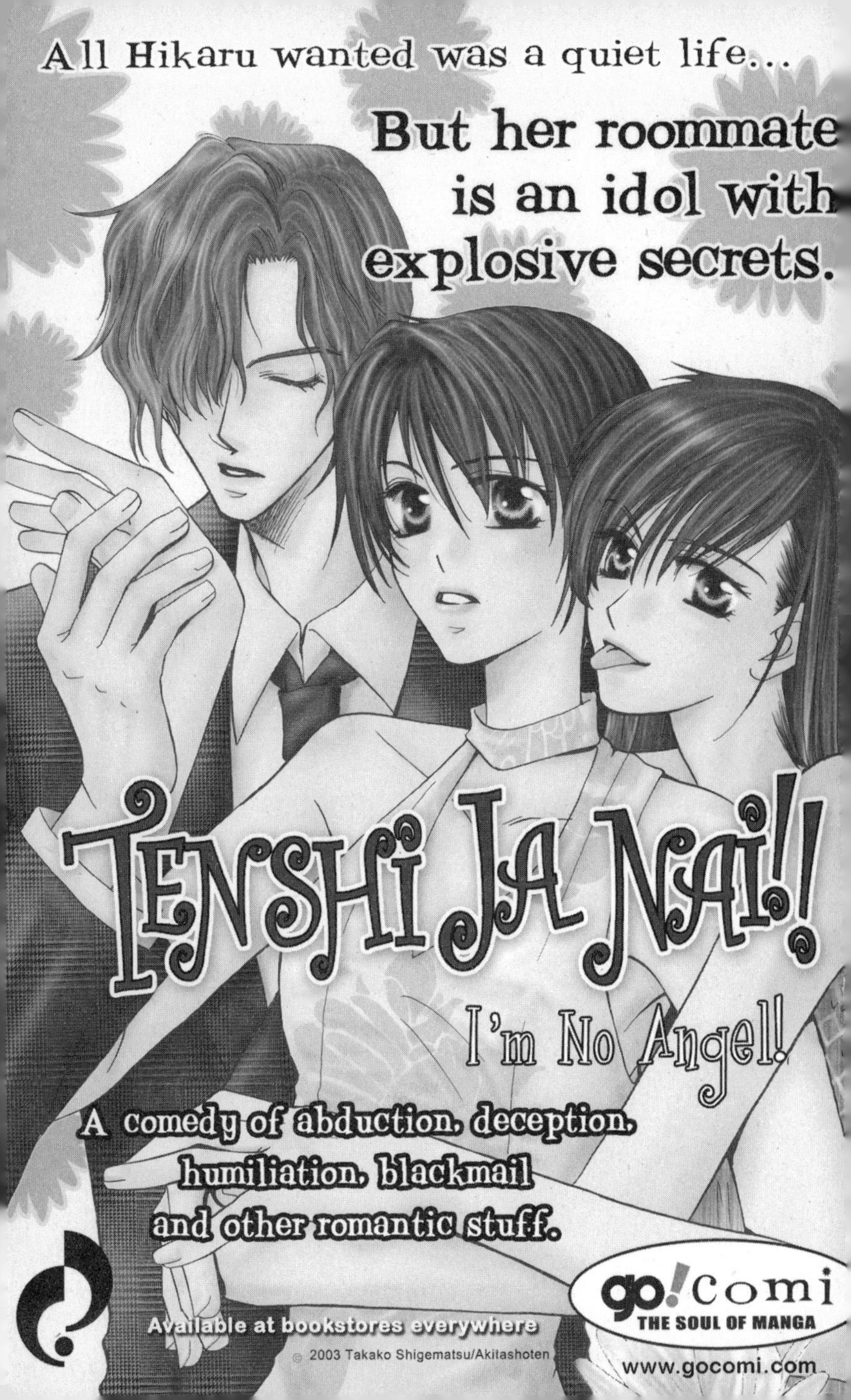
All Hikaru wanted was a quiet life...
But her roommate is an idol with explosive secrets.
TENSHI JA NAI!!
I'm No Angel!
A comedy of abduction, deception, humiliation, blackmail and other romantic stuff.
Available at bookstores everywhere
© 2003 Takako Shigematsu/Akitashoten
go!comi
THE SOUL OF MANGA
www.gocomi.com

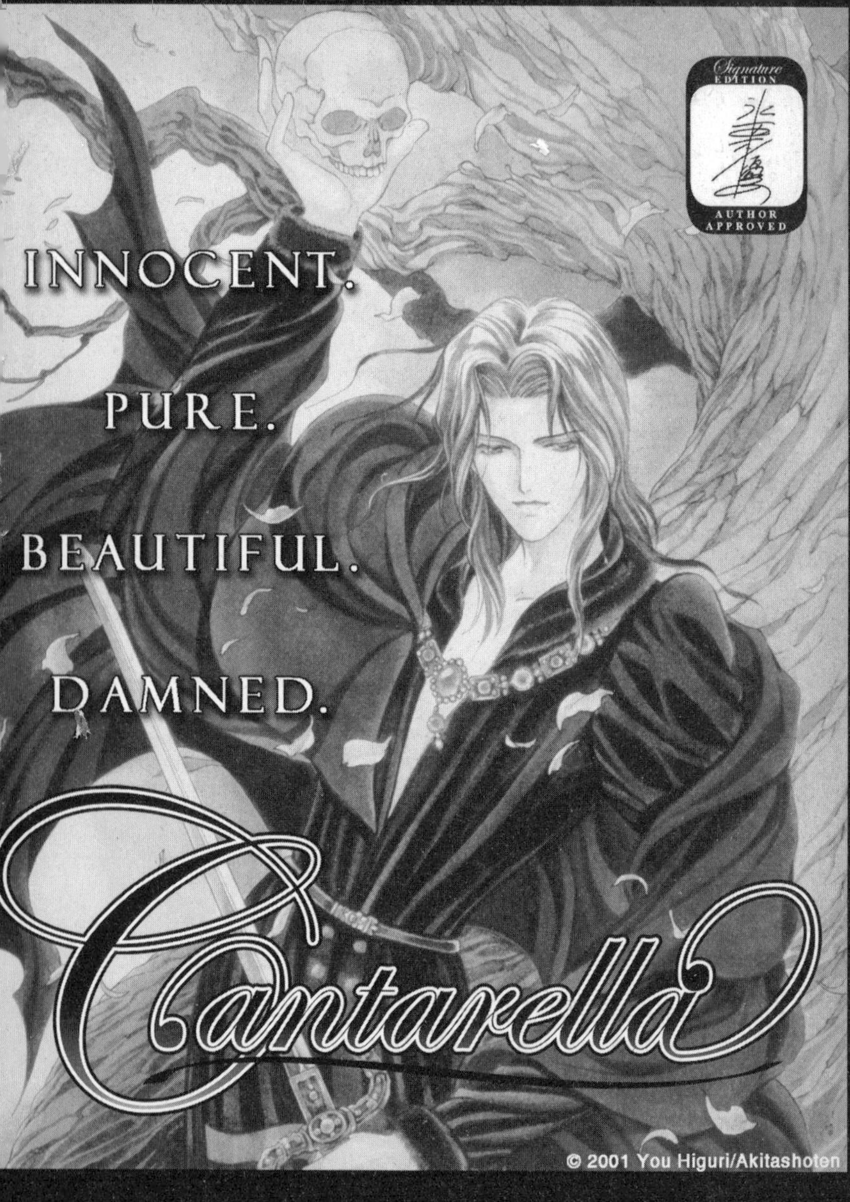
Signature Edition
Author Approved
INNOCENT.
PURE.
BEAUTIFUL.
DAMNED.
Cantarella
© 2001 You Higuri/Akitashoten

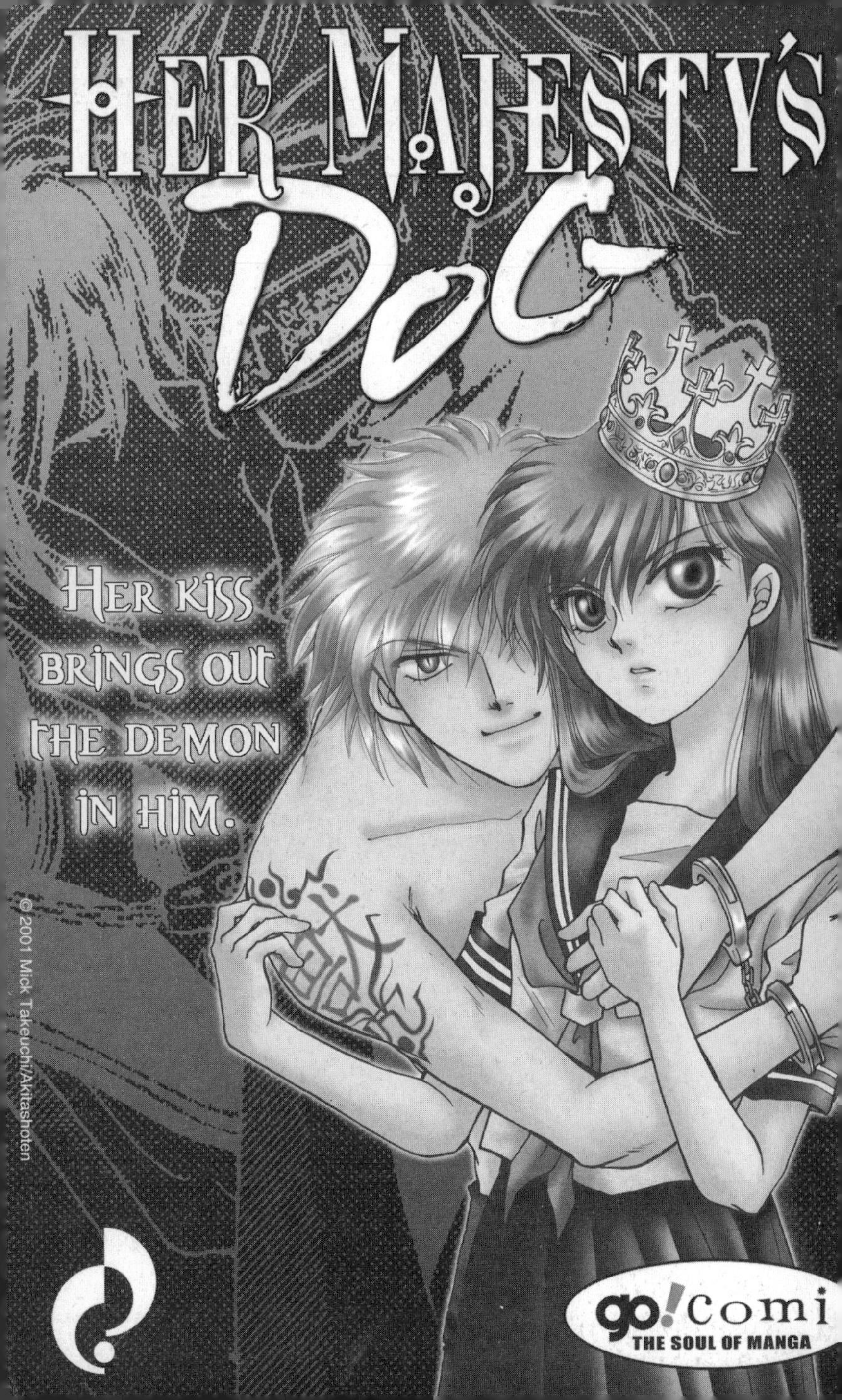
HER MAJESTY'S DOG
HER KISS BRINGS OUT THE DEMON IN HIM.
© 2001 Mick Takeuchi/Akitashoten
go!comi
THE SOUL OF MANGA

Author's Note

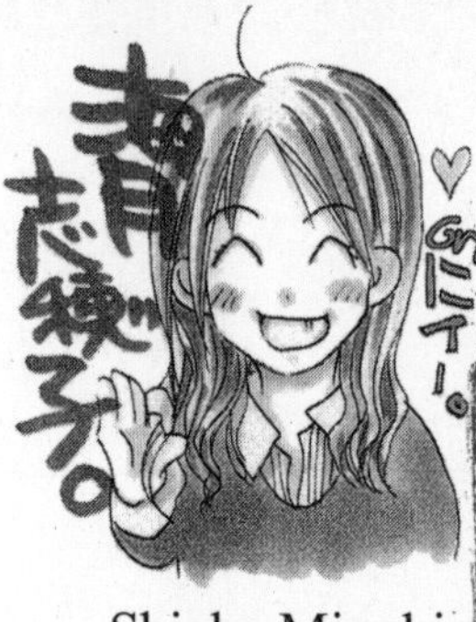
Grin
にィー。

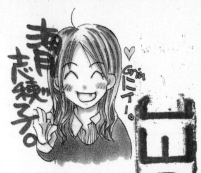

Shioko Mizuki

"I'm working on growing my hair out. But for some reason, it's taking a really long time. I'm sure I'm making all the hair-dressers cry. Maybe it'd grow faster if I did some voodoo or something… Am I even alive? (Now do they say it's the perverts whose hair grows fast? Or was it slow??)

Other Works by Shioko Mizuki
(only available in Japan)

CAN THREE PEOPLE BE IN LOVE?
<5 VOLS>

LOVE FRUITS
<1 VOL>

Visit the manga-ka online at www.shioko.com